Consciousness, Gandhi and Yoga

Interdisciplinary, East–West Odyssey
of
K. Ramakrishna Rao

Consciousness, Gandhi and Yoga

Interdisciplinary, East–West Odyssey of K. Ramakrishna Rao

Edited by
B. Sambasiva Prasad

GITAM University Press

PRINTWORLD
Publishers of Indian Traditions

Cataloging in Publication Data — DK
[Courtesy: D.K. Agencies (P) Ltd. <docinfo@dkagencies.com>]

Consciousness, Gandhi and Yoga : interdisciplinary, East-West odyssey of K. Ramakrishna Rao / edited by B. Sambasiva Prasad.

p. cm.

Includes bibliographical references and index.

ISBN 13: 9788124607152

1. Consciousness. 2. Philosophy, Indic. 3. Psychology and philosophy — India. 4. Gandhi, Mahatma, 1869-1948 — Philosophy. 5. Rao, K. Ramakrishna. I. Rao, K. Ramakrishna. II. Sambasiva Prasad, B. III. GITAM University.

DDC 153 23

First published in India, 2013
ISBN 13: 978-81-246-0715-2

Published by:
GITAM University Press
Rushikonda, Visakhapatnam – 530 045 (A.P.)
Phone: (0891) 284 0312; *Fax*: (0891) 279 0037
e-mail: director_cgs@gitam.edu
Web: www.gitam.edu

and

D.K. Printworld (P) Ltd.
Regd. Office : *'Vedaśrī'*, F-395, Sudarshan Park
(Metro Station: Ramesh Nagar), New Delhi - 110 015
Phones : (011) 2545 3975, 2546 6019; *Fax* : (011) 2546 5926
e-mail : indology@dkprintworld.com
Web : www.dkprintworld.com

Printed by:
D.K. Printworld (P) Ltd., New Delhi

सत्यमेव जयते

Dr. Karan Singh

MEMBER OF PARLIAMENT
RAJYA SABHA
(UPPER HOUSE OF PARLIAMENT)

PRESIDENT
INDIAN COUNCIL FOR
CULTURAL RELATIONS
(ICCR)

Message

I am happy to know that a Festschrift is being prepared for the 80th Birthday of my good friend Prof. K. Ramakrishna Rao. In his long and productive career Prof. Rao has made a substantial contribution to philosophical research in the country and, for many years, has been Chairman of the Indian Council of Philosophical Research (ICPR).

A keynote of his work has been his constant attempt to build cross-cultural and interdisciplinary bridges. He has also written extensively on parapsychology, an area that has generally been neglected by Indian scholars. In Yoga, we have the most profound and integrated approach to the study of human mind and consciousness, and Prof. Rao's work on Patañjali's iconic *Yoga-sūtras* is an important contribution to studies in this field. He has also addressed Gandhi in his various dimensions, thus making a useful contribution to Gandhian studies.

It would be correct to say that Prof. Ramakrishna Rao is an outstanding figure in contemporary Indian philosophy. This volume brings together a broad spectrum of views on his work by scholars from India and around the world. On the occasion of his 80th Birthday, I express my warm greetings and wish him many more years of creative activity in the service of philosophy.

Karan Singh

Karan Singh

Foreword

It is an honour to write the Foreword to the Festschrift to be presented to Prof. K. Ramakrishna Rao on the occasion of his 80th Birthday. Rao's signal contributions to the fields of philosophy and psychology as also a builder of institutions have been detailed by more than one contributor to this volume. In this short space, I can only outline what I have personally found most valuable in his varied and impressive oeuvre.

As a psychologist, Prof. Rao was a pioneer in bringing into focus the vague feeling of many psychologists, especially in our country, that psychology as it is taught and practised all over the world does not adequately reflect the full range of the inner experience of human beings and that Indian psychology has an important role to play in redressing this sense of unease. In a series of important publications, Prof. Rao has convincingly shown that at the present historical moment where we see a great fragmentation in psychological models and approaches, syncretic theorizing and a richness of ideological competition taking place, there is ample space for the emergence of an Indian psychology to stake a claim in the future development of the discipline of psychology. His has been the leading voice in warning Indian psychologists that if we miss this opportunity we might be condemned to eke out a ghetto existence at the margins of world psychology.

Prof. Rao, though, is much more than an eminent psychologist, philosopher or educationist. When an intellectual history of twentieth-century India comes to be written, his name will occupy an honoured place as one of the few thinkers who did not uncritically accept the dominance of Western scientific discourse but creatively mined the Indian philosophical traditions to raise fundamental questions on the nature of consciousness and attempted to free our thinking from the stranglehold of modern Western discourse. He is thus part of a long line of thinkers, going back to the colonial era, who sought to salvage the best of Indian civilizational thought and to express it in a contemporary idiom that is both persuasive and emancipatory for young minds which have had no other nourishment than the one offered by an all-embracing, West-inspired globalization.

When I think of Rao, my mind goes back to some of his illustrious predecessors. In the nineteenth century, it is the great Bengali writer Bankim Chandra Chatterjee who deplored that Indian tradition must pass through the sieve of Western knowledge. In the first half of twentieth century they are Mahatma Gandhi, Ramakrishna Rao's lifelong inspiration, and Rabindranath Tagore, who, too, sought an emancipation of the Indian mind which had been suppressed by the wholesale acceptance of modern, Western education. The Indian mind had been treated like a wooden library shelf to be loaded with volumes of second-hand information, and Tagore observed:

> In consequence, it has lost its own colour and character, and has borrowed polish from the carpenter's shop . . . we have bought our spectacles at the expense of our eyesight.

Like Tagore, Ramakrishna Rao, too, is concerned that we are in danger of losing our priceless inheritance and in trying to replace it clumsily with feeble imitations of the West, we are making ourselves superfluous and ludicrous.

Such a fate may not be looked at with equanimity. In a globalized world that links not only entertainment and capital flows but also ideas, the bankruptcy of Indian thought will also have an impact on Western mind, make it poorer. To adapt Tagore's words, if the great light of culture becomes extinct in the East, the horizon in the West will mourn in darkness.

Prof. Rao's is not a defensive and regressive repudiation of Western sciences of man, some kind of fundamentalist response. What he objects to is the disproportional space Western ideas and world-view continue to occupy in the modern Indian mind. This colonialization has killed or hampered the opportunity to create a new combination of truths that could arise if we were also aware of the hidden riches in our own tradition. What he urges is the mining of psychological truths in the Indian tradition, its revival and strengthening, not to resist in opposition to the Western tradition but to become its true partner. Otherwise, psychologists in India will continue to live, as they have done for a century, on the outskirts of modern West (in Tagore's words) "as the hewers of texts and drawers of book learning". It is at our peril if we do not heed the voice of a rare, visionary thinker.

Sudhir Kakar

Preface

THIS volume is a review and appraisal of the sixty-year academic journey of Prof. K. Ramakrishna Rao covering many areas including Indian psychology, yoga, parapsychology, consciousness and Gandhian studies by a select group of international experts fully conversant with Prof. Rao's work. The book shows not only the contributions of Prof. Rao in advancing the frontiers of Gandhian and consciousness studies and bridging the East–West divide in these areas but also his intellectual influence among a number of scholars around the world.

From Prof. Rao's perspective, parapsychology, Indian psychology and yoga fall under the general rubric of consciousness studies. Further, according to Prof. Rao, Gandhian thought and practices are best understood against the backdrop of researches in the broad area of consciousness. Hence the title of the book *Consciousness, Gandhi and Yoga*.

Prof. Rao's East–West journey started at the very beginning of his research career. He did his MA (Hons.) dissertation on paranormal cognition, discussing Western research and Indian theories. This was published under the title *Psi Cognition* (Rao 1957) with Foreword by J.B. Rhine, the father of experimental parapsychology. This was followed by his book *Gandhi and Pragmatism: An Intercultural Study* (Rao 1968). This cross-cultural journey in areas as diverse as paranormal phenomena and Gandhian studies has never stopped. It has been continuous and relentless, eventhough Prof. Rao shouldered numerous other responsibilities. The milestones of his journey are the following other publications. He edited a volume *Cultivating Consciousness: Enhancing Human Potentials, Wellness and Healing* (Rao 1993). An expanded and revised edition of this volume is being published in 2013 by D.K. Printworld. *Consciousness Studies: Cross-Cultural Perspectives* was published by Jefferson, McFarland, USA (Rao 2002).[1] The more recent ones are *Cognitive Anomalies, Consciousness and Yoga* (Rao

[1] K.R. Rao (2002), *Consciousness Studies: Cross-cultural Perspectives*, Jefferson, NC: McFarland.

2011a)[2] and *Gandhi and Applied Spirituality* (Rao 2011b).

Thus Prof. Rao's academic voyage is truly an East–West odyssey and an important interdisciplinary exercise. He has not only travelled back and forth from continent to continent and held important academic assignments in USA and India, but he has also attempted to understand their unique cultural nuances for gaining wholesome insights into human nature.

Koneru Ramakrishna Rao began his professional career as a lecturer in the Department of Philosophy at Andhra University sixty years ago. By then he studied Indian philosophy and Western philosophy under the tutelage of Prof. Saileswar Sen and Prof. Satchidananda Murty, respectively. He was also exposed to psychology as pursued in the West at that time. Prof. A. Lakshmana Rao taught psychology in the philosophy department at Andhra University during those days. The formative field of exploration of young Ramakrishna Rao may be seen as a matrix of Indian thought and Western philosophy and psychology. His endeavour since has been one of seeing patterns in this matrix and create a mosaic where the three can be seen coexisting in harmony, complementing each other for a complete and consummate understanding of man and his destiny.

There is another interesting aspect in Prof. Rao's academic journey. He has not been content with acquiring knowledge. He has been equally interested in exploring the ways of applying knowledge for common good of human kind. This exercise is one of converting knowledge into wisdom. He considers wisdom as knowledge applied to life. Thus we find in Prof. Rao's sixty-years academic odyssey a relentless pursuit of wisdom. This he has attempted to do by churning the East–West ocean of knowledge; and it was no small undertaking. Many in the past found it a daunting and challenging task as the contours of East–West knowledgescape appeared so desperately different and tortuously troubling to reconcile.

It is for the readers of this volume to find the extent of Prof. Rao's success in bringing the East and the West together. The assessments are likely to vary; but few would fail to be impressed by his Herculean scholarly effort, his encyclopaedic knowledge, the commendable

[2] K. Ramakrishna Rao (2011a), *Cognitive Anomalies, Consciousness and Yoga*, New Delhi: Centre for Studies of Civilizations and Matrix Publishers; K. Ramakrishna Rao, *Gandhi and Applied Spirituality*, New Delhi: Indian Council of Philosophical Research and Matrix Publishers.

command on ideas and clear insights into the nuances of both the traditions, East and West. What is even more amazing is that he is as active and productive at the age of eighty as he ever was. His is one of the very few mature, active and encyclopaedic minds I encountered in my own fairly long academic career.

Over and above his excellent academic work, Prof. Rao occupied several prestigious administrative positions. He was the Chairman, Indian Council of Philosophical Research (ICPR), New Delhi, for two terms, and the Vice-Chancellor of Andhra University, Advisor to Andhra Pradesh State Government on Higher Education, Vice-Chairman of Andhra Pradesh Planning Board, and the Chair of several national and state-level committees. Consequently he is well known beyond the academic institutions where he worked.

I consider it a great privilege to have the opportunity to put together this collection of essays reviewing his academic work by some eminent scholars fully familiar with Prof. Rao's writings. We offer it as a small token of academic tribute to his outstanding scholarship and creative contributions.

The contributors to this volume are an interesting mix of scholars with different cultural and academic backgrounds. Prof. Anand Paranjpe, Dr Kanthamani and Dr Hanu Rao are Indians who worked most of their professional lives in the West. Dr Jerry Solfvin is an American with a deep interest in India and Indian philosophy. Prof. V.V. Raman is a distinguished physicist and philosopher with Indian roots and Western upbringing. Prof. Max Velmans is a leading Western researcher in consciousness studies. Prof. R.C. Pradhan, Ashok Vohra and G. Vedaparayana are among the leading Indian philosophers familiar with Prof. Rao's work. While Dr Alok Tandon is an interested outside scholar, Prof. Gouri Rammohan is a former student and later a colleague of Prof. Ramakrishna Rao like Dr Kanthamani and Hanu Rao. Dr Matthijs Cornelissen is a Dutch psychiatrist settled in India. He is a scholar of Sri Aurobindo and is a close associate of Prof. Rao in the Indian psychology movement. Prof. Devadoss, one of the senior philosophers in the country, has known Prof. Ramakrishna Rao for almost forty years and they have had opportunities to work together on a number of occasions.

Prof. Girishwar Mishra and Prof. Janak Pandey are distinguished psychologists and long-time friends and associates of Prof. Rao in promoting Indian psychology. Prof. Ajit K. Dalal of Allahabad University and Prof. Jean Kristeller of Indiana State University, USA, are well-known psychologists located in two continents divided by long distance and huge cultural differences. They, however, illustrate how the work of Prof. Ramakrishna Rao touched and influenced them in interesting ways.

We thank Dr Karan Singh, the best-known philosopher–statesman of the country after Dr Sarvepalli Radhakrishnan for his message. Dr Karan Singh is fully acquainted with Prof. Ramakrishna Rao at a personal level and is familiar with Prof. Rao's academic contributions. We are equally privileged to have the Foreword from Dr Sudhir Kakar, a well-known Indian psychoanalyst, psychologist and a respected author.

I am grateful to all the above for readily agreeing to contribute to this volume and timely delivery of their articles. I know well that all the contributors of this volume responded so spontaneously to my request for papers because of their deep respect, love and admiration for Prof. Rao and his work. In this connection, I may call attention to a sister-volume *Mind and Consciousness,*[3] edited by Prof. K.R. Rajani, which contains a number of articles reviewing the work of Prof. Ramakrishna Rao.

I thank Mr Susheel K. Mittal of D.K. Printworld, for readily accepting to publish this book and for the splendid job of bringing out an aesthetically appealing volume and to GITAM University Press for including this volume in their scholarly book series. I also express my thanks to the family of Prof. Ramakrishna Rao for sharing the photographs printed in this volume. I am thankful to Dr Nalini Bikkina, Dr M. Varalakshmi and Dr Aruna Pariti for their help in reading the proofs and other editorial assistance.

It is customary in this part of the world to celebrate two events in one's life. The first is the completion of sixty years, which is called *ṣaṣṭipūrti*. The second is the rising of one thousand full moons after one's birth. This happens after one reaches the age of eighty years. We are indeed very happy that in a way the two events in this case are coalescing into one in a very interesting way. Prof. Koneru Ramakrishna Rao completes sixty years as an academician having started his professional career as a lecturer at Andhra University on 12 August 1953. So, this is the year of Prof. Rao's academic *ṣaṣṭipūrti* (sixtieth anniversary). Again, Prof. Ramakrishna Rao sees during this year 1000th full moon since his birth on 4 October 1932, the *sahasracandrodaya* for him.

---

[3] K.R. Rajani (ed.) (2013), *Mind and Consciousness: Some Contemporary Reflections*, New Delhi: Akansha Publishing House.

I take this opportunity to say on behalf of the contributors to this volume, and many of Prof. Ramakrishna Rao's students, colleagues, friends and admirers, "Happy Ṣaṣṭipūrti and Happy Sahasracandrodaya". May the Almighty shower His Choicest Blessings on him and his family for many more years of excellent health, active scholarly work and continued success in the advancement of human science and service!

B. Sambasiva Prasad
Director
Centre for Gandhian Studies
GITAM University
Visakhapatnam - 530 045
Andhra Pradesh, India

Contents

The beginning of an intellectual quest:
Ramakrishna Rao as a student at Andhra University, 1950

Rao being a Smith-Mundt Fulbright scholar
with fellow students at the University of Chicago, 1958

Guru Devobhava: Prof. Saileswar Sen, Prof. Rao's Philosophy Teacher

From theories to empirical investigations: Dr J.B. Rhine, Prof. Rao's Mentor in Parapsychology

Hoisting the Indian National Flag at Bennington College, USA, 15 August 1958

Mr Clement Stone making a point. Next to Prof. Rao, seen are Dr Louisa Rhine and Dr Russell Moores

Parapsychology Conference, France, 1968

Receiving Mother Teresa at Visakhapatnam Airport

With his students of Department of Psychology, Andhra University

With his students at the University of North Carolina, Chapel Hill, USA

With daughter-in-law Madhu, wife Sarojini, daughter Vani.
Standing (L-R): Vani's husband Murali, son Chandu,
daughter Rani and her husband Sarath

Grandchildren (L-R): Vivek, Shilpa, Sunila, Tarun, Kavya and Mira

With daughter Vani

With sister Rama

50th birthday meeting. (L-R): Sri Bhattam Sreerama Murthy, Prof. Satchidananda Murthy, Prof. Avula Sambasiva Rao and Sri M. Venkaiah Naidu

55th birthday celebrations, meeting at Andhra University

70th birthday party, Park Hotel, Visakhapatnam

80th birthday bash, Chapel Hill, USA

Release of the book *Consciousness Studies*
by Shri Barnala, Governor of Andhra Pradesh, Left to Governor Barnala
is Sri Akkineni Nageswara Rao, at Raj Bhavan, Hyderabad

Release of the book *Yoga and Parapsychology*
by Dr M.V.V.S. Murthi, President, GITAM University

Hon'ble Union Minister D. Purndeshwari releasing the book *Handbook of Indian Psychology* by K.R. Rao et al. (2008)

Shri Kapil Sibal, Hon'ble Union Minister of Human Resource Development, releasing the book *Cognitive Anomalies, Consciousness and Yoga* (2010)

Releasing the book *Gandhi and Applied Spirituality* by Prof. K. Ramakrishna Rao — Sri Kishore Chandra Deo, Hon'ble Minister for Tribal Welfare, Government of India (second from the left), Right to Prof. Rao, Dr B.L. Mungekar, MP, former Member, Planning Commission, Sri D.V. Subba Rao, former Mayor of Visakhapatnam and Chairman, Bar Council of India

With Dr Hiroshi Motoyama and his wife in Tokyo, Japan

Honouring Dr Stanley Krippner with J.B. Rhine
Life Time Achievement Award

Being honoured on his appointment as Chairman,
AP State Council of Higher Education

Presenting Annual Report 58th Convocation, Andhra University

Presenting Sunil Gavaskar for the
Honorary Doctoral Degree of Kreedaprapoorna

Farewell function after completing his tenure
as Vice-Chancellor, Andhra University

Sri N.T. Rama Rao felicitating Prof. Rao on the eve
of his leaving the government and returning to USA

An event in which Prof. Rao was elected as the
President of Asian Philosophy Congress

With dignitaries after delivering the Valedictory Address,
World Philosophy Day 2010 (21 November, Tehran, Iran)

Receiving Padma Sri Award 2011 from
Mrs Pratibha Patil, the President of India

In his role as Chancellor of GITAM University, 2012

1

K.R. Rao on East–West Expressway
A Journey of Sixty-plus Years

Gowri Rammohan

Introduction

I had the privilege of editing (Rammohan 2002) a Festschrift volume to Prof. Dr Ramakrishna Rao on his seventieth birthday, ten years ago. I am happy to update in this article what I wrote on that occasion in the chapter "K.R. Rao: The Man and His Mission".

It is difficult to write about someone objectively when he is your teacher, colleague and mentor. I had the privilege of being Rao's student and colleague in the Department of Psychology and Parapsychology at Andhra University. He has been in many ways my teacher, philosopher and guide. I continue to look up to him and seek his advice and support. I believe, I am just one among many, who are influenced and inspired by him.

A man of many interests, Rao excelled as a teacher, researcher, administrator, institution-builder, visionary and thinker. His mind is a unique combination of toughness and tenderness. He is a dreamy, idealist visionary and at the same time a thoroughly pragmatic person. His interests are multidisciplinary, and his outlook is cross-cultural and cosmopolitan. In his research he combined theoretical wisdom with rigorous skills of a sensitive experimental investigator. His writings are a blend of Eastern and Western traditions, the *saṅgamam* (confluence) of East–West streams of thought. Following the metaphor incorporated in the title of this chapter, he travelled to and fro on the East–West Expressway for sixty years. Dr K. Ramakrishna Rao is to Indian psychology what Dr S. Radhakrishnan was to Indian philosophy. Both of them did much to bring into focus the depth and richness of classical Indian thought and its relevance in the contemporary context.

The Formative Years

Rao told us that his years as a student were uneventful. Even though he was a good student and topped his class in BA (Hons.) he recalled little that distinguished him as a special student. It is only after he graduated studying philosophy and psychology at Andhra University that he was awakened to the intellectual quest that characterized all of his professional life. As a student, he learned in his psychology classes that humans like animals are conditioned beings. In his study of Indian philosophy also he saw how we are conditioned by the past *karma*. Though the two views appeared similar, he readily saw that they are as different as night and day.

The Hindu and Buddhist conceptions do not consider the conditioned existence as inevitable and a necessary aspect of life. It is only a contingent condition that could and should be overcome. The ultimate goal is to be free from the existential constraints of habits and compulsive desires, and from ego-involvement. It is his perception of the striking contrast between the two perspectives that sparked Rao's intellect and ignited an unending drive to seek the ways to reconcile the two. This has led him to investigate the paranormal phenomena and extraordinary experiences. His MA (Hons.) dissertation was a critical evaluation of Eastern and Western theories of paranormal cognition, which was published under the title *Psi Cognition* with a Foreword by Dr J.B. Rhine.

Rapid Academic Rise

Rao was appointed to a full-time faculty position in the Department of Philosophy at Andhra University to teach psychology before he celebrated his twenty-first birthday. He was elevated to the rank of a full professor at the age of thirty. He became the head of Andhra University, Vice-Chancellor, when he was fifty-two. He travelled widely to study and learn, and to lecture and teach. He attended the University of Chicago as Smith-Mundt Fulbright scholar and a fellow of the Rockefeller Foundation. He worked with Rhine at Duke University. He spent time with Montague Ullman and Stanley Krippner at the Dream Laboratory of the Maimonides Medical Center in Brooklyn, New York. He visited a number of active research centres such as Joe Kamiya's Laboratory in San Francisco and Elmer Green's at the Menninger Foundation to learn about biofeedback. He published extensively in India and abroad. He founded and edited the *Journal of Indian Psychology*. He was the editor of the *Journal of Parapsychology* during 1977-94. He has authored/edited more than 20 books so far.

Rao's papers appeared as chapters in more than twenty-five books. His research publications are numerous as may be seen from the bibliography appended to this volume. His interests are broad and multidisciplinary. His contributions cover many areas that include philosophy (Eastern and Western), Indian psychology, parapsychology, consciousness studies, library development, school and university education, and Indian studies. His writings appeared in all the major parapsychological journals and such prestigious mainstream journals like *Behavioural and Brain Sciences* and the *Journal of Consciousness Studies*.

Distinguished Teacher

Teaching came naturally to Rao. Even though he spent many years away from active teaching, teaching was his first love. He taught for five years in the Department of Philosophy and eight years in the Department of Psychology and Parapsychology at Andhra University. He also gave psychology courses at the University of North Carolina at Chapel Hill, University of Tennessee at Chattanooga and the California Institute for Human Science. Government of Andhra Pradesh honoured him with the Distinguished Teacher Award.

As his student in parapsychology and social psychology classes, I recall how clear, precise and profound his lectures were. I always wondered how he was able to give his lectures with an unceasing flow of information with no notes to consult. That only showed his command and mastery of the subject. I recall also how surprised we were, one day, when the head of the university showed up unannounced to attend one of Rao's seminar classes. To my knowledge, a similar event never took place in the history of Andhra University. Such was Rao's reputation as a teacher and scholar. He inspired his students, recognized their special skills and talents, and motivated them to achieve their best. He stimulated academic interests and encouraged the students to excel in the class as well as outside.

Builder of Institutions and Administrator of Distinction

Rao is not merely a thinker and a visionary. He is also a doer, a man of action. He is both an architect who prepares the plans and the blueprints, and an engineer who helps to build and concretize the plans. As an administrator he is astute and savvy. His first administrative challenge was to develop Andhra University Libraries. He did this in a relatively short time. Under his leadership, the main library moved into its new abode in 1961, a beautiful five-storey structure organized in a user-friendly manner with an impressive collection. Rao was also able to build around it the Department of Library and Information Sciences to train library professionals.

Next came the challenge to build a new Department of Psychology and Parapsychology, the first of its kind in the country. It is no secret that this Department came into being at Andhra University entirely due to the efforts of Rao. Dr D.S. Kothari, who was at the time the Chairman of the University Grants Commission, learnt about the work of Rao and invited him to start a centre for parapsychological study and research at a university of his choosing in India. The choice fell naturally on Andhra and the Department of Psychology and Parapsychology was inaugurated on 28 December 1967. Started with one professor and two research scholars, the Department grew rapidly to the strength of ten full-time faculty and dozens of research students. Rao's leadership was seen not only in organizing teaching and research, but also in providing first-rate infrastructure and physical facilities. I recall his mentioning once that he knew every stone that went into the building that houses the Department. During his tenure as the head, the Department was a showpiece of the university, tastefully decorated and furnished and kept meticulously clean. The Department was buzzing with research. The first two Ph.D. dissertations under Rao's supervision were awarded gold medals for being the most outstanding in humanities and social sciences at Andhra University. The Chief Minister of Andhra Pradesh visited the Department to observe the groundbreaking research being conducted with a *yogī* locked in an airtight box to monitor his psychophysiological states in deep meditation.

As Chairman of the Faculty of Humanities and Social Sciences and as an elected member of the Syndicate (Executive Council), Rao carved for himself a distinctive niche in the affairs of Andhra University, even before he became its Vice-Chancellor in 1984. As Vice-Chancellor, Rao is remembered for the administrative reforms he initiated, the curricular changes he helped to bring, the new departments he added, the financial stability he brought to the university, and above all the relentless crusade for excellence in teaching and research. Again, he was the founder of Yoga Village, a beautiful facility facing the Bay of Bengal, where students learn *yoga*, and the Institute for Yoga and Consciousness, a centre for fundamental research on mind–body interaction.

After a three-year stint as the Vice-Chancellor, Rao took over as the Chairman of Andhra Pradesh Commissionerate of Higher Education. Later, he served as Advisor on Higher Education to the Government of

Andhra Pradesh. His last assignment in the Government of Andhra Pradesh was to head Andhra Pradesh State Planning Board with the rank of a cabinet minister. In all these roles, Rao excelled as a state-level administrator and planner. As a close confidant and advisor to the then Chief Minister of Andhra Pradesh Dr N.T. Rama Rao, Rao was associated with a number of important innovative schemes undertaken by the state government. His contributions as a scholar, researcher and administrator were recognized throughout the state. He received honorary degrees of Doctor of Letters from Andhra and Kakatiya universities and the degree of Doctor of Science (*honoris causa*) from Nagarjuna University.

On the Frontiers of Human Science

In the beginning, Rao's interest in the paranormal was entirely theoretical. What attracted his attention most were the implications of parapsychological findings to an understanding of human nature and their potential to bridge the East–West intellectual divide. Rao has had an abiding interest in cross-cultural studies. His Ph.D. dissertation was on "Mahatma Gandhi, William James and American Pragmatism". He made extensive cross-cultural studies of consciousness (Rao 2002, 2011a). It is his belief that all traditions contain truth. Truth, however, gets fragmented as each tradition attempts to find its identity by emphasizing one aspect, neglecting the others. Therefore, in his view, the quest to discover the whole truth must begin with exploring the complementary contributions of different cultures and traditions.

Psi Research

It was Dr Rhine who had the greatest influence in turning Rao's theoretical interests into empirical investigations. His readings of published research in parapsychology, especially the laboratory investigations of Extra Sensory Perception (ESP), convinced him of the existence of some of the extraordinary phenomena to which *yoga* treatises refer. However, considering the controversial nature of ESP investigations in the scientific community and the difficulty of replicating the results, Rao felt the need to get acquainted first-hand with the research and those who conduct it. Then, what could be a better place to start than the Parapsychology Laboratory at Duke University? So, Rao took the first opportunity to travel to Durham, North Carolina to meet with Dr Rhine. It was in early September of 1958 that he spent a few weeks at Duke before moving on to the University of Chicago.

Rao told us that with Rhine it was love at first sight. The professionalism and dedication he saw at the Parapsychology Laboratory left a deep impression on him. The personal warmth and cordiality of Dr Rhine and the friendship of William Roll and Wadih Saleh touched him. Not the least is the acquaintance with J.G. Pratt. Dr Rhine and Pratt reminded him of Rāma and Lakṣmaṇa in the great Indian epic *Rāmāyaṇa*. They made a great team. Rao acknowledges that he learnt from both of them. Dr Rhine gave Rao a blanket invitation to visit him any time and work with him, as long he wished. So, Rao was back again at Duke in 1960, after completing his assignment at the University of Chicago and again in 1962 to work as a member of Dr Rhine's research team.

His stay at Duke University during 1962-65, Rao told us, was a period of remarkable learning experience. The tender-minded philosopher was transformed into a tough laboratory investigator. "The three years I spent at the Laboratory," he wrote, "seem to be one of the most productive periods of my career so far. I was able to publish a number of experimental papers and to write the book *Experimental Parapsychology*" (Rao 1973). Rao was elected as the president of the Parapsychological Association (PA) for the year 1965. His address at the Annual Convention in New York centred on psi missing and the differential effect to which he made important contributions both at theoretical and empirical levels.

Parapsychology for Rao was never an end in itself. He saw in it a means to expand the frontiers of human science and to find a reasonable resolution of the manifest differences in the conflicting paradigms of classical Indian thought and contemporary science. His mission was to bridge the divide between Eastern and Western perspectives. Parapsychology, it seemed, covered the common ground between the two in a very important sense. However, the more experiments he conducted and more data he collected, the less he became comfortable with his work. It was disconcerting that parapsychology, working within the experimental paradigm of methodological behaviourism, appeared to have lost sight of the main import of its findings. It seemed to have reached a dead end, and caught in a vicious circle of doing better experiments and encountering more vigorous criticism. In an autobiographical brief, Rao (1973) expressed thus the raging conflict within himself:

> Most of my work, which has had any consequence, is the experimental work carried out under rigid and artificial conditions. Yet, my thinking is that only a more phenomenologically-oriented experiential approach

> would reveal the mysteries of psi. So I am struggling to reconcile these two points of view and evolve studies that focus on the variety and richness of psi experience without sacrificing the advantages of quantitative data. I believe the future of parapsychology lies in a synthesis of these two approaches — the experimental and the experiential.

Back in India after three eventful years at Duke, Rao collected around him a small group of talented researchers and helped to establish the Department of Psychology and Parapsychology. Andhra University soon became a leading centre for parapsychological research. Important projects were undertaken to investigate:

1. The relationship between ESP and personality factors,
2. the facilitating role of meditation in enhancing human potentials,
3. the differential effect with tests in real life situations,
4. the paranormal claims of *bābā*s, *yogin*s and "godmen", and
5. nocturnal dreaming.

While these empirical studies are underway, Rao focused his attention on classical Indian psychology, attempting to interpret it in contemporary context and integrate it with his laboratory researches. He founded and edited a new journal, the *Journal of Indian Psychology* to promote the publication of research into classical ideas with contemporary methodologies.

As the work began yielding fruits, the call came from Dr Rhine that Rao's services were needed to run his battered Institute for Parapsychology in Durham. At the time, Dr Rhine was grooming a young physician to succeed him as the director of the Institute. Regrettably, the young man was caught by his colleagues while compromising on the integrity of his experimental data. He had to go. The Institute was in shambles. The morale was low. There was need for new leadership at the Institute and the field at large. Rao was Dr Rhine's choice. So he returned to Durham in 1976 to head Dr Rhine's Institute for Parapsychology.

Rao reluctantly agreed to spend three years at the Institute taking leave of absence from Andhra University. Before he completed his work at the Institute in Durham, Dr Rhine died. Mrs L.E. Rhine and the board of directors of the Foundation for Research on the Nature of Man (FRNM) to which the Institute was affiliated persuaded Rao to stay on permanently. So, finally Rao resigned his permanent position as professor of psychology at Andhra University in 1982. We all felt the loss. We felt that he had left the Department of Psychology and Parapsychology rudderless in mid-stream. He kept on hold his own interests in Indian psychology and his pursuits of larger goals. One of the speakers at a function arranged to mark his retirement from the university pointedly asked Rao to reconsider his decision to leave the university because the university and the country needed his services.

As soon as he arrived in the US, Rao took a leadership role not only at the Institute but also of the field at large. He was re-elected as the president of the Parapsychological Association (PA) for 1978. In his address at the twenty-first annual convention of the PA held at Washington University in St. Louis, Rao argued that

> psi is both real and profound. It is real because the evidence is inescapable and the criticisms of it are unfair, false, and unable to explain away much of experimental evidence. It is profound and exciting because it has substantive implications for our understanding of the nature of man and his place in nature. — Rao 1978

Pursuing his cross-cultural interests in his presidential address to the PA, Rao compared the Advaita Vedānta views of *Brahman* and pure consciousness with the holographic theories of David Bohm (1973) and Karl Pribram (1978). He then proceeded to develop his own views:

> Reality, it seems to me, has many layers. In the core, it is undifferentiated and stable. On the surface, it has distinct forms that are ever changing. The core reality is progressively differentiated so as to give us the appearance we have of it in surface reality. In the outer layer things are relatively insulated from each other. The interaction between them can be understood in causal terms. But within the inner layers distinctiveness and individuality are obscured and even obliterated as things merge into each other. Subject–object dichotomies become meaningless. Consequently, causality as it is commonly understood and the space–time characterization of reality lose their significance and relevance. The reality as actualized in the outer layers is implied in the inner layers in the same way the oak is implied by the acorn. The relation between layers themselves is teleological.
>
> In other words, the outer layers of reality are explicate forms of what is implicate in the inner layers. The process of the universe is one of making explicate what is implicate in core reality. To put it differently, reality at its core contains the grand plan or design to which the unfolding universe conforms. The process, by which the grand plan gets implemented, I venture to hazard, is psi. So conceived, psi is a fundamental process in nature, a process through which nature communicates with its constituents. — Rao 1978

Rao served as the director of the Institute for Parapsychology and as the executive director of the FRNM until 1994. He continued at the Institute his empirical investigations of the differential effect. He carried out research to explore the relationship between cognitive variables such as memory and ESP. More importantly, as the situation stabilized at the Institute, he refocused his attention on his main intellectual mission to connect parapsychology with other frontier areas in human science, seeking at the same time to bring together the Eastern and Western conceptions of the mind. He began spending more time on theoretical issues in the broader area of consciousness. He brought out the volume *Cultivating Consciousness* (1991a). This work continued beyond his stay at the Institute and culminated in his book, *Consciousness Studies*: *Cross-cultural Perspectives* (2002).

In his third presidential address to the Parapsychological Association in 1990, Rao's broad interest in consciousness studies became more explicit. Reviewing extensive theoretical literature on consciousness, he argued that materialist renderings of consciousness, whether it is philosophical behaviourism or identity theory, are inconsistent with the possibility of psi. Paranormal phenomena, he pointed out, call for a study of consciousness *qua* consciousness. In his model, attention takes the centre stage (Rao 1991b):

> In human condition, attention fluctuates. If fluctuations of attention are random or determined by stimulus properties and subjective conditions such as motivation, habit, interest, and attitudes which are themselves determined by other factors, there is indeed little room for free will. If, however, the focus of attention can be achieved by voluntary intentions as suggested by certain meditative practices, then such voluntary attention can be a means of studying consciousness *qua* consciousness. Volition, imprisoned as it were in cerebral cells and serving the chores of attending to the commands of sensory and proprioceptive inputs, can be freed to escape the existential impasse of pervasive determinism in our mental life. When this happens and one gains volitional access to consciousness, the unusual phenomena become ordinary.

Indian Psychology and Consciousness Studies

Before he left for USA to join Dr Rhine's establishment in 1976, Rao was working on a writing project sponsored by the University Grants Commission (UGC) on Indian psychology and another major research project on laboratory studies of nocturnal dreaming funded by the Indian Council of Social Science Research. He set up the first dream laboratory in India and three of his students obtained their Ph.D. degrees in the area of dream research. After moving to the US, his time was fully committed to parapsychology in administrative and research roles. His work on Indian psychology took a back seat for almost a decade.

In 1987 Rao was elected president of the Indian Academy of Applied Psychology, a professional society of academic and practising psychologists in India. He used this as an occasion to bring back into focus his thoughts on Indian psychology. Raising the question: "What is Indian psychology?" at the twenty-fifth annual convention of the Academy held at Osmania University in Hyderabad, Rao defined the scope of Indian psychology and drew its contours. With his characteristic frankness, he castigated psychology taught and practised in India as lacking in direction and relevance to national life and ethos. The dependence on Western models and the use of inappropriate research tools borrowed from the West, he argued, should be corrected by a "judicious introduction of Indian psychology" into research and teaching of psychology in India. He pointed out that a systematic study of classical Indian ideas on mind and consciousness would suggest heuristic models from which investigators could derive programmes of research that would enable psychology "to carve a niche of its own in the ongoing process of national change and development". He illustrated his views by describing a model for a psychology of transcendence drawing from the Hindu and Buddhist psychological thought.

Elected as the president of the Academy for the second term and also acting as the chairman of the Psychology National Committee of the UGC, Rao encouraged the study and research in Indian psychology. In his second presidential address to the Academy at Calcutta University in 1989, he dealt with meditation research. He explained how a concept considered so esoteric not too long ago is now a subject of serious scientific study around the world. Again, he was forthright in pointing out that "much of contemporary literature on meditation is characterized by methodologically deficient experiments, conceptually confused discussions and often exaggerated claims" (1989). He argued that the apparent physiological correlates of practice of meditation are likely the results of the cognitive factors common among the meditating subjects rather than being the direct effects of meditation. The states of low arousal and other concomitants of meditation, he pointed out, are not the effects of meditation *per se*. Rather, they are the outcomes of preparatory steps preceding meditation. The goal of meditation from classical times is one of achieving states of pure consciousness and not reducing blood pressure or slowing heart rate, which may occur as by-products.

The consciousness project started by Rao before he returned to India in 1994 is a major undertaking. The first output of this project is the publication of a comprehensive review article on consciousness studies in volume 2 of Janak Pandey's third survey of psychology in India (Rao 2001). Also, a paper entitled "Two Faces of Consciousness" appeared in the *Journal of Consciousness Studies* (Rao 1998). The most significant outcome, however, is *Consciousness Studies: Cross-cultural Perspectives*. In this book, Rao reviews the deeply different perspectives of Eastern and Western traditions in studying consciousness. He describes the different respects in which they differ. He then goes on to succinctly point out their complementary aspects. Drawing heavily from Sāṁkhya-Yoga, Advaita Vedānta and Buddhist systems, he develops a model for studying consciousness. In this model, following the Indian tradition, there is a fundamental difference between "mind" and "consciousness". Consciousness in this view is the knowledge side of the universe, the ground condition for all awareness. Mind is physical; comprising of the subtlest form of matter that has non-local characteristics. Mind and consciousness do not interact. Consciousness is the light that shines on the mind. Human experience is the rainbow formed by the reflection of the light of consciousness on the mind. Rao describes the role of the mind in human condition in the following way:

> Mind in this view is the interfacing instrumentality that faces consciousness one side and the brain on the other side. The mind thus gives the impression of having two faces . . . from the physical side, the mind collects information by processing the inputs it receives. When this information is exposed to consciousness at the other end, i.e., when the light of consciousness is reflected on it, there is subjective awareness and conscious experience of the phenomenal data.
>
> Mind thus enjoys dual citizenship in the physical world as well as in the realm of consciousness. As a material form, mind's citizenship in the material world is by birth as it were. Its naturalization in the domain of consciousness is a matter of choice and an outcome of significant effort. Its citizenship in the land of matter bestows on it the right to process information through its sensory channels and neural networks. The mind also has involuntary and passive access to consciousness in that the light of consciousness shines on it to illumine its critically poised contents, which become subjectively revealed. The mind also has within its reach the possibility of partaking in consciousness as such by disciplined practice so that it may have direct and unmediated knowledge.

Blazing New Trails in Indian Education

His colleagues in the West may not know about Rao's influence on Indian education, especially in the state of Andhra Pradesh. He served as the executive and administrative head of Andhra University, as mentioned, which is one of the oldest and largest in the country. He also served as the Advisor on Higher Education to the Government of Andhra Pradesh. He chaired a number of state and national-level committees on education. The recommendations of these committees were the forerunners of some recent reforms in education.

As Vice-Chancellor of Andhra University, he initiated major reforms in university administration, introduced several new academic programmes, strengthened teaching, and attempted to improve standards of research. He introduced large-scale decentralization in administration. He created several new positions of deans and appointed the rector and delegated several of his responsibilities to the new functionaries. Decentralization of administration and diffusion of power was a new phenomenon at the university. We hope that this welcome trend would continue. Under Rao's leadership, undergraduate curricula were extensively revised and updated. New core courses, such as Indian heritage and culture, were introduced. More significantly, he encouraged student involvement in community development and fieldwork as part of academic curricular activity. New degree programmes such as bachelor courses in computer application and business administration were introduced in a number of colleges affiliated to Andhra University. He established the Institute for Yoga and Consciousness, and the Yoga Village in the main campus of the university. The institute is funded entirely by the UGC and the state government. The Yoga Village is developed with private contributions. His astute administrative skills enabled the university to improve its financial position during his three-year stint as the Vice-Chancellor.

In his role as advisor to Andhra Pradesh government, Rao prepared a blueprint for reforming higher education in the state. He recommended a system with three parallel streams. One stream with accent on excellence is for the most talented of the students. It is to be funded for the most part by the state. The second stream, which is largely self-financing, caters to the needs of those who can afford to pay for their education, but are unable to get admission into the first stream. The third is a subsidized non-formal stream accessible to everyone who seeks higher education. He also encouraged the establishment of colleges in the co-operative sector.

On his recommendation, Andhra Pradesh State Council of Higher Education was formed. This is an autonomous semi-governmental agency that provides state's funds for higher education. It co-ordinates the activities of the universities and colleges in the state. Rao was the first Chairman of this organization. Several states in the country followed Andhra's lead and established similar councils. Rao also chaired committees to establish a rural university in the state and the Institute for Professional Studies.

Rao's leaving FRNM coincided with his appointment as the head of the Andhra Pradesh State Planning Board with the rank of a Cabinet Minister. In this role, Rao was associated with a number of innovative schemes. He headed a committee to suggest reforms in school education. Again, the recommendations of the committee are far-reaching in a number of ways. More important among them is the proposal to involve the local community, especially the parents of the students enrolled, in the management of schools. Another innovative proposal was to recruit voluntary teachers, drawing from the locally available talent. The goal was to universalize primary education with the available limited resources and to ensure that those who do receive elementary education do not lapse back into illiteracy after leaving the school.

In his Dr Sarvepalli Radhakrishnan Memorial Lecture, delivered at Andhra University, Rao (2000) spells out with his characteristic outspokenness what is wrong with the current state of affairs in Indian higher education and shares his thoughts for a national system of education. The main problem with the system of education as practised in India today is that it is alien in its essentials, only remotely relevant to national needs. He says (Rao 2000: 20):

> For over fifty years after Independence we have subscribed to a policy of drift, a belief in automatic adjustment of our educational system to the changing circumstances and needs. The British had a vision of spreading their cultural empire through the instrument of education. Independent India lacked a vision of its own and did little to fashion education as a tool for national reconstruction. The old system was allowed to continue without any serious attempts to change it. It got further and further entrenched and became a controlling influence on the growing minds. The result is a crisis of identity among the educated young and a lack of a sense of participation in the ongoing process. There is a paralysis of sorts precipitated by the conflicting conditions that obtain in the classroom and the society at large. Consequently, the nation since Independence has to endure the aches and pains of the conflict between

> tradition and education. It is not simply a conflict between a "jealous pride in Indian genius and tradition" and the dire "desire to profit by the example of the west". It is the existential conflict of the split-soul torn between the conflicting conditions prevailing in our society and the institutions that prepare us to play a role in it.

Rao passionately pleads for a national system of education along the lines sketched by the father of the nation, Mahatma Gandhi. Gandhi's thought, Rao (2000: 34) points out, "blends well with the mosaic of Indian pluralism".

> Gandhi saw the unmistakable cultural context of education, the importance of learning by doing and the need for earning while learning. In today's unbridled enthusiasm for a technological society, explosive forces of economic globalization engulfing the country and the brazen media promotion of Western material values and life styles, Gandhian ideas are an important antidote for preserving the Indianness of India.

At seventy, most people look back at what they had accomplished so far. Rao had much to look back and be proud of his many splendoured contributions; but he is not one to rest content and bask in past glory and laurels. He has always been forward looking. After he celebrated his seventieth birthday, which was capped by a grand reception and felicitations function at the Convocation Theatre of Andhra University on 4 October 2002, Rao continued as active as ever. Mrs Sarojini Ramakrishna Rao, his wife, says that he is working more and longer hours now than when he was employed and paid full-time salary. The only difference is that he is not paid for what he does now.

Rao continues to travel and participate in academic events worldwide. He participated in the 28th International Congress of Psychology held in Beijing in 2004. He gave an invited presentation at the 30th International Congress of Psychology, in Cape Town, South Africa, earlier this year. He led a delegation of Indian philosophers to World Philosophy Congress in Seoul, a few years ago. He participated in the Unesco sponsored World Philosophy Day functions held in Moscow, St. Petersburg and Teheran. He lectured widely in Japan, USA, Canada and other countries.

On 6 June 2006, Rao took charge as the Chairman of the prestigious Indian Council of Philosophical Research (ICPR) and continued as Chairman until 19 September 2012. Under his leadership, ICPR served as a vibrant think-tank of the nation. In addition to his numerous administrative responsibilities, Rao has been very prolific in his writings. He published several books including *Towards a Spiritual Psychology* (with Marwaha 2005), *Handbook of Indian Psychology* (with Paranjpe and Dalal

2008), *Yoga and Parapsychology* (2010), *Cognitive Anomalies, Consciousness and Yoga* (2011a), and *Gandhi and Applied Spirituality* (2011b). During the past five years, Rao published over 3,000 pages in books, book chapters and papers in scholarly journals.

Cognitive Anomalies, Consciousness and Yoga is his *magnum opus*. I had the opportunity to review it in *Psychological Studies* (Rammohan 2011). It is a 900-page dense text covering parapsychology, consciousness studies and Indian psychology. There is no other comparable book in its comprehensive multidisciplinary coverage, providing a holistic perspective for understanding human nature.

A product of mature scholarship in Eastern and Western philosophies, and deep understanding of different schools and systems of contemporary psychological thought, this book is indeed a source book of serious ideas concerning the person, her nature and destiny in the universe. This book is an extraordinary blend of deep scholarship in different areas, written with great clarity and exceptional creativity, to develop a workable model of the person that would doubtless provoke in the years ahead wide discussions worldwide.

Part I of the book deals with the conundrums of cognitive anomalies. In Part II, Rao discusses the enigma of consciousness — its ubiquitous presence in the human condition and our notorious inability to precisely say what it is. Part III is devoted to *yoga* and its relevance for discovering the missing links in consciousness studies and psychical research.

The concluding chapter builds on the main conclusions drawn in the previous reviews and discussions in the previous chapters to sketch a model of the person as a composite of body, mind and consciousness. In the Trisula (Trident) Model, as Rao calls it, body, mind and consciousness are related in a linear and not a triangular manner. The mind is the interfacing instrumentality and connecting link between consciousness and the body. In its cognitive activity, mind reflects consciousness. However, the reflections are generally flawed and are not the true images of reality because they are blemished by the distortions brought about by the constantly changing states of the mind with its biases and the unconscious *saṁskāra*s and the consequent conditioning of the person. Psychology is the discipline whose business is to understand the nature of the biases that distort one's perceptions and the conditioning process so as to decondition the person and render the mind pure and thus make the person perfect. Ego plays a critical role here and the deconditioning and deconstruction of the ego takes the centre stage in the practices believed to raise humans to higher levels of consciousness and being. In this model, the human condition permits three levels of cognitive excellence — (a) observational knowing, (b) rational understanding, and (c) intuitive and transformational realization.

The Trisula Model, as Rao points out, is derived from the basic premises of Indian psychology and is consistent with the main trends of Indian thought without the baggage of the metaphysical commitments of different systems. It has implications for further theoretical developments and for generating new programmes of research in areas that have so far resisted close scientific scrutiny such as the case with putative paranormal phenomena and hard problems of consciousness. The Trident Model, as the author acknowledges, is at a nascent stage as a psychological theory. One hopes that we would soon have a more detailed account of the model and its implications for psychological research. That could indeed be the necessary base for non-reductionist psychology of the future.

Cognitive Anomalies, Consciousness and Yoga, as I wrote in my review, is a rich treasure of information and ideas, drawn from and relevant to diverse fields of inquiry. A vast amount of scholarship is creatively woven to give us an attractive fabric displaying the many splendours of human excellence. It is a book that would stay on our shelves beyond the present generation and one that deserves to be translated into other major languages. Its content is timely. The book augments the scope and substance of psychology in general and Indian psychology in particular.

Rao has a special passion for Mahatma Gandhi. His Ph.D. dissertation is on Gandhi; and his latest book is also on Gandhi — *Gandhi and Applied Spirituality* (2011b). As the Chairman of the ICPR, he encouraged research in the area of Gandhian studies. He is instrumental in persuading GITAM University to establish the GITAM Institute for Gandhian Studies and to start the *GITAM Journal of Gandhian Studies* of which he is the Chairman of the Editorial Board.

Under his leadership, ICPR organized an international and interdisciplinary event — Gandhirama-2012. Dubbed as feast of ideas and festival of art, Gandhirama was arguably one of the largest academic conferences on Gandhi ever held in India. Rao's interest in Gandhi goes beyond politics and philosophy to include parapsychology and *yoga*. He interprets Gandhi's thought and practices in the light of spirituality, modern studies in epidemiology of religious beliefs and practices, and the scientific research into psychic phenomena. He persuasively argues that Gandhiji is a *yogin* and that the practices like *satyāgraha* and the concepts such as *sarvodaya* make little sense without presupposing that, underlying human nature, there is a spiritual dimension of altruism and a hidden bond between people. There is also an epistemological implication that human beings are endowed with extrasensory modalities of communication and action. This is a new and original interpretation of Gandhian thought and practices that has profound implications for understanding Gandhi's notion of non-violence, suffering and salvation.

Rao is a man of deep convictions, unwavering commitment to higher values of life and learning, knowledge and service, and a thoughtful and loving person. As a researcher and scholar he has sought excellence. As a caring teacher, he has won the hearts and minds of his students. As a citizen of the world, he hopes for a global community free from war and terror, a community in which the many extant traditions of the world may blend harmoniously constituting a beautiful mosaic of multiple traditions.

His mission has been one of building cross-cultural bridges in human science to engineer East–West *saṅgamam* (confluence), to close the gap between knowing and being, and to reconcile the essentials of scientific knowledge and religious thought. He was able to raise some of the basic underlying issues, chart a few avenues of possible advances, and more importantly, enthuse and inspire some of us that these are indeed achievable goals.

I believe that we have not seen the end of the journey that Rao has taken over sixty years ago. There is much more to come. At eighty, his intellect is vigorous and his enthusiasm is vibrant as ever. With his mature scholarship, creative mind and deep academic commitment, Rao is poised to add further to his already stupendous contributions. Given another ten or more years of uninterrupted journey, he will find for us many more interesting places from which we may have a better view of the landscape of human science. His deep excavations of classical Indian thought and his concurrent scientific explorations on the frontiers of human science are well structured to provide us with a new architecture of the mind. It has been such a delight to have travelled with him part of the journey as a student and colleague, and see for myself a few exciting things on the way.

References

Bohm, D. (1973), "Quantum Theory as an Indication of a New Order in Physics — Part B: Implicate and Explicate Order in Physical Law", *Foundations of Physics*, 3(2): 139-68.

Pribram, K.H. (1978), "Consciousness: A Scientific Study", *Journal of Indian Psychology*, 1: 95-118.

Rammohan, G. (2011), "*Cognitive Anomalies, Consciousness and Yoga* by K. Ramakrishna Rao", Book Review in *Psychological Studies*, 56: 413-15.

Rao, K.R. (1957), *Psi Cognition*, Tenali, Andhra Pradesh: Tagore Publishing House.

——— (1965), "The Bidirectionality of Psi", *Journal of Parapsychology*, 29: 230-50.

——— (1966), *Experimental Parapsychology: A Review and Interpretation*, Springfield, IL: Charles C. Thomas.

——— (1973), "Koneru Ramakrishna Rao: An Autobiographical Note", *Parapsychology Review* (July–August), pp. 13-15.

——— (1978), "Psi Its Place in Nature", *Journal of Parapsychology*, 42: 276-303.

——— (1988), "What Is Indian Psychology?" Presidential Address, Twenty-fifth Annual Convention of the Indian Academy of Applied Psychology, Hyderabad, Osmania University.

——— (1989), "Meditation, Secular and Sacred: A Review of Some Recent Research", *Journal of the Indian Academy of Applied Psychology*, 15(2): 51-74.

——— (ed.) (1991a), *Cultivating Consciousness: Enhancing Human Potential, Wellness, and Healing*, Westport, CT: Praeger.

——— (1991b), "Consciousness Research and Psi", *Journal of Parapsychology*, 55: 1-43.

——— (1998), "Two Faces of Consciousness: A Look at Eastern and Western Perspectives". *Journal of Consciousness Studies* 5(3), 309-27.

——— (2000), *Higher Education in India: Ground 00 and Vision 2020*. (Dr Sarvepalli Radhakrishnan Memorial Lecture), Visakhapatnam: Andhra University Press.

——— (2001), "Consciousness Studies: A Survey of Prespectives and Research." In J. Pandey (ed.) *Psychology in India Revisited: Development in the Discipline* (pp. 19-162). New Delhi: Sage Publications.

——— (2002), *Consciousness Studies: Cross-cultural Perspectives*, Jefferson, NC: McFarland and Co.

——— (ed.) (2010), *Yoga and Parapsychology: Empirical Research and Theoretical Studies*, Delhi: Motilal Banarsidass.

——— (2011a), *Cognitive Anomalies, Consciousness and Yoga*, New Delhi: Matrix Publishers.

——— (2011b), *Gandhi and Applied Spirituality*, New Delhi: Matrix Publishers.

Rao, K.R. and S. Marwaha (2005), *Towards a Spiritual Psychology*, New Delhi: Samvad.

Rao, K.R., A. Paranjpe and A. Dalal (2008), *Handbook of Indian Psychology*, Delhi: Cambridge University Press.

2

Koneru Ramakrishna Rao: A Philosopher–Scientist–Leader

An Overview of His Career in and Contributions to the Field of Parapsychology[1]

Hanu Rao and *H. Kanthamani*[2]

Introduction

WE are glad to have the opportunity and privilege to write about Prof. Dr K.R. Rao's contributions to experimental parapsychology. Rao is someone whom we have known for a long time professionally and with whom we have also enjoyed a close friendship. The longer we have known him, the more we have come to admire him as a person. Given our unique relationship to the subject and the wonderful occasion for this book, it was clear that this review would not be anything other than a tribute and an accolade to the staggering number of scholarly and scientific contributions Rao has made over fifty plus years "to matters of the mind and beyond". It also occurred to us fairly early that this article would

[1] We are indebted to Jim Kennedy, whom we wish to thank for patiently going through the manuscript and adding to and improving the crucial paragraphs towards the end of the article. Another individual to whom we would like to express our deep gratitude is none other than K.R.R. himself! His recent volume, *Cognitive Anomalies, Consciousness and Yoga* (2011b) came in very handy, as it contains autobiographical references made by Rao, which proved invaluable for our present review. The authors may be forgiven "for repeatedly going to the well" as it were, making frequent references to this hefty scholarly work.

[2] Both the authors studied under Rao. While both have known Rao for several decades, it was Kanthamani who has been collaborating with him virtually from the beginning, and is thus quite familiar with most of the events and developments with respect to his career mentioned in this article. Hanu Rao is no relation of Rao, except that they both hail from the great state of Andhra Pradesh, India.

hardly be a retrospective of his life's work, because at eighty, as Doug Stokes (2002) has previously observed albeit in a different context, Rao seems to be "just getting started". Anyone who has been following the prolific writing put forth by Rao and the frenzy of scholarly activities he was involved in over the past decade would know what we mean by this. While we are on the subject of age, we take this opportunity to wish the good professor a happy birthday and the return of many more. It is clearly in the collective interest of those of us intrigued by the workings of the human mind with its undoubted and yet to be understood potential, that Rao should remain active, so that he can continue to write and make further contributions to the field.

One more word pertaining to this article. When we sat down to write about Rao and his work in the field of parapsychology, it became apparent that the remarkable "arc of his life" was as compelling as the many contributions he has been able to make while living it. Thus what started out as a review of his work naturally turned into a narrative biography, because in Koneru Ramakrishna Rao we have a man whose extraordinary personal qualities coloured his many achievements and took him to the places they did.

Impassioned and Impressionable

It was the decade following India's Independence, when Koneru Ramakrishna Rao attended graduate school in the Philosophy Department of Andhra University, Visakhapatnam. With the protracted and hard-fought "freedom struggle" led by Mahatma Gandhi behind it, the new nation, under the leadership of Prime Minister Jawaharlal Nehru, focused on developing higher education and technology. Andhra University was and continues to be a reputed institution in south India, complimented by vigorous departments in both arts and sciences. That he would one day go on to lead the same university as its Vice-Chancellor (president, in American parlance) might not have occurred to the talented young man at the time, preoccupied as he was attending classes and engaged in deep philosophical debates in and out of the classroom. Rao might very well have lacked such precognitive ability himself, even though that is precisely what he would proceed to study as an experimental parapsychologist in the years to come.

Rao's tutelage under Prof. Saileswar Sen, and later under Prof. Satchidananda Murthy, helped lay a strong foundation as a philosopher and thinker. Prof. Sen was a philosopher and teacher of great distinction, one who attracted serious scholars from overseas. It fell on Sen to advise and guide the precocious pupil who was being pulled in radically different directions, in terms of different schools and intellectual influences. At one extreme was the newly fashionable and contemporary school of Behaviourism from America, with its emphasis on the exclusively observable and measurable, and, on the opposite extreme, the timeless staple of arcane Indian philosophy, preoccupied by metaphysical and abstract concepts. Rao turned to Sen to reconcile these opposing views. Sympathizing with the intensity of Rao's conflict, Sen prescribed him the writings of the eminent philosopher F.W.H. Myers of London's Society for Psychical Research (SPR), as well as the book *Extrasensory Perception* by the American parapsychologist, Joseph Banks Rhine (Rhine 1934/1964). These writings and findings by individuals whom Rao had never heard of before, together with the exotic subject matter they were specializing in, made a strong impression on him. He felt that the ideas behind the writings could serve as a conceptual bridge between the radically different worldviews he had to contend with, just as his professor had hoped. Thus it was fairly accidental that Rao first made contact with parapsychology, a subject which quickly took a strong foothold in his imagination. Here was a field of study, he realized, which was quite provocative in that it potentially had dramatic implications for the existing theories posited to explain the nature of human mind.

Rao delved further into the subject of psychical research and paranormal phenomena, literature on which, rare as it was, was fortunately available in the library at Andhra University. It is noteworthy that at this incipient stage, even as he was first researching the literature, Rao found himself fully convinced as to the reality of psychical phenomena, based on the evidence for psi (standing for the Greek symbol which is universally used by parapsychologists to refer to psychical phenomena) provided by the well-known Pearce-Pratt and other early experiments carried out by Rhine and associates (Rhine et al. 1964/1940). It is equally important to note that there has never been an instance since, over the intervening decades, when Rao wavered in his basic belief in the existence of the paranormal. However, he did express his feelings of discouragement from time to time at the snail's progress made by the field in its aim to confidently demonstrate and manipulate psi phenomena. But that would be getting ahead of our story.

Convinced as he was of the subject matter, Rao was impelled to write his dissertation for a Masters (Hons.) Degree on the topic of psi. He had already begun corresponding with Rhine, a pre-eminent figure in the field who had been conducting pioneering research at Duke University in the United States. It is noteworthy that around this time, while still a student, Rao (1955) had published his first article on parapsychology relating to Vedānta and psi. Following completion of his dissertation, Rao ventured to have it published as a book, *Psi Cognition* (Rao 1957). The fact that it took such a short time from the first reading to writing his own book on parapsychology at a relatively young age, may reflect not only Rao's undoubted mental acumen, but also a compelling interest in what he found to be tantalizing questions raised by the subject. What was more, in addition to his promising scholarly capacities at this early stage in his academic career, Rao was already showing strong potential for leadership and initiative. He was able to approach Rhine, whom he was yet to meet in person, and have him write the foreword to his book. Rao then circulated the publication, sharing his enthusiasm for the newly-found subject of parapsychology with influential scientific and academic figures in India.

To put this in perspective, Rao had written a book and was already promoting the hitherto unfamiliar field of scientific parapsychology in his native country, before the ink had hardly dried on the pages of his Masters thesis! Only one other figure Rao would later meet would possess such missionary zeal for spreading parapsychology. It was none other than J.B. Rhine, referred by many as the father of experimental parapsychology (Mackenzie 1977). Here then were already signs of a synthesizing mind at work, daring to tussle with the big questions and looking wherever for answers. Thus, it was but natural for the neophyte from Andhra to contact the sage in America and be invited to study parapsychology at Duke University, under the latter's guidance.

The Andhra–America Axis

However, as things turned out, Rao first went to the University of Chicago on a Fulbright scholarship, where he wrote his doctoral dissertation in philosophy under the joint tutelage of Richard McKeon of the University of Chicago and K. Satchidananda Murty of Andhra University. His stay at the University of Chicago helped him widen his scholarship as well as attune him to academic rigour. To give a glimpse into the young man's depth of scholarly ambition, it might be pointed out that Rao had also applied and secured a British Council fellowship to study parapsychology at Oxford University under Gilbert Ryle, which he eventually gave up preferring to go to USA and work with Rhine.

While we are beginning to follow Rao's career and trying to keep up with his journeys around the world, it is important to note the one constant that had always been present. His travel to and fro, involving Andhra University, on one end, and Durham, North Carolina, USA, on the other, where Duke University and the Foundation for Research on the Nature of Man (FRNM) were located. He would find himself repeatedly travelling on this axis, which also connected the two strong-minded leaders, Rhine and Rao.

After arriving in the United States in the summer of 1958, Rao first stopped in Durham, to personally meet and introduce himself to Rhine and his team of parapsychology researchers at Duke University. He was able to spend a couple of exciting weeks at Duke, before proceeding to the University of Chicago to study under Richard McKeon. Even though his philosophy studies at Chicago did not directly pertain to parapsychological issues, Rao found the programme to be very beneficial in that it was scholastically demanding and imbued in him academic rigour and discipline. In this connection, Rao later remarked (2011b): "My philosophical mind was cast at Andhra University; but it was shaped and sharpened at the University of Chicago."

Rao Visits Duke Parapsychology Lab

After the successful completion of his studies at Chicago, on his way back to India, Rao went straight to Duke University to once again visit Rhine and his research colleagues at Duke's Parapsychology Lab. On this leisurely visit, which occurred in the year 1960, when Rao walked into Duke Parapsychology Laboratory, it was already a place with a sense of history and mission. It was founded originally to engage in research that would serve to highlight man's unique purpose and show meaning in his existence. These goals bordered on espousing the spiritual, thus were radically opposed to the limited mechanistic view of man associated with the behaviouristic movement, dominant in the early part of the twentieth century.

The prime movers behind the Duke Parapsychology initiative were two men, William McDougall and J.B. Rhine. The two were like-minded, in that they both wanted to find scientific validation for their idealistic views of man's essential nature and psychical research seemed to offer the avenue. By this time, Rao was quite familiar with the history of parapsychology, including that of the Duke Lab. He was aware of how its founding was inspired by the historical investigatory work involving psychic mediums conducted at London's SPR.

Three decades after it came into being, "the Parapsychology Research Unit" lapsed into an uneasy coexistence with the more conventional and image-conscious Duke Psychology Department. During this period much had been accomplished by Rhine and colleagues to move the field of parapsychology into modern times. Rhine did not see an inherent conflict in maintaining opposition to behaviourism's theoretical implications, and, at the same time, unabashedly borrowing from the behaviouristic methodology, with its reliance on *objective* and *measurable* methods. Rhine insisted on employing only objective methods in designing parapsychology experiments, which led to the adoption of Forced Choice tests and the use of statistical analyses.

The Research Scene at Duke Lab

The scene Rao was witnessing at Duke Parapsychology Lab on his first leisurely visit could be described as follows. The well-known work with high-scoring individuals such as Pearce and Linzmayer had already taken place at Duke by that time, which was seen within parapsychology circles as proof of evidence that psi exists. Researchers focused less on testing "psychically-gifted subjects" and more on finding "consistent scorers" from among the general population. By that time, the field had arrived at a general consensus with respect to operationally defining the complex psi ability. Psi was conceptually divided into two broad categories: Extra Sensory Perception (ESP) and Psychokinesis (PK). ESP was further categorized as: Telepathy, Clairvoyance and Precognition. Such categorization was done for sheer methodological convenience, as the phenomena did not lend themselves for clear differentiation.

The experimenters were no longer content with merely establishing evidence for the psi phenomenon, wanting to try and tap its characteristics, particularly the psychological aspects. The counter-intuitive phenomenon of psi missing, wherein it appeared as if a person would, at times, systematically *and unintentionally* miss receiving the target information to a remarkable degree, elicited much research curiosity. Rhine (1952) had written a long paper on the subject of psi missing in the *Journal of Parapsychology*, followed by another describing the unconsciousness nature of psi (1958). These two articles served to frame subsequent research and discussion on these characteristics of psi. Researchers who were psychologically oriented were especially inquisitive to know whether beliefs, attitudes, traits, moods, etc. of the experimental subject had any bearing on the direction of the individual's ESP performance. For instance, the famous Sheep–Goat Effect first noted by Gertrude Schmeidler (1945) addressed how a subject's belief in the existence of psychic phenomena may be related to his or her scoring tendency. Her findings suggested that those who believed in the existence of psi, labelled as sheep, scored in the positive direction, while those who were skeptical, labelled goats, tended to score in the negative direction. This line of research divided subjects into those who were "psi hitters" and "psi missers". Schmeidler and McConnell (1958) discuss a large number of relevant studies in their book on ESP and personality patterns. Betty Humphry (1946) tried to investigate whether the subject's mood state similarly affected the direction of scoring. Based on "free drawings" rendered by the subjects, Humphry divided them into those manifesting expansive mood and those showing compressive mood. She did find subjects with expansive mood tended to be psi hitters, while those showing compressed mood tended to show psi missing. Another dimension of psi research that was being explored at the Duke Lab pertained to the manifestation of psi in the form of PK. Ed Cox, a long time colleague of Rhine, was using innovative equipment to study PK, a phenomenon that continued to generate much research interest in the years to come (Schmidt 1969, 1974). Present-day researchers are increasingly studying PK in real life settings.

Quite apart from the lab studies that were being conducted at the Duke Lab, Louisa Rhine, wife and life-long collaborator of Rhine, had been quietly spending her time amassing and analysing reports she had received at the Lab, of spontaneous occurrences of psi in real life. People who had dramatic experiences apparently involving extrasensory information in their daily lives would often be so impressed by the experiences that they would, on their own, contact and correspond with serious psi researchers such as Louisa Rhine at the Duke Lab. This line of work (Rhine, L.E. 1967, 1965), referred to as "spontaneous case-studies", was recognized to be vital by Rhine himself, as the effects involved were compelling and dramatic, unlike the statistical effects used to measure presence of psi in the lab studies. Like other researchers, later in his career, Rao would increasingly recognize the value of studying such spontaneous manifestation of paranormal effects in the day-to-day lives of people. The importance of L.E. Rhine's life-long work examining the spontaneous case-studies in real life received much recognition by many researchers including Rao who later became a strong advocate of real-life applications of psi.

In 1960, Rao was able to stay long enough at Duke to absorb the parapsychology research climate and get to know the various issues being put to experimental test at the time, both at the Duke Lab as well as at other parapsychology centres in the US and elsewhere. He also had the opportunity to meet and get to know other parapsychology figures who were present, including, J.G. Pratt, Karlis Osis, William Roll, Robert McConnel, Margaret Anderson and Rhea White, all of whom grew to become important figures and would go on to make significant contributions to the field of parapsychology.

Rao's visit left a positive impression in J.B. Rhine's mind. To Rao's delight, Rhine extended an invitation for him to return to Duke in the future for a longer stay, to study parapsychology and do research. Liking what he saw of parapsychology research and impressed by American universities in general, Rao returned to India in 1960. However, it was the charisma and personality of J.B. Rhine, which most impressed Rao, who saw the former as a committed and unwavering guardian of the emerging field of parapsychology.

Turning to Rao himself at this point, during the span of five short years (1955-60) he was able to achieve much already by way of equipping himself as a serious scholar and clearing a path for himself for a career in the dimly lit terrain of parapsychology, on which his mind was clearly set. For those who may not be aware, such determination and goal-orientation was fairly uncommon among young Indians of Rao's generation, especially in the fields of humanities and other non-technological disciplines.

Brief Stay in India

Upon return to India, Rao went back to Andhra University, where he worked out of the Philosophy Department, in addition to spending time developing the university's library. His mind stayed with parapsychology, but he realized that he was not adequately trained in research methodology to conduct experimental studies on his own. Securing a three-year leave of absence from Andhra University, he went back to the United States in 1962, this time to join Rhine and his team at Duke University as a researcher. Many times in his career, Rao left institutions for similarly long periods, for reasons and causes that he found to be compelling at the time. More on this, as we document the unfolding of events.

Rao Joins Rhine (1962-65)

Rao was back at Duke Parapsychology in 1962, this time as a Research Associate. He was welcomed by Rhine, who was always on the lookout for promising researchers who were able and open minded.

Rao was intrigued by the effect of "psi missing", which had been observed for a long time and was an object of investigation. Results from earlier studies showed that some subjects would obtain ESP scores, which were significantly greater than what was expected by chance, while others would score significantly below chance. For some unknown reason subjects seemed to be actively *avoiding* psi-borne information, not just failing to receive the information. As we shall see, throughout his career as an experimenter Rao had an enduring interest in the topic of psi's bidirectionality as he termed it (Rao 1965a). The experiments he designed were aimed at exploring this dual aspect of psi expression, which led to other descriptive terms such as the preferential effect, differential response, and differential effect.

Rao's first published piece of laboratory research was on what he termed the preferential effect (Rao 1962). He deliberately used two types of target material as part of his ESP study: one set consisting of classic ESP symbols developed in the Duke Parapsychology Lab and the other set involving symbols drawn by the subjects themselves, which probably had personal significance to them. The results showed above-chance scoring on "the choice cards" and below-chance scoring, on the standard ESP cards. The difference between them was found to be statistically significant. In further studies Rao (1963a-c) employed two sets of words to serve as targets, selecting words that were innocuous in terms of meaning and of common usage. One set was derived from English and the second set of words was derived from the Indian language, Telugu. It should be noted that none of the subjects who participated in this study were familiar with Telugu. The results showed above-chance scoring on the English-words and below-chance scores on the Telugu set. Rao attributed the difference in ESP scores on the two sets to the variable of familiarity with target material. The subjects, who were all English speaking, probably felt more comfortable with the familiar English language ESP targets and hence found them to be more psi-conducive than targets involving an unfamiliar language.

Rao (1964a, b) continued with this line of work involving dual target conditions differing in language. The studies yielded similar results as before, psi hitting on one condition, and missing on the other. Rao felt that the term differential response was more appropriate for the observed effect than the previous term preferential effect, noting that more than preference seemed to underlie the effect noted. In a related study, B.K. Kanthamani used words from a different Indian language. Results from her experiments (Kanthamani 1965) were in favour of the foreign language words, which was opposite in direction while still supporting the differential effect hypothesis. Reviewing all comparable research involving two distinct experimental conditions such as the ones described above, Rao went on to point out "the bidirectionality of psi" as a characteristic feature of the phenomenon (Rao 1965a). Rao and Davis (1978) in a complex study addressed differential effect and experimenter effect and "the subjects' intentionality". It may be noted that Rao would return to the language-ESP format later to study ESP testing carried out in conditions of relaxation (induced through verbal suggestion), as compared with "normal-wakeful conditions". In a study that involved only one subject, there was evidence for differential effect in a direction that Rao found interesting (1979a). Sailaja (1965), visiting from Andhra, had also carried out a language-ESP study along the lines of Rao above. Attention was turned next to subject-variables including how well the subject had adapted to the testing conditions. Rao (1965b) explored the relationship between anxiety and its effect on ESP performance using Taylor's Manifest Anxiety Scale. The results showed that those showing higher anxiety levels tended to score lower on the ESP task, reflecting an inverse relationship between anxiety level and ESP performance. This study would serve as a precursor to a number of other projects exploring the psychological aspects of the subjects in the years to follow. Several subsequent investigations from the yet to be established Andhra University parapsychology programme, would involve Rao and various associates studying personality variables.

During his first three years in parapsychology, Rao had conducted a sizeable number of studies and published several papers while at Duke. This period of research at Duke Parapsychology Lab beginning in 1962 would prove crucial as it helped transform him "from a tender-minded scholar with interests in philosophy and theoretical psychology into a tough-minded empirical researcher". He would be transformed in many other respects due to a number of significant events that were packed into this short period. Thus Rao was catapulted from his status as a beginner research scholar in parapsychology to leadership roles that proved to be of great consequence for his career, and the field as a whole.

The longer he spent in the company of Rhine, the more Rao was able to appreciate the many challenges the pioneer had to deal with which came from many corners. The more vexing ones included challenges presented by the very subject of investigation. ESP was notoriously capricious in that, consistent results and consistent psi effects were hard to come by. When they did detect a psi signal, so to speak, its magnitude would be typically weak. The phenomenon, it seemed to the researchers, was given to vagaries the nature of which could not be pinned down. The fickle features associated with the psi function in the context of laboratory-based investigations, rendered a repeatable parapsychology experiment difficult to achieve.

As if these technical challenges were not troublesome enough, psi researchers like Rhine had to contend with "professional critics" of their work. The ranks of the critics included those opposed to the enterprise of scientific parapsychology based on their avowed skepticism towards the very existence of paranormal phenomena. That such close-minded individuals also populated "the sister discipline of conventional psychology" came as a disappointment to Rhine and his colleagues. The critics of parapsychology, whose demands were mostly based on standards observed in the well-established physical sciences, perhaps unjustly, found ready ammunition in the day-to-day technical challenges and obstacles encountered by psi researchers. The critics proved to be a distraction that the investigators could well do without. Thus Rao, like other parapsychologists before him, realized that working in the field called for persistence and developing a high tolerance for criticism and frustration. In the years to come, in the role of leader, Rao himself would be offering logical and systematic rebuttals to criticisms levelled at the field (Rao and Palmer 1987). Keeping the critics in mind, even earlier Rao (1979b) had written an article defending the scientific credibility of ESP.

The theoretical and experimental aspects of research espoused by Rhine raised some issues in Rao's mind, the longer he worked at the Duke Lab. He perceived "a disconnect" between Rhine's experimental methods which were objective and quantified and his theoretical notions which tended to be highly subjective and vague. Rao was repelled by terms such as "non-physical and non-materialistic" employed by Rhine to describe the nature of psi. As he grew more comfortable, Rao ventured to voice his criticism of his mentor's "transcendental rhetoric". While doing so, however, Rao could not have been blind to the irony involved as he realized how far he had come in the evolution of his own philosophical standards and values. Gone (or so it seemed at the time, for they would come back with force, in later years) were the metaphysical concepts he had routinely entertained as a student of philosophy at Andhra University. His training as an experimental parapsychologist seemed to have pushed him in the direction of a pragmatic and objectively oriented researcher to whom theory was of a lesser concern. In a fairly short period we see that Rao's research experience in America exerted a significant influence on his thinking, which was still impressionable.

Impressive Progress

Not long after Rao arrived at the Duke Lab and settled down to the job of carrying out experiments, he was called back to India with an unexpected but welcome invitation to set up a parapsychology lab back home — much more on that later. The leadership experience thus gained instituting a university-based parapsychology department in India and his grasp of crucial issues pertaining to parapsychology helped him gain stature in the field. In 1965, still a relative newcomer, Rao, at the age of thirty-three, was elected president of the Parapsychological Association, the international professional body for the field. His charismatic yet earnest personal style, coupled with the unabashed enthusiasm and energy with which he would take up any project, would serve Rao well at this and other points in his career. As is clear from the above, Rao immersed himself in parapsychological research and related issues to such a degree that within three years of his arrival at Duke, he was able to write a book on experimental methodology and have it published in the United States. *Experimental Parapsychology* (Rao 1966) would serve as a handy manual for new entrants to the field, for a long time to come. While going over the past experimental research for writing the book, Rao familiarized himself with all the important historical developments as well as current methodological and theoretical issues. More importantly, he scrutinized the nature of the arguments behind the voluble criticism being levelled at the field.

Other factors which probably explain Rao's rapid rise include the limited scope of the field of parapsychology in terms of the small number of fundamental concepts studied and easy access to the small research community. Speaking of writing books, we will see that Rao was always in the practice of writing books, even as he was reading up on a subject and researching it, which does seem to be a good scholarly habit, as the process of writing forces one to immerse oneself in the new area.

Kothari Calls from India

As we touched on in the previous paragraph, just when he began settling down to carry out parapsychology research in earnest, Rao was abruptly called back to India, as it happened, for a good reason. Back in India, D.S. Kothari, a distinguished theoretical physicist, who was at the time serving as chairman of India's powerful University Grants Commission (UGC), happened to read a review of Rao's first book, *Psi Cognition*. Sufficiently impressed with Rao's ideas and his obvious enthusiasm for parapsychology, Kothari contacted Rao, who was still in the United States with Rhine.

Kothari extended an invitation for Rao to return to India and start a department of parapsychology, at one of the Indian universities, to be fully funded and supported by UGC. This unexpected development was enthusiastically received by both Rao and Rhine, aware as they both were how rare it was for parapsychology research to receive such full-fledged formal recognition from a premier government agency; rarer still, for it to be accompanied by adequate financial support for an indefinite period.

The news of this development had added significance, having come at a time when Rhine was reaching the mandatory age of retirement at Duke University. Not long after Rao returned to India, Rhine retired from Duke University and his long isolated Parapsychology Lab had to severe formal connections with Duke University. The Parapsychology Lab moved out of Duke campus into a privately-funded research foundation in Durham, within a stone's throw from the Duke University. Rhine named the new organization, The Foundation for Research on the Nature of Man (FRNM), of which The Institute for Parapsychology was a part. Rhine was particularly happy about the founding of a new department at Andhra University in India, because he was always a strong proponent of "mainstreaming" parapsychology, which he wanted to see assimilated into universities so as to facilitate systematic research and education. Rao returned briefly to India in 1963 to attend to preliminary work involving the setting up of a university department of parapsychology, clearly a maiden venture, aided by money and encouragement from the UGC.

The speed at which things were developing in his life, considering that Rao was not much older than thirty at this point, must have seemed simply astounding to him as well as those around him. He clearly got what he bargained for and more, in terms of wishing to be involved in parapsychology research while he was a graduate student! It was just as well that he had been spending his time diligently and productively soaking up the field while he was at Duke Parapsychology Lab, as the experience must have provided Rao with an excellent blue print on which to design the Andhra experiment.

Setting Up of Andhra University Department of Psychology and Parapsychology

Rao was faced with the daunting task of setting up a full-fledged department in which to study an entirely new discipline, one he had found out from his American experience could be potentially controversial, not to mention challenging. However, once again, his innate nature of initiative and enterprise came to the fore, as he went about the latest project with his trademark enthusiasm and energy. The year was 1963.

Taking advantage of the presence of J.G. Pratt, Rhine's long time collaborator who happened to be travelling in India at the time, Rao invited the former to join him as he toured various universities in India trying to pick a suitable site to house the proposed new department of parapsychology. The two men finally decided in favour of the familiar Andhra University to serve as the home for the UGC-sponsored venture.

It was Rao's deliberate strategy to develop the new field of parapsychology in India, not in isolation, but alongside conventional psychology. Accordingly, the specially endowed department at Andhra University was named the Department of Psychology and Parapsychology (DPP). There remained a lot of work to be done before the dream could be realized. A favourable and receptive climate had to be cultivated among the influential figures at Andhra University, towards gaining their acceptance of the new department. Even more importantly, individuals to serve as faculty in the new field had to be found and trained from scratch.

Rao was able to find and recruit three promising scholars from Indian universities, who would be trained in the United States, in Rhine's lab. Rhine welcomed the idea and readily accommodated Rao's request to help train the visiting researchers, an arrangement which continued in subsequent years, involving more such trainees to come. Thus Rhine continued to be supportive towards the new venture in India. In this connection, it may be noted that Rhine had already expressed his views on the need for trained research workers in the field of parapsychology (1956). The first group to undergo training in parapsychology during 1963-65, included B.K. Kanthamani, P. Sailaja and a third individual, Bhadra, who, it so happened, had to leave the programme prematurely for personal reasons. The newly-trained researchers would join Rao to form the core staff for the new department in India.

Parapsychology Centre in India

DPP at Andhra University eventually came into being in 1967. With the ample financial support provided by the UGC, Rao was able to find a separate building for the new department on campus, which was fully equipped in all respects, including a good collection of books, and relevant literature in the departmental library. Considering that it had to serve both psychology and parapsychology graduate studies, care was also given to finding adequate laboratory facilities.

The DPP was off to a fine start, opening its doors to graduate students eagerly enrolling in psychology courses as well as the hitherto unfamiliar subject of parapsychology. The new field was actively promoted to attract promising students to enroll in the parapsychology offerings. A full-fledged syllabus was developed, which addressed the definitions, significant issues and controversies, along with research methodology pertaining to experimental parapsychology. In this sense, it fell on Rao "to cull and synthesize" the haphazard historical developments in the field, into a coherent, systematic university-level curriculum of study. In meeting this daunting academic challenge, he was helped not only by his recent apprenticeship under Rhine, but also the solid academic background he had acquired in philosophy, described earlier.

Interestingly, the founding of Andhra University DPP in 1967 seems to involve a "displacement effect". What was originally Rhine's dream of setting up a full-fledged parapsychology department under the inspiration and guidance of McDougall at Duke University finally came to fruition, displaced in time and space, occurring four decades later, and some 10,000 miles away! The Rhine–Rao connection does seem kārmic in nature, when we see how the remarkable events involving the two men unfolded.

Under Rao's careful leadership and guidance, the Andhra University parapsychology programme proved to be highly productive. During the decade Rao was able to stay in India, and personally direct the newly-founded department, much was achieved by way of parapsychology research including several doctoral dissertations, and papers published. Rapid growth was also achieved on the teaching side, involving courses of study in psychology and parapsychology.

Andhra PhDs

Under the direction of Rao, researchers and scholars engaged in several parapsychological investigations at Andhra University DPP. These studies were generally oriented to studying psychological variables of individual ESP subjects, such as personality traits, mood variables and perceptual states, and assessing their impact on subjects' ESP performance. Even altered states of consciousness such as meditation and *yoga* practices were among the person-related variables tested. The researchers also showed innovation in trying to study psi, as it operated in real life settings.

The initial contribution from Andhra parapsychology programme was made by B.K. Kanthamani, the first graduate-student to register for PhD. She had already spent two years at Duke Parapsychology Lab, and thus familiar with research literature involving subjects' psychological characteristics and related variables. Her dissertation was influenced by the findings of Schmeidler (1945) and Humphry (1946). Collaborating with Rao, Kanthamani explored the perplexing phenomenon of psi missing from the standpoint of personality variables including subjects' mood. In a personality–ESP study, Kanthamani tested a large number of subjects who were in the age range 15-18, drawn from local schools. She employed the Cattel's High School Personality Questionnaire (HSPQ), and had subjects render free drawings from which to assess their mood at the time of taking the ESP test. Standard ESP cards were used for ESP testing. The results showed that psi-hitting was associated with extroverts, and missing with introverts. The Neuroticism scale also yielded significant results, showing that low anxious subjects scored higher on the ESP test than high anxious subjects. The general conclusion drawn from this study suggested that those who were able to make a positive psychological/emotional adaptation to the ESP testing situation seemed to score higher. These findings are published (Kanthamani & Rao 1971, 1972a, b, 1973a, b).

Anxiety elicited in the process of dealing with a stressful life situation, and its effect on ESP scoring, was the aim of an innovative study conducted by Rao et al. (1968). The study involved applicants to a sought-after graduate programme at Andhra University who were called for a personal interview, where they were asked to first participate in an ESP test, which was introduced as "a test of applicants' intuitive ability". The ESP test came as a surprise to all the applicants who were not expecting the novel task. Nevertheless, everyone complied. Next the applicants attended the personal interview, following which subjects were asked to complete another round of ESP testing. This second round was justified by explaining to the subjects that it was "for gathering more data for research purposes". The results of the elaborate study confirmed the expectations of the researchers, in that ESP scoring prior to the personal interview showed psi missing and the post-interview scoring tended towards psi hitting. It was interesting to note that the negative impact of anxiety on psi scoring was the same, whether the anxiety manifested as an inherent trait of the subject, or, if it was present as "situational anxiety" attributable to a stressful life situation. It should be noted that Sailaja continued this line of work involving ESP and real-life situations which she submitted as a doctoral dissertation (Sailaja & Rao 1973).

Hamlyn Dukhan of Trinidad, West Indies, is a researcher credited with the discovery of Lal Singh Harribance, a gifted psychic and a high scoring subject who was widely tested in the United States later. Dukhan visited Andhra University for a two-year period, during 1970-72, at the invitation of Rao. While at Andhra, Dukhan engaged in pioneering research involving a systematic study of *yoga* and its relation to paranormal abilities. A series of experiments were conducted at two different *yoga āśramas* in south India, one in Pondicherry and another in Bangalore. At these sites, exponents of *yoga* were tested for their ESP ability. The target material involving standard ESP cards as well as free-response targets were administered to the *yoga* practitioners before and after meditation. The results showed better ESP performance following the meditative period, than when tested prior to meditation. This effect was found on both types of targets described above (Rao et al. 1978).

P.V.K. Rao, also from Andhra University DPP, followed up the above line of work involving meditation, which he submitted as his doctoral dissertation. He explored the relationship between ESP and Subliminal Perception (SP). The two types of perception were tested under two conditions, one involving normal state of consciousness, and the other, an altered state of consciousness produced by meditation. The results showed a significant positive correlation between the SP and ESP scores among those who practised Transcendental Meditation (TM) before taking the test, suggesting that, to the extent both perceptual phenomena were influenced alike by TM, they might be processed in similar ways (Rao & Rao 1982).

Another dissertation from Andhra submitted by Shanti Krishna (Krishna & Rao 1981), investigated differential response involving language-ESP tests. She had collaborated with Rao and Kanthamani and carried out part of this research at the FRNM (1979). Krishna had used similar target material employed by Rao in his early work, using words from English and Telugu. She had conducted both individual and group testing on a large number of subjects, generating thousands of trials. Overall, the results from this study did not lend support to earlier findings with respect to differential scoring reported by Rao. Later, another study was reported on the effects of ESP feedback on personality data (Krishna & Rao 1991).

Gowri Rammohan (1990), also from Andhra University DPP, investigated "psi in need-relevant, high motivational contexts". She was specifically interested to see how psi operated in the routine classroom setting, and during academic examinations. In a series of experiments, Rammohan attempted to relate her findings to such variables as student attitudes towards the teacher, whether subjects felt luck played a role in their performance on examinations, their mood at the time, and their belief in ESP, etc. Prior to this study, Rao and O'Brien (1977) had carried out similar work at the FRNM.

U. Vindhya based her parapsychology doctoral dissertation (unpublished) on a multivariate study on psi, using the ganzfeld technique. She was interested in the variables of personality and belief in ESP on the parts of both agents and percipients, in determining psi retrieval in the ganzfeld condition.

In addition to the impressive experimental parapsychology research, which was being undertaken at Andhra University DPP during its formative years, Master's degree programmes with conventional psychology majors were also flourishing. All in all, it was a heady period of growth for the new department, bringing it much notice on the Andhra University campus.

It is important to point out that quite a bit of this success at Andhra is attributable to the strong personal connection Rao had established over the years with Rhine, and his Institute for Parapsychology, which was a part and parcel of Rhine's FRNM. Rhine was more than happy to help Rao and see that Andhra University DPP got on its feet and thrived. As mentioned earlier, this was accomplished mainly by inviting Andhra scholars to travel to United States, stay at the institute for a period of training, long enough to work on and complete doctoral-level research in parapsychology, before they returned to Andhra. Thus Rhine might have perceived the parapsychology set up at Andhra University as a distant satellite of his historical centre in Durham.

Prior to the appearance of Andhra on the parapsychology landscape, not many doctorates were awarded in the subject of parapsychology. In this connection, it is of interest to note that Rhine, who was originally trained in natural sciences, was ambivalent about the value of a pure parapsychology degree as useful preparation for a research career in the field. Rhine preferred that workers arrive with credentials and expertise that they have obtained in other disciplines, so as to participate in an interdisciplinary effort. However, Rao, unlike Rhine, was part of a major university, directing a full-fledged post-graduate department, which awarded degrees to students/candidates.

The story of Andhra University DPP does not quite end here, as we will come back to it later in this narrative.

The Levy Affair

Late 1960s and early 1970s was a vibrant period for the handful of parapsychology centres located in the United States and other parts of the world. The number of labs and research units investigating the paranormal was on the rise; special subjects — individuals who were believed to be psychically gifted — were being tested in different parts of the world; parapsychology-related educational activities by way of summer study programmes, seminars and conferences were in full swing; there was also a surge in popular interest in ostensible psychical happenings and phenomena, as reflected by the showing of more movies, and frequent press reports containing parapsychology content. In another significant development, the prestigious American Association for the Advancement of Science (AAAS) formally admitted the Parapsychology Association as a member during the decade of the 1970s. Even the NASA space programme to the moon involved an unofficial parapsychology experiment conducted by an interested astronaut!

There were changes taking place within Rhine's lab also. Some researchers elected to leave, following strained relationships that had developed between them and Rhine. Charles Honorton and Rex Stanford were two of the more prominent members from "the group of young lions" who walked out. Before we proceed with the narrative, we should pause here to recognize the many contributions made by these two stalwarts of scientific parapsychology. Stanford was a theorist and an astute experimenter who has widely published. Honorton was a natural leader who branched out on his own and based in New York City, he spearheaded a highly successful programme involving the ganzfeld technique. It would be no exaggeration to say that he devoted his entire life to advancing the cause of parapsychology. Honorton (1977) wrote a seminal paper on internal states published as part of Wolman's *Handbook of Parapsychology*. Following Honorton's untimely death, Rao (1993) recognized the former's significant leadership contributions.

Back at the FRNM, it was remarkable that Rhine was able to find competent replacements fairly quickly. The new crop of researchers included Helmut Schmidt, an applied physicist who was working previously for the Boeing Corporation. Jay Levy was a young physician, trained in neurology. Also added to the research staff at the FRNM was Edward Kelly, a psycholinguist by training with a broad range of research interests including psychophysiology.

Levy's medical and research qualifications, as well as his apparent interest in parapsychology and successful innovative experiments, were what Rhine found attractive in the youthful doctor. Rhine thought that in Levy he had found someone who could fully take over the reins from him, when the time came. Meanwhile, Levy was made director of the Institute for Parapsychology. Indeed, for all appearances, the Institute for Parapsychology was humming along with more vigour and vitality than ever before. Quite a bit of the research activity was attributable to a novel line of experiments studying PK in animal-subjects, which were being conducted by Levy. Then came "the Jay Levy bomb shell", referred to as such, based on the concussive impact it has had on the tiny lab where it occurred, and on the field of parapsychology as a whole.

It was discovered in 1974 that Jay Levy was engaging in deliberate fraud, by manipulating results from one of his PK experiments. This fact was unearthed and demonstrated beyond doubt by Levy's own research colleagues, who took care to produce indisputable evidence of the data falsification, when they approached Rhine. This understandably came as a shock and a profound disappointment to Rhine, something he could ill afford at this late stage in his life, not to speak of the effect this would have on the already fragile reputation the field was accorded in the scientific world. However, to his credit, Rhine, who had, until then, pinned his hopes on Levy to lead the field, was able to quickly bring himself to fire Jay Levy on the spot. He severed all ties with Levy, retracting and discrediting all of Levy's parapsychology research, published or otherwise.

As can be imagined, the Levy scandal sent shock waves through the small universe of parapsychology, resulting in a palpable sense of disillusionment. The news reached Rao and brought him to the United States. Along with many others, Rao stood by his mentor and offered his moral support, as the latter struggled to carry on in the aftermath of the unfortunate development. By this time Rao had gained a significant measure of professional stature in the field, having already served as the president of the Parapsychology Association (PA). Rao would have occasion to exercise leadership at the annual convention of the PA held in Santa Barbara, later that summer. In the convention hall, he spoke up and strongly opposed moves being made by the PA leadership to discredit and censure all work being reported from Rhine's institute, not just that of Jay Levy. Rao maintained that such a blanket policy simply was not fair, logical or in the best interests of the field of parapsychology. Rao's compelling comments received a resounding applause. In making these forthright comments, Rao also showed his loyal support for Rhine, both in speech and action that summer, when the latter needed it the most. Apparently, this did not go unnoticed, as Rhine began to court Rao trying to interest him to return to the FRNM. Rao was told by Rhine that he was the person "who could help complete the job" that Rhine had started (Rao 2011b).

Back Home, Minding Own Business

If Andhra's remoteness from America and all the parapsychology happenings there was seen before as a disadvantage following the Levy affair, Andhra provided welcome isolation. Rao was able to get his mind back on parapsychology, specifically thinking of widening the horizons of research. Rao was now turning back to Eastern concepts such as consciousness, as well as ideas and practices from traditional Indian psychology to explore suitable avenues of psi research. It was important to dive in deeper, so to speak and look into see where psi could be residing. The goal, it seemed to Rao, was to reintegrate parapsychology with a more comprehensive view of psychology, to achieve a holistic and non-reductionistic approach. In addition to tackling such intricate "matters of the mind", Rao was also actively participating in the affairs of the university at the leadership level. Rao seems to have always possessed the unusual ability to switch between radically different endeavours, scholar one minute, and leading and organizing affairs of men, the next.

To Go or Not to Go? Andhra or America?

This relatively quiet and contemplative phase at Andhra would not last long, however. Rhine kept up correspondence and eventually prevailed in having Rao consider returning to the FRNM, this time as its leader. Rao felt flattered considering that the offer was probably more of a plea, one that came from Rhine, Rao's long time American idol. To be replacing the patriarch of the field of parapsychology in the United States, likely came as "a considerable ego-boost". More than anything else, the invitation from Rhine implied that the venerated elder had enough confidence in Rao's leadership abilities, which would be needed in order for him to continue to nurture and develop the field. After all, Rhine was a trained botanist, and an avid gardener, so it would be fitting to depict his life's work as that of a devoted gardener. Together with his loyal wife and fellow botanist, Louisa Rhine, J.B. Rhine raised an enchanted garden, as it were, which held the mysteries and secrets to the human mind, for the two of them. Only people familiar with the history of Duke Parapsychology Lab, and later with the FRNM, and those who knew of the diligence and seriousness of purpose with which the Rhines pursued their cherished subject matter, would understand the aptness of this floral analogy.

Thus, it was nothing less than being invited into the inner sanctum, something Rao simply could not turn down. At the same time, however, he was faced with a dilemma. It was fine for him "to go to the rescue of Rhine's baby" as it were, but what about his own? In less than a decade, he created his own parapsychology lab at Andhra University. He was infused with the same enthusiasm and sense of mission for parapsychology, as were the Rhines. The parapsychology programme at Andhra University DPP was off to a great start and continuing to thrive. The university and the community were receptive to the study of a subject that enjoyed strong roots in the Indian culture, at large. More importantly, Rao's department enjoyed predictable and sure financial support on an indefinite basis, as was assured by UGC at the very outset of setting up the DPP. Rao's broader role on the campus, which involved participation at the university leadership level, further ensured continued support from within the university for the parapsychology initiative.

If he were to leave all this behind at Andhra University DPP, in which he invested so much time and energy, instead chose to go to America, who will assume leadership in his absence? There were trained faculty at Andhra who should reasonably be expected "to hold the fort", in his absence. In other words, someone could be designated to carry on with the basic mission of the Andhra parapsychology programme during Rao's absence — someone who could manage the department on a day-to-day basis, until his return. However, at the time, Rao did not find any one in the small group who evinced sure signs of leadership ability, zeal and commitment for fostering parapsychology, as he himself had been doing. But then, how would he ever to know unless someone was allowed the opportunity in the first place to exercise his/her leadership skills, away from under his own admittedly imposing presence? Pushing all doubts aside and making what arrangements he could in the short amount of time he had, Rao left Andhra on a three-year leave to Rhine. Even if Rao had any misgivings about his decision to go on long leave from Andhra University, there was not much room in his mind for them, preoccupied as he was with thoughts about the challenge awaiting him in the West.

In any event, this wouldn't be the only time Rao would find himself obliging requests to lend his talents and skills, to intervene in distant crises and causes.

The year was 1976 — it would be years later before Rao would fully realize how his departure from Andhra University DPP effectively orphaned it. The parapsychology component would go neglected and allowed to wither, mainly for lack of genuine interest in the paranormal and associated lack of leadership among departmental faculty. We will return to the status of the Andhra programme later in this article.

Rao, the Rescuer

When Rao arrived at the FRNM in 1976, the agreement between Rhine and him was that the latter would stay and steer the Institute for Parapsychology only till such time as someone else was found, one who could stay and serve in the leadership role for a longer period. The two expected that it might take a couple of years for this to occur, following which Rao could return to Andhra. This was the thinking at the time when Rao secured the three-year leave from Andhra University to travel to America and take up leadership of the FRNM. This was the second such prolonged leave of absence Rao was granted by Andhra University, which as it turned out, had to be further extended.

It would be useful to stall here for a moment and look for factors which might explain how Rao was able to move so freely between job assignments, back and forth. First, the moves he had made were always undertaken "for a good cause". They always involved some type of a "rescue mission", which called on his expertise and hence was always found to be a persuasive reason. Second, Rao always proved himself invaluable to his employers or the institution he was serving, by working hard to develop the organization and institute significant changes and improvements. Last, he had always realized the importance of maintaining good social relations with those in important positions within the organization, often occupying one himself. This was not simply for reasons stemming from personal ambition, but to have access to resources needed to advance the cause he was promoting.

Upon arrival at FRNM, Rao found the scene quite familiar, everyone carrying on as they always did — researchers churning out more data employing the classic Rhinean experimental methodology. Rao joined the group, and began conducting some studies of his own, along the same lines he had adopted before, and collaborating with others in their work.

The relationship between ESP and memory has been of interest to parapsychologists for a long time. For instance, Roll (1966) postulated that frequently reinforced memory traces would serve better as ESP vehicles than less frequently reinforced ones. Along these lines, Kanthamani and H.H. Rao (1974, 1975a, b) conducted a series of experiments in which subjects memorized a list of paired associates consisting of a trigram and a meaningful word. The ESP test was embedded in the recall phase wherein the subjects had to pick one of the two spaces provided on the response sheet to write-in the recalled word. The results showed that the subjects were more successful in their ESP on correctly recalled words than on incorrectly recalled words. Further, this effect seemed stronger on low-association word pairs.

Rao et al. (1977a) continued studying memory and ESP. They also had subjects attempt to recall meaningful words associated with the stimulus trigrams. In the first experiment they observed that when "psi hitters" failed to recall the correct word, they tended to respond with words that were relatively close in their association to the target. Psi missers did the opposite, but to a much lesser degree. Subjects seemed to substitute a forgotten word with another, which seemed to have the closest association. If this were the case, it would appear that at some level memory retrieval and ESP response might involve similar processing.

The results from a follow up study were in the same direction but not statistically significant (Rao et al. 1977b).

Rao (1978a) attempted to explore whether meaningfulness of target words to the subject would have any effect on the scoring direction. The results showed a positive memory–ESP correlation. However, the result was in a direction opposite to what was suggested by the previous study, leading to an interesting discussion on the question of the relationship between memory and ESP. Based on the above research Rao wrote an interesting paper on psi and its place in nature (Rao 1978b). It may be added that memory–ESP relationship was also studied at Andhra University, along the lines adopted at the FRNM, by Sailaja and P.V.K. Rao (1978). Later, Rao and Weiner (1982) and Rao et al. (1990) had conducted more studies exploring "normal–paranormal interaction" in the context of memory–ESP testing. In his new book, *First Sight: ESP and Parapsychology in Everyday Life,* Carpenter (2012) devotes a section to psi and memory. He describes the memory studies cited above and puts them in perspective along with the others found in the literature. Carpenter's book also serves as an excellent source covering much of the experimental work done by Rao and his colleagues, over the years.

The research studies cited thus far were all conducted either by Rao himself or by his collaborators under his close direction. Keeping the limited scope of this review in mind, suffice to say that Rao remained a dynamic research leader and scientist, during all his parapsychology years. He was directly instrumental in conceiving, implementing and otherwise facilitating a multitude of innovative research studies. For instance, many of the parapsychological dissertation studies from Andhra University DPP, at their heart, had research questions that Rao wanted addressed. While the individual authors of these studies deserved much credit for their own part in executing them, many would acknowledge the close day-to-day guidance of Rao. Virtually all topics subjected to experimentation by the Andhra researchers, which run the entire gamut of modern experimental parapsychology, were carried out "at Rao's prompting, and under his aegis". The topics explored included: the roles of memory, altered states, perceptual states, psychophysiology, dreams, not to speak of *yoga*/meditation and other altered states of consciousness. Rao's "free-ranging mind", it seems, "ran here and ran there", looking for any lead or at least a suggestion of one, in his frantic search for the capricious phenomenon. He was able to venture out of the confines of the lab and sought out serious exponents of *yoga*, who actively cultivated their fields of consciousness, to study them in their natural locales. He had similarly preferred real world settings for some of the studies that were undertaken in India.

A more recent study, supported by a grant from India's Defence Ministry, involved a very large subject pool, massive by Western standards. Rao (2010) refers to the project as dealing with "cognitive anomalies". Assisted by his colleagues at the Institute for Human Science and Service (IHSS), Rao developed a specialized ESP test to screen unselected subjects to find "star performers". His aim was to develop "a culturally relevant and ecologically valid" ESP test, one which would be suitable for use in the context of real-life settings. The new ESP test, which was titled "How intuitive are you?" Rao hoped would be suitable for mass screenings looking for ESP ability. It included twelve forced-choice items and one free response item. The forced-choice items involved short verbal descriptions of a hypothetical problem taken from real life, for which four plausible solutions were offered, and the subjects was to select "the correct solution". The administration of the free response trial was preceded by a brief relaxation exercise. Two remarkable aspects of this study involve the utilization of a very large pool of subjects, and the use of precognition modality for testing ESP. College students — 1,800 — comprising of both sexes, were tested in this study. Many ancillary questionnaires and surveys of interest were also administered to the subjects, in addition to the "How intuitive are you?" The questionnaires surveyed subjects' religiosity, their belief in the paranormal. The Myers–Briggs personality questionnaire was also administered. It is interesting to note that this massive data yielded an overall evidence of psi significant at the .05 level, which is rather rare. It is noteworthy that Rao was careful to use the broader term "cognitive anomalies of the ESP type" to indicate the paranormal thrust of this investigation, which was funded by grants from India's military. Also of interest is the use of college-age students as subjects for this study, considering young military recruits also fall in the same age group. Rao's newly-designed ESP test could conceivably be used to screen soldiers on a large scale or any other naturally occurring group.

Taking advantage of the large data base, Jacksan and Sonali (2010) went on to analyse the questionnaire data. However, extensive analyses revealed no systematic relationships of a significant nature between the different personality variables, religiosity and paranormal beliefs.

Turning to research in *yoga* and meditation, the Institute for Yoga and Consciousness (IYC), founded by Rao, proved to be quite fruitful. Kristeller and Rikhye (2008) noted that as many as sixty studies were undertaken at the IYC. However, a majority of the studies were focused on the health benefits that accrue from the practice of *yoga* and meditation, rather than on parapsychology. A study of meditation and its effects on attentional regulation and the overall health of practitioners by N.J. Rani and P.V.K. Rao (1996, 2000), exemplifies some of the work done at the institute. It may be noted that P.V.K. Rao of Andhra University DPP served as director of the IYC, during this period. Rao had already written a review article on meditation research for an Indian periodical (1989). He was also interested in variables relating to psychophysiology and ESP. He participated in an exploratory study looking at alpha rhythm and ESP scoring (Rao & Feola 1979). Another area of interest, which received attention at Andhra University DPP in the 1970s, explored relationship between meditation and perceptual states — subliminal and extrasensory (Rao & Puri 1978). Rao et al. (1977) explored relationship between "kinesthetic subliminal perception" involved in a weight discrimination task and ESP. Munson et al. (1980) also explored subliminal perception and ESP "in a learning paradigm", in a study which took place at the FRNM.

During 1977-84, research at the FRNM was proceeding as it always had. The experimenters "might be tweaking something here or tightening something there", but basically everyone was adhering to the classic methods and statistics, originally introduced by Rhine. Even experiments that were deemed successful would produce results that were mere statistical effects, whose significance seemed to impress no one else outside the small huddled research group. If he experienced any sense of dissonance at the time, Rao did not give in to it, stoically continuing to implement "research as usual". However, in retrospect, it does appear that during this period Rao missed the sense of independence he was enjoying while he was directing his own department at Andhra University DPP. At Andhra, he was trying to pursue a parapsychology research programme, which was derived from a wider conceptual base. He was in the process of refocusing his thinking, trying to accommodate and investigate psi-conducive states informed by ideas from the consciousness literature and that of classical Indian psychology.

Here is Rao, in his own words, looking back, years later, and commenting on this phase of his career at the FRNM, which lasted nearly eight years (Rao 2011b: 233):

> Back in the US, I continued strictly the Rhinean experimental legacy, shelving my personal preference for integrating psi research into related areas of human science because it did not appear prudent or feasible in the American setting. We continued to accumulate more and more data, testing what now seem to be trivial hypotheses. Our work, as most of the work in parapsychology, was fundamentally data driven, rather than theoretically oriented. It was methodologically sound and rigorous, but theoretically lacking strength and significance. We were too timid to draw the logical conclusions of the reality of psi. The goal, it seemed, was to seek admission into the portals of science, than try to make a difference.

Meanwhile, things did not turn out quite as originally hoped, in that a permanent director for the FRNM could not be found within the three-year period. This meant that Rao, at Rhine's request, had to stay on at FRNM for another three-year period.

The pre-eminent, staunch pioneer of parapsychology, Rhine, passed away in 1980. Rao edited a book, *J.B. Rhine: On the Frontiers of Science,* commemorating Rhine's historical contributions to the field (1982a). It may be mentioned that Rao (1982b) wrote in this book a chapter on Rhine and his critics. Rao felt obliged to stay and continue to lead the research programme at the FRNM, even if it reflected "a greater concern with methodology than with its meaning." He retrospectively conveys (2011b) that such prolonged exposure to reliance on "scientifically respectable" methods of experimentation, in an atmosphere where everyone seemed content with pursuing relatively shallow concerns and questions, made him look back fondly to his days as a graduate student in philosophy. He felt as if he went full circle, back to the days when he was preoccupied with the *Brahman* and other subjective, but rich metaphysical concepts. It was becoming increasingly clear to Rao that he, along with his research colleagues, was "marching on a dead end road" as it were. They were engaged in pursuing bona fide but inconsequential "data-happy experiments".

Lest the reader should go away with the impression that Rao was content to passively go along with a tepid research programme during his years at the FRNM, it should be made clear that he was very active on the writing and speaking fronts as befits a leader. He was quite vocal when it came to dealing with the critics (Rao & Palmer 1987) and suggesting changes in direction that the field should consider. In addition to his many books, Rao had written many book reviews [including one of B.B. Wolman's *Handbook of Parapsychology* (1977c)], several commentaries, and delivered presidential and keynote addresses at many conferences and gatherings. Some of the commentaries pertained to the theories of psi. Rao also addressed the persistent and thorny issue of replicability in parapsychology experiments at the Parapsychology Association's annual convention held at Syracuse in 1981. He (1977a, b) wrote extensively on issues dealing with the frustrations and challenges faced by psi researchers and on the nature of psi.

American Idol to Andhra Idol

While Rao was plodding along carrying out day-to-day research, but keeping busy with the different functions associated with his role as executive director of the FRNM, "out of the blue" he received a phone call from none other than the Chief Minister (CM) of Andhra Pradesh in India, the state in which Andhra University is located.

This was indeed a pleasant surprise because the CM happened to be none other than the famous N.T. Rama Rao (no relation), the former movie star and popular Telugu matinee idol, lovingly referred by legions of fans as NTR. So what exactly did the CM want from Rao? During a search for the position of Vice-Chancellor for Andhra University, NTR was advised by his staffers to tap K.R. Rao for the important position. The position of Vice-Chancellor, it may be explained, is comparable to that of a president of an American university, as he or she serves as the head of the academic institution and as well as its administration. So, was Rao interested? Again we see that Rao was being courted, this time by another kind of idol, who was a childhood cultural icon for Rao, and everyone else in Andhra, for that matter. NTR's charisma on the silver screen was such that it had not spared any soul from Andhra Pradesh, scholars and intellectuals included! Once again, Rao had to weigh the pros and cons of decision-making. This time around, the conflict was not so intense. The chance for an academic to serve as the top leader of a major university, especially one of which he was an alumnus, was something one simply grabbed. Rao had spent seven years at the FRNM, long beyond his original commitment to Rhine. Unlike at Andhra University DPP, there were trained and experienced staff who could fill his shoes and carry on. Rao was ready for a change, as he found parapsychology research at the FRNM was reaching a point of stagnation.

It was a relatively easy decision for Rao to take a three-year leave of absence from the FRNM and return to India and his *alma mater*. He was now the Vice-Chancellor of Andhra University, a position historically held by a succession of eminent Indian personalities. The mission on which Rao came back to India and Andhra University was literally worlds apart from the one he was involved in, while in America. It was a sudden leap from the quiet, deep, dimly lit world of psi search, out into the noisy, bustling world of an Indian university, where policy, it seemed, was made "under the harsh glare of the tropical sun". Yet, Rao had always been eminently adaptable. He had never allowed lack of comforts and such other external factors interfere with his work. As he writes (2011b: 235):

> Fortunately I never had any trouble in adjusting to such changes. I felt quite at home whether I lived in the comforts and conveniences of USA or the hardships of rural India, whether the universe of activities is as large as Andhra Pradesh or as small as FRNM. I always found myself enough to do, whatever is the stage.

In this respect, Rao was not unlike the great Mahatma Gandhi, someone whom Rao happens to venerate, about whom he wrote books and has set up an institution for Gandhian studies (1968, 2011a). Let us go back to Andhra University in the year 1984, when Rao was a newly-appointed Vice-Chancellor, in which position he served for three years. On arrival, "he had to hit the ground running" as he had to get busy attending to many boiling issues involving an institution whose student body was in the thousands and the number of rapidly growing and multiplying departments, simply staggering. Not only did he manage the situation well, "he was able to turn the university around", overcoming many challenging and intractable problems, and instituting bold changes, which were long overdue.

The high-profile job of Vice-Chancellor simply did not leave any time for Rao to indulge his enduring interest in parapsychology. After all, the Andhra University DPP for the development of which he devoted so much of his energy was located right on the campus, nestled right behind his vice-chancellor's lodge! In this connection, Rao airs his frustrations openly and honestly, when he observes (2011b: 234):

> Back in India, I realized quickly that parapsychology lost its shine and glamour. There was little interest or enthusiasm in the Department of Psychology and Parapsychology at Andhra University (Andhra University DPP), which I founded. I arranged for an international conference sponsored by the Parapsychology Association at Andhra University and appointed a couple of additional faculty with

> parapsychology specialization. All these did not ignite the necessary interest to set parapsychology in motion again. I did not wish to interfere with the working of the DPP academically or administratively at the personal or professional level. At the same time, my interest in and commitment to exploring extraordinary human abilities is too intense and deep to accept the unexciting prospects for parapsychology at Andhra University.

It is clear from the above that Rao was deeply disappointed at the state of affairs as far as the parapsychology programme at Andhra University was concerned. However, in retrospect, Rao accepts all the blame on himself for the neglected state in which he found Andhra University parapsychology upon his return, seven years later. He engages in a good measure of introspection, even expresses feelings bordering on self-reproach, over this issue. Rao deeply regrets his decision to leave one parapsychology programme, one which he had personally founded, which was developing and was gradually coming into its own, in order to tend to another programme which needed attention. In so doing he might have saved one baby but lost another, it seemed to him. Here is Rao, speaking of the twin parapsychology interests located in different hemispheres of the globe, which consumed his energies and interests during much of his active years (2011b: 233):

> In hindsight, it would appear, I was wrong (in deciding to leave Andhra University DPP for America in 1976). Whether or not I succeeded in "saving" the FRNM, as J.B. Rhine wished, I clearly failed in my responsibilities for the Department of Psychology and Parapsychology, and especially to the parapsychology programme there that was entrusted to me by D.S. Kothari and the University Grants Commission. . . .

Among the reasons he offers for the debacle include the fact that he stayed far longer than he had originally planned, due to events beyond his control.

However, it is obvious from the above that Rao's interest in the paranormal was too deep for him to remain as a helpless bystander. Certainly not while he was standing right there, as the most powerful man on campus.

While being careful not to interfere with the working of the Andhra University DPP, Rao turned his energies instead to starting a bold, new initiative, which would advance the cause of parapsychology from a different direction, by way of *yoga* and consciousness studies. In explaining the thrust behind the latest project, Rao writes (2011b: 235):

> (I was interested in) integrating parapsychology with related disciplines and breaking the crippling insulation of the field and helping parapsychologists to come out of the cocoons of their own making. I thought parapsychology belonged as an integral and indispensible core of consciousness studies. *Yoga* indicated the possibility of developing psychic technologies for the development of the mind.

In typical Rao fashion, he was able to quickly secure funds from his personal mentor and benefactor, N.T. Rama Rao, the CM, as well as funds from the UGC, to set up the Institute for Yoga and Consciousness (IYC). Rao deliberately left out any explicit reference to parapsychology in its name, although the intended aim of the IYC was to facilitate psi research. IYC is located in a lovely spot on the Visakhapatnam beach, a popular spot for the locals interested in learning and practising *yoga*.

Towards the end of his tenure as Vice-Chancellor, Rao was asked to stay on for some more time so as to help reorganize the large university-level educational system in the state, which was in the throes of explosive growth. Rao was elevated to the bureaucratic rank of chief secretary for the purpose, responsible for co-ordinating the affairs of several different universities, in addition to Andhra. Rao had to overstay his leave by almost one year to complete the above mission.

From the Big Pond, Back in the Puddle

One can imagine "the problems of sheer scale" and "contrasts in purpose" which Rao would have had to overcome that winter of 1988, when he returned to the tiny FRNM, with its usual "insular preoccupations" and the pursuit of the elusive. But Rao simply donned the wetsuit and dropped back into the microcosm as it were, away from sunlight, diving back into the deep, back to delving into minutiae. Again, it was something that needed little adaptation, "as it was not the stage that mattered to him as much as the action that was taking place on it".

By now in 1988 back at the FRNM, Rao's attitude towards parapsychology was more proactive. He was no longer content to keep persisting to "normalize the paranormal", in effect designing experiments devoid of any theoretical underpinnings. He was intent on "bringing parapsychology and related disciplines together on a common platform".

The year 1991 proved to be "a banner year" for Rao as far as his developing interest in the subject of consciousness was concerned. Coincidentally at the time, there was a resurgence of academic interest in consciousness studies, an area Rao has been eyeing for some time for its potential to help psi research. Accordingly, Rao arranged for a large-scale conference on the topic of consciousness in Durham, sponsored by the FRNM. The successful proceedings led to the publication of a book titled *Cultivating Consciousness* (Rao 1991a). Rao had also published a comprehensive review article published for the *Journal of Parapsychology* on consciousness research and psi (1991b). Later that year, delivering his third and final presidential address at the Parapsychological Association, he stressed the importance of studying and understanding the fascinating nature of consciousness for fruitful parapsychological research. In the coming years, Rao would be spending more time reading, writing and thinking about the subject of consciousness. He writes (2011b: 236):

> It seemed obvious to me that the reality of psi has important ontological and epistemological implications bearing on consciousness. Psi research findings . . . seem to lend strong support to the notion that consciousness is a primary principle governing reality, and epistemological dualism is a necessary corollary of the existence of psi.

Another paper relevant to religion and consciousness was published as a chapter in a book edited by Tart (1997). Rao's grounding in philosophy was obviously dominating his thinking once again, as he went about seeking a broader conceptual platform for parapsychologists.

Along with consciousness and related issues, Rao's mind began gravitating back to classical Indian psychology and the doors it could potentially open for psi research. What better way was there to refresh oneself on a subject than to do some writing on it? Accordingly, he wrote a chapter (Rao 2001b) on the relevance of classical Indian ideas to contemporary concerns in psychology, which was published as part of a comprehensive book, *Psychology in India Revisited: Developments in the Discipline* by Janak Pandey. *Basic Research in Parapsychology* (2nd edn.) by Rao (2001a) was also published around this time.

Speaking of Rao's natural proclivities for the spiritual and internal states, the following do need mention. Rao's interest in linking psi with consciousness, *yoga* and other Eastern derivatives goes all the way back to early 1970s. He delivered a series of lectures on mystic awareness and the paranormal at the University of Mysore (Rao 1972). He wrote an article on the relevance of parapsychology for science and religion (1986). Later he edited a book on spiritual psychology, as part of his writings on Indian psychology (Rao & Marwaha 2005).

Rao was not alone in looking for fresh ground and more fertile soil for psi research. William Braud was quite conversant with the ancient Indian classic *Yoga-Sūtras* of Patañjali — he has written a chapter on the subject as part of a book edited by Rao (2008) along with other Indian scholars. Braud (2003) had also conducted several studies on internal attention states. His research interests included what he termed distance mental influence. He found that yogic principles and techniques in theory and practice were uniquely suited for facilitating psychic experiences, and hence offered potentially invaluable tools for parapsychology researchers. Robert Jahn of Princeton University Engineering Department was intrigued by psychic phenomena, which he approached as paradoxes and anomalies in need of explanation. In 1981, he presented a paper at the AAAS symposium on the role of consciousness in the physical world, revealing his broad purview of parapsychology (Jahn 1981). Even earlier, E.H. Walker (1975), a physicist by training and one who was keenly interested in parapsychological research, wrote on consciousness and the quantum theory, both areas of interest to psi investigators. Rhea White (1997, 1998) could be credited with pioneering the move away from laboratory-based investigations towards "a more experiential approach". J.E. Kennedy (2003), who is highly impressed by the capricious nature of psi, believes that psi very likely falls "in the spiritual realm". He discourages self-serving attitudes and motivations based on superiority when investigating psi. He believes that humility and gratitude and such other nobler motivations are better suited to investigate a phenomenon that seems to be clearly spiritual in nature (Kennedy 2010).

Brush with Politicos

Back to the nineties at the FRNM, where Rao was trying to spread his wings on the theoretical front and spending increasingly less time conducting the usual experiments, he was once again interrupted. Again it was NTR wanting to give Rao an even bigger assignment this time than he had back in 1984. Fresh from a landslide general election victory in the state of Andhra Pradesh, the CM wanted Rao to come back and join his cabinet of ministers/advisors to help his administration focus on improving the lot of the masses. Rao was offered the all-important planning portfolio, along with the position of principal advisor to the CM.

This time K.R. Rao was not quite surprised, for the charismatic CM "had extracted a promise" previously from Rao for the latter to return and serve the Andhra Pradesh government, one more time. Rao, who had been contemplating retirement from the FRNM so as to move back to India, found the offer not only very attractive but also timely. Again there were enough seasoned and experienced researchers at the FRNM to take over leadership from Rao, which made it easy for him to return to India in December 1994.

As can be expected, Rao's new assignment straight took him into the frenzy of the state capital in Hyderabad. Unlike his previous challenge involving leadership of the university system, in which he could keep politics and politicians at a safe distance, in the high-profile assignment he was now given, Rao found himself in the thick of state politics. Nevertheless, the nature of the work he was engaged in being primarily that of a higher-level civil service executive he could do his work fairly quietly without too many distractions. Rao favoured and fully endorsed the economic policies he was developing to meet the CM's mandate, as they were directed mostly at the poor and the indigent who needed help with the very basics in life. Unfortunately, the assignment working for the government as satisfying as it was for Rao personally, ended abruptly. NTR had to give up his chief minister-ship amidst much political turmoil, a short period after which the charismatic leader died. In early 1995, Rao, feeling distraught and having no further business left in the state capital, left Hyderabad and returned to private life.

Rao had returned to the FRNM one last time. However, financial support for parapsychological research declined after the 1980s due to a lack of scientific progress. Many parapsychological laboratories were closing and FRNM was feeling pressure. At this point, Rao was at retirement age and had neither the motivation nor confidence in success to attempt to raise funds to support the type of experiments that were the tradition of the institute. Under these circumstances, retiring was the best alternative for him and for the institute. Unfortunately, those who were more optimistic about raising funds were not successful and the institute subsequently experienced declining support with several changes in leadership and downsizing.

What Does This All Mean?

This is the same kind of question Rao poses for himself in his recent book, *Cognitive Anomalies, Consciousness and Yoga* (2011b). Here, however, we are asking the question pertaining not to the development and state of the whole field but in the context of Rao's own development secondary to involvement in parapsychology research for a very long time. The answer, to some extent, should lie in his current views towards the field, as compared to say when he wrote *Psi Cognition* (1957) as "the impassioned scholar". Rao has not changed his views about the reality of psi, but he has come to believe that a fundamentally different strategy of investigation is needed.

After reviewing the field and his entire life experience with parapsychology, he concludes (Rao 2011b: 240):

> Parapsychology in the West started its journey on a path without realizing that it is a dead-end road. Having travelled long enough and garnered a bundle of evidence for the existences of psi, we are now stranded with the discovery of an anomaly, without knowing what it means or where we are headed.

The startling honesty of this conclusion by a person who devoted many decades to parapsychological work must be clearly acknowledged. Perhaps even more noteworthy is how extremely rare it is for a person in the late stages of a prominent career to be willing to recognize and admit the limitations of past work and to advocate a major change in direction (i.e. a paradigm shift).

Rao believes that Indian psychology offers a more expansive worldview and methodology that can move beyond the past limitations of psychology and parapsychology in the West. He advocates that researchers consider (a) that ". . . psi is neither an anomaly nor an aberration, but a genuine, inherent principle embedded in reality and accessible to human experience", (b) ". . . the relevance of the reality of psi to an interdisciplinary understanding of who we are and where our destiny lies", and (c) "judicious application of psi for personal transformation as well as enhancing human potentials" (ibid.). Indian psychology particularly brings into focus the relevance of psi for personal transformation and human potentials. In establishing a direction that others may continue, Rao (2011b) presents the principles and philosophy of Indian psychology in the form of standard scientific writing and in the form of *sūtras*. He believes that studies of psi, consciousness and *yoga* psychology can be integrated into a path for scientific progress.

Rao is in a unique position, having taken "the holy dip" into not only the Indian Ocean but the Atlantic as well, "to tell us a thing or two, as to what is down there". We are, of course, referring to Rao's immersion into both Eastern thought and the Western tradition for decades, looking for a hint as to how parapsychology fits in with the rest of "the interior scheme" we take for granted. Alas, fifty years apparently is not long enough, even for an incessant and tireless worker like Rao to solve the great conundrum. However, Rao has broadened the search to include, somewhat ironically, other related mysteries pertaining to consciousness and *yoga*. His argument seems to be that these may well represent the medium in which psi resides, offer it a locale as it were. While he does "use the broad brush" to present some novel approaches, he is quite sure about not continuing on the path we have been marching all along, as he feels it is clearly not taking us any where. Enough with gathering data in a theoretical vacuum, he is saying in unambiguous terms (2011b).

Rao is also sensitive to "the atmospherics" of parapsychological research, as he feels that the atmosphere of criticism is seriously stymieing research efforts. He finds this to be the case especially in the Western cultures whereby the psi worker is simply going through the motions of research which might be designed more to meet with the approval of the scientific establishment, rather than whetting their own genuine curiosities. This is not to suggest that scientific methodology is in any way secondary, just that one could be obsessed with it to the point of sacrificing the main goal.

Thus one solution Rao offers is to move the research sites to cultural climates where there is an inherent acceptance of the phenomena, "where these things are not that big a deal". In such a benign atmosphere the researchers can afford to be more "bold" and venturesome in their methods and hypotheses, Rao feels (2011b). Thus the parapsychology elder seems to be exhorting us "to look for the ring where it was lost, rather than under the nearest lamp post . . ." to borrow a well-known saying from the wisdom literature.

Is There Life After Parapsychology?

Having accomplished as much as he had on a variety of stages, in a life's work involving radically different types of challenges and endeavours carried out without regard to country or cultural setting, what more is there left for Koneru Ramakrishna Rao to do? Plenty, as it turns out.

In the fifteen years that Rao had moved back to India and receded from the active parapsychology scene, his intellectual life if anything seems "to have switched to a higher gear". He has been serving as a model chairman of the Indian Council of Philosophical Research (ICPR) in New

Delhi, where he is asked to stay on for a second three-year term. We will not go into the details of the work of the Council, but suffice to say, it is "not the typical New Delhi cushy job", at least not for him. Sitting in the middle of burgeoning bureaucracies of which he is unmindful, Rao has taken upon himself "to breathe and infuse" intellectual life back into the Indian university departments and cultural institutions. As the judicious arbiter of government grants, organizer of national and international conferences, invited speaker at important academic and cultural occasions, Rao is a busy man while in the Indian capital.

Rao's work, of late, has simply been that of a guardian of knowledge. He says India has such vast stores of ancient writings; it is imperative that they be preserved, made accessible, and not allowed to slide back into oblivion. He is also stressing ethics and moral behaviour in government, business and the fabric of society in general, trying to restore Gandhian principles (Rao 2011a). If one were to watch him at his desk in New Delhi, or back home in Visakhapatnam these days, more than likely one would find him writing. Write, write and write some more seems to be Rao's motto, these days. A life of the mind comes naturally to the man who spent his entire life trying to study its mysteries. The President of India honoured him last year with the Padma Shri Award for his literary and scientific contributions. Not many of us know that in addition to his many academic credentials, Rao has a couple of D.Litt. degrees conferred upon him. However, the sheer number of books and articles he has written in his career thus far are enough to show him to be "the man of letters" that he is, than any number of academic decorations pinned on him.

We have not touched on the myriad types of activities and initiatives that Rao has been involved in. In addition to his main work at the ICPR, he spends time at the Institute for Human Science and Service (IHSS), his own brainchild, located in Visakhapatnam. The institute engages in many vital research and social service activities. The GITAM Institute for Gandhian Studies is another favourite haunt of Rao. The institute is located also in Visakhapatnam, on the beautiful campus of GITAM University. Teaching, talking and travelling mostly in connection with promoting new directions in parapsychology, as well serving other academic and cultural causes in India and abroad, all keep Rao very busy.

Dr. Koneru Ramakrishna Rao simply keeps marching on! Just as we were wrapping up this article we have received word that he has accepted invitation to be Chancellor of GITAM University! We are certain that there are many more honours and responsibilities waiting in the wings for this perspicacious and exemplary scholar. In conclusion, we wish him a happy eightieth birthday, cheering him on "to endeavour for ever" and "write, Dr Rao, write!"

References

Braud, W.G. (2003), *Distance Mental Influence: Its Contributions to Science, Healing, and Human Interactions*, Charlottesville, VA: Hampton Roads.

Braud, W.G. (2010), "Patanjali Yoga-Sutras and Parapsychological Research: Exploring Matches and Mismatches", in K.R. Rao (ed.) *Yoga and Parapsychology: Empirical Research and Theoretical Essays*, Delhi: Motilal Banarsidass.

——— (2008), "Patanjali Yoga and Siddhis: Their Relevance to Parapsychological Theory and Research", in K.R. Rao, A.C. Paranjpe and A.K. Dalal (eds.) *Handbook of Indian Psychology*, Delhi: Foundation Books.

Carpenter, J.C. (2012), *First Sight: ESP and Parapsychology in Everyday Life*, New York: Rowman and Littlefield.

Honorton, C. (1977), "Psi and Internal Attention States", in B.B. Wolman (ed.) *Handbook of Parapsychology*, New York: Van Nostrand Reihhold.

Humphry, B.M. (1946), "Success in ESP as Related to Form of Response of Drawing: I. Clairvoyance Experiments", *Journal of Parapsychology*, 10: 78-106.

Jacksan, J.F. and B.M. Sonali (2010), "Personality, Religiosity and Paranormal Experiences", in K.R. Rao (ed.) *Yoga and Parapsychology: Empirical Research and Theoretical Essays*, Delhi: Motilal Banarsidass.

Jahn, R.G. (1981), "The Role of the Consciousness in the Physical World", *AAAS Selected Symposium*, 57, Boulder, CO: Westview Press.

Kanthamani, B.K. (1965), "A Study of the Differential Response in Language ESP Tests", *Journal of Parapsychology*, 29: 27-34.

Kanthamani, B.K. and K.R. Rao (1971), "Personality Characteristics of ESP Subjects: I. Primary Personality Characteristics and ESP", *Journal of Parapsychology*, 35: 189-207.

——— (1972a), "Personality Characteristics of ESP Subjects: II. The Combined Personality Measure (CPM) and ESP", *Journal of Parapsychology*, 36: 56-70.

——— (1972b), "Personality Characteristics of ESP Subjects: III. Extraversion and ESP", *Journal of Parapsychology*, 36: 190-212. [Also in K.R. Rao (ed.) *Basic Research in Parapsychology*, 2nd edn. (2001), Jefferson, NC: McFarland.]

——— (1973a), "Personality Characteristics of ESP Subjects: IV. Neuroticism and ESP", *Journal of Parapsychology*, 37: 37-50.

——— (1973b), "Personality Characteristics of ESP Subjects: V. Graphic Expansiveness and ESP", *Journal of Parapsychology*, 37: 119-29.

Kanthamani, H. and H.H. Rao (1974), "A Study of Memory–ESP Relationship using Linguistic Forms", *Journal of Parapsychology*, 38: 286-300.

——— (1975a), "The Role of Association Strength in Memory–ESP Interaction",

Journal of Parapsychology, 39: 1-11.

——— (1975b), "Response Tendencies and Stimulus Structure", *Journal of Parapsychology* 39: 97-105. [Also in J.D. Morris, W.G. Roll, and R.L. Morris (eds.) (1974), *Research in Parapsychology*, Metuchen, NJ: Scarecrow Press.]

Kennedy, J.E. (2003), "What is the Purpose of psi?: Capricious Actively Evasive Untenable Nature of Psi: Summary and Hypotheses", *Journal of Parapsychology*, 67: 53-74.

——— (2010), "Spirituality and the Capricious, Evasive Nature of Psi", in Rao, K.R. (ed.), *Yoga and Parapsychology: Empirical Research and Theoretical Essays*, Delhi: Motilal Banarsidass.

Krishna, S.R. and K.R. Rao (1981), "Personality and Belief in Relation to Language ESP Scores", in W.G. Roll and J. Beloff (eds.), *Research in Parapsychology, 1980*, pp. 61-63, Metuchen, NJ: Scarecrow Press.

——— (1991), "Effect of ESP Feedback on Subjects' Responses to a Personality Questionnaire", *Journal of Parapsychology*, 55: 147-58.

Kristeller, J.L. and K. Rikhye (2008), "Meditative Traditions and Contemporary Psychology", in K.R. Rao, A.C. Paranjpe and A.K. Dalal (eds.) *Handbook of Indian Psychology*, Delhi: Foundation Books.

Mackenzie, B. (1977), "Three Stages in the History of Parapsychology", paper presented at the Quadrennial Congress on History of Science, Edinburgh, Scotland.

Munson, R.J., J.W. Davis and K.R. Rao (1981), "Subliminal Perception and Extrasensory Perception in a Learning Paradigm", in W.G. Roll and J. Beloff (eds.), *Research in Parapsychology*, 96-98, Metuchen, NJ: Scarecrow Press.

Rammohan, V.G. (1990), "Psi in the Academic Context: Two Further Studies", *Journal of Parapsychology*, 54: 229-44.

——— (2002) (ed.), *New Frontiers of Human Science: A Festschrift for K. Ramakrishna Rao*, Jefferson, NC: McFarland.

Rani, N. J. and P.V.K. Rao (1996), "Meditation and Attention Regulation", *Journal of Indian Psychology*, 14(1-2): 26-30.

——— (2000), "Effects of Meditation on Attention Processes", *Journal of Indian Psychology*, 18(1-2): 52-60.

Rao, K.R. (1955), "Vedanta and *modus operandi* of Paranormal Cognition", *The Philosophical Quarterly*, vol. 5.

——— (1957), *Psi Cognition*, Tenali, AP: Tagore Publishing House.

——— (1962), "The Preferential Effect in ESP", *Journal of Parapsychology*, 26: 252-59.

——— (1963a), "Studies in the Preferential Effect, I: Target Preference with Types of Targets Unknown", *Journal of Parapsychology*, 27: 23-32.

——— (1963b), "Studies in the Preferential Effect, II: A Language ESP Test Involving Precognition and Intervention", *Journal of Parapsychology*, 27: 147-60.

——— (1963c), "Studies in Preferential Effect, III: The Reversal in the Psi Preference", *Journal of Parapsychology,* 27: 242-51.

——— (1964a), "Studies in the Preferential effect, IV: The Role of Key Cards in Preferential Response Situations", *Journal of Parapsychology,* 28: 28-41.

——— (1964b), "The Differential Response in Three New Situations", *Journal of Parapsychology,* 28: 81-92.

——— (1965a), "The Bidirectionality of Psi", *Journal of Parapsychology,* 29: 230-50. [Also in *Proceedings of the Parapsychology Association,* 1965, No. 2, pp. 37-59.]

——— (1965b), "ESP and the Manifest Anxiety Scale", *Journal of Parapsychology,* 29: 12-18.

——— (1966), *Experimental Parapsychology: A Review and Interpretation,* Springfield, IL: Charles C. Thomas.

——— (1968), *Gandhi and Pragmatism: An Intercultural Study,* Calcutta: Oxford IBH.

——— (1972), *Mystic Awareness: Four Lectures on the Paranormal,* Mysore: Mysore University Press.

——— (1977a), "Some Frustrations and Challenges in Parapsychology", *Journal of Parapsychology,* 41: 119-35.

——— (1977b), "On the Nature of Psi", *Journal of Parapsychology,* 41: 294-351. [Also in S. Krippner (ed.) (1978), *Advances in Parapsychological Research 2: Extrasensory Perception,* New York: Plenum Press.]

——— (1977c), "Book Review of *Handbook of Parapsychology,* ed. B.B. Wolman, New York: Von Nostrand and Reinhold", in *Journal of Parapsychology,* 41: 352-58.

——— (1978a), "Further Studies of Memory and ESP", *Journal of Parapsychology,* 42: 167-78.

——— (1978b), "Psi: Its Place in Nature", *Journal of Parapsychology,* 42: 276-303.

——— (1979a), "Language ESP Test under Normal and Relaxed Conditions", *Journal of Parapsychology,* 43: 1-16.

——— (1979b), "The Scientific Credibility of ESP", *Perceptual and Motor Skills,* 49: 415-29.

——— (1981), "On the Question of Replication", *JP,* 45: 311-20.

——— (1982a) (ed.), *J.B. Rhine: On the Frontiers of Science,* Jefferson, NC: McFarland.

——— (1982b), "J.B. Rhine and His Critics", in *J.B. Rhine: On the Frontiers of Science,* Jefferson, NC: McFarland.

——— (1986), "Parapsychology: Implications for Religion and Science", *Perkins Journal,* 39(2): 1-21.

——— (1989), "Meditation: Secular and Sacred: A Review and Assessment of Some Recent Research", *Journal of Indian Academy of Applied Psychology,* 15(2): 51-74.

——— (1991a), "Consciousness Research and Psi", *Journal of Parapsychology,* 55: 1-44.

——— (1991b) (ed.), *Cultivating Consciousness: Enhancing Human Potential, Wellness, and Healing,* Westport, CT: Praeger.

——— (1993) (ed.), *Charles Honorton and the Impoverished State of Skepticism: Essays on a Parapsychological Pioneer,* Jefferson, NC: McFarland.

——— (1997), "Some Reflections on Religion and Anomalies of Consciousness", in C.T. Tart (ed.), *Body Mind Spirit: Exploring the Parapsychology of* Spirituality, Charlottesville, VA: Hampton Roads.

——— (2001a) (ed.), *Basic Research in Parapsychology,* 2nd edn., Jefferson, NC: McFarland.

——— (2001b), "Consciousness Studies: A Survey of Perspectives and Research", in J. Pandey (ed.), *Psychology in India Revisited: Developments in the Discipline,* vol. 2, pp. 19-162, New Delhi: Sage Publication.

——— (2002), *Consciousness Studies: Cross-cultural Perspectives,* Jefferson, NC: McFarland.

——— (2010) (ed.), *Yoga and Parapsychology: Empirical Research and Theoretical Essays,* Delhi: Motilal Banarsidass.

——— (2011a), *Gandhi and Applied Spirituality,* New Delhi: Indian Council of Philosophical Research and Matrix Publishers.

——— (2011b), "Cognitive Anomalies, Consciousness and Yoga", vol. XVI, part 1, in D.P. Chattopadhyaya (ed.), *History of Science, Philosophy and Culture in Indian Civilization,* New Delhi: Centre for Study of Civilization and Matrix Publishers.

Rao, K.R. and J.W. Davis (1978), "The Differential Effect and Experimenter Effects in Intentional and Nonintentional Psi Tests", *Journal of Parapsychology,* 42: 1-19.

Rao, K.R. and J. Feola (1979), "Electrical Activity of the Brain and ESP: An Exploratory Study of Alpha Rhythm and ESP Scoring", *Journal of Indian Psychology,* 2: 118-33.

Rao, K.R. and S.B. Marwaha (2005) (eds.), *Towards a Spiritual Psychology: Essays in Indian Psychology,* New Delhi: Samvad.

Rao, K.R. and T.J. O'Brien (1977), "A Cross-cultural Study of Psi in Academic Examinations", *Journal of Parapsychology,* 41: 1-9.

Rao, K.R. and J. Palmer (1978), "Theories of Psi", in S. Krippner (ed.) *Advances in Parapsychological Research,* vol. 2, *Extrasensory Perception,* New York: Plenum Press.

——— (1987), "The Anomalies Called Psi: Recent Research and Criticism", *Behavioral and Brain Sciences,* 10: 539-51.

Rao, K.R. and I. Puri (1978), "Subsensory Perception (SSP), Extrasensory Perception (ESP) and Transcendental Meditation", *Journal of Indian Psychology,* 1: 69-74.

Rao, K.R. and D.H. Weiner (1982), Memory and E.S.P.: An Attempted Replication, *Journal of Parapsychology,* 46: 56 (Abstract), (paper presented at the Ninth annual S.E.R.P.A. Convention).

Rao, K.R., H. Dukhan and P.V.K. Rao (1978), "Yogic Meditation and Psi Scoring in Forced-choice and Free-response Tests", *Journal of Indian Psychology,* 1:

160-75. [Also in K.R. Rao (ed.) (2001), *Basic Research in Parapsychology*, 2nd edn., Jefferson, NC: McFarland.]

Rao, K.R., H. Kanthamani and S.R. Krishna (1979), "Psi and Volitional Activity: An Experimental Study of Psi in a Competitive Situation", *Journal of Parapsychology,* 43: 101-12.

Rao, K.R., H. Kanthamani and J. Palmer (1990), "Exploring Normal/Paranormal Interaction within a Memory–ESP Testing Paradigm", *Journal of Parapsychology,* 54: 245-59. [Also in L. Henkel and J. Palmer (eds.) (1989), *Research in Parapsychology,* Metuchen, NJ: Scarecrow Press.]

Rao, K.R., B.K. Kanthamani and P. Sailaja (1968), "ESP Scores before and after a Scheduled Interview", *Journal of Parapsychology,* 32: 293 (Abstract). [Also in W.G. Roll, R.L. Morris and J.D. Morris (eds.), *Proceedings of Parapsychological Association,* 5: 57-59, Durham, NC.]

Rao, K.R., M. Morrison and J.W. Davis (1977a), "Paired-associates Recall and ESP: A Study of Memory and Psi-missing", *Journal of Parapsychology,* 41: 165-89.

Rao, K.R., M. Morrison, J.W. Davis and J.A. Freeman (1977b), "The Role of Association in Memory Recall and ESP", *Journal of Parapsychology,* 41: 190-97.

Rao, K.R., A.C. Paranjpe and A.K. Dalal (2008) (eds.), *Handbook of Indian Psychology,* Delhi: Foundation Books.

Rao, K.R., K.G. Sundari, Y.J. Rao and R.N. Rao (1977), "SSP and ESP with a Weight Discrimination Task (Abstract)", in J.D. Morris, W.G. Roll and R.L. Morris (eds.), *Research in Parapsychology,* pp. 79-81, Metuchen, NJ: Scarecrow Press.

Rao, P.V.K. and K.R. Rao (1982), "Two Studies of ESP and Subliminal Perception", *Journal of Parapsychology,* 46: 185-207.

Rhine, J.B. (1934/1964), *Extrasensory Perception* (rev. edn.), Boston: Bruce Humphries. (Later publication: *Extrasensory Perception,* 1973, Brookline Village, MA: Branden Press.)

——— (1952), "The Problem of Psi-missing", *Journal of Parapsychology,* 16: 90-129.

——— (1956), "The Need for Research Workers in Parapsychology", *Journal of Parapsychology,* 20: 184-96.

——— (1958), "On the Nature and Consequences of the Unconsciousness of Psi", *Journal of Parapsychology,* 22: 175-86.

Rhine, J.B., J.G. Pratt, B.M. Smith, C.E. Stuart and J.A. Greenwood (1966/40), *Extrasensory Perception After Sixty Years,* Boston: Bruce Humphries.

Rhine, L.E. (1967), *ESP in Life and Lab: Tracing Hidden Channels,* New York: Macmillan.

——— (1975), *Psi, What Is It?* New York: Harper and Row.

Roll, W.G. (1966), "ESP and Memory", *International Journal of Neuropsychiatry,* 2: 505-21.

Sailaja, P. (1965), "Confirmatory Study of the Role of Key Cards in the Language-

ESP Test", *Journal of Parapsychology,* 29: 290-91 (Abstract).

Sailaja, P. and K.R. Rao (1973), *Experimental Studies of the Differential Effect in Life setting,* Parapsychological Monographs No. 13, New York: Parapsychology Foundation.

Sailaja, P. and P.V.K. Rao (1978), "Response Patterns and psi Scoring", *Journal of Parapsychology,* 42: 304-12.

Schmeidler, G.R. (1945), "Separating the Sheep from the Goats", *Journal of the American Society for Psychical Research,* 39: 47-49.

Schmeidler, G.R. and R.A. McConnell (1958), *ESP and Personality Patterns,* New Haven: Yale University Press.

Schmidt, H. (1969), "Precognition of a Quantum Process", *Journal of Parapsychology,* 33: 99-108.

——— (1974), "Comparison of PK Action on Two Different Random Number Generators", *Journal of Parapsychology,* 36: 47-55.

Stokes, D.M. (2002), "Book Review: *Consciousness Studies: Cross-cultural Perspectives,* K.R. Rao (ed.) in V.G. Rammohan (2002) *New Frontiers of Human Science: A Festschrift for K. Ramakrishna Rao,* Jefferson, NC: McFarland.

Tart, C.T. (1997) (ed.), *Body, Mind, Spirit: Exploring the Parapsychology of Spirituality,* Charlottesville, VA: Hampton Roads.

Walker, E.H. (1975), "Consciousness and Quantum Theory", in E.D. Mitchell (ed.) *Psychic Exploration: A Challenge for Science,* New York: Putnam.

White, R.A. (1997), "Exceptional Human Experiences and the Experiential Paradigm", in C.T. Tart (ed.) *Body, Mind, Spirit: Exploring the Parapsychology of Spirituality,* Charlottesville, VA: Hampton Roads.

——— (1998), "Becoming More Human as We Work: The Reflexive Role of Exceptional Human Experiences", in W. Braud and R. Anderson (eds.) *Transpersonal Research Methods for the Social Sciences* (pp. 128-45), Thousand Oaks, CA: Sage Publication.

Wolman, B.B. (ed.) (1977), *Handbook of Parapsychology,* New York: Van Nostrand Reinhold.

3

Contributions of Prof. K. Ramakrishna Rao to Indian Psychology

Anand C. Paranjpe

It is not easy to summarize the lifetime work of an accomplished scholar, much less so when his scholarly output involves half a century of the relentless pursuit of objectives set while starting a career in his early twenties. I cannot pretend to cover the entire range of topics that such an exceptional man has covered, but restrict to only one major area of his work — Indian psychology.

There are three areas covered in Prof. Rao's *magnum opus*, a volume of about one 1000 pages, published in his late seventies: *Cognitive Anomalies, Consciousness, and Yoga* (Rao 2011a). These three areas, all related to Indian psychology, appear to be at the core of his scholarly work, although they do not exhaust the entire field of his contributions. "Cognitive anomalies" is another name for parapsychology, a field to which Rao devoted a major part of his productive years. At the first blush, the connection among these areas may not be clear, and one might wonder what makes the three areas hang together, and how they are related to Indian psychology. This should be clear if we note that *yoga* is usually considered the quintessence of Indian psychology, of which attainment of higher level of consciousness is the goal, and parapsychological phenomena such as clairvoyance are the by-product of its pursuit. It is interesting to see how these topics became the lifelong concern of Rao. To understand this, it is useful to go back to the days of his graduate training.

As Rao narrates in an autobiographical account in his work (Rao 2011a: 225-41), as a student studying philosophy and psychology, he was hit by the stark contrast in what he heard in two successive classes: the importance of *Brahman* in a class on the Advaita Vedānta, followed by a lecture in psychology where the students were told that behaviour was the only thing worth studying. Obviously there is a huge gap between *Brahman* and behaviour, and the young Ramakrishna couldn't just "take it" without bitterly complaining about the abysmal divide between the two perspectives. The story goes that Prof. Sen, the Advaita teacher, suggested the reading of two books: F.W.H. Myers' book on the survival of personality after bodily death, and J.B. Rhine's book on Extra Sensory Perception (ESP). How would such books help bridge the exceedingly wide gap between *Brahman* and behaviour? Notice that the two sides stand at the opposite poles of a whole set of classic dualities — the list includes not only East–West and ancient–modern, but also super-natural–natural, idealist–practical, abstract–concrete, holistic–molecularistic, top-down–bottom-up thinking, subjectivist–objectivist approaches — and so on. Surely, bridging such a yawning gap is not easy.

To put the issue into a generational perspective, a number of young scholars of Prof. Rao's generation were faced with such dilemmas. The East–West divide was particularly pressing for students who saw career prospects by going abroad for a Ph.D. Many young men and women of this generation found a quick way out: by simply accepting the Western worldview; no questions asked. This was not very problematic for students of the natural sciences, for there is not much in the Indian worldview or ethos that would contradict the basic premises of physics or other natural sciences. But for students of humanities, particularly those who were deeply into traditional Indian way of thinking conveyed by such great modern Indian thinkers as Gandhi, Tilak or Sri Aurobindo, accepting the Western approach whole hog was highly problematic. For young Ramakrishna, Gandhi's spirituality was a matter of deep absorption and a personal calling. This is evident from the fact that for his post-doctoral research at the University of Chicago he chose to focus on Gandhian philosophy, and continued to write about it in his late seventies.

It is interesting that philosophy and psychology remained areas of equal importance to Prof. Rao, even as they were equal parts of his MA courses. Soon after devoting himself to philosophy at the doctoral and post-doctoral stages, it was time to turn to psychology. Parapsychology seemed to be the right choice in this context, as Prof. Sen had injected the idea that this is the area where the *Brahman*–behaviour gap could be bridged. J.B. Rhine, whose book Rao had read at the suggestion of Prof. Sen, was clearly the most widely recognized authority on parapsychology in those days. Rhine had developed experimental methods for studying

ESP. Experimentation was the most preferred method for the validation of truth claims in behaviourism, which ruled the roost in psychology in those days. Against this background, Rhine's experiments would seem to be the best bet for providing a satisfactory proof for the paranormal phenomena such as clairvoyance mentioned in Patañjali's *yoga* aphorisms. Rao, who was already in the US for post-doctoral work in Chicago, took the earliest opportunity to visit Rhine's laboratory at Duke University in Durham, North Carolina. With the meeting of two minds in this situation, a long period of close collaboration started resulting in significant contributions to parapsychology.

It is not possible to overstate the importance of the experimental method for the mainstream of modern psychology. Initially when Wundt introduced it, introspection was the main route to consciousness. But as is well known, when Wundt's followers in Germany and the US violently disagreed with each other on what they respectively found through introspection, Watson, the father of behaviourism, declared the method of introspection null and void, thereby closing the royal road to consciousness. That shutting the doors to consciousness and the mind meant throwing away the baby with the bathwater did not matter to Watson's followers. So what was left in the Wundtian formula thereafter was mainly the method of experiment. For Watson's followers, *how* you study became far more important than *what* you study. Against this background, no psychologist could gain respectability without first demonstrating his mastery over methodology. It is to Rao's credit that he took the challenge of mastering methodology; he published a whole book examining the use of the method of experiment in parapsychology very early in his career (Rao 1966). This book is widely recognized as a standard piece of work in this field. Once a psychologist demonstrates his mastery over the nuances in estimating the probabilities in deviation of data from the null hypothesis, and knows how to avoid experimenter bias, nobody can question his credentials in the house of modern psychology. Rao was careful in passing this test right at the time of entering the citadel of psychology.

During the decades of his work in the field of parapsychology, Rao became a virtual successor to J.B. Rhine, the founder and unquestionable leader of the field. He carried the responsibilities of the director of parapsychology's main laboratory at the Institute for Parapsychology, in Durham, USA, and of editing its prestigious *Journal of Parapsychology* for almost two decades. He was also elected president of Parapsychological

Association, the international professional organization of scientists interested in parapsychological research, three times, first in 1965, when he was only thirty-three years old. I cannot pretend to have the competence necessary to review the work in this area, and it is rightly left for a separate essay in this volume. As Rao himself says it, during the years he spent in pursuing parapsychological research, he had turned from a philosopher and a theoretical psychologist to a "tough-minded empirical researcher" to the point of becoming a Westerner with a "holier than thou" attitude (2011: 228-29). Had he remained thus converted, it would have been an irreparable loss to Indian psychology. However, his fascination for experimental parapsychology was to come to an end, turning him back to Indian psychology.

Here it is necessary to indicate what his assessment was of his work in parapsychology and of the state of the field as a whole, and how it turned him back to his roots in Indian psychology. To put it into his own words:

> Statistical estimates of the improbability of the non-existence of psi based on the data of the kind we now have are unlikely to be convincing to someone who accords a very low subjective probability for its existence.
>
> — 1911: 238

Interestingly, it is not physicists themselves who were reluctant to accept the reality of psi, for the Nobel Laureate in physics, Prof. C.V. Raman, had expressed to Rao in a personal conversation that he was convinced about the reality of psi on the basis of experimental observations presented to him. As Rao points out, Dr Kothari, a well-known physicist, was also convinced about the reality of psi. Indeed, as chief of the University Grants Commission (UGC) of India, he provided sumptuous grants to Andhra University's centre for research in parapsychology under Rao's guidance.

The staunchest opposition to parapsychology came not from scientists, but from philosophers of science such as Mario Bunge, and from many so-called "skeptics", who took it upon themselves to protect science from the perceived dangers. After all, paranormal phenomena are by definition instances of events that are not scientifically explainable. So, to admit the reality of ESP and other paranormal phenomena is to accept the serious limitations of science. Indeed, accepting the validity of psi research threatens entire worldview based on science. This prospect was so unsettling to those who view themselves as protectors of the scientific establishment that they launched scathing attacks at parapsychology. The vitriolic nature of attacks on the findings of parapsychological research is evident in responses by a dozen of defenders of science to the presentation of such findings by Rao and J. Palmer in their lead article published in 1987 in the *Journal of Behavioral and Brain Sciences* (Rao & Palmer 1987a). A fitting response to the critics was given by Rao and his colleague (Rao & Palmer 1987b), but from my direct acquaintance with some of the critics I know that their commitment to the worldview of science is far too entrenched to be converted to alternatives howsoever strongly presented. Thus, in effect, a bold attempt at bridging the *Brahman*–behaviour gap remained unsuccessful. The loss to parapsychology inadvertently but fortunately worked for the benefit of Indian psychology.

It is interesting to see how Rao reacted to this disappointment, and what may have helped his turning to Indian psychology. Without going into the details, he basically thought that there was need for parapsychologists to re-think their entire enterprise to get out of the dead end. One idea was to think of the *usefulness* of various paranormal phenomena in solving practical problems rather than focusing on establishing their *validity*. This is an interesting idea, especially in the American context, where the philosophy of pragmatism originated and remains highly popular. Another interesting conclusion was to turn to other cultures where the atmosphere was more welcoming — India, for instance, where saints have continued to demonstrate a variety of paranormal powers, and innumerable people have witnessed the same. Interestingly, the title of one of his earlier papers (Rao 1968) was "Psi in Communities and Other Interpersonal Situations in the Eastern World". It indicates that he was looking to the East for a more fertile soil for further work in parapsychology. He had already started a separate Department of Psychology and Parapsychology at Andhra University where his many students were continuing with parapsychological research. But after returning to India with a stint in the US, Rao started a new Institute for Yoga and Consciousness. In his autobiographical account he explains this new initiative thus:

> I thought that parapsychology belonged to integral and indispensable core of consciousness studies. *Yoga* indicated the possibility of developing psychic technologies for the development of the mind. — 2011a: 235

Here I wish to pause and make an observation regarding the nature of the pursuit of scientific knowledge in the light of insights from the philosophy of science and the sociology of knowledge. As noted by Kuhn (1970), a historian and philosopher of science, the pursuit of science happens within the confines of paradigms or belief systems shared by scientists in a particular field. Such pursuit is founded on axiomatic assumptions and is guided and nurtured by principles such as consistency, validity and utility, but it is often also circumscribed and limited by boundary conditions defined by the basic assumptions — beliefs taken for granted and never challenged. Paranormal phenomena violate the basic assumptions of naturalism and universal validity of the laws of nature. As Kuhn has noted, the history of science shows how data indicating anomalies tend to be routinely ignored by scientists. In the case of apparently valid results of psi experiments, the reaction was more than simple disdain, it seemed violent! Here, it is relevant to note an insight from the work of Berger (1966), a sociologist of knowledge. While the scientists' search for knowledge happens within the confines of their shared paradigms, communities of scientists are not totally isolated from the broader society which provides institutional support. The larger society forms a culture which provides a widely but implicitly shared worldview, which Berger calls "the sacred canopy". Indian cultural tradition has provided its own sacred canopy, which is different from the mix of elements of Abrahamic religions and secularist rationality of the Greek forebears. While the former has nourished *yoga*, the latter has promoted the natural sciences. Against the backdrop of these ideas, Rao's return from the experimental parapsychology in the West to Indian psychology in the East may be viewed as a return to the supportive pavilion on the home ground.

Consciousness: East and West

Upon his return to India, Rao reached right to the core of Indian psychology, which is consciousness. Consciousness is clearly at the heart of the tradition that goes back to the Upaniṣads and Buddhism. As noted, *Brahman*, which is of the nature of pure consciousness, was a topic in his MA. Within two years of his completion of his doctoral work Rao (1964) had published a review of R.H. Thouless's book, *Mind and Consciousness in Experimental Parapsychology.* Although consciousness was practically banished from mainstream psychology since the beginning of the Behaviourist Revolution in 1913, it emerged as a new topic of interest in the 1970s, albeit in the fringe areas rather than in the mainstream of psychology. Against this background, it is interesting to note that it was in 1972 that Rao presented a paper "Consciousness in Indian Psychology" at the International Conference of Humanistic Psychology in Tokyo. That he was getting increasingly deeper in studies of Indian perspectives on consciousness is clear from his publications over the subsequent years. Thus, he published a paper "Psychology of Transcendence: A Study in early Buddhistic Psychology" in 1978 in the newly-started *Journal of Indian Psychology*. He later wrote a foreword to the book *Sankara: Humanist, Integrator, Poet and Philosopher* by I.V. Chalapati Rao (Rao 1990). Clearly, this was slow but sure return from behaviour to *Brahman*, and that with due attention to the old Buddhist opponents of the doctrine of *Brahman*.

The effect of decades of exposure to the West was to broaden the perspective well beyond the traditional Indian debates between Buddhist emptiness versus Advaitic fullness at the core of consciousness. There was a deep impact of Western views of consciousness that have continued to unfold from Descartes onwards. This is reflected in the fact that Rao invited over a dozen of Western scholars to a conference he organized on "Cultivating Consciousness". It is not simply that he was in touch with, and was listening to, these Western specialists in the field of consciousness studies, his own paper in the book based on this conference indicates his deep personal engagement with Western perspectives. Moreover, it is interesting to see how he introduces critical aspects on traditional Indian views of consciousness against the backdrop of a brief discussion of some distinctive aspects of Western views. Since this paper nicely illustrates Rao's approach to Indian psychology, it will be useful to briefly discuss it here (1991: 83-100).

The title of the book based on the papers presented at the conference is *Cultivating Consciousness: Enhancing Human Potential, Wellness and Healing*. The very opening word, "cultivating" suggests the *practical* approach to the study of consciousness, and the subtitle clarifies the *results to be attained* through cultivating consciousness. The essay begins with a brief explanation of what the author means by the term consciousness, quickly noting the views he does *not* subscribe to: the denial of consciousness, the epiphenomenalist view and the view that equates consciousness with neural events. Thus, the currently popular Western perspectives aligned with behaviourist psychology are clearly rejected off the bat, declaring to the reader that something different is to be expected. After clarifying that he is not presenting a psychoanalytical perspective with a focus on the unconscious, the most common alternative to the behaviourist psychology is also rejected. The discussion then turns from psychology to philosophy. First there is a brief discussion of Descartes' mind–body dualism, which provides conceptual foundations for modern psychology, followed by a reference to the then popular views of the mind–body problem, namely D.M. Armstrong's materialist monism on the one hand, and Roger Sperry's mind-over-matter view on the other. This discussion of the relatively more popular perspectives in the mainstream Western philosophy and psychology is followed by the less well-known views of the phenomenologist Husserl and the existentialist philosopher Jean-Paul Sartre. Then there is a short discussion of upward versus downward causation, which is presented as a "methodological issue". It is after covering such diverse Western perspectives that Rao proceeds to a discussion of two distinctive aspects of the traditional Indian views on consciousness: (i) pure consciousness or consciousness as-such, and (ii) the main issue of the "cultivation" of consciousness, i.e. altering the processes of consciousness through yogic meditation.

There are several important things to note about the style and substance of this paper. Clearly a major part of the paper is devoted to Western approaches before coming onto select aspects of Indian approaches. This is partly the result of the context, namely a conference in the US, where the paper was presented. Clearly the audience was mainly Western, which is familiar with Western approaches; it makes sense in this context to go from what is commonly known to the audience to what may be unknown to many — or most — of them. Ironically the strategy would not be different if the audience was Indian psychologists in India, since most of them are trained in Western psychology and have little or no exposure to Indian thought. In an interesting way, by presenting Western perspectives first Rao can be said to follow the typical Indian style of discourse, where one begins by clearly stating the position of the opponent (*pūrva pakṣa*), then systematically refute it (*khaṇḍanam*), and then present one's own thesis (*uttara pakṣa, siddhānta*) as a better alternative, and defend it (*maṇḍanam*). We may also note that Rao defends the Indian approach, that of *cultivating* consciousness to attain higher levels of well-being, thereby outdoing American pragmatism. Thus, in style and substance, Rao presents an authentically Indian perspective on consciousness.

Indeed, it is not common in discourses in mainstream psychology to discuss past philosophers like Descartes and Kant, or more recent philosophers like Husserl or Sartre, for that matter. But in engaging in a discussion of historical roots and philosophical foundations Rao is adopting the approach called philosophical psychology, or what is recently called "theoretical psychology". Adopting such an approach is particularly relevant for a discussion of issues in Indian psychology because the differences between Indian and Western psychologies are grounded on differing ontological theses and epistemic principles — which belong to the traditional domain of philosophy.

The reader may remember that a brief mention was made above to Rao's discussion of the difference between downward and upward causation, which he calls a "methodological" issue. In my opinion, the idea of upward causation implies a very important idea about what is widely but implicitly taken for granted about how the world works. Thus, in modern science, it is tacitly assumed that causal chains originate in changes that take place at the molecular or even sub-atomic levels, and work their way through increasingly broader units, such as molecules, cells, and organs up to the complex circuits in the brain — which then produce awareness. The direction of causation is therefore "bottom up" in the sense from concrete to abstract, from molecular to molar, and finally from physical to mental. Mental phenomena such as thoughts and plans for action are often viewed to be at the *end* of such a causal chain. They are "epiphenomena" in the sense that they are considered causally impotent, thus denying any role for "will" and voluntary action. It may be noted that Rao explicitly rejects the epiphenomenalist position right at the beginning of his essay. At a later stage of the discussion he points out that the more recent works of Sperry (1983) and Globus et al. (1976) show that, reciprocally, downward causation, implying the effect of the whole on parts, or mind onto the body, also works. This is a very important point in trying to build a bridge between Western and Indian ways of thinking because Indian thought is predominantly holistic rather than molecularistic, and most schools of Indian thought accept the position of mind-over-matter. Indeed, the idea at the core of Patañjali's *yoga* in particular, and most systems of meditation in general, is to voluntarily control both the bodily movements and mental processes so as to achieve higher levels of human potentials (including paranormal powers), wellness and healing. To put it simply, Rao's analysis reaches right down to be foundation of axiomatic principles on the one hand and on the other hand to the guiding goals for the search of knowledge that stand at the apex.

Indian psychology is not new; its history goes back to millennia. It is a living tradition that continues to function in traditional forms embedded in literature, in philosophy, in practices in *āśramas*, and so on — although the colonial influence has led to amnesia about the traditional legacy among university psychology departments. Most of us in Rao's generation were taught only Western psychology; few like him had the good fortune of being also exposed to Indian psychology embedded in Indian philosophy. This embedded knowledge had to be brought out and explicated to fellow psychologists in India and abroad in the language and idiom of modern psychology in the same way that in the late medieval times Ādi Śaṅkarācārya had to establish the doctrines of the ancient Upaniṣads through debates with followers of Buddhism and Pūrva-Mīmāṁsā. A tradition can survive only by re-interpretation of old insights in face of new challenges, whether home-grown or imported. That is the challenge Rao has taken, and his more recent work shows how he has continued to do so in increasingly sophisticated ways.

Following the paper published in 1991 described above, the next major step in the explication of Indian perspectives on consciousness appears in his paper "Two Faces of Consciousness: A Look at Eastern and Western Perspectives" published in the *Journal of Consciousness Studies* in 1998. It would be simple and straightforward to reproduce the abstract of that paper, so we get the gist of it in his own words.

> Two dominant perspectives on consciousness representing the Eastern and the Western viewpoints are discussed. In the Western scholarly tradition, (a) consciousness is generally equated with the mind; (b) intentionality is regarded as its defining characteristic; and (c) the goal is one of seeking rational understanding of what consciousness/mind is. In the Eastern tradition, as represented by the Indian approach to the study of consciousness, (a) consciousness and mind are considered to be different; (b) consciousness as-such is believed to be nonintentional while the mind is regarded as intentional; and (c) the goal is one of developing practical methods for transformation of the human condition via realization of consciousness as-such.
>
> It is suggested that consciousness encompasses two different domains, the transcendental and the phenomenal, and that humans enjoy dual citizenship in them. The Eastern and the Western viewpoints each seems to be directed more toward one domain than the other, resulting in a biased emphasis. Seen as complementary rather than in opposition to each other, the Eastern and the Western perspectives may give us a more comprehensive understanding of consciousness and its role in our being.
>
> — Rao 1998: 309

Quite clearly, the East–West encounter is continuing to dominate in this essay as in the previously mentioned publication, but the focus here is different as is the audience. Here he is addressing not only psychologists but a wider international audience. The *Journal of Consciousness Studies* is a relatively new journal started in 1994. From its beginning it has become the forum for an international and interdisciplinary group of scholars interested in consciousness viewed from various angles. Here, as in earlier work, the contrast between Indian and Western positions is clearly pointed out, perhaps in a more forceful way. The first point about the differing views of mind and consciousness is concerned with an *ontological* issue. This is very appropriate since the various contemporary views of consciousness have arisen against the backdrop of mind and matter, which Descartes proposed as two ontological categories with highly contrasting properties. Following Descartes, Western thinkers have continued to equate consciousness with mind, ignoring the spectrum of consciousness beyond the mind. In India, too, there have been fierce debates over similar ontological issues, between Sāṁkhyan dualism versus Advaitic monism for instance. But the postulation of a mind-independent pure consciousness as Sāṁkhyan *Puruṣa* or Advaitic *Ātman* is clearly different from all of the Western variations of Cartesian dualism. The most distinctive psychological feature of pure consciousness is its non-intentional character. In Western thought, Brentano revived the concept of intentionality from its medieval scholastic roots, but he as well his followers such as Husserl and Sartre insisted that consciousness is *always* intentional with no exceptions. This is a pervasive presumption among phenomenological thinkers, and like the Cartesian equation of consciousness with the mind, stands as an obstacle in communicating the idea of pure, non-intentional consciousness to Western audiences. In his article Rao meets this challenge head-on.

We may pause here to note some of the implications of all this for psychology. Modern psychology is not something that suddenly came up as a brand new discipline; it was an outcome of a long tradition. As every generation passes its insights to the next, the blind spots get transmitted as well, and these often tend to magnify over time. Examining current ideas in light of their historical roots helps in identifying the development of insights as well as blind spots that may have developed across generations of teachers and students. A cross-cultural view of historical development of ideas in relatively insulated traditions has an additional advantage comparable to the stereoscopic advantage of binocular vision which monocular vision lacks. In his paper under consideration, Rao traces the development of ideas about consciousness from Descartes through Locke and William James, views of the unconscious from Freud through Jung, as well as the notion of intentionality from Brentano through Husserl and Sartre. Backed by years of study of the development of Indian views of consciousness from the Upaniṣads through Buddhism, Jainism, Śaṅkara and Rāmānuja down to Krishna Chandra Bhattacharyya in the twentieth century, Rao is able to accurately pinpoint both the points of convergence as well as divergence between the East and the West. Such analysis, it is hoped, can help in getting over traditional blind spots and thereby paving the way for building a more inclusive and comprehensive psychology based on complementary insights and techniques.

Within four years of the publication of his paper in the *Journal of Consciousness Studies* Rao came up with a whole book, *Consciousness Studies: Cross-cultural Perspectives* (2002). Once again he pursues East–West comparison with the first half devoted to an exploration of the Western perspectives and the second half to ideas in the Eastern tradition. This book demonstrates further advance with exploration of a broader range of phenomena, and deeper analysis of concepts and theories. Thus, a separate chapter is devoted to the discussion of paradoxical and pathological awareness, and another to paranormal awareness. This means that a wider spectrum of consciousness is covered, and the issues of parapsychology are integrated within the discussion of consciousness. A detailed philosophical discussion of the concepts of mind and intentionality is included, taking the analysis of previously mentioned paper to a deeper level. A separate chapter "Consciousness, Brain and the New Physics" not only further extends the scope, but also brings the discussion up-to-date. With all this covered in the first part, the second part provides detailed accounts of Yogic, Vedāntic, and Buddhist views of consciousness in three separate chapters. This account itself amounts to a distinctive contribution to Indian psychology especially because it is done from a psychological rather than a purely philosophical perspective common to most of the earlier accounts. A survey of the recent literature on meditation shows how concepts and techniques of Indian psychology are enriching psychology across the world today. Finally, the complementarity of Western and Indian contributions to the study of consciousness is explained, and the resulting blend is appropriately titled *saṅgamam* — a Sanskrit word meaning the confluence of rivers.

Against the background of the earlier work mentioned so far, it would only be surprising if Rao's most recent work did not add new dimensions to the already rich discussion on the nature of consciousness. From the point of view of Indian psychology, it is significant that in *Cognitive Anomalies, Consciousness and Yoga* (2011a), while Part I deals with paranormal awareness, Part II provides a broader perspective on consciousness with a more deeply penetrating analysis than the book of 2002. It begins with a brief overview of the background of the classical Indian thought followed by a summary of the major schools of Indian thought, orthodox as well as the "heretical". Indeed there are many standard as well as textbook accounts of Indian philosophy widely available. Then what is so special about Rao's account? Clearly, he is a philosopher/psychologist who brings out what is relevant in the traditional treasure trove that matters for students and teachers of psychology today. Psychologists are usually uninterested in the nuances of ontological doctrines and the finer points of the endless debates among schools and their subdivisions. Psychologists are bound to focus on topics at the core of their discipline, such as perception, cognition, personality and self-actualization. True, there are a few philosophers who have written about topics like perception, and placed it in the context of contemporary philosophy. There is a book by the late B.K. Matilal (1986), for instance, but psychologists tend to be more interested in the processes of perception rather than in epistemology *per se*, which is of greater concern to the philosophers. Unlike such writings by philosophers, what Rao presents is not only the selected aspects of Indian thought relevant for psychology, but also places them in the context of current developments in the mainstream of psychology. This is going to be most useful to students and teachers of psychology today, who need an introduction to Indian philosophy which their current curricula need, but lack.

While knowing about the classical Indian perspectives on consciousness is useful, it is not enough from the point of view of psychologists today. Caught in the turbulent confluence of Eastern and Western worldviews, they equally need adequate background in the history of Western thought from which the contemporary views of consciousness have originated. This requires a good understanding of how Cartesian mind–matter dualism has led to the continuing debates over dualism, physical monism, interactionism and so on. This need is fulfilled as Rao traces the development of Western thought through major landmarks such as Gilbert Ryle's dismissal of the Cartesian dilemma as a "category mistake", to the latest developments in the work of Searle (2004) and the Churchlands (P.M. Churchland (1988) and P.S. Churchland (1986)). It is against this background of a comprehensive analysis that a student of modern psychology must understand the ongoing conflict between behaviourism versus phenomenology in contemporary Western psychology. Equipped with all this background, one can proceed to examine what makes the difference between Indian and Western perspectives on consciousness. We cannot and need not repeat Rao's detailed discussion of all this here; we may only note his conclusion.

> Interestingly, the concept of mind in classical Indian thought and twenty-first century psychology is surprisingly similar except that "consciousness" is not seen as part of aspect of mind. Rather consciousness becomes the primary principle, the ground condition and the knowledge base of the universe. — 2011a: 360-61

Having thus succinctly noted the commonality in the Indian and Western views, he goes on to specify the difference. The Western perspectives, he suggests, essentially address the phenomena of what the Buddhists call the *kāmaloka*, i.e. "the empirical world known through the senses and driven by desire" (2011a: 352). What they leave out are the regions of the spectrum of consciousness that lie beyond — or transcend — this limited portion. And it is in the exploration and understanding of the transcendental regions of consciousness that Indian psychology complements Western perspectives. Rao's favourite terms to designate the transcendental domain of consciousness are "consciousness as-such" and "pure consciousness".

On Patañjali's Yoga

In the history of Indian psychology, Patañjali's *Yoga* is the most important text that explains the nature of the transcendental domains of consciousness, particularly the states of the *saṁprajñāta* and *asaṁprajñāta samādhi*. Patañjali also provides an account of the procedures and techniques one can adopt to attain such states. This is a very important contribution of Indian psychology, and Rao devotes a major portion of his *magnum opus* equivalent to a whole book to *yoga* (pp. 564-735). This part of his contribution deserves special attention (to which we shall turn later on in this essay). But Rao's account of Indian views of the transcendental regions of consciousness goes beyond *yoga* to include the Buddhist views of how meditation can take us beyond empirical consciousness of the *kāmaloka* to increasingly sublime forms of consciousness in the *rūpaloka* and *arūpaloka* and ultimately to the *lokottara* region where the meditator overcomes all mental limitations. But he does not stop with such a comprehensive account of the distinctly Indian contributions to the understanding of the nature of consciousness and the yogic and Buddhist techniques of meditation that can take an aspirant to the transcendental states. In his discussion of consciousness, as in others, he covers parallel issues from the Western tradition.

As is well known, states of consciousness such as *samādhi* have been covered under the title of "mysticism" in Western thought. William James (1902, 1958) discussed this issue in his *Varieties of Religious Experience*. But as consciousness was turned into a non-issue by the behaviourists, mysticism and religious experience got dumped with even more disdain than ordinary varieties of consciousness. Maslow and few others who have touched on this topic are all marginalized. However, outside of psychology mysticism has continued to be a topic of serious inquiry, especially in philosophy and religious studies. Rao touches upon some of the important developments in Western thought on this issue. More specifically, he discusses in some detail the controversy that arose in the late 1970s through the 1980s on the nature of mystical experience. In this controversy a group of scholars led by Steven Katz (1978) argued against the universality of mystical experience saying that cognitive construction plays a major role accounting for the differences as shown by the variety of accounts from various religious traditions. In opposition to such a constructivist position, Robert Forman (1990) strongly argued that there indeed is a common core of "pure" consciousness emptied of all manner of cognitive constructions in reports of mystical experiences in numerous accounts over the centuries and across cultures. The conclusion of this controversy is not important here; indeed, such controversies tend to repeat and continue in various forms over and over. What is important to note from the point of Indian psychology is that accounts of the experience of pure consciousness are common to many schools of Indian thought, and the topic remains a most distinctive and important part of the Indian contributions to psychology. Credit goes to Rao for not only discussing this issue in his books, but also, as noted earlier, for bringing forth the Indian perspectives on this issue in the international and interdisciplinary forum represented by the *Journal of Consciousness Studies*.

The importance of consciousness lies, among other things, in its very close relationship with the self and personal identity. As Rao looks at this issue in the light of East–West comparison, he makes an important observation about a common and predominant feature of Western perspectives. On the whole, he says:

> The identification of consciousness and the mind tends to lead one to ignore or deny the possibility of pure conscious states . . . and provokes the denial of the existence of an enduring self and tends to identify self with the mind, the mind with consciousness, and consciousness with

> brain states; and thus promotes some kind of reductionism.
>
> — 2011a: 423

After reviewing the development of the views of the self in the Western tradition from Descartes through Hume, Kant, William James, Husserl, Sartre and G.H. Mead, Rao notes the overall tendency to consider self as object rather than subject, thus leading to the idea that being himself implies having *perceptions* of himself, and not being the self *per se*. This observation makes sense given the proliferation of the "concept" of self, rather than the *experience* of the self in modern Western psychology. Turning then to a fairly comprehensive overview of the views of the self in the Indian tradition, Rao notes the radical difference between the Vedāntic affirmation of an enduring self, as opposed to the Buddhist denial of the same. Regardless of this and other matters of difference in the views of self among the major schools of Indian thought, he notes that removal of suffering has been the most common and predominant aim of inquiry into the nature of self (rather than focus on a purely rational quest in the West). He concludes his account of the Indian views with the observation:

> The self at the psychological level appears quite similar for both Buddhist and Hindu thinkers. What the Buddhists have rejected is in actuality the psychological self, the ego that binds us to things. In Hindu thought, the ego is not the self; it is an aspect of the mind. Clinging, craving, desires, attachment and so on do not belong to the self but to the ego. The Hindu thinkers share with their Buddhist counterparts that alleviation and removal of human suffering consists essentially in the realization that the I-ness is not the self. The deconstruction of the ego is the recommended path for liberation from suffering and human bondage. The Buddhists as well as Hindu thinkers agree that meditation and states of *samādhi* are conducive conditions for the deconstruction of the ego.
>
> — 2011a: 459

In these words Rao very briefly and clearly communicates some of the most essential features of Indian psychology that explain the close connection between consciousness and the self, and the role of pure consciousness or states of *samādhi* in eradicating suffering from human life.

Yogic meditation is clearly the most well-known process for the attainment of *samādhi*, and this is becoming increasingly popular throughout the world today, although it is the physical aspect of *yoga* that is being "sold" in stores called "*yoga* studios". Despite the fact that *yoga* is simply the core of the applied aspect of Indian psychology, psychologists in India are disdainful of it. Outside of academic psychology in India today, the literature on *yoga* is abundant. The tradition of thinkers of the Sāṁkhya-Yoga school of thought from Patañjali through Vyāsa, Vācaspati Miśra and many others continues till this date. The more recent contributions to this literature comes primarily from Indologists, Sanskrit scholars, philosophers and several Westerners — among whom there are some clinical psychologists wishing to use meditation in their clinical practice. There is lack of scholarly work published by a psychologist with deep knowledge of Indian psychology. This is the void that is filled by the section of Rao's book-length section on *yoga* in his major work, *Cognitive Anomalies, Consciousness and Yoga*.

The work of Rao on *yoga* combines traditional and modern, Indian and Western, theoretical as well as empirical perspectives; it is indeed very inclusive and comprehensive. The focus is, first, on the Patañjali's *Yoga-Sūtras* — as it should have been. He provides translation, explanation and commentary on every aphorism in Patañjali's text. Aside from the basic text and major traditional commentaries on the same, Rao has used the important interpretive work of Surendra Nath Dasgupta, as well as many of the well-known English translations and commentaries on the *Yoga-Sūtras*. This section itself could stand as a separate monograph, but there is much more he has offered in addition. Patañjali's *yoga* clearly presents a specific technique of meditation which is but one of the many systems of meditative practice that have been developed in India and elsewhere in Asia. Many of these have become recently popular as part of the technical repertoire of clinical psychologists. While early studies of *yoga* applying modern scientific methodology such as Electroencephalography (EEG) were primarily exploratory and aimed at understanding the basic physiological processes involved in yogic practice, the more recent studies of meditation are aimed at examining the benefits of practice in reduction of stress and improving health and well-being. As part of his work on *yoga*, Rao has critically examined the burgeoning literature in meditation research including the most recent contributions. In this context he covers classical concentrative as well as mindful meditation, Transcendental Meditation (TM), Benson's relaxation response, Vipassanā, Zen, Mindfulness-Based Cognitive Therapy, Tai Chi and Qui Gong, thus spanning the entire range of meditative techniques. There is an entire section on neurophysiological effects and correlates of meditative practices using various techniques such as EEG, Positron

Emission Tomography (PET), and functional Magnetic Resonance Imaging (fMRI). His analysis is not restricted to health benefits alone, but covers the effects of meditation on emotion, volition and cognition as well as paranormal abilities.

Given Rao's life-long interest in researching the paranormal phenomena, it would only be a surprise if he had not examined the place of paranormal powers — *siddhis* — in *yoga*. This is clearly an important aspect of *yoga*, as Patañjali devotes one whole chapter out of four to describe the *siddhis*. Like many a student of *yoga* he realizes that, despite listing a number of *siddhis* and claiming that they can be attained through high-level concentration on a variety of targets of attention, Patañjali explicitly warns that they are obstacles on the way to the highest goal of *yoga*, which is to attain *kaivalya* or liberation. Then how do we understand the place of the *siddhis* in the yogic enterprise? In his search for an answer to this question, Rao is quite open to alternative possibilities, including the idea that *siddhis* do not even exist. "If *siddhis* do not exist", he writes, "and the claimed supernormal abilities are no more than clever chicanery or pseudo experiences laced with widespread misperceptions, seeking solace in *kaivalya* would be like chasing the mirage in the desert. Therefore, *siddhis* are integral and essential pursuit of *kaivalya*" (2011a: 629). Does this conclusion imply that, despite his apparent skepticism, he is truly a believer? That he is not a believer pretending to be a skeptic becomes clear from one of his experiences narrated in the following words:

> In fact, I worked with a *yogin* who claimed that in his *samādhi* state he could go to the moon. It did not take long for me while studying him to convince myself that the *yogin* who is otherwise normal is totally deluded when he speaks of his celestial voyages. — 2011a: 630

Let me quote a few more words from the same page.

> If Patañjali was merely chronicling the beliefs current at the time, it is entirely possible that many of the *siddhis* are imaginary. The other positive side of it is that there is a tenable rationale behind them all. If so, it is a matter of scientific inquiry and credible observation to separate wheat from the chaff. — 2011a: 630

It would be useful to cite another example in Rao's writings where open mindedness and genuine skepticism are highly demanded. This is in regard to the belief in survival after death. The importance of this issue for Indian psychology should be clear, for it relates to the doctrine of *karma*, which is foundational for Indian psychology. This doctrine implies the assumption of a universal ethical principle whereby justice will be *ultimately* done, and since saints often suffer while crooks get away with murder, reincarnation is a corollary that would ensure that the books will be balanced some time in the future. In this context, it makes sense that Rao carefully examines the evidence available thus far on reported cases of reincarnation. He is very candid in his assessment. After examining reported cases where persons speak languages or demonstrate skills they had no chance to learn, he says that "the survivalist interpretation of such cases involves some logical difficulties" (2011a: 559). His overall conclusion is that: "For the most part the evidence for survival is anecdotal" (2011: 558). Despite his apparent sympathies for the conceptual foundations of Indian psychology in the doctrine of *karma*, he does not blindly accept all its corollaries. In view of the concept of *liṅga śarīra*, an aspect of a person that is said to survive death, for instance, Rao demands conclusive evidence and reserves judgement.

Here, to help explain how this critical and open-minded approach reflects the spirit of Indian psychology, I wish to take the liberty to make some observations and add a few comments. The opinions about paranormal powers of *yogī*s range between two extremes. At one end are too many credulous people who flock around self-proclaimed *yogi*s who demonstrate magical powers. Included among their followers are highly-educated people, engineers, lawyers, professors, even highly-placed judges, let alone politicians of all stripes. There are on the opposite side some who are convinced that each and every person who claims to have special powers must be a crook bent on cheating the credulous folk. In between these extremes are people who are skeptical. However, I have personally known self-proclaimed skeptics, professors of various disciplines among them, who have formed formal societies of skeptics whose main activity is to debunk claims to paranormal. Granted that it is useful to expose fraudsters who sell magical tricks in the name of yogic powers or divine gifts, many of the so-called skeptics are self-appointed protectors of science, who have blind faith in scientism rather than genuine open-mindedness in the true spirit of science. In their view, observations that do not fit the laws of science as they understand them, or anomalies, must imply either faulty observations or simply frauds. Kuhn, the well-known historian and philosopher of science, has mentioned many examples showing that a majority of scientists often ignore or dismiss anomalies. He goes ahead to point out how, only when enough examples of anomalies accumulate, some genius like Copernicus or Einstein comes along and provides a new, revolutionary view of the world in which the so-called anomalies find clear place. Kuhn's thesis of scientific revolutions is now widely accepted. This is the history of modern science, which is often claimed to be a Western product (although many Asians have made significant contributions to it). How does all this look from the standpoint of the intellectual history of India?

Let us note that the "orthodox" schools of Indian thought accept the authority of the Vedas, which include the Upaniṣads. The approach to truth respected and followed in this tradition is reflected by Śaṅkarācārya (788–820) in what he says in his commentary of the *Bhagavad-Gītā* (18.66). He suggests that, if one finds an expression in the Vedas saying that fire is without light or heat, then it need not be taken to be valid. All claims to truth, he affirms, must be tested in light of established criteria of validation, including observation and reason. This view of knowledge, which denies blind faith and demands empirical and rational validation of all truth claims, represents a central teaching of the Indian tradition. In my view, Rao's views about yogic *siddhi*s represent this spirit of the Indian intellectual tradition. In this way, he is a genuine representative and an authentic proponent of Indian psychology.

Modern Contributions to Indian Psychology

Gandhi's Spirituality

As a young philosopher Rao chose Gandhian philosophy very early in his career, comparing it with American pragmatism. He returned to the topic in his most recent work. One can see that, at this later stage, he writes more like a theoretical psychologist with deep roots in Indian thought. Although some of the most important contributions of Indian psychology go back to ancient times, as part of a living tradition it has continued with important developments through the twentieth century. Prof. Rao recognizes the more recent contributions to this tradition, such as the writings of Sri Aurobindo through the first half of the twentieth century. In writing about Gandhi, and recognizing him for bringing in the spiritual element in politics, Rao has in effect recognized modern Indian contributions to *social psychology* in so far as Gandhi's *satyāgraha* is essentially a technique of applied social psychology aimed at conflict resolution.

In keeping with his usual approach, Rao's analysis of Gandhi's applied spiritual social psychology (if I may call it by such a label) digs deep into the history of ideas from ancient to the latest and extends his scope to include modern insights into the nature of conflict from E.O. Wilson's sociobiology through experimental social psychology of Henri Tajfel and others. It is interesting to note how he traces the uniqueness of Gandhi's approach to the striking contrast between Western views of human nature grounded in Hobbes' work in the seventeenth century on the one hand and traditional Indian counterpart in the ancient *Kaṭha Upaniṣad* on the other. For Hobbes, he notes, the natural tendency of human beings is to be selfish and power hungry, and their attempts to establish one's superiority over others result in violence. Those who adopt an approach founded on such assumptions of human nature are bound to take violence as simply natural, and would be less inclined to find ways for removing it. In contrast, Rao notes, traditional Indian views, illustrated by the *Kaṭha Upaniṣad,* for example, do not consider human spirit to be naturally and forever bondaged by desires, and seek to conquer the world through overcoming desires rather than through selfish use of power. He traces this basic theme of Indian culture to persist through the centuries, citing in support a statement from the poet Kālidāsa saying "ow[n]ing the whole world while disowning oneself" (2011b: 97). Then he goes on to say that "it is within this tradition that *satyāgraha* was born, and it is this tradition that provides the rationale for the Gandhian thought and practice". In other words, Gandhi's approach to social conflict can be understood as an innovation in applied social psychology in the age-old tradition of Indian psychology. By explaining this idea in the context of the latest insights from the diverse fields of sociobiology and experimental social psychology, Rao is continuing the tradition of Indian psychology in the global context of the twenty-first century.

Proposing a More Inclusive Model for Psychology at Large

The main challenge facing Indian psychology in the globalized context of the twenty-first century is to come face-to-face with the challenges of Western psychology. This implies the need for a broader framework that would accommodate both Indian as well as Western insights and approaches. In the concluding section of his *Cognitive Anomalies, Consciousness and Yoga,* Rao presents a conceptual model to help meet this challenge. He calls it the "Trident" model since it deals with a three-pronged solution that puts together three basic domains of inquiry — consciousness, mind and body. As he has shown again and again in his writings, his view of consciousness includes the entire spectrum of consciousness extending from the exalted pure consciousness extoled in the Upaniṣadic tradition on the one hand, to the depths of the unconscious explored in psychoanalysis on the other. In Indian psychology consciousness is not seen simply as an aspect of the mind but as the ground condition of existence. While rejecting the reduction of mind to neurological events in the brain, he does not recommend ignoring the connection of the mind with the body. Rather, he sees the need for Indian psychology to take into consideration the great strides taken in recent neurophysiological research exploring the connection between the mind and body. To put it simply, he presents a comprehensive model that includes the best of Indian and Western traditions. It is particularly interesting that in explaining this model he uses Sri Aurobindo's explication of the various levels of consciousness which brings his discussion up-to-date on the Indian side. On the Western side, he makes it up-to-date by showing how Max Velman's recent work gets pretty close to including essential Indian insights indicating possible ways to bring the twain together. His Trident model, we hope, will provide a guideline for an expanded and enriched global psychology in the near future.

Contributions to Indian Psychology Beyond Writing and Publishing

Rao's contributions to Indian psychology are not restricted to his individual scholarship and publications. In addition to being a committed scholar and a prolific author, he has been an able administrator, organizer and leader, and through these roles he has also made incomparable contributions to Indian psychology. He was instrumental in founding the *Journal of Indian Psychology* as far back as in the late 1970s, and founded the Institute for Yoga and Consciousness at Andhra University in the mid-1980s. Although in India, the land of *yoga*, a Yoga institute was neither a novelty nor something special; what makes it extraordinary is that it was started as part of a university system in an atmosphere where Indian psychology has become outcaste. It would be useful to note here an introduction to the Institute of Yoga and Consciousness from its webpage to help appreciate the direction that Indian psychology took with this pioneering initiative of Rao.

The Institute for Yoga and Consciousness was established by Prof. K. Ramakrishna Rao when he was the Vice-Chancellor of the university during the VIth Plan period and it is one of the developing departments of the university. The institute was set up by the university for fundamental research on mind–matter interaction. It undertakes empirical and conceptual research on *yoga* and allied disciplines and carries out

extension programmes related to them. Interdisciplinary in approach and international in scope, the institute attempts to bring together the high technology of the West and the wisdom of the East for a fuller understanding of human nature, an understanding that reflects at once the experimental objectivity of science and the experiential richness of traditional practices. The approach of the institute is scientific and secular. Therefore, it has no religious orientation or affiliation. It subscribes to the rules of reason and logic, and defends facts against fiction and knowledge against superstition.

In more recent years, Rao was appointed by the Government of India as the head of the Indian Council of Philosophical Research (ICPR) for two successive terms. While this was a clear recognition of his contribution to Indian philosophy, he was already well known for his deep interest in, and unique contributions to, parapsychology and Indian psychology. Aside from the institutional support that the ICPR could provide under his administration to research in Indian psychology, his high profile in the country naturally projected the continuing developments in the field of Indian psychology.

Apart from his influential role within formal institutional frameworks, Rao has promoted Indian psychology as a leader of an informal group of like-minded scholars. An excellent example of this is the fact that, at the National Conference on Yoga and Indian Approaches to Psychology held in 2002 at Pondicherry, he proposed the "Manifesto of Indian Psychology". This was a declaration unanimously adopted by over 150 delegates from across India to adopt a whole set of measures for strengthening psychological study, research and practice in India. The focus of many papers presented at this conference, as of the manifesto itself, was on promoting psychology in tune with traditional Indian culture and ethos. Before the conclusion of the conference, a small and informal group was formed with a resolve to meet again and formulate strategy and adopt programmes for the enhancement of research and promoting publications in Indian psychology.

Subsequently, this group along with some more colleagues met at Rao's residence and decided to organize local and national conferences at various places in India. More specifically, Rao proposed an ambitious programme to publish a set of three volumes: a handbook, a sourcebook and a textbook of Indian psychology. In pursuance of this goal, the *Handbook of Indian Psychology* was published in 2008 with Rao as the editor in association with Anand Paranjpe and Ajit Dalal. The projects for the sourcebook and textbook are in various stages of development. Together the three books are expected to help in promoting Indian psychology especially as aid to students and teachers. A series of conferences have taken place since the first one in 2002 in Pondicherry. Rao was the keynote speaker in many of them. At the national level, activities of the informal Indian psychology group are becoming increasingly visible through the presentation of papers and symposia at the annual conferences of the National Academy of Psychology (NAoP). In the middle of all these indications of the continuing growth of Indian psychology, Rao has clearly emerged as the most significant contributor. The recognition of his leadership role is clearly reflected by the fact that he was invited to address the 30th International Congress of Psychology held in South Africa in July 2012 on the topic "Psychology in the Indian Tradition".

References

Berger, P.L. (1966), *The Sacred Canopy: Elements of a Sociological Theory of Religion*, Garden City, NY: Doubleday.

Churchland, P.M. (1988), *Matter and Consciousness: A Contemporary Introduction to the Philosophy of Mind*, Cambridge, M.A.: MIT Press.

Churchland, P.S. (1986), *Neurophilosophy: Toward a Unified Science of the Mind–Brain*, Cambridge, M.A.: MIT Press.

Forman, R.K.C. (ed.) (1990), *The Problem of Pure Consciousness: Mysticism and Philosophy*, New York: Oxford University Press.

Globus, G.G., G. Maxwell and I. Savodnik (eds.) (1976), *Consciousness and the Brain*, New York: Plenum.

James, W. (1958), *The Varieties of Religious Experience*, New York: New American Library (originally published 1902).

Katz, S. (ed.) (1978), *Mysticism and Philosophical Analysis*, New York: Oxford University Press.

Kuhn, T. (1970), *The Structure of Scientific Revolutions* (2nd edn.), Chicago: University of Chicago Press.

Matilal, B.K. (1986), *Perception: An Essay on Classical Indian Theories of Knowledge*, Oxford, UK: Oxford University Press.

Rao, K.R. (1964), "Review of *Mind and Consciousness in Experimental Parapsychology* by R.H. Thouless [Cambridge, Cambridge University Press, 1963]", *Journal of Parapsychology*, 28: 136-38.

——— (1966), *Experimental Parapsychology: A Review and Interpretation*, Springfield: Charles C. Thomas.

——— (1968), "Psi in Communities and Other Interpersonal Situations in the Eastern World", in R. Cavanna (ed.) *Psi and Favorable States of Consciousness: Proceedings of an International Conference on Methodology in Psi Research*, New York: Parapsychology Foundation, pp. 74-83.

——— (1972), "Consciousness in Indian Psychology", paper presented at the Third International Conference on Humanistic Psychology, Tokyo.

——— (1978), "Psychology of Transcendence: A Study in Early Buddhistic Psychology", *Journal of Indian Psychology*, 1: 1-21.

——— (1990), foreword in I.V. Chalapati Rao's *Sankara: Humanist, Integrator Poet and Philosopher*, Hyderabad: Telugu University.

——— (1991) (ed.), *Cultivating Consciousness: Enhancing Human Potential, Wellness and Healing*, Westport, CT: Prager.

——— (1998), "Two Faces of Consciousness: A Look at Eastern and Western Perspectives", *Journal of Consciousness Studies*, 5(3): 309-27.

——— (2002), *Consciousness Studies: Cross-cultural Perspectives*, Jefferson, NC: McFarland.

——— (2011a), *Cognitive Anomalies, Consciousness, and Yoga*, Delhi: Matrix and Centre for Studies in Civilizations.

——— (2011b), *Gandhi and Applied Spirituality*, Delhi: Matrix and Indian Council for Philosophical Research.

Rao, K.R. and J. Palmer (1987a), "The Anomaly Called Psi: Recent Research and Criticism", *Behavioral and Brain Sciences*, 10: 539-51.

——— (1987b), "Where Lies the Bias?", *Behavioral and Brain Sciences*, 10: 618-27.

Rao, K.R., A.C. Paranjpe and A. Dalal (eds.) (2008), *Handbook of Indian Psychology*, Delhi: Foundation Books (Cambridge University Press, India).

Searle, J.R. (2004), *Mind: A Brief Introduction*, New York: Oxford University Press.

Sperry, R. (1983), *Science and Moral Priority: Merging Mind, Brain and Human Values*, New York: Columbia University Press.

4

Yoga and Parapsychology

Jerry Solfvin

Introduction

THIS year, the world of parapsychology celebrates the eightieth birthdays of two great educators, scientists, visionaries, philosophers and leaders. These two men — K. Ramakrishna Rao in India and Stanley Krippner in America — have contributed to the world in so many ways. There are many parallels that can be drawn between Krippner and Rao, even as they are distinctly individual. Both have strong followings in their own countries, extending out like peels of great temple bells for all who have ears to hear, in all directions, in space and time. Both are great teachers, with long — and still growing! — lists of students inspired by them. Both are great scientists and have made important contributions in their published research studies. Both are great leaders, organizers and team players, who have brought people together in collaborative ventures for the benefit of all. Both have created opportunities for others which would not have existed otherwise. Both are prolific authors, each having already published hundreds of articles in professional journals and dozens of books, with the list still increasing. Both have been editors of journals and books, and brought together important and rich volumes for the benefit of other authors and readership everywhere. Both are humanitarians, alert and attentive to human rights, injustice and corruption. Both are recognized "bridge-builders" who actively promote cross-cultural understanding in their lives and in their professions. Both have been models of a tireless work ethic and both are still incredibly active, to the benefit of all, in their eighth decade of life.

These two men were both born on 4 October 1932, Stanley Krippner in Wisconsin (USA), and K.R. Rao in Andhra Pradesh (India). Somehow, while honouring the one, we cannot help but honour the other.

In their cross-cultural efforts, these two very special human beings cover the globe and reach out in all directions. Krippner, it might be said, has focused more upon the north–south co-ordinate, opening up the vast and important connections between Eurocentric North America, and Latin- and South America, including the native peoples of the Americas.

Rao has focused primarily on the East–West co-ordinate by personifying the India–America academic exchange. Rao, of course, is ideally suited for this with his long and deep associations with India and America. Brought up and educated in his native country, he came to America originally as a Fulbright Fellow, and began an association which lasted many years. In my review of his 2010 book, *Yoga and Parapsychology: Empirical Studies and Theoretical Perspectives*, I call attention to Rao's very intentional role (Solfvin 2011) in promoting intercultural dialogue by pointing out that he has

> . . . published in recent years several important contributions towards an East–West bridge on academic topics, including *Consciousness Studies: Cross-cultural Perspectives* (Rao 2002), *Towards a Spiritual Psychology* (Rao & Marwaha 2005), and the outstanding and sorely needed *Handbook of Indian Psychology* (Rao, Paranjpe & Dalal 2008). Now he follows this with an edited volume aimed squarely at the specific field with which his name was most closely associated for so many years — parapsychology.

Carving out an East–West pathway for scientific interchange on *yoga* and parapsychology is no easy task. There is prejudice to deal with, especially the prejudice among American scientists towards the field of parapsychology in which Rao spent many years. In the same book, he offers an explanation of why the very idea of psychic phenomena may be repugnant to some American scientists (Rao 2010):

> First, the theoretical implications of these findings are unsettling to the assumptive base of science in general and the physical sciences in particular. They seem to question the basic principles that limit the extent of human information acquisition resources that are considered sacrosanct in science. In other words, psychic phenomena are of a kind that would not happen in a universe determined by physical laws. If the universe is entirely determined by physical causation, as is generally assumed, any claims of psychic phenomena that appear to call into question such determinism should be considered spurious and a priori unreal. It is so because the antecedent probability accorded to their occurrence is zero.

In this, Prof. Rao correctly points to the dangers of the materialist, determinist assumption that dominates Western science. Rao is not alone in this, not a voice in the wilderness, but rather a member in good standing of a choral group whose chant becomes louder by the year. Rao's insightful concern is shared by Krippner, as well as a long list of luminaries from the past, such as William James, Gardner Murphy, Abraham Maslow, Margaret Mead, J.B. Rhine, F.W.H. Myers, to name a few.

In 1991, physicists Paul Davies and John Gribben wrote of the demise of materialism at the hands of scientific progress generally and quantum mechanics specifically:

> Then came our quantum theory, which totally transformed our image of matter. The old assumption that the microscopic world of atoms was simply a scaled-down version of the everyday world had to be abandoned. Newton's deterministic machine was replaced by a shadowy and paradoxical conjunction of waves and particles, governed by the laws of chance, rather than the rigid rules of causality. An extension of the quantum theory goes beyond even this; it paints a picture in which solid matter dissolves away, to be replaced by weird excitations and vibrations of invisible field energy. Quantum physics undermines materialism because it reveals that matter has far less "substance" than we might believe. But another development goes even further by demolishing Newton's image of matter as inert lumps. This development is the theory of chaos, which has recently gained widespread attention.
>
> — Paul Davies and John Gribben, *The Matter Myth,* chap. 1

Despite this, materialism persists as the default assumption among Western scientists, often in the form of what John Polkinghorne calls "promissory materialism", the claim to eventually be able to explain all phenomena via materialistic science (Harris 1998). Recent books by Charles Tart (2009), B. Alan Wallace (2000, 2008a, 2008b), Gary Schwartz (2011), and Emily Kelly et al. (2006) may call attention to and help erode the materialist bias but, as physicist David Scharf (2010, 2012) points out the materialist dogma is stubbornly persistent.

It is not only Western scientific materialism that concerns Rao. On the Indian side, there is the current state of Indian psychology, which he defines as (2008: xvii):

> . . . a complex subject variously viewed as esoteric and spiritual, philosophical and speculative, practical and ritualistic, and of course, as we believe, systematic and scientific understanding of human nature.

Rao holds back no punches when criticizing affairs in India:

> . . . psychology in India is in such a sorry state that it is widely felt it needs to take a round-about turn and look back into its own tradition and learn from it. It need not march mindlessly in a "catch up with the West" game in an uneven field, with mismatched tools.

The bright side, they say, is that a close look at contemporary Western psychology will find

> . . . some native Indian psycho-developmental techniques and personal transformation practices and strategies like meditation have not only become popular in the West, but they also have been subjected to serious scientific scrutiny, raising the expectation that what were once considered esoteric phenomena are now amenable for scientific investigation.
>
> — Rao 2008: xvii

Thus, East and West both benefit by taking a good hard look at each other, absent of the traditional prejudices and biases. Thus, in the remainder of this chapter, I wish to capture the magnitude and importance of Rao's efforts to build a bridge for Eastern–Western dialogue, especially along the *yoga*–psychology–parapsychology continuum, because, I assert, Rao understands more than other scholars the tremendous riches/wealth that lies in wait for this marriage to complete. Rao, I believe, stands out among colleagues East and West in being fully aware that *yoga* and parapsychology are "transformative" activities, capable of far-reaching impact on individual and collective perceptions.

In my opinion, Rao is clanging the bell to alert us that both East and West have lost sight of the "mystery" that drives the "seekers" in all cultures. Re-awakening to the mystery, individually and collectively, may be parapsychology's greatest and most profound offering to the world.

> The most beautiful thing we can experience is the mysterious. It is the source of all true art and all science. He to whom this emotion is a stranger, who can no longer pause to wonder and stand rapt in awe, is as good as dead: his eyes are closed. — Albert Einstein

Transformative Power of Yoga

From the frontispiece of K.R. Rao's masterful book — *Yoga and Parapsychology: Empirical Research and Theoretical Studies* (2010), we find this foundational quote:

> *Yoga* and parapsychology are two areas in which a significant amount of professional research is awaited. Parapsychology, considered as the

> discipline to study psi (psychic abilities), is essentially the science of *siddhis* (extraordinary human abilities). *Yoga* is considered to be an effective psycho-spiritual pursuit that results in the manifestation of a variety of supernormal phenomena. In fact, Patañjali's *Yoga-Sūtras* is the foundational text of psychic science. One of its four parts, *Vibhūti Pāda*, is filled with the description and discussion of a variety of paranormal phenomena. There is thus an intrinsic commonality between *yoga* and parapsychology, which remains essentially unexplored in any systematic way. A serious and scientific study of the two and the resultant synergy of their confluence could result in resolving many of the riddles that puzzle parapsychology today and be a harbinger of a vibrant science opening up new frontiers. Further, it could be seen as a productive East–West meet in a profound sense.

With this, Rao throws down the gauntlet and challenges us to develop a truly transformative science. The pieces of this puzzle are right here in front of us, Rao suggests, waiting for us to pick them up, dust them off, and put them together. It is as if we were seeking the re-union of siblings who were born of the same parents, separated at birth, and grew up in entirely different cultures. Now we all await their grand re-union. *Yoga* and parapsychology are those siblings that were separated and await reuniting.

The family resemblance can still be seen. For one thing, both *yoga* and parapsychology have transformative qualities. Both are mysterious. Both attract seekers after knowledge. In *yoga*, the primary avenue of transformation is body and spirit. For parapsychology, it is mind and spirit.

For the Western reader, it may be necessary to anticipate some likely — and quite valid — questions. Why *yoga*? What is transformative about *yoga*? Has *yoga* got anything at all to do with science? What does Western science say about *yoga*?

Or maybe not. Twentieth-century America is quite familiar with *yoga*, at least as an increasingly common soundbite. According to Wikipedia, "In the West, the term *yoga* is today typically associated with *haṭha-yoga* and its *āsanas* (postures) or as a form of exercise." The phrase, "I'm off to my *yoga* class!" has become as common as, "I'm off to the fitness centre", and usually expressed with the same inflection. It is no wonder that *yoga* is often misconstrued in America and the West as being "exercise".

Yoga, of course, is exercise. And like any form of vigorous, structured fitness activity it is good for one's physical health and can even provide the aerobics recommended for heart patients. Fitness, regular exercise of any sort, can be thought of as the first and perhaps most important step towards maintaining a healthy body. However, those who choose *yoga* soon discover that it is something more than palliative exercise. When one steps through the *yoga* door at their fitness centre, they move up a level into a therapeutic practice which has "transformative" qualities. In fact, many of the estimated fifteen plus million *yoga* practitioners in America may have been seeking not only to maintain, but to *transform* their health.

And well they should. On the website "nursingdegree.net" for example, Meredith Walker reviews the documented health benefits of *yoga* practice and finds an astonishing seventy-seven of them! She writes:

> Over the past several years, *yoga* has experienced an upsurge in popularity in the Western world among medical professionals and celebrities alike. While many associate *yoga* with new age mysticism or the latest fad at the gym, *yoga* is actually an ancient practice that connects the mind, body, and spirit through body poses, controlled breathing, and meditation. The practice of *yoga* has many health benefits associated with it, so read below to discover seventy-seven benefits of incorporating *yoga* into your or your patient's fitness programme. — Walker 2012

Walker points out that practising *yoga* is now known to benefit internal indicators such as blood pressure, pulse rate, circulation, respiratory, cardiac endurance, gastrointestinal, immune system, pain, and metabolism. External health indicators that benefit from *yoga* include: ageing, posture, strength, energy, weight, sleep, balance, body awareness, integrated body function, and sexuality. Body chemistry also benefits from *yoga*, including: cholesterol, lymphatic system, glucose, sodium levels, endocrine function, triglycerides, red blood cell count, and vitamin C level. In addition, studies have shown *yoga* practice can help prevent heart disease, osteoporosis, Alzheimer's disease, and type II diabetes. *Yoga* can also be beneficial for carpal tunnel, asthma, arthritis, multiple sclerosis, cancer, muscular dystrophy, migraines, scoliosis, chronic bronchitis, epilepsy, sciatica, Obsessive Compulsive Disorder (OCD), constipation, allergies, and menopausal symptoms. (see http://www.nursingdegree.net/blog/24/77-surprising-health-benefits-of-*yoga*/)

Yoga is more than exercise. In an article on website www.abc-of-yoga.com, contributor Shaynebance (2012) explains:

> Ancient *yogīs* had a belief that in order for man to be in harmony with himself and his environment, he has to integrate the body, the mind, and

> the spirit. For these three to be integrated, emotion, action, and intelligence must be in balance. The *yogīs* formulated a way to achieve and maintain this balance and it is done through exercise, breathing, and meditation — the three main *yoga* structures. (see http://www.abc-of-yoga.com/beginnersguide/whatisyoga.asp)

A survey released in December 2008 by the US National Center for Complementary and Alternative Medicine found that *yoga* was the sixth most commonly used alternative therapy in the United States during 2007, with 6.1 per cent of the population participating.

While some Westerners still distinguish between *yoga* and meditation, in the Eastern tradition they are part and parcel of the same thing, essentially synonymous, as Shaynebance implies above. *Yoga* is the broader term. It is described variously — and correctly — as a comprehensive philosophy born out of Hinduism, a way of life, a therapeutic intervention, or as a set of techniques to awaken a person to his/her own fullness. But some form of mental, attentional focusing, contemplative/meditative practice, is always central to it. The central involvement of mind in *yoga* is the part that makes *yoga* more than exercise, and the central involvement of mind may be the key to its transformative impact.

In a more recent (December 2011) website review of studies at University of Virginia by Sara Lazar (2012), it is concluded that:

> Meditation is more than just a way for us to get in touch with ourselves and calm a busy mind. It appears that meditation has a direct effect on the physical body, brain activity and underlying brain structure. (see http://www.sikhnet.com/news/study-shows-meditation-changes-brain-structure-just-8-weeks)

The specific benefits of *yoga*/meditation cited in this review are (Lazar 2012):

- *Pain*: There is a body of research work indicating that meditation can reduce chronic pain. One notable study conducted at the Texas Tech University found that meditation in conjunction with traditional medicine enhances the effectiveness of Western medical treatment. In another study published in the *Journal of Behavioural Medicine*, patients suffering from backache, chronic migraine and tension headaches were able to significantly reduce pain medication. Another study found that people who meditate regularly find pain less unpleasant.
- *HIV*: There is emerging evidence from other studies that shows

that meditation and behavioural stress-management programmes can buffer HIV declines in HIV-positive people.

- *High cholesterol*: In two prospective, random assignment studies, meditation reduced total cholesterol over a relatively short period (three months) as well as a long period (11 months).
- *Anxiety and depression*: Since the early sixties, scientists have speculated that meditation improves mental functioning. Meditation decreases oxygen consumption, heart rate respiratory rate, and blood pressure, and increases the intensity of alpha, theta and delta brain waves, the opposite of the physiological changes that occur during the stress response.
- *Diabetes*: Meditation also aids in controlling blood sugar levels. Researchers at the University of Virginia have shown that following meditation, reduced stress levels correlate with a decrease in blood glucose levels.
- *Hypertension*: Besides its role as a stress buster, meditation also reduces blood pressure and contributes to the overall reduction in risk of cardiovascular disease.

It is for its health benefits that *yoga* enjoys an increasing audience in America. However, we only scratch the surface of *yoga*'s transformative potentials when speaking of physical health benefits only. Persistent practitioners note — as the ancient Hindu writings contended — more profound but less readily measurable transformative effects. Over time, *yoga* practice shows a sustained positive impact on one's everyday life experience. The emotional and social dimensions of one's life show positive change. Here's a personal anecdote that illustrates of this. A close friend, a hospital administrator, once described what happened to him after he began daily Transcendental Meditation (TM) practice. He said:

> My work used to be a virtual battlefield. Each day I'd dread going to work because it meant another confrontation with the director of nurses, with the supply room chief, with the medical director, with the chief surgeon, with my boss, and with my own employees. After TM, something changed. The struggles seemed to melt away and smooth out. Then I realized that it wasn't them that changed, it was something in me!

A truly healthy individual will interact differently with his environment than an unhealthy person will. But the profound part is the realization that this executive reveals. Here we see the subtle beginnings of the self-realization, or awakening, of which meditation teachers' speak. The person's attributions get realigned. Things he mindlessly thought were coming at him from the outside, he now is forced to see as his own projections. His concepts of "self" and "other" may be turned upside down. This may even be enough to initiate the "who am I?" sequence of reflections, or a classic existential crisis. The door to personal transformation is now open but the rest is up to him. For some, repeated openings are needed.

This, then, is a quick review of the transformative power of *yoga*. We now turn our attention to its younger sibling, parapsychology.

Transformative Potentials of Parapsychology

Gallup polls (Gallup 1987) have shown an increase in percentages of people who report: mystical experiences (from 35 per cent in 1973 to 43 per cent in 1986), contact with the dead (from 27 per cent in 1973 to 42 per cent in 1986), ESP (from 58 per cent in 1973 to 67 per cent in 1986), visions (from 8 per cent in 1973 to 29 per cent in 1986) and other unusual experiences. Based on his fifteen years of survey research, Greeley (1987) concluded:

> More people than ever say they've had such experiences . . . whether you look at the most common forms of psychic and mystical experience or the rarest. . . . These experiences are common, benign and often helpful. What has been "paranormal" is not only becoming normal in our time-it may also be health-giving. —p. 49

Even such unusual experiences as UFO abductions (Ring 1992), paranormal (Braud 1995; Hastings 1983), and out-of-the-body experiences (Gabbard and Twemlow 1984) are often experienced as meaningful, positively transformative, and spiritual. Accordingly, as the number of persons who engage in spiritual practices and have spiritual experiences increases, it seems likely that the incidence of spiritual problems seen in psychotherapy will also grow (Lukoff 1998).

It would not be too far afield to say that parapsychology is the mirror reflection in the West of the Indian tradition of *yoga*. Of course, *yoga* is a comprehensive system with practical and philosophical components, based upon a vast ancient literature of accumulated wisdom on living one's life, while parapsychology is but one field of science among many. However, a bit of historical inquiry reveals that it was founded upon much bigger dreams, by a group of highly regarded scholars to explore what may be the greatest question that faces mankind using scientific methodology: the question "What happens to a human being after death?" In boldly setting their sights upon such a profound and wide-ranging question, this new field of "psychical research", which would later morph into "parapsychology", took up a question of concern to *yoga*, also thought of as a science. It was in fact the essential science of life. It is considered science because it is empirical, rooted in an ancient trial and error method, and guided by a rather coherent theory. It is built upon the cumulative wisdom of many who had gone before, and put together in the world's oldest written literature, in a language capable of conveying human experience, especially inner and transcendental experience.

Thus, the *yogin*s of India and the small group of Western scholars that gathered in the 1880s to found psychical research aka parapsychology, were on the same page. In fact, the huge head start that the Indian *yogī*s had would later assist Western parapsychologists with some of their greatest achievements.

The transformative potential of parapsychology has at least two dimensions — individual and collective. While its Eastern sibling *yoga* may chart an elaborate, comprehensive, and life-long path for individuals who seek to understand mortality, a single profound psi experience may be the proximal cause of an individual's transformation in understanding life and death. It is useful to use an analogue from nature for this — a storm cloud builds slowly over time until it encounters a sufficient concentration of condensation nuclei in the atmosphere, and then bursts into rain. Psi experience may serve as the condensation nuclei for profound individual change for those who are ready.

It is interesting to note how often psi experience involves death in some way. Louisa Rhine's collection of spontaneous psi reports (Rhine 1983) from across America included a high percentage of death related experiences, such as visions, intuitions, nighttime awakenings, unexplained physical sensations, odd environmental occurrences (clock stopping, lightning striking a special tree or spot, black bird tapping at the window) which are later discovered to correspond to someone's death or near-death, or to someone already dead. Potentially deadly accidents were a common theme for waking and sleeping precognitions. Ghost and poltergeist reports were also common. In addition, memories of a past life (Stevenson 1966), deathbed visions (Osis & Haraldson 1997), and Near Death Experiences (NDE)(Greyson 2000) may or may not include veridical psi anomalous information transfer, but they are almost always "anomalous" in being unusual or unexplainable as to when, how, and why they happened. In short, they are mysterious to the experiencer as well as to anyone (scientist or clinician) who seeks to understand them.

These psi, psi-imitative and psi-related experiences, as described above, are all potentially transformative, or "watershed" experiences. They often have lasting impact on an individual's personal philosophy, beliefs, or way of life, and on one's view and understanding of life and death issues.

NDEs are a particularly interesting variant of the psi experience for our purposes. In fact, they only sometimes include reports of the anomalous information transfer such as the experient reporting receiving information while being clinically dead on the gurney, and this being later verified. Such events are sometimes referred to as Apparently non-physical Veridical Perception (AVP). But the importance individually or collectively is askew from whether or not psi or veridical events occurred. Even when they do not, the experience is mysterious in and of itself. In fact, these NDE experiences may answer, at least for the individual experient, the BIG question around which psychical research gathered in its early years. In 2001, a Dutch group published the results of a prospective study of NDEs among heart attack victims (Van Lommels et al. 2001). Pam Kircher (2012) comments on this study as follows:

> Van Lommels's article in Lancet is a landmark that should be read by every doctor. It reports on the largest prospective study to ask people about NDEs after a cardiac arrest. The results show that NDEs are a significant phenomenon in the setting of cardiac arrest. Equally important, the study followed people for eight years after their NDE. The observations gleaned from that follow-up demonstrate that NDEs really are life transforming, and that the transformation in values is consistent over time. The study showed that NDEs create much greater changes in a person's life than does simply having a cardiac arrest or being near death.

Western parapsychologists may try to carve out the veridical psi from this experience, sometimes using the self-deprecating phrase, "nonsensory sources of knowing". A more Eastern approach may be to honour the experience as well. Rao has pointed out, for example, that in reincarnation studies, ". . . what we may look for are not memories . . . or physical appearances as in birthmarks but the unconscious spring of dispositions . . . that could not have been due to current life experiences." I would extend this to include also the transformative qualities of the discovery of "unconscious springs of disposition" from the past or present, upon the individual's present life situation. Is it possible, perhaps, that psi research in the future may be extended to include the study of profoundly transformative non-pathological experiences, as well as a new set of scientific tools with which to do it? Might this be a front upon which East and West can meet, shake hands and move ahead together as one?

The second way in which parapsychology is potentially transformative is for the community as a whole. Rao points out that in classical Indian thought, ". . . psychic phenomena like clairvoyance are not considered freak and exceptional occurrences." "Rather", he reminds us, ". . . there is a rich heritage and widespread belief in paranormal phenomena" (Rao 2010: 394).

This is not currently the case in West, and certainly not in America. While the majority of Americans may believe in a personal psi experience that they have personally been a part of, such experiences have not been integrated into the American mythos, and therefore are not discussed openly, especially not with one's doctors, counsellors, social workers, ministers, or any other "professional". Even the extensive portrayals of psychic phenomena in Hollywood films, and in the media and popular press are notoriously unsupportive. A person who has an experience that they believe may be psychic — contain "anomalous cognition" — is confronted with a number of hurdles when and if she or he attempts to share it with others. There are the faux-scientific "skeptics" groups, who are eager to deny and ridicule any report suggestive of psi as being a sort of badge of stupidity, or being cuckolded. There are the Christian churches which sometimes play the "devil" card, and there are the psychiatrists whose Diagnostic and Statistical Manual (DSM) maps such reports to various psychopathologies. Thus, there's little room for the psi experient in America to consider his/her experience in any way normal.

Yet many do. It is truly amazing that anyone at all can continue to normalize their spontaneous psi experiences privately. And this is where the science of parapsychology, the Western extension of India's *yoga* tradition, may contribute to a transformation in society at large. Parapsychology is a Western science that stands — possibly alone — at the crossroads of the development of a new group mythos in America. Parapsychologists have collected, recorded and studied thousands of these stories throughout the past century.

New mythos? What's that? Let's delve into this a little bit. Cosmologist Thomas Berry calls attention to the important role played in any society by a contextual "story" which governs the life of the society. Berry, sensitive to the rude, human disrespect shown towards our natural environment in recent years, calls for the creation of a new story. As

Mary Tucker explains, on the Berry website:

> Berry observed: "We are in between stories". He notes how the old story was functional because: "It shaped our emotional attitudes, provided us with life purpose, energized action. It consecrated suffering, integrated knowledge, guided education." This context of meaning provided by the old story is no longer operative. People are turning to new age novelties or to religious fundamentalism for orientation and direction. However, neither of these directions will ultimately be satisfying. We are confronted with dysfunctionalism in both religious communities and in secular societies. Berry proposes a new story of how things came to be, where we are now, and how the human future can be given some meaningful direction. In losing our direction we have lost our values and orientation for human action. This is what the New Story can provide.
> — Tucker 2012 (www.thomasberry.org/biography/Tucker-Bio.html)

Berry is quite aware of the key role that science plays in providing the theoretical sanction for this "story". Brian Swimme reflects Berry's viewpoint on this in his book (Swimme 1984: 10):

> The creation story unfurling within the scientific enterprise provides the fundamental context, the fundamental arena for meaning, for all the peoples of the Earth. For the first time in history, we can agree on the basic story of the galaxies, the stars, the planets, minerals, life forms, and human cultures. This story does not diminish the spiritual traditions of the classical or tribal periods of human history. Rather, the story provides the proper setting for the teaching of all traditions, showing the true magnitude of their central truths. We have a vast new empirically grounded story of the universe, one that explodes beyond any previous telling of reality, one that encompasses all peoples because it is rooted in concrete experience. Within this emerging story, each tradition will flower beyond telling in fruitful interaction with the rest, and together we can continue our journey to our fullest destiny.

Medical psychologist Lawrence LeShan (2009) agrees, and is even more adamant and articulate on this issue. He writes:

> We desperately need a new concept of what a human being is if we are to learn how to stop killing each other and poisoning our only planet. The old, materialistic worldview has not enabled us to do this.

LeShan then adds, somewhat cryptically but importantly,

> Psychic research, however, does offer the opportunity for a new picture of the world.
> — LeShan 2009: 4-5

Human beings all over the world, East and West, live our daily lives by the rules and laws of classical physics, the billiard ball world of cause and effect, action–reaction. And it works just fine. However, for over 100 years now, the most advanced levels of our mainstream science have been telling us about another world, a quite different world with quite different sets of laws and rules. This is the strange world of quantum mechanics and it is slowly creeping into the consciousness of the non-scientist through "new science" books, TV specials, sci-fi movies and documentaries, and media coverage. It is, in effect, a new context for understanding the world we live in, although quite different from our old story, which still seems to work quite well for everyday purposes. This new physics provides a theoretical context, a new story, in which apparent miracles may be allowable, integrable with driving to the office or eating lunch at a fast-food restaurant. However, this new story lacks the tangibility of the old story. There are no tangible examples of quantum leaps, observer effects, or wave-particle duality in John and Jane Doe's everyday life. The theories of the quantum reality resemble folklore more than everyday reality. It makes for nice stories for entertainment and sometimes, perhaps, a useful metaphor. But for John and Jane Doe, it's simply a fantasy world, fun to slip into when you have a free moment, perhaps.

Enter parapsychology! In this scenario, where materialist theory has outrun materialism, and quantum science has outrun the common man's everyday experience, parapsychology may serve the essential, transformative function of supplying empirical data with which to ground the new physics, the new mythos. The empirical data which parapsychology has patiently accumulated, from anecdote and laboratory may turn out to be the condensation nuclei needed to start the burst of rain. Rao (2010: 31) refers to the ". . . conundrum of cognitive anomalies, created by the available evidence, which is massive and in many ways unassailable". Could this be the straw that breaks the camels back?

Before we envision parapsychology and quantum mechanics riding off into the sunset in a lived-happily-ever-after ending, we must heed the prudent cautions of LeShan (2009: 15):

> Forty years ago, I was one of the people who started the idea that psi could be explained in terms of quantum mechanics or relativity theory. I now believe that we were wrong, and I regret my part in it. Dignity, love, loyalty, awe, and psi must be dealt with on their own terms in a science built on these observables, not one built on the observables of subatomic particles.

This is an important warning. LeShan reminds us that psi is a human experience. Psi is not a collision of subatomic particles in a cyclotron, nor will it be explained entirely by what happens at the nano level. For one thing, the quantum theorist who is observing the cyclotron is viewing psi from a third-person perspective, as if it were some distant, separate, and independent event somewhere "out there". The description arrived at in this way is partial, at best, based as it is upon the yet-to-be-debated assumption of independence. The second-person perspective, that of the data collector or experimenter, provides a different, possibly "better" view of it, albeit now with observer effect and experimenter expectancy to contend with. The first person perspective, that of the experient himself or herself, is still more different, and hindered by another set of issues.

This is the situation we currently find ourselves in. Perhaps we can agree that "finding ourselves", however we get there, or wherever we are, is never a bad thing!

In short, it is the authentic raw data of parapsychology which is its true wealth. The currency of this wealth is universal, because it is minted in real experiences, reported by real people, collected using state-of-the-art quantitative and qualitative methodologies, in life and in lab. The greatest strength of parapsychology, strangely enough, is that psi is unexplainable. It is a mystery! And so we end this section with a reminder from philosopher William James, drawn from his conclusions in his classic study of "mystical experiences" (James 1902: chap. XX):

> That unsharable feeling which each one of us has of the pinch of his individual destiny as he privately feels it rolling out on fortune's wheel may be disparaged for its egotism, may be sneered at as unscientific, but it is the one thing that fills up the measure of our concrete actuality, and any would-be existent that should lack such a feeling, or its analogue, would be a piece of reality only half made up.

It is the experience itself that may be most important about psychic phenomena, the "pinch" of feeling that is associated with it. Since science knows not how to deal with that pinch, scientists tend to move away from it when posing questions and hypotheses designed to advance our understanding. Science moves outward, to the places where the light is better, to where the pinch is not, and the concrete actuality is lost, leaving a "would-be existent" that is a "reality only half made up".

Summing It All Up

The importance of the reunion of parapsychology and *yoga* in the modern world is multifold. Both are potentially transformative. *Yoga* outlines a comprehensive programme for personal enrichment, of phenomenal and transcendental growth and actualization. Its Western sibling, parapsychology has patiently collected the data. Perhaps most importantly, parapsychology has the data and time honoured methodology to call into question the materialist assumption that still dominates Western science. Years ago, parapsychologists became aware that extraordinary claims, which many in the Western world consider reports of psychic phenomena to be, require extraordinary evidence to remain viable. Parapsychologists devoted years of patient careful research to supply just such "extraordinary" evidence to anyone who would listen. The latest chapter in the on-going skeptic-parapsychology debate can be read in a book edited by Stanley Krippner and Harris L. Friedman (2010). Ironically, the tables may be turning now due to the increased incursions of new physics, quantum effects, entanglement and string theory, whose strange results at least in the nano world make psychic phenomena appear not only possible but likely and normal in contrast. Now then, it is the materialist assumption which appears more and more to be the "extraordinary" claim for which science must demand extraordinary evidence.

Many of the issues confronted by modern science and society have been dealt with before in the East. It is not that we find the final solution in the East, but rather that we find a colleague with a different angle on the issue who can be a valuable co worker when we overcome our own biases and prejudices and look — really look — at the potential for a combined approach. This is precisely what Rao suggests.

Rao notes:

> The dualism of *yoga* consists in its assertion that *prakṛti* and *puruṣa* are the two irreducible but complementary principles of reality. They enable us to understand the relative roles of permanence and change in our being. *Puruṣa* underscores permanence and *prakṛti* the changing phases of reality.

He continues (2010: 21):

> Awareness is thus of two sorts, transcendental and phenomenal. Transcendental awareness ensues from directly accessing consciousness as-such, which in the language of Sāṁkhya-Yoga is realization of *puruṣa*-hood. Phenonminal awareness consists in accessing the information content . . . through the mediation apparatus of the embodied mind.

In summing this up, Rao notes (2010: 34):

> Indian science is not opposed to science, even though it leaves room for understanding the spiritual side of human nature. First-person methodologies have extensive application in Indian psychology. Second-person mediation provides a way of bridging the explanatory gap between first and third-person perspectives. Employing first-person and second-person methodologies and applying the mind-controlling techniques such as *yoga* to develop psychic abilities, I believe, it would be possible to advance parapsychological research to the levels that western approaches are simply unable to achieve.

I couldn't agree more. And thank you, Rao for your work in bringing together the long separated siblings of *yoga* and parapsychology. Thank you also for your long and illustrious service to mankind. And thank you for your role in bringing the mystery back!

References

Braud, W. (1995), "Parapsychology and Spirituality: Implications and Intimations", *Revision: A Journal of Consciousness and Transformation*, 18(1): 36-43.

Davies, Paul and John Gribben (1991), *The Matter Myth: Dramatic Discoveries that Challenge our Understanding of Physical Reality*, New York: Simon and Schuster.

Gabbard, G. and S. Twemlow (1984), *With the Eyes of the Mind: An Empirical Analysis of Out-of-the-Body States*, New York: Praeger.

Gallup, G. (1987), *The Gallup Poll: Public Opinion 1986*, Wilmington, DE: Scholarly Resources.

Greeley, A. (1987), "Mysticism Goes Mainstream", *American Health*, January/ February, 47-49.

Greyson, B. (2000), "Near Death Experiences", in E. Cardeña, S.J. Lynn and Stanley Krippner (eds.), *Varieties of Anomalous Experience* (pp. 315-52), Washington DC: American Psychological Association.

Harris, Lyndon F. (1998), "Divine Action: An Interview with John Polkinghorne", *Cross Currents*, Spring, 48(1).

Hastings, A. (1983), "A Counselling Approach to Parapsycholgical Experience", *Journal of Transpersonal Psychology*, 15(2): 143-67.

James, William (1902), *The Varieties of Mystical Experience: A Study in Human Nature*, London: Longmens, Green, and Co.

Kelly, E.F. et al. (2006), *Irreducible Mind: Toward a Psychology for the 21st Century*, Lanham, MD: Rowman and Littlefield.

Kircher, Pam (2012), Commentary. Copied from http://www.mikepettigrew.com/afterlife/html/dutch_study.html, (accessed on 26 August 2012).

Krippner, Stanley and Harris L. Friedman (eds.) (2010), Debating Psychic Experience: Human Potential or Human Illusion? Santa Barbara, CA: Praeger.

Lazar, Sarah (2012), "Study Shows Meditation Changes Brain Structure in just 8 Weeks". Article found on http://www.sikhnet.com/news/study-shows-meditation-changes-brain-structure-just-8-weeks (accessed on 15 August 2012).

LeShan, Lawrence (2009), *A New Science of the Paranormal: The Promise of Psychical Research,* Wheaton, IL: Quest Books: Theosophical Publishing House.

Lukoff, David (1998), "From Spiritual Emergency to Spiritual Problem: The Transpersonal Roots of the New DSM-IV Category", *Journal of Humanistic Psychology*, 38(2): 21-50.

Osis, Karlis and Erlandur Haraldson (1997), *At the Hour of Death: A New Look at Evidence for Life After Death,* Norwalk, CT: Hastings House.

Rao, K.R. (ed.) (2010), *Yoga and Parapsychology: Empirical Research and Theoretical Perspectives,* Delhi: Motilal Banarsidass.

Rao, K.R. (2008), "Preface" in K.R. Rao, A.C. Paranjpe, and A.K. Dalal (eds.), *Handbook of Indian Psychology*, pp. xvii-xix, New Delhi: Cambridge University Press.

Rao, K.R. (ed.) (2002), *Consciousness Studies: Cross-cultural Perspectives,* Jefferson, NC: McFarland.

Rao, K.R. and S.B. Marwaha (eds.) (2005), *Towards a Spiritual Psychology,* New Delhi: Samvad India Foundation.

Rhine, L.E. (1983), *Something Hidden*, Jefferson, NC: McFarland.

Ring, K. (1992), *The Omega Project: Near-death, UFO Encounters, and Mind at Large,* New York: Willaim Morris.

Scharf, David (2010), "Near Enough: An Implicit Argument for a non-Cartesian Interactionism (Part II)", *NeuroQuantology,* December, 8(4): 614-25.

——— (2012), "Mistaken, Misinformed, Misleading", essay found on www.skepticsonTM.blogspot.com (accessed on 15 August 2012).

Schwartz, Gary E. (2011), "Consciousness, Spirituality, and Postmaterialist Science: An Empirical and Experiential Approach", in Lisa Miller (ed.), *Oxford Handbook of Psychology and Spirituality*, Oxford: Oxford University Press.

Shaynebance (2012), "What Is *Yoga*?" essay on http://www.abc-of-*yoga*.com/beginnersguide/whatis*yoga*.asp (accessed on 15 August 2012).

Solfvin, Jerry (2011), "Book Review", *Yoga and Parapsychology: Empirical Research and Theoretical Essays*, ed. K.R. Rao, *Journal of Parapsychology,* Spring, *75*(1): 148-57.

Stevenson, Ian (1966), *Twenty Cases Suggestive of Reincarnation,* Charlottesville, VA: University of Virginia Press.

Swimme, Brian (1984), *The Universe Is A Green Dragon: A Cosmic Creation Story,* Rochester, VT: Bear and Co. (Quoted on http://www.context.org/iclib/ic12/swimme/, accessed on 15 August 2012.)

Tart, Charles T. (2009), *The End of Materialism: How Evidence of the Paranormal Is Bringing Science and Spirit Together,* Oakland, CA: New Harbinger.

Tucker, Mary (2012), "Commentary", found on www.thomasberry.org/biography/Tucker-Bio.html (accessed on 15 August 2012).

Van Lommels W., Van Wees R., Meyers V. and Elfferich I. (2001), "Near-death Experience in Survivors of Cardiac Arrest: A Prospective Study in the Netherlands", *The Lancet*, 358: 2039-45.

Walker, Meredith (2008), "Surprising Health Benefits of *Yoga*", on http://www.nursingdegree.net/blog/24/77-surprising-health-benefits-of-*yoga*/ (accessed on 15 August 2012).

Wallace, B. Alan (2008a), *Hidden Dimensions: The Unification of Physics and Consciousness*, New York: Columbia University Press.

——— (2008b), *Embracing Mind: The Common Ground of Science and Spirituality*, Boston, MA: Shambhala.

——— (2000), *The Taboo of Subjectivity: Toward a New Science of Consciousness*, New York: Oxford University Press.

5

How to Arrive at an Eastern Place from a Western Direction

Convergences and Divergences Among Sāṁkhya Dualism, Advaita Non-dualism, the Body–Mind–Consciousness (Trident) Model and Reflexive Monism

Max Velmans[*]

Over the millennia, there have been irresolvable tensions between monist and dualist thought in both Eastern and Western analyses of the relations among body, mind and consciousness. This paper compares two approaches to resolving such tensions, Reflexive Monism (RM), a model of the self-observing universe that resolves many of the oppositions in Western thought, and K. Ramakrishna Rao's Eastern, Body–Mind–Consciousness (BMC) or "Trident" model, which focuses on the convergences between dualist Sāṁkhya-Yoga and monist Advaita Vedānta. According to RM many opposing analyses of body–mind–consciousness relationships in Western thought can be treated as different (often complementary) views of the one global system by parts of itself, from within itself. According to the BMC or Trident model, many of the tensions between dualist Sāṁkhya and monist Advaita can be resolved by noting the similarity in their analyses of the human condition and the developmental processes required to provide a release from the limitations of that condition. In spite of the very different (Western and Eastern) traditions that inform them, there are many convergences between RM and BMC although there are also some major differences, for example, in their grounding ontology and their respective analyses of body–mind–consciousness causal relationships. In this paper I

---

[*] I would like to thank K. Ramakrishna Rao and Anand Paranjpe for checking manuscript to make sure that I have represented Eastern views accurately, and for their supportive comments. Any remaining errors of interpretation are of course my own.

examine both the convergences and divergences in detail.

Introduction

In his *magnum opus, Cognitive Anomalies, Consciousness and Yoga* (2011), K. Ramakrishna Rao reviews both Eastern and Western approaches to understanding consciousness. In this, he develops a model of body–mind–consciousness relationships (a "BMC" or "Trident" model) that tries to find the points of convergence between Eastern dualism of the kind found in Sāṁkhya-Yoga philosophy and classical Eastern monism of the kind found in Advaita Vedānta. He also presents a very interesting point-by-point comparison of his BMC or Trident model with Reflexive Monism (RM), a psychological/philosophical analysis of the same relationships, viewed from a Western perspective that I have developed over many years. Intriguingly, in spite of their being lodged in very different traditions, Rao finds many points of convergence between his own synthesis of Eastern philosophy/psychology and RM — along with a few divergences. Given their very different points of departure, any genuine convergence between Eastern and Western understanding of body, mind and consciousness offers the promise of a more global synthesis of Eastern and Western thought. In the hope of furthering this project, I give my own analysis of some of these convergences and divergences below.

A Few Important Terminological Distinctions

Before entering into the details of the models, it is important to note that in Eastern *versus* Western writings the terms "mind" and "consciousness" have a range of different meanings that divide up the space of BMC relationships in somewhat different ways. This complicates any direct comparison of Eastern and Western writings, including comparisons of BMC with RM. It is also the case that these terms have been used in varying ways within the respective traditions.

For example, in classical Western dualism (following Descartes) physical stuff is thought of as *res extensa* (stuff that has extension in space) that is clearly distinguished from mental stuff, which Descartes termed *res cogitans* (stuff that thinks). However, Descartes made no clear distinction between the substance of mind, consciousness and soul. In subsequent Western thought, this fundamental splitting of the universe into two incommensurate substances forms the philosophical background for the classical "mind/body" problems — how, for example, could substances as different as "extended substance" and "thinking substance" causally interact?

In Sāṁkhya-Yoga philosophy there is a somewhat similar bifurcation of the universe into *puruṣa* (consciousness) and *prakṛti* (physical matter/energy). However "mind" is thought to be a subtle form of physical matter/energy that is distinct from consciousness. Given that the mind is thought to be physical, Sāṁkhya doesn't have a "mind/body problem" in the Western sense. But, arguably, it does have a "consciousness/body problem": Given the fundamental bifurcation of the universe into *puruṣa* and *prakṛti* how could entities/energies as different as these causally interact?

Western theories of mind and consciousness have also evolved considerably over the last century — to the extent that the commonly understood meanings of the terms "mind" and "consciousness" have themselves evolved since the time of Descartes. For example, *contra* Descartes, current Western writings make clear distinctions among "mind", "consciousness" and "soul". With the emergence of cognitive psychology in the late 1950s and related developments in artificial intelligence, mental processes have increasingly been viewed as forms of *information processing* and the "mind" as the system that embodies that processing (typically a brain, or perhaps a computer). Following on developments in psychodynamics and cognitive investigation of mental processes it also became clear that many mental processes are unconscious or preconscious. Given that operations of mind may or may not be accompanied by conscious experiences, consciousness is commonly thought of as a *state or property* of mind (which may or may not be manifested under given conditions) — while "soul" continues to have its more classical meaning, i.e. some essence of human identity that survives bodily death. Teased apart in this way, mind and consciousness have become major topics of scientific research, while soul has been largely left to theologians.

It should be evident that if one uses modern Western usages of the relevant terms, East–West comparisons come out in a different way. The Eastern view that the mind is a subtle form of physical matter/energy is, for example, consonant with the Western view that it can be thought of as a form of information processing that is embodied in a physical system. And, just as Sāṁkhya can be said to have a "consciousness/body" problem, modern consciousness studies recognize that consciousness remains a "hard problem" for Western materialist views of the mind: how could the rich qualities of lived experience arise from or interact with the neurochemistry of the brain?

That said, a very sharp difference remains in Eastern and modern Western views about the nature of consciousness and about the way that mind relates to consciousness. Western views of consciousness have been largely shaped by how this manifests in everyday human experience. For example, following on the writings of Brentano (1874), Western philosophers largely agree that a fundamental property of consciousness is that it is always about something,[1] which distinguishes it from physical matter, which isn't about anything. Everyday conscious experiences also have phenomenal content with particular qualities or "qualia". Consequently, in order to disambiguate the many different natural language usages of the term "consciousness", in current Western scientific and philosophical writings is often expanded to (or assumed to mean) "phenomenal consciousness".

Given the evidence that mental processes appear to be embodied in the brain, that many of these processes operate without consciousness, and that certain combinations of mental processes appear to provide the necessary and sufficient conditions for consciousness, it is not surprising that much (but by no means all) of twentieth-century Western philosophy of mind has tried to demonstrate that consciousness too is nothing more than a particular state of the brain (reductive physicalism) or a particular form of information processing (reductive functionalism). As the appearance of consciousness in humans appears to be dependent on mind/brain processing the mind and/or brain are also commonly thought of in the West as ontologically more fundamental than consciousness.[2]

While Eastern philosophical/psychological writings entirely accept the existence of phenomenal conscious experiences that have been shaped by the workings of the mind and sensory systems, they do not take the view that these exhaust or even reveal the true essence of consciousness. For example, in both Sāṁkhya and Advaita Vedānta these mentally conditioned phenomenal contents are said to obscure the actual source from which they arise — a form of pure, contentless consciousness that Rao (2012) describes as a "pure subjectivity", also commonly described as *sat–cit–ānanda* (being–consciousness–bliss). According to Sāṁkhya this is the true nature of *puruṣa* (which remains eternally distinct from *prakṛti*). According to Advaita Vedānta, such a pure consciousness is the nature of *Brahman* — the ultimate basis of everything, including the manifest material world. While in embodied human beings this state of pure consciousness

[1] The formal term used in philosophy of mind is that consciousness is "intentional".

[2] It is often assumed for example that consciousness is somehow "supervenient" on physical processes in the brain.

both illuminates and is conditioned by the material mind/brain; according to Eastern thought it does not arise from the mind/brain, and cannot therefore be thought of as a property or state of it. Rather than being ontologically dependent on mind it is either viewed as distinct from mind (in Sāṁkhya) or as giving rise to mind, along with the rest of the material world (in Advaita Vedānta).

The above brief sketch of Eastern and Western mappings of the body–mind–consciousness terrain is deliberately oversimplified but, hopefully, provides a sense of the conceptual convergences as well as divergences that currently separate much of mainstream Western from classical Eastern thought that provides the context for both Rao's work and my own. As should be evident there is a tension between dualist and monist thought within both traditions although the way that their monist traditions resolve dualism is very different. While Western monism over the last century has largely tried to reduce classical dualism to a form of materialism, classical Indian monism favours idealism. Rao's BMC model searches for the commonalities in Sāṁkhya and Advaita Vedānta. RM searches for a unified way of thinking about body–mind–consciousness relationships that avoids the classical mind/body problems associated with Western dualism, while avoiding the implausibilities of reductive physicalism and functionalism. Although it did not deliberately set out to do so, RM moves in an Eastern direction — and, according to Rao (2011, 2012), might therefore help in the construction of a unifying East–West bridge. So it is to this that we now turn our attention.

Where Reflexive Monism is Placed within the Western Tradition

At the turn of the twentieth century Bertrand Russell noted in his seminal *The Problems of Philosophy*, "We commonly mean by 'matter' something which is opposed to 'mind', something which we think of as occupying space and as radically incapable of any sort of thought or consciousness" (1912: 19). If "mind" is viewed in this classical, dualist Western way there are three basic ways in which the apparent differences between physical stuff and mental/conscious stuff can be understood in monist terms:

1. Mind and/or phenomenal consciousness might turn out to be nothing more than a particular aspect or arrangement of physical matter (physicalism; functionalism).
2. Physical matter might turn out to be nothing more than a particular aspect or arrangement of mind and/or consciousness (idealism).
3. Mind/consciousness and physical matter might be aspects or

arrangements of something more fundamental that is in itself neither mental nor physical as normally understood (neutral monism; dual-aspect theory, panpsychism, panexperientialism, reflexive monism).

As noted above, Western philosophy and science over the last century have largely favoured Option 1 and (in contrast to the Indian tradition) there has been little support for Option 2. RM largely explores Option 3 — along with a number of related philosophical views in which there has been increasing interest over the last decade.[3] In its fully developed form, RM provides a global analysis of body–mind–consciousness relationships that arguably synthesizes many of the apparent oppositions and conflicting "isms" (dualism, physicalism, functionalism, realism, idealism, etc.) that currently populate consciousness studies (see the analysis in Velmans 2012a). However, unlike Sāṁkhya and Vedānta which have their roots in classical Indian thought, developed over the millennia, its point of departure is a simple observation about how consciousness, brain and the physical world relate to each other in everyday perception.

The Reflexive Model of Perception

Fig. 1 provides an initial map of how consciousness, brain and the physical world relate to each other in normal visual perception. It shows a typical psychology experiment in which an experimenter E observes a subject S attending to a light stimulus, and the aim of the experiment is to understand the causal processes responsible for S's conscious experience of the light. In this initial form, the figure only shows how the causal sequence might appear to E and how the physical light appears to S. Viewed in these terms the figure is both consistent with science and with common sense. Given suitable measuring instruments, E might be able to observe the physical light bulb, emitted light energy, neural representations of the information in the light within the subject's brain, and any subsequent brain events that cause and/or correlate with S's experience. However, E has no direct access to S's visual experience (the problem of "other minds"). If he wants to find out what she experiences, he has to ask her to describe it. Note that a description of her experience has to do with its phenomenology, not its ontology and if S has normal vision, she should report that she sees a light bulb out in the world — as *fig.* 1 shows. This is hardly surprising as the observational arrangements that enable S to see the light are similar to those that enable E to see the light.

[3] See for example Skrbina (2005) and readings in Velmans and Nagasawa (2012).

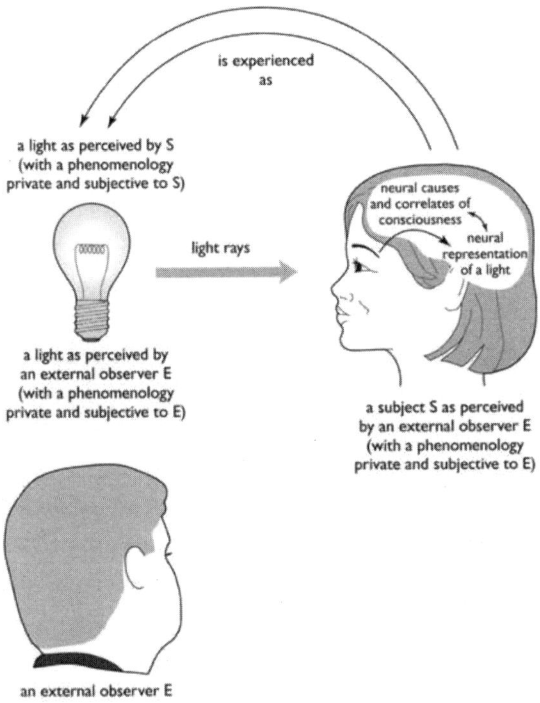

fig. 1: A schematic diagram of how consciousness, brain and the physical world appear to relate to each other in normal visual perception. It shows a typical psychology experiment in which an experimenter E observes a subject S attending to a light stimulus, and the aim of the experiment is to understand the causal processes responsible for S's conscious experience of the light. In this initial form the figure only shows how the causal sequence might appear to E and how the physical light appears to S

Consequently when she looks at the light S sees more or less what E sees.

Although this simple diagram follows the contours of ordinary experience, this map of what is going on differs from more conventional Western maps in one crucial respect: both substance dualists and their materialist reductionist opponents clearly separate physical objects as perceived (out in the world) from experiences of those objects which are either "nowhere" (according to dualists) or "in the brain" (according to materialist reductionists). By contrast, the reflexive model in *fig.* 1 places the experience where it seems to be out in the world beyond S's body surface.

I should stress again that *fig.* 1 only deals with appearances — and how things appear should not be confused with how they are in themselves. Strictly speaking it is the light bulb itself that is the source of light energy in this situation, not the light as perceived by E (which is only an appearance), and quantum mechanics would describe the energetic processes in the light in ways that are very different to how they appear in unaided perception. Otherwise, however, the map remains the same: physical processes initiated within a light bulb out in the world, once they are processed by the subject's visual system, are perceived as a light out in the world located more or less where the initiating processes are. That is what makes the entire process reflexive (the entire sequence loops back on itself). Similar reflexive loops typically apply to events initiated within the body, at the body surface or within the brain itself. For example, if one pricks one's finger with a pin, signals associated with skin damage activate complex pain circuitry located in the brain that results in a sharp pain that appears to be located back in the finger where the pin went in. Thoughts, by contrast, seem to be very poorly located, or, at best, to be located "in the head or brain". Yet this follows the same pattern: the cognitive processes that initiate thought are distributed around the brain, so the resultant experiences appear to be located more or less where the initiating causes are, and once again the entire process is reflexive.

In sum, within the reflexive model of perception the contents of consciousness can appear to be out in the world, in the body or on its surface, or "in the head or brain". Taken together, these form a phenomenal world, along with its constituent phenomena which appear to be located and distributed in different ways within phenomenal space. Such observed phenomena may be thought of as biologically evolved mental models of their initiating causes that are sufficiently useful to serve the purposes of everyday life, although for other deeper purposes the sciences might describe those initiating causes in very different ways.[4]

It should be obvious that this way of viewing the phenomenology of conscious experiences poses an immediate challenge to substance dualism. According to Descartes, conscious experiences are entirely exemplified by thoughts, which led him to the view that they consist of *res cogitans* (substance that thinks) in contrast to the physical world which consists of *res extensa* (substance that has extension in space) — a distinction also

[4] The view that observed phenomena generally provide useful albeit incomplete, approximate representations of their autonomously existing causes (things themselves) is a widely adopted view in Western science known as "indirect realism" or "critical realism".

implicitly adopted by Russell (see quote above). While this might arguably apply to experienced thoughts, which seem to be poorly located and extended, it does not seem to apply to most experienced phenomena, which appear to have location and extension in phenomenal space. This self-evident aspect of conscious phenomenology also places a much greater burden on materialist reductionism. If the entire phenomenal world is part of conscious experience, it is not just the ephemeral "qualia" of thoughts which seem to exist "nowhere" that need to be naturalized. Rather, for reductionism to succeed, entire phenomenally extended worlds with their constituent phenomena need to be reduced to states or functions of the brain. This turns out to have various absurd consequences that we do not need to consider here (but see Velmans 2008a, 2009 (chap. 7), 2012a).[5] To arrive at a point of convergence with Eastern thought we need only draw on the reflexive aspect of perception.

How Conscious Appearances Relate to the Unconscious Ground of Being

But first we must complete our rough map of body–mind–consciousness relationships. The relationships charted in *fig.* 1 and the discussion above deal largely with the world of appearances, and give only the briefest of indications of the complex entities, events and processes that give rise to those appearances — which reflect how things seem to be in everyday life. Our inner feelings and thoughts, experienced bodies, and surrounding phenomenal world simply appear in our experience with little if any indication of the wider energies and events from which they sample, or of the complex, preconscious and unconscious processes that support them.

Yet science makes it clear that such energies, events and processes exist. For example, data from physics, sensory physiology, perception and psychophysics makes it clear that the perceived world "models" only a selection of the events and energies described by physics. There are electromagnetic energies of many kinds that permeate space and even penetrate our bodies, to which our eyes (and other sense organs) are blind. There are acoustic signals produced and perceived by animals and insects to which our ears are deaf. Compared to many animals, our chemical senses (smell and taste) are poorly developed and convey little

---

[5] These sources also give a detailed discussion of how the experienced, extended nature of the phenomenal world relates to spatial extension as described by physics. A critique of physicalism and functionalism that ranges more widely is given in Velmans (2009: chaps. 3-5).

of the chemistry of the substances that we inhale and ingest. Sensory systems are also limited in their spatial and temporal resolution to detect events of a size, distance and duration that is relevant to normal human action and survival (to make observations beyond these limits we need telescopes, microscopes, atomic clocks and so on). The perceptual processes that translate the information detected by our sense organs into the perceived "qualia" that we experience, furthermore, do so in a very specialized, species-specific way. Even three-dimensional phenomenal space existing through time turns out to be an approximation of the universe that modern physics describes. General Relativity Theory, for example, requires a four-dimensional space–time in which the shortest distance between two points is an arc (that follows the curvature of space) not a straight line. There are many other ways in which the physical world we experience differs from the world that physics describes, but as these points are entirely conventional I will not labour them. The three-dimensional phenomenal world that we think of as the "physical world" is actually a world peculiar to humans, and only a partial, approximate, species-specific model of the greater universe described by physics.[6]

In assessing the limits of conscious contents it is also important to note that we normally perceive entities and events of an intermediate scale. The human phenomenal world is predominantly visual, and, unaided, our visual systems normally provide information only about exterior surfaces. Beyond what we can normally see, there is immensely detailed structure within the nature of the things as well as a structure that extends beyond our perceptual horizons. The external visual appearance of the human body, for example, yields little information about its macrocosmic internal structure and functioning. Interoception provides some added details about the body's internal condition (the position of limbs, temperature, internal damage, and the need for sustenance, sleep and so on) but reveals little of how the body actually works, let alone any details of its microscopic organization at cellular, molecular, atomic and subatomic levels. Similar limitations apply to our ability to experience the detailed operation of our own minds. A few details of mental processing are normally available to introspection, such as the progressive stages in problem solving, long-term planning and so on. However, the bulk of so-called "conscious mental processing" is not conscious at all! Experimental

[6] For a far more detailed account of how the human world as experienced relates to those of other animals and to the world described by physics, see Velmans (2009: chap. 8).

psychology has made it clear that even processes that we normally think of as "conscious" for the reason that they result in conscious experiences rely on unconscious or preconscious processing that gives rise to those experiences. For example, one has little or no conscious awareness of the detailed processing which enables one to "consciously read" this sentence. This also self-evidently applies to the way that the external phenomenal world normally appears in visual experience without any indication of prior analysis or synthesis by sensory, perceptual and cognitive processing.

There is far more to be said about the relation of conscious phenomenology to the unconscious and preconscious energies, events and processes that support it, but again I do not have space to give details here.[7] For the purposes of this essay it is enough to indicate that the map of relationships among consciousness, mind, brain and the physical world shown in *fig.* 1 is incomplete. At the very least, it requires an added unconscious dimension that supports the phenomena that appear in conscious experience and the causal relations amongst them.

Metaphorically, the contents of consciousness have often been likened to the tip of an iceberg. The bulk of the mind, like the iceberg, remains unseen below the water. The present analysis extends this metaphor. Once one expands consciousness to include the experienced body and surrounding phenomenal world (in the way shown in *fig.* 1), what is "above the waterline" is not just the tip of an iceberg but everything that one can experience extending to one's perceptual horizons. What is "below the waterline" expands correspondingly to include the entire universe of entities, events and processes that, at a given moment, supports and embeds what we experience, but has little or no representation in what we experience. Because our consciously experienced worlds emerge from this unconscious ground one can think of it as the unconscious ground of being.[8]

---

[7] I have provided extensive analyses in Velmans (1991a, b, 2009: chaps. 8, 10 and 12-14).

[8] The fact that complex interactions of entities, events and processes that support our consciously experienced worlds are normally unconscious to us leaves open the possibility that at least some aspects of this ground (or even at some fundamental level all of this ground) may be autonomously conscious (in some non-anthropomorphic sense) as suggested for example by pan-experientialism (see Skrbina 2005; Seager 2012; Weekes 2012). It also leaves open the possibility that, by appropriate introspective and meditative methods the range of human consciousness can extend more deeply into its own unconscious ground to arrive at what in Eastern philosophy is described as a state of "pure consciousness" (see Paranjpe 2010; Rao 2012).

Reflexive Monism

In this reflexive monist way of looking at things, human phenomenal consciousness is embedded in and supported by the greater universe (just as the tip of an iceberg is supported by the base and the surrounding sea). The contents of human consciousness are also a natural expression or manifestation of the embedding universe. In humans, the proximal causes of consciousness are to be found in the human brain, but it is a mistake to think of the brain as an isolated system. Its existence as a material system depends totally on its supporting surround, and the contents of consciousness that it in turn supports, arise from a reflexive interaction of perceptual processing with entities, events and processes in the surrounding world, body, and the mind/brain itself.

Individual conscious representations are perspectival. That is, the precise manner in which entities, events and processes are translated into experiences depends on the location in space and time of a given observer, and the exact mix of perceptual, cognitive, affective, social, cultural and historical influences which enter into the "construction" of a given experience. In this sense, each conscious construction is private, subjective, and unique. Taken together, the contents of consciousness provide a view of the wider universe, giving it the appearance of a 3D phenomenal world that represents aspects of the embedding universe in ways appropriate to normal human life. However, such conscious representations are not the *thing-itself.*

The reflexive model of perception outlined above also exemplifies a general process. According to RM, there is one universe (the thing-itself), with relatively differentiated parts in the form of conscious beings like ourselves, each with a unique, conscious view of the larger universe of which it is a part. In so far as we are parts of the universe that, in turn, experience the larger universe, we participate in a reflexive process whereby the universe experiences itself.

RM also suggests that once entities, events and processes are consciously experienced they become "real-ized"[9], i.e. once one experiences entities, events and processes for oneself they become subjectively real. This provides a form of knowledge that mere descriptions or theories

[9] In Velmans (2009: chaps. 10, 13 and 14), I arrive at this view of the role of phenomenal consciousness only after an extensive analysis of the many alternative roles that have been proposed for consciousness in human information processing. The term "real-ization" is deliberately hyphenated to stress the point that it is through becoming consciously aware of something that it becomes subjectively real.

cannot convey.[10] Experiencing something other than oneself makes it subjectively real and allows one to know "what it is like". Similarly, experiencing otherwise latent aspects of one's own nature makes those aspects subjectively real — although to achieve such real-izations one has to become that which one seeks to know — a potentially transformative process. For example, one cannot know what it is like to be in love, without entering into a state where one can experience it for oneself. Again, according to RM, what happens in human experience is just one manifestation of a more general process. When humans deepen their experience of their own, inner nature they can be said to become more fully real-ized, but RM suggests that Nature may have as many distinct ways of real-izing its own nature as there are distinct sentient beings, whether human or non-human.[11]

It is not possible to present a full justification for these global features of reflexive monism in anything less than a book, but, hopefully, an appeal to natural intuition will suffice for the limited purposes of this essay. As I note in the concluding paragraph of Velmans (2009: 351):

> Whatever the full truth of this may be, who can doubt that our bodies *and* our experience are an integral part of the universe? And who can doubt that each one of us has a unique, conscious perspective of the larger universe of which we are a part? In this sense, we participate in a process whereby the universe observes itself — and the universe becomes both the subject and object of experience. Consciousness and matter are intertwined in mind. Through the evolution of matter, consciousness is given *form*. And through consciousness, the material universe is real-ized.

In spite of its origins in the Western tradition, those familiar with Eastern philosophy will recognize that these features of RM given it a distinctively Indian flavour. According to Rao (2011: 766):

> These concluding lines from Velmans' book state more elegantly than we have the purport of what we have described as the role of consciousness in the Trident model. Such a notion of consciousness as it comes from a cognitive psychologist, a scientist deeply steeped in the western tradition . . . is indeed provocatively non-Western.

Rao then goes on to make more detailed comparisons between RM and

---

[10] Bertrand Russell makes a similar distinction between "knowledge by acquaintance" which he contrasts with knowledge conveyed or represented by language which he terms "knowledge by description".

[11] A range of options are for example discussed in Velmans (2009: chap. 8).

his own synthesis of Eastern philosophy and psychology, which he summarizes in the way shown in Table 1.

Table 1: Comparison of Trident and Reflexive Models
(taken from Rao 2011: 767, Table 4)

Trident Model	*Reflexive Monism*
1. *Prakṛti* (matter) and *puruṣa* (consciousness) are two basic principles underlying the universe.	Consciousness and material forms are equally basic aspects of the universe.
2. Consciousness is fundamentally different from matter and is essentially irreducible to material forms.	Consciousness may have neurological correlates and certain processes in the brain may accompany it, but consciousness and bodily states or their functions are not ontologically identical. Phenomenal awareness is brain irreducibly distinct from states and functions.
3. Each *puruṣa* is distinct and has unique experiences in its association with the mind–body complex.	Each of us has "a unique perspective on the larger universe".
4. The *puruṣa* illuminates the material forms of the universe through the instrumentality of the mind.	We are part of a process by which the universe observes itself, creating the subject–object distinction.
5. Consciousness (*puruṣa*) and mind (*citta*) are different. Mind is not the same as brain.	"Consciousness", "mind" and "brain" are distinguishable concepts, but mind includes phenomenal consciousness and certain states of the brain.
6. Mind is the interface between consciousness and the brain. The distinctions such as subject and object arise because of the mind's ability to reflect consciousness and its predispositions to take the reflections as its own.	Consciousness and matter are intertwined in the mind. Subject and object distinctions arise in the mind's exteroceptive and interoceptive interactions and involvement.

Table 1 (Cont.)

Trident Model	*Reflexive Monism*
7. Consciousness as-such has no form. In the human condition, it illuminates the form of material objects in the mind.	Matter gives consciousness its form.
8. By accessing consciousness as-such the mind realizes the universe.	". . . through consciousness the material universe is real-ized."
9. Consciousness as-such is undifferentiated subjectivity. Subjectivity in experience arises from the mind's association with consciousness.	Consciousness renders perceived objects, events and processes subjectively real. "That, and that alone, is its function."
10. Consciousness as-such has no content.	Phenomenal consciousness has content.
11. Intentionality is a characteristic of the mind and not of consciousness.	Intentionality is a characteristic of mind and of phenomenal consciousness, but it is not a defining characteristic of consciousness as it also applies to unconscious mind.
12. There are two ways of knowing: (1) direct knowing without sensory involvement and (2) meditation knowing with sensory meditation.	There are two fundamental ways of knowing: (1) knowing directly (by acquaintance) and (2) knowing indirectly (by description).

Tabulated in this way, some of these convergences are striking. However, as Rao (2011) notes, close examination of the respective systems reveals that there are also important differences. For example, given its development within the context of current Western thought, RM deals largely with the evidence of everyday phenomenal conscious experiences (and the problems that they pose) along with well-accepted scientific findings. While it does not deny the existence of paranormal phenomena, it does not specifically address them. And, although RM entirely accepts the possibility of advanced yogic experiences of consciousness "as-such" as a route to real-ization of otherwise "unreal-ized" aspects of the nature of the Self[12] it does not go as far as, say, Advaita, in giving this experience

[12] In principle, various paranormal phenomena (e.g. those that occasionally →

of consciousness as-such an independent, primary *ontological* status.

Why not? Recall that there are three basic ways in which Western thought has tried to resolve mind/body or consciousness/brain dualism into a form of monism (see Options 1, 2 and 3 above). Current Western monism largely follows Option 1 (physicalism) — the view that both material forms and our experience of them are ontologically physical. Eastern monism in the tradition of Advaita Vedānta adopts a form of Option 2 (idealism) — the view that the ultimate stuff of the universe is "consciousness as-such" — also characterised as "pure consciousness" and, by Rao (2011), as "pure subjectivity". Material forms are thought to be a concretisation of that consciousness.

It is well recognized in the West that physicalism (along with related positions such as functionalism) faces a "hard problem": it has no adequate account (and many would say, no account at all) of how the varied "qualia" of experience could arise from the brain's physical activity let alone how such "qualia" could be nothing more than such physical activity. However, it is less well recognized that Eastern idealism faces the inverse problem: how could the autonomously existing material of the macrophysical world arise from something characterized as "pure consciousness" or "pure subjectivity"? Rao searches for ways of resolving the ontological differences between dualist Sāṁkhya and monist Advaita Vedānta philosophy, and stresses the point that their soteriological aim is the same — "to release humans from their conditioned state of being into a state of unbound freedom or liberation". However he accepts that the ontological divide between dualist Sāṁkhya and monist Advaita is difficult to bridge. As he notes:

In *yoga*, *puruṣa* and *prakṛti* are two fundamental, irreducible and

---

→ appear to demonstrate distant events as meaningfully connected) might be understood as normally unreal-ized connections within the unconscious ground of being that, under special conditions, have observable manifestations. Yogic *siddhis* too can be understood as procedures by which some of these normally unconscious, autonomously functioning connections are brought under voluntary control — in analogous fashion to the way that becoming conscious of otherwise unconscious processes within the human body (e.g. by the use of biofeedback techniques) can be a precursor to bringing some of these processes under voluntary control. However given the vexed status of the evidence for such phenomena within current Western scientific debates, I have restricted the current evidence base for RM entirely to everyday conscious experiences and well-accepted scientific findings.

> substantive entities of reality. *Prakṛti* is undifferentiated materiality and *puruṣa* is undifferentiated subjectivity. — Rao 2012: 125

By contrast,

> In Advaita, what is *real* is that which is unchanging and eternal. There is only one such unchanging and eternal, the ground of all that is. It is *Brahman*. What is *unreal* is that which is "absolutely nothing". In other words, the unreal is that which is non-existent like hare's horn or the barren woman's son. The world of things around us that are ever changing are not real like the *Brahman*, the unchanging and permanent ground of all being. Nor are they unreal like hare's horn. They have intermediary or conditional existence. The external physical world surrounding us exists, but it is not true existence. It is an illusory manifestation, a mere appearance of *Brahman*. *Māyā* is the mother of all illusions. — Rao 2012: 123

In short:

> Advaita and *yoga* uphold two deeply divergent ontologies; and yet their psychological thought is quite similar. *Yoga* is an explicitly dualist system whereas Advaita (literally meaning non-dual), true to its name, is an uncompromisingly non-dualist philosophy. That we can have a psychological model equally applicable to dualist and non-dualist systems suggests to me that we possibly could have at a psychological level discussions that would be expected to reasonably bypass ontological distinctions and rise above rank physical reductionism on the one hand and radical entity dualism on the other, the discussion of which can be safely left to philosophers to ponder over and wrestle with.
> — Rao 2012: 122

In its stress on "real-ization" as fundamental to what consciousness adds to existence, RM converges in an intimate way with these ancient Eastern, practical concerns. However, an added, central feature of RM is the way it resolves dualism into a form of monism. Rather than adopting ontological Option 1 or 2 it develops a variant of Option 3 — a form of dual-aspect monism in the tradition of Spinoza. While it is not possible to give a detailed rationale for this in the limited space available[13] a simple re-examination of the situation in *fig.* 1 should suffice to convey the general principles involved.

The earlier discussion of *fig.* 1 focused on how the external world, perceptual processing in the mind/brain of a subject, and consequent phenomenal experience relate to each other when a subject (S) focuses on

[13] But see Velmans (2008a, 2009, 2012a).

an external object (in this case, a cat) and we concluded that, viewed in terms of its phenomenology, perception is reflexive. We now turn our attention to what is going on in S's *mind*.

Third-Person and First-Person Views of the Nature of Mind

Let us suppose that, while S experiences a light bulb out in the world, E has access to the neural causes and correlates of S's experience. Suppose too that for each distinct experience a distinct set of neural causes and correlates could be found, and that in the case of the light bulb there is a perfect correlation between S's experience and the brain events that E can observe. Would that establish S's experience to be nothing more than (ontologically identical to) the brain events observed by E? No — for the simple reason that causation, correlation and ontological identity are very different relationships (see Velmans 1998, 2008a, 2009). In any case, in this situation, both S and E experience something out in the world that they would describe as "physical". S has a visual experience of a light bulb, located beyond her body, in the world. E has a visual experience of the physical correlates of S's experience, located beyond E's body, in S's brain.

What S and E can see in this situation nevertheless relate to each other in a very precise way. S experiences a phenomenal light bulb — a visual representation containing information about the shape, size, location, colour and texture of an entity that currently exists out in the world beyond her body surface. E sees the same information (about the light bulb) encoded in the physical correlates of what S experiences, in her brain. That is, the information structure of what S and E observe is identical, but it is displayed or "formatted" in very different ways. From S's point of view, the only information she has (about the entity in the world) is the phenomenal light bulb she experiences. From E's point of view, the only information S has (about the entity in the world) is the information E can see encoded in her brain. The way information (about the entity in the world) is displayed appears to be very different to S and E for the reason that the "observational arrangements" by which they access that information are entirely different. From E's external, third-person perspective he can only access the information encoded in S's neural correlates by means of his visual or other exteroceptive systems, aided by appropriate equipment. Because S embodies the information encoded in her neural correlates and it is already at the interface of her consciousness and brain, it displays "naturally"[14] in the

[14] I assume here that it is simply a "natural" empirical fact about the world that certain physical events in the brain (the correlates of consciousness) are

form of the light bulb she experiences.

S experiences a light bulb, rather than her neural encodings of the light bulb for the reason that it is the information about the world (encoded in her neural correlates) that is manifested in her experience rather than the embodying format or the physical attributes of the neural states themselves. E observes/experiences the neural encodings of the light bulb in S's brain (rather than the light bulb) for the simple reason that his visual attention is focused on S's brain, not the light bulb. If he wanted to experience something similar to what she experiences, he would have to shift his attention (and gaze) away from S's brain to the light bulb.[15]

From E's "external observer's perspective", can he assume that S's experience is really nothing more than the physical correlates of her experience, as a materialist reductionist might claim? From his external perspective, does he know what is going on in S's mind/consciousness better than she does? Not really. E knows something about S's mental states that she does not know (their physical embodiment). But S knows something about them that E does not know (that these mental states are manifested as a visual experience). These first- and third-person ways of knowing the mind are complementary and mutually irreducible. One needs both S's first-person story and E's third-person story for a complete account of what is going on.

A straightforward way to make sense of this situation is to assume that there is one underlying entity or process, S's mind (viewed in a Western sense) that grounds and connects the two forms of knowledge that E and S have of it — a position that can be formally described as ontological monism combined with epistemological dualism.

But this leaves the ontological nature of mind an open question. What is mind really like? As Einstein puts it (Einstein and Infeld 1938: 31):

→ accompanied by experiences. Consequently, when such neural activities (the correlates) occur in one's brain one has the corresponding experiences. I also assume that the formatting of neurally encoded information relates to the formatting of corresponding, phenomenally encoded information in an orderly way, with discoverable neural state space/phenomenal space mappings. In short, this relationship follows some natural law, however mysterious this presently seems. I return to this issue, and to analogous situations in other branches of science below.

[15] For a more detailed analysis of these similarities and differences see the discussion of "changing places" and related issues in Velmans (2009: chap. 9).

> In our endeavour to understand reality we are somewhat like a man trying to understand the mechanism of a closed watch. He sees the face and the moving hands, even hears its ticking, but he has no way of opening the case.

One can of course try to develop better instruments to make more refined observations.[16] However, beyond the limits of observation one can only make "best conjectures".

If mind grounds and unifies the first- and third-person knowledge we have about it, what can we conjecture about its nature?

- In so far as conscious experiences are of something or about something it is reasonable to suppose that they, and their neural correlates, encode information (see above). If so, the mind encodes information.
- To the extent that brain activities and accompanying experiences are fluid and dynamic, the mind can be described as a process, developing over time.

Taken together, these points suggest that mind can be thought of as a form of information processing, and the information displayed in experiences and their physical correlates can be thought of as two manifestations of this information processing — which makes this a *dual-aspect theory of information processing*.

However, this does not fully specify the ontology of the mind. Information processing needs to be encoded in some medium that is capable of carrying out that processing. Given this, what kind of "medium" is the mind?

One can give a very short list of the observable facts:

- In the human case, minds viewed from the outside seem to take the form of brains (or some physical aspect of brains).
- Viewed from the perspective of those who embody them, minds take the form of conscious experiences.

If first- and third-person perspectives (on the mind) are complementary and mutually irreducible (see above), then the nature of

[16] In third-person observations of the brain this usually involves the development of new technologies (fMRI, EEG, PET, etc.). However, such refinements can also be obtained with first-person methods, for example with more highly trained attention to the minutiae of experience (see, for example, readings in Varela and Shear 1999; Hurlburt and Akhter 2006; Petitmengin 2006; Price and Barrell 2012).

the mind is revealed as much by how it appears from one perspective as the other. If so, the nature of mind is not either physical or conscious experience, it is at once physical and conscious experience. For lack of a better term we may describe this nature as psychophysical.[17] If we combine this with the features above, we can say that mind is a psychophysical process that encodes information, developing over time.

Note that an alternative way of making the point that the nature of mind is as much psychological as it is physical (and consequently "psychophysical") is to argue that the nature of mind is neither psychological nor physical, at least in the ways that these terms are normally understood. That for example is the description preferred by Atmanspacher (2012). These seemingly different characterizations of dual-aspect theory differ only in emphasis. Both agree (a) that conscious experiences and their neural correlates are best thought of as complementary, mutually irreducible psychological and physical aspects of the underlying nature of mind, (b) that whatever the nature of mind might be, under respectively first- and third-person observation arrangements it must have the power to give rise to its observed psychological and physical aspects, (c) that this underlying nature somehow unifies its manifest aspects (monism), (d) that it is knowable only through its manifest aspects, and (e) that this nature must be something other than "psychological" or "physical" as normally understood.[18]

This dual-aspect understanding of the nature of mind suggests a way of understanding the seemingly unbridgeable divide between Western

[17] Note that a similar combination of terms occurs in physics to describe the nature of entities, energies or processes that have dual aspects, for example electromagnetism, which is manifested both in the form of electric currents and associated magnetic fields. Physics also struggles to find a suitable term to describe the nature of photons and electrons which exhibit both wave and particle properties depending on the observational arrangements and are consequently referred to as "wave packets" or "electron clouds". As with the psychological dual-aspect monism described above, physics struggles to find a descriptive term for the underlying state that somehow combines both observable aspects, for example describing photons as "wave-packets" or electrons as "electron-clouds". And, as with psychological complementarity, wave and particle aspects are viewed as complementary and mutually irreducible.

[18] Point (e) also distinguishes dual-aspect monism from both idealism and physicalism. Note that similar differences in terminology and emphasis can be found in prior formulations of dual-aspect monism. Gustav Theodor →

physicalism and Eastern idealism. As noted above, the mind has dual (physical and experiential) aspects that can be known in respectively third- and first-person ways. How does that help to understand East–West differences? Over the millennia Western and Eastern thinkers have asked themselves the same question: what are the enduring, unchanging realities that underlie the ever-changing world of phenomenal appearances? Although many investigative methods have been developed both in the East and West, the predominant methods used to address this particular question have been very different. The West has specialized in the development of third-person methods — and, using these methods, mind, body and world all appear to be physical, and the unchanging, underlying realities are described by physical laws. By contrast, Eastern first person methods (within both Sāṁkhya and Advaita Vedānta) have focused on stilling the mind to the point where phenomenal content no longer appears, in order to ascertain what, if anything, remains. As noted above, what remains has been variously described as a state of "pure consciousness", "pure subjectivity" or *sat–cit–ānanda* (being–consciousness–bliss).

In short, RM suggests that one's understanding of the ultimate nature of mind is conditioned by the investigative route one takes. If one pursues exclusively third-person methods it is entirely understandable that this ultimate nature might appear to be physical. If one pursues purely first-person, yogic methods it is entirely understandable that one might conclude that this ultimate nature is "pure consciousness" — and, through a direct experience of that state, to have real-ized that nature. However RM is cautious about giving epistemic primacy to either investigative route. In viewing the mind as a psychophysical form of information processing, it honours observations made in both traditions, thereby occupying the

→ Fechner for example preferred to think of the nature of mind as "psychophysical" as I do here, while, in their private discussions, recorded in letters to each other, Wolfgang Pauli and Carl Jung often referred to the underlying ground of mind–matter relationships as "psychophysically neutral" (which can be interpreted as neither physical nor psychological — see Atmanspacher 2012). The ways that physics relates observable phenomena to conceptions of entities that underlie those phenomena offer rough analogies for both versions. An analogy to "psychophysical" would be the way in which electric and magnetic fields are thought to be manifest aspects of electromagnetism in the manner described by Maxwell's equations. A closer analogy to "psychophysically neutral" would be how the dual nature of photons and electrons is conceived as a neutral system state that manifests itself as either wave-like (interference patterns) or particle-like (clicks in a Geiger counter) under different experimental arrangements.

middle ground of a potential East–West bridge. RM also suggests that the dual-aspect nature of the human mind exemplifies a more general, natural process within the embedding universe as such, i.e. rather than being pure consciousness or purely physical, Nature might be, in its depths, psychophysical (or neither purely psychological nor purely physical in the way that these terms are normally understood).[19]

Is the Relationship Between Body, Mind and Consciousness Linear or Triangular?

According to Western physicalism, the ultimate nature of Nature is physical. Mental states are particular arrangements of physical states (e.g. physical forms of information processing) and conscious experiences are a subcategory of these states (e.g. those forms of information processing receiving focal attention). In short the relation between body, mind, and consciousness is linear: body → mind → consciousness. According to Advaita, *Brahman* is the ultimate basis of everything, and the nature of *Brahman* is variously described (e.g. by Rao) as "pure consciousness", "undifferentiated consciousness" and "pure subjectivity". If consciousness is the basis of everything it must give rise to mind and body and, again, the relationship is thought to be linear: consciousness → mind → body. Notes Rao (2012: 135):

> The relationship between consciousness, mind and body is not triangular but linear. The mind is connected with the bodily processes at the one end and with consciousness at the other. Thus the mind is the interfacing instrumentality and the connecting link between consciousness and the body.

However, Rao recognizes that Sāṁkhya does not entirely conform to this model and, given that both Sāṁkhya dualism and Advaita monism have clearly stated entity metaphysics, it does not seem possible to unify their ontology. Consequently, he suggests (2012: 140) a different route to convergence:

> As an alternative to entity metaphysics one could explore a process view of reality, especially in the context of Buddhist thought. In fact, such a view may prove in some ways more heuristic to further expand and

[19] There are various suggestions about how Nature might incorporate such dual features in its microcosmic structure (panpsychism, pan-experientialism, etc.) although that is not a subject that I have space to examine here. But see, for example, Skrbina (2005) and readings in Velmans and Nagasawa (2012).

> refine the Trident model. It is possible, for example, to consider body, mind and consciousness as states in a continuous process of reality rather than a consortium of one, two or more ontologically distinct constituents. The basic reality is just one process, the ground of all manifest being. The transition from body to mind involves something like a "quantum leap" in the process. I use the phrase "quantum leap" to indicate the explanatory gap that exists, which in my view is unlikely to be understood by current science with quantitative methods. In a similar manner one could see a qualitative leap from the conceptualization of mind to consciousness. The distinctiveness of body, mind and consciousness is embedded in the qualitative leaps that take place in the reality process. Some kind of micro–macro transition is involved in the relation between body and mind. In Sāṁkhya-Yoga, the material objects evolve out of the *mahat*, the cosmic mind. Patañjali himself makes it no secret that mind in its utmost purity is essentially indistinguishable from *puruṣa*. Therefore, such a jump is not a priori ruled out. The leap or jump refers to bridging of the two states without reducing one to the other.

Arguably, however, viewing the nature of reality as the development of one process is still a form of monism (albeit process monism rather than entity monism)[20] and, while the development of one process in which major state changes occur might apply, in principle, to Advaita Vedānta monism, a problem remains of how one something that Rao describes as "pure consciousness" or "undifferentiated subjectivity" (in which materiality is entirely absent) might make a series of "quantum leaps" to something like an autonomously existing material world. Or, to rephrase the problem in terms more familiar to Sāṁkhya, how, in ways comprehensible to science, might one make a transition (or even a series of transitions) from undifferentiated (pure) subjectivity to undifferentiated (pure) materiality.

On this issue, however, RM might have something useful to suggest. According to RM, the underlying process, characterized as a "psychophysical form of information processing that develops over time" already has the potential to manifest itself in dual ways within its own nature — for the simple reason that the underlying process is specified (in so far as it can be specified at all) in terms of its observable material and conscious manifestations and the psychophysical relationships that hold between them. In a way analogous to how electric currents and

[20] RM for example remains neutral on the issue of whether, for some purposes, the thing-itself is best thought of as an entity and for other purposes as a process (these options are not mutually exclusive).

associated magnetic fields can be regarded as the manifestations of one underlying process (electromagnetism) whose relationships are defined by Maxwell's laws, physical processes and associated experiences can be thought of as the manifestations of one psychophysical process (the mind itself) whose relationship can in principle be defined by psychophysical laws.[21] Physical manifestations are observable under one set of observation arrangements (third-person observations); conscious experiences are observable under another set of observation arrangements (first-person observations). Third- and first-person observations are complementary and mutually irreducible. As the underlying psychophysical process evolves over time, its dual manifestations into material forms and their associated conscious experiences co-evolve.[22] Viewed in this way, there never was a gap between physical processes and their associated conscious experiences.

In this, RM, once again converges with and diverges from Rao's BMC model in intriguing ways. RM converges with BMC in suggesting that the ultimate reality might be thought of one fundamental process with different states or manifestations. However, in its adoption of dual-aspect monism RM clearly follows an inverted equilateral triangular model (rather than a linear one) with one grounding reality at the base of the triangle[23] and its two manifest aspects (consciousness and its associated material forms) at the upper two corners of the triangle. And, given that these manifest aspects are *already* intimately linked by the one underlying process of which they are aspects, in RM there do not need to be any

[21] This and other analogies with physics are only intended to be approximate. For a more detailed discussion see Velmans (2008b).

[22] Such a process allows for the full range of conscious experience. For example, as conscious experiences become more complex (in informational terms) their physical correlates would become correspondingly complex. Conversely as experiences become simplified and primal their corresponding physical correlates might be correspondingly primal. A state of "pure consciousness" for example might correspond to some primal physical state — perhaps at the quantum mechanical level (whether or not it does so is in principle investigable). For a more detailed account of co-evolution and its further applications to the changing relationships between conscious experiences and their associated physical states see Velmans (2012b).

[23] There are many ways of referring to this ultimate reality. In his early formulation of dual-aspect theory, Spinoza sometimes referred to it as "Nature" and sometimes as "God". Other terms include the "*Unus Mundus*" (Jung), and the "universe itself". One might also call it the "cosmic mind" (or *mahat*) as Sāṁkhya-Yoga suggests, although in RM such a cosmic mind does →

added "quantum leaps" from conscious experiences to their associated physical states.

Causal Interactions Between Conscious States and Material Forms

These basic differences between RM and BMC also lead to very different ways to account for the apparent causal interactions of consciousness with material forms that have plagued Western thinkers since the time of Descartes. Rao observes (2012: 124):

> The problem of interaction between the *Brahman* and the material world is sidestepped in Advaita by according a lower level of reality to the latter. From the perspective of *Brahman*, i.e. at the transcendental level, the world we see out there is false and therefore what goes on in it is equally illusory and therefore needs no causal explanation. Again, the plurality of subjects is an illusion. However, at the empirical (*vyavahārika*) level, the material world of objects as well as the individual subjects enjoy a second grade reality, a conditional and transient existence. The phenomenal world at the empirically observable (*vyavahārika*) level is experientially real. What is experientially real, however, is not on that account ultimately real. Inasmuch as what is experientially real cannot be wished away as non-existent, the subject–object interaction needs explanation at the transactional level. Advaita does not shy away from this as we will note later in the paper.

He then goes on to explain (2012: 125):

> . . . in Yoga as well as Advaita, the mind is physical, whereas consciousness is nonphysical. The chasm between the two dissimilar and radically different entities, consciousness and the material world of

→ not just give rise to the material aspects of the human mind, but also to their associated conscious experiences. Given its neutrality, I find it useful to borrow the term the "thing-itself" from Kant, although unlike Kant, I do not view the "thing-itself" as *entirely* unknowable. According to RM, although human knowledge is partial, approximate, uncertain and species-specific, it does represent aspects of what the thing itself, *in its manifest form*, is really like, in ways appropriate to the biological needs of human life. If it does not, we can know nothing, as the thing-itself is all there is to know (see the analysis of this issue in Velmans 2009: chap. 8). This, of course, leaves open the possibility that one can know nothing about the *unmanifest* thing-itself — although, even on this, it might be strategic to avoid premature closure; current cosmology for example proceeds on the assumption that the earliest observable states of the universe might give clues about its state prior to its initial manifestation (in the "big bang").

> objects is bridged by the mind which occupies an intermediary position and is able to catch the reflections of consciousness without interacting with it. The mind is more like a painted canvas in a dark room. It requires the light of consciousness to illuminate it. For example, in perception, the mind, interacting with the world of objects via the sensory processes, takes the form of the objects and the person becomes aware of those forms when the light of consciousness is reflected on them.

And finally Rao states (2012: 134):

> In the person, body, mind and consciousness coexist and in a way function together. However, their relative roles differ from person to person and from time to time in the same person. In abstract, consciousness is an undifferentiated subjectivity. It is the essence of all being, the meaning and information content of all things. It is self-manifesting as well as other-manifesting, i.e., illuminates the contents of sensory inputs so as to bestow meaning on them. It is self-luminous and reveals itself and is also a source of illumination to all others. Though primary on its own, it has a secondary role in the person. It exists more as a "witness" and plays the role of an observer rather than of an active participant. The main player in human functioning is the mind which has the intrinsic ability to reflect consciousness. These reflections are mistaken for consciousness as-such and mind is taken as the seat and source of consciousness.

Once again, there are both convergences and divergences with RM. For example, RM agrees that, "the creation of an experienced, phenomenal world brings a conscious 'light' into an otherwise 'dark' universe" (Velmans 2009: 298). In stressing the role of phenomenal consciousness to be real-ization RM agrees that consciousness acts more as witness than an active participant. It agrees that the relation between consciousness, brain and the external physical world is *reflexive* (and in that sense "reflects its own light"). And it also agrees that the phenomenally experienced Self is routinely mistaken for the real Self.[24] However there are also differences: Viewed in Western terms, "information" cannot be carried, transmitted or transformed in any system without differentiation within that system (Shannon 1948), so RM does not adopt the view that undifferentiated subjectivity (or even undifferentiated materiality) is the "meaning and information content of all things". And, in viewing phenomenal consciousness and its associated physical states as dual aspects of a grounding, psychophysical mind, RM takes the immediate source of

[24] See Velmans (2013) for a detailed discussion of this point.

conscious phenomenal "light" to be immanent rather than something shone on the material aspects of the mind from a transcendent source (i.e. from a source outside of the mind).[25]

Consciousness–Brain Causal Relationships

RM also offers a different and more detailed account of consciousness–brain causal relationships. As in Sāṁkhya-Yoga and Vedānta, RM accepts that consciousness does not appear to directly affect brain states, when these are viewed from a purely third-person perspective. However, first- and third-person views of the mind are thought of as complementary and mutually irreducible. Nor is this confined to perception. If one views consciousness as a state of mind in the classical Western way, there are four distinct ways in which body/brain and mind/consciousness might, in principle, enter into causal relationships. There might be physical causes of physical states, physical causes of mental states, mental causes of mental states, and mental causes of physical states. Each of these potential causal relationships is routinely accepted in one or another therapeutic practice.

Within conventional medicine, physical → physical causation is taken for granted. Consequently, the proper treatment for physical disorders is assumed to be some form of physical intervention. Psychiatry takes the efficacy of physical → mental causation for granted, along with the assumption that the proper treatment for psychological disorders may involve psychoactive drugs, neurosurgery and so on. Many forms of psychotherapy take mental → mental causation for granted, and assume that psychological disorders can be alleviated by means of "talking cures", guided imagery, hypnosis and other forms of mental intervention. Psychosomatic medicine assumes that mental → physical causation can be effective. Consequently, under some circumstances, a physical disorder (for example, hysterical paralysis) may require a mental (psychotherapeutic) intervention. Given the extensive evidence for all these causal interactions how are we to make sense of them?

---

[25] On this last point, it should be noted however that Rao's description is clearly meant to be metaphorical, and that the differences between the Eastern and Western usages of the terms mind and consciousness make comparisons difficult. Nevertheless, the linear relationships in BMC and the triangular ones in RM suggest different sources for the "light" of phenomenal consciousness. RM nevertheless leaves open the possibility that "mind itself" (or the "thing-itself") also has transcendent aspects about which little, and perhaps nothing can be said — as in the Indian tradition, not-this, not-this (*neti, neti*).

Although I do not have space to present a full analysis here,[26] a brief analysis of how first- and third-person accounts relate to each other given above can be used to indicate the route that RM takes: Physical → physical causal sequences describe events from an entirely third-person perspective (they are "pure third-person" accounts). Mental → mental causal sequences describe events entirely from a first-person perspective (they are "pure first-person" accounts). Physical → mental and mental → physical causal sequences are mixed-perspective accounts that employ *perspectival switching*.

Perspectival Switching

Physical → mental causal sequences start with events viewed from a third-person perspective and switch to how things appear from a first-person perspective. For example, a causal account of visual perception starts with a third-person description of the physical stimulus and its effects on the visual system but then switches to a first-person account of what the subject experiences. Mental → physical causal sequences switch the other way. From a subject's point of view, for example, an experienced pain in a tooth might cause a visit to the dentist. It might be possible to give an entirely third-person account of this sequence of events (in terms of dental carries producing pain circuitry activation, efferent signals to the skeleto-muscular system, etc). But the mixed-perspective account gives a more useful description of what is going on in terms of the knowledge available to the subject.

In principle, complementary first- and third-person sources of information can be found whenever body or mind/brain states are represented in some way in subjective experience. A patient might for example have insight into the nature of a psychological problem (via feelings and thoughts), that a clinician might investigate by observing his/her brain or behaviour. In medical diagnosis, a patient might have access to some malfunction via interoceptors, producing symptoms such as pain and discomfort, whereas a doctor might be able to identify the cause via his/her exteroceptors (eyes, ears and so on) supplemented by

---

[26] But see Velmans (2002a) the accompanying eight commentaries and my reply in Velmans (2002b) in a Special Issue of the *Journal of Consciousness Studies* devoted to this question, or the overview in Velmans (2009: chap. 13). A very detailed research programme that integrates first-person experiential science with neuroscience in a way that is based on the explanatory principles developed in these sources has recently been developed by Price and Barrell (2012).

medical instrumentation. As with conscious states and their neural correlates the clinician has access to the physical embodiment of such conditions, while the patient has access to how such conditions are experienced. In these situations, neither the third-person information available to the clinician nor the first-person information available to the patient is automatically privileged or "objective" in the sense of being "observer-free". The clinician merely reports what he/she observes or infers about what is going on (using available means) and the patient does likewise. As noted above, such first- and third-person accounts of the subject's mental life or body states are complementary and mutually irreducible. Taken together, they provide a global, psychophysical picture of the condition under scrutiny.

In short, RM provides a simple way of unifying all four forms of physical/mental causation. Operations of mind viewed from a purely external observer's perspective (physical → physical), operations of mind viewed from a purely first-person perspective (mental → mental), and mixed-perspective accounts involving perspectival switching (physical → mental, mental → physical) can be understood as different views (or a mix of views) of a single, psychophysical form of information processing developing over time. And, in providing a common psychophysical ground for brain states and their accompanying experiences, such a grounding process (at the base of the triangle) also provides the "missing link" required to explain psychosomatic effects.

Conclusion

Although they depart from very different traditions, there appear to be clear convergences between theories of how body, mind and consciousness relate in Rao's BMC Trident model (drawn from Sāṁkhya-Yoga and Advaita Vedānta) and RM (which draws its evidence base from science and everyday phenomenal experience). Some of their apparent divergences can be understood in terms of differences in the way terms such as "mind" and "consciousness" are commonly understood in Eastern *versus* Western traditions. However there are also some real differences both in their detail and in how they conceptualize the ontological ground of body–mind–consciousness relationships. In his overall summary of the BMC Trident model and how RM relates to it, Rao writes (2012: 141):

> To conclude, the BMC Trident model does not play well with currently fashionable psychological theorizing that favours physicalism which has no room for mind and consciousness as primary and irreducible

> aspects of humans. The one that comes somewhat close to this model is reflexive monism (RM) as articulated by Max Velmans. . . . In both RM and BMC, the world of perceptions is constructed. Mind/consciousness is irreducible to physical states. The "embedding universe" [the thing-itself] in Velmans is more like the all encompassing *Brahman* of Advaita. It would be of interest to note that the *Brahman* is best described as characterless, "not this and not this" (*neti neti*). One could argue that *Brahman* is neither physical nor non-physical. Distinctions between physical and non-physical arise at a different level of discourse on reality. . . . In a sense, they are necessitated by our information processing exercise. The "reflexive interaction" Velmans speaks of is somewhat akin to the reflection of consciousness illuminating the mind. A more detailed comparison of RM and the Trident model is given in my book *Cognitive Anomalies, and Consciousness and Yoga* (2011). Velmans took one important step forward in bridging East–West views on consciousness by asserting the irreducibility of consciousness to the physical states and the brain functions and by pointing to the immediacy and directness of conscious experience. If he took another step to provide for consciousness *as-such* and its existence apart from its contents, his views would have been a lot closer to the view we have attempted to develop from Yoga, Advaita and Buddhist systems of thought.

It should be apparent that my own conclusions are similar. For clarity however, it is worth stressing again that RM does accept the possibility of experiencing a state of pure consciousness as a first person way of real-izing the embedding universe, ground of being, or "thing-itself". In so far as such a state is free of sensory contents it can also be thought of as existing apart from its contents.[27] But RM remains cautious about the view that a real-ization of the thing-itself by an embodied human being can be a full real-ization of the thing-itself as it is for itself, i.e. RM leaves open the question of whether the whole can be fully real-ized by any of its parts. RM also remains cautious about the view that such a real-ization (even one experienced as pure consciousness) can constitute the ground of all being. For reasons that hopefully will be clear from the brief outline above, rather than opting for either Western physicalism or Eastern idealism, RM adopts the intermediate view that the ground of being (at least in its manifest form) is psychophysical, or perhaps something that is neither psychological or physical as normally understood, thereby forming a potential bridge between Eastern and Western thoughts. As is said in the East, the nature of *Brahman* is not-this, not-this — *neti, neti*.

[27] Although whether a state of being–consciousness–bliss is entirely free of content is arguable. One might argue for example that it is not free of bliss.

References

Atmanspacher, H. (2012), "Dual-Aspect Monism à la Pauli and Jung", in M. Velmans and Y. Nagasawa (eds.) *Monist Alternatives to Physicalism: Journal of Consciousness Studies Special Issue* 19(9-10): 96-120.

Brentano, F. (1874), *Psychology from an Empirical Standpoint,* (tr.) A.C. Rancurello, D.B. Terrell and L. McAlister, London: Routledge, 1973, 2nd edn., introd. by Peter Simons, 1995.

Einstein, Albert and Infeld, Leopold (1938), *The Evolution of Physics: The Growth of Ideas from Early Concepts to Relativity and Quanta,* New York: Simon and Schuster.

Hurlburt, R.T. and S.A. Akhter (2006), "The Descriptive Experience Sampling Method", *Phenomenology and the Cognitive Sciences* 5: 271-301.

Paranjpe, A.C. (2010), "Theories of Self and Cognition: Indian Psychological Perspective", *Psychology and Developing Societies* 22(1): 5-48.

Petitmengin, C. (2006), "Describing One's Subjective Experience in the Second Person: An Interview Method for the Science of Consciousness, *Phenomenology and the Cognitive Sciences* 5: 229-69.

Price, D.D. and J.J. Barrell (2012), *Inner Experience and Neuroscience: Merging Both Perspectives,* Cambridge, MA: MIT Press.

Rao, K.R. (2011), *History of Science, Philosophy and Culture in Indian Civilization* Volume XVI, Part 1: *Cognitive Anomalies, Consciousness and Yoga,* New Delhi: Matrix Publishers.

——— (2012), "Complementarity of Advaita Nondualism and Yoga Dualism in Indian Psychology", in M. Velmans and Y. Nagasawa (eds.) *Monist Alternatives to Physicalism: Journal of Consciousness Studies Special Issue* 19(9-10): 121-42.

Russell, B. (1912), *The Problems of Philosophy,* Home University Library of Modern Knowledge, London: Williams and Norgate.

Seager, William (2012), *Natural Fabrications: Science, Emergence and Consciousness,* New York: Springer.

Shannon, C.E. (1948), "A Mathematical Theory of Communication", *Bell System Technical Journal* 27: 379-423, 623-56.

Skrbina, D. (2005), *Panpsychism in the West,* Cambridge, MA: MIT Press.

Varela, F. and J. Shear (1999) (eds.), *The View from Within: First Person Approaches to the Study of Consciousness,* Exeter, UK: Imprint Academic.

Velmans, M. (1991a), "Is Human Information Processing Conscious", *Behavioral and Brain Sciences* 14(4): 651-69.

——— (1991b), "Consciousness from a First-person Perspective", *Behavioral and Brain Sciences* 14(4): 702-26.

——— (1998), "Goodbye to Reductionism", in S. Hameroff, A. Kaszniak and A. Scott (eds.) *Towards a Science of Consciousness II: The Second Tucson Discussions and Debates,* Cambridge, MA: MIT Press, pp. 45-52.

——— (2002), "How could Conscious Experiences Affect Brains?", *Journal of Consciousness Studies* 9(11): 3-29.

——— (2002), "Making Sense of Causal Interactions between Consciousness and Brain", *Journal of Consciousness Studies* 9(11): 69-95.

——— (2008a), "Reflexive Monism", *Journal of Consciousness Studies* 15(2): 5-50.

——— (2008b), "Psychophysical Nature", in H. Atmanspacher and H. Primas (eds.) *Wolfgang Pauli's Philosophical Ideas and Contemporary Science*, Berlin, Germany: Springer, pp. 115-34.

——— (2009), *Understanding Consciousness*, 2nd edn., New York, USA: Routledge/ Psychology Press.

——— (2012), "The Mind–Body Problem and Whitehead's non-reductive Monism", in M. Velmans and Y. Nagasawa (eds.) *Monist Alternatives to Physicalism: Journal of Consciousness Studies Special Issue* 19(9-10): 40-66.

——— (2012a), "Reflexive Monism: Psychophysical Relations among Mind, Matter and Consciousness", in M. Velmans and Y. Nagasawa (eds.) *Monist Alternatives to Physicalism: Journal of Consciousness Studies Special Issue* 19(9-10): 143-65.

——— (2012b), "The Evolution of Consciousness", in D. Canter and D. Tunbull (eds.) *Biologising the Social Sciences*, Special Issue of Contemporary Social Science, *Journal of the Academy of Social Sciences* 7(2): 117-38.

——— (2013), "Conscious Free Will and the Unconscious/Preconscious Self", in S. Menon, A. Sinha and B.V. Sreekantan (eds.) *Interdisplinary Perspectives on Consciousness and the Self,* Berlin: Springer (in press).

Weekes, A. (2012), The Mind-Body Problem and Whitehead's Non-Reductive Monism, in M. Velmans and Y. Nagasawa (eds.) *Monist Alternatives to Physicalism: Journal of Consciousness Studies, Special Issue* 19(9-10): 40-66.

6

The Search for Authentic Self
A Key Concern of Indian Psychology

Girishwar Misra and *Shivantika Sharad*

Prof. K. Ramakrishna Rao represents a long tradition of Indian scholarship, which is open to good ideas from all directions. Indeed his work illustrates the Vedic pronouncement of "आ नो भद्राः क्रतवो यान्तु विश्वतः (*ā no Bhadraḥ kratavo yāntu viśvataḥ*) . He emphasizes the need to be firmly rooted in the soil of indigenous thought systems. At the same time, he is not averse to the scientific vision and methods. However, he remains cognizant of the fact that the positivist mode of science promotes certain forms of knowledge and understanding that are neither universal nor intrinsically beneficial for the welfare of humanity. During his academic career spanning over six decades his interaction and experience in various teaching and administrative capacities in India and the US, in the fields of psychology, philosophy and education convinced him to address problems from an indigenous perspective, a perspective that provides an insider's view of reality. It is reflected in his effort and dedication to the cause of repositioning the discipline of psychology through the rich and variegated knowledge resource available in classical Indian texts and discourses. In particular Rao has nurtured articulations, debates and discussions under the theme or sub-field called "Indian psychology". To him the term "Indian" does not denote any geographical area or a race/community or religion but represents a super-ordinate thematic category to refer to the knowledge available in the Indian thought traditions.

Through a variety of efforts including the launch of the *Journal of Indian Psychology*, establishment of the Institute of Yoga and Consciousness at Andhra University, writing journal articles and monographs on consciousness, yoga, cognition, spirituality, Gandhism, Buddhist view of mind and articulation of Indian psychology, Prof. Rao has made seminal contributions to the field of Indian psychology. All this, however, was not enough to satisfy him. So he assumed the role of an academic leader and edited several volumes, helped organizing national and international seminars, conferences, consultations and research projects. As a mentor he encouraged colleagues to engage critically and constructively with the academically interesting, culturally pertinent and methodologically rigorous initiatives. Rao has indefatigably pursued the cause of culturally relevant academic interventions at various levels. His efforts amount to nothing less than bringing a paradigm shift. We have been fortunate to be associated with him in various academic activities and to have been receiving his guidance in our academic journey.

On the occasion of the 80th Birthday of Rao we express our joy and offer some thoughts that extend the theme of Indian psychology. We argue that psychology as a modern discipline has drawn its orientation mainly from the physical sciences. As a result, an objectivist ontology and a positivist epistemology have been directing its learning and research practices. As a consequence the behaviourist approach has become the dominant strategy to attain scientific status. This single-track focus has led to a systematic and selective promotion of certain ideas and themes and neglect of others. In particular, the emphasis on "behaviour" pushed the study of themes like self and consciousness to the margins of research. The psychologists were engaged in pursuing the agenda of converting the subjective and covert psychological processes into "objects" that could be mathematically manipulated and addressed through objective techniques. The impact of behaviourism was so pervasive that it made objectivity and quantification as the keys to the ontology of psychological aspects of reality.

After the demise of conceptual behaviourism, methodological behaviourism continued to inform the disciplinary deliberations of psychology. It worked as a "gatekeeper" by prescribing a set of conditions for the entry or exclusion of the concepts to the domain of genuine investigation, a domain defined and controlled by behaviourist ontology. As a result, the revival of interest in the study of self, took a new direction and emphasis. In this tradition, aspects of self-as-object were deemed legitimate and self-as-subject remained neglected. The self as (perceived) object became the focus of a plethora of research. This view was also congenial for the culture of the North American region. It is therefore not surprising to find an orientation in mainstream psychology that emphasizes the egoistic tendencies, self-esteem, and outer directed analyses of the attributes of self. Contrarily, the tradition of psychology rooted in the Indian thought system bears inner orientation towards the self and lays emphasis on the "subject" with the centrality of search for a true or authentic self. The same has been reflected in the lives of many great Indians. Sri Aurobindo and Mahatma Gandhi in their unique ways have illustrated an authentic self through their works and deeds. Their lives offer an approach to understanding the self that is much more comprehensive and holistic.

Disciplinary Discourses, Reality Construction and Human Action

Disciplinary discourses provide not only the conceptual tools to represent reality at an abstract level, but also furnish specific grounds for constructing particular worldviews and allowing certain forms of reality construction. The social science disciplines, however, are in a peculiar situation as they deal with a domain that is rooted in specific cultural milieu inhabited by specific communities. These communities constantly participate and dynamically contribute to the construction of that milieu and in turn get constructed by it. In this way we live in the worlds of our own making and aspire to play the game of cultural construction. Consequently all our discourses unfold under the prevailing socio-economic and political circumstances which are human constructions. Of course, with the processes of cultural contact (e.g. acculturation, Westernization, Sanskritization) intercultural transactions do take place and cultures undergo change.

The diversity found in local circumstances often contains elements of resistance that selectively filter the inflow and outflow of ideas. Being parts of "practice", these ideas (or idea-based activities) constitute necessary ingredients of everyday reality and organize our actions, the goals toward which the actions are directed, as well as the achievement of these goals. For instance, the ideas of God, freedom, love, autonomy, and human rights are created by humans themselves, and arrange life activities in certain preferred ways. Similarly the key psychological constructs like intelligence, motivation, personality, interest, value, emotion and so on, constitute the ways of describing reality as well as conducting ourselves. They create boundaries for our actual and possible worlds. In this sense Sigmund Freud's concepts of ego, id, super ego, the unconscious and the like define who we are, how we conduct ourselves and help explain behaviours. Taken together, this kind of repertoire works both ways — they are constraints as well as affordances and offer a range of conceivables, knowables and doables. They help tremendously in meaning-making in the socio-cultural world. A mismatch between culture and the disciplinary orientation is bound to make the discipline insipid and its role in making sense of culture or contributing to it constructively suspect. A culturally alienated discipline often results in pseudo understandings and leads to the formation of a parallel reality with little substance beyond the scheme of the conceptual frame.

Rao is a part of the academic movement to decolonize higher education, especially in the areas of social sciences. In a recent article, he (Rao 2012) points out how psychology taught and practised in India has come to be a culturally-alienated discipline and what needs to be done to restore its cultural identity.

The Case of Social Sciences in India

The introduction of social sciences in modern India took place during the early part of the twentieth century. Instead of being a natural organic growth it was a foreign implant. The university set-up was born under the colonial rule with a definite agenda of creating a particular kind of academicians with an attitude congenial to the ruling British. Accordingly the educational system drawn from Britain deliberately created a distance from and aversion toward the knowledge systems and vast intellectual resources available in the Indian traditions. The indigenous resources were made obscure and came to be treated as "things of the past" with little relevance to the present conditions. This followed from the British perspective that saw the Indian as "the other" and the Indian society, consequently as an out group. The new sciences were maintained and nurtured in a scheme of education that had almost banned the entry of indigenous ideas into its corridors. The subsequent developments in these disciplines further widened the gap due to increasing magnitude of Euro-American scholars and their categorization by Indians as "significant others" with whom Indians tended to compare their work; a pattern that persists even in current times.

In the course of events the productive use of ideas of Indian origin was drastically diminished on account of attributions of its other worldliness, its non-secular approach and non-scientific temperament. Thus an alien perspective was imposed as the framework and "India" became a case/field for exploring and establishing that alien structure with the help of a baggage of concepts and methods that were claimed as universal and objective categories. The discipline of psychology in India suffered a double disadvantage. First was the disadvantage of being a social science whose forefathers strongly believed in making it a "science" and overcome what Thomas Hardy Leahey (1987) refers to as their "physics envy". Second was the disadvantage of being an implanted discipline that was nurtured in the Western culture, without any considerations for bridging the fundamental disparities of the "home" and the "host" cultures. Psychology in India was thus forced to operate in a straitjacketed way.

The history of psychology in India as a modern discipline presents an example of the difficulties and struggles in discipline formations. After the initial fervour to develop a new science, the effort culminated in a tendency to emulate the works of Western counterparts. This resulted in large-scale duplication and adoption of research issues and methods, and in such a scheme, only limited attention could be paid to the problems and challenges of Indian society. That too was done with a lens that obfuscated the vision due to the serious cultural incompatibility of the underlying assumptions, concepts and tools. This has led to increased dissatisfaction with the disciplinary affairs amongst the academicians. Today, it is widely felt that to a large extent the disciplinary developments in teaching and research are flawed in certain respects. Barring a few attempts that have cultural sensibility and intellectual courage, a vast majority of research works are mere extensions of the Western works. In a nutshell, there is a growing consensus that the applied value of researches, their cultural relevance and contribution to the cumulative growth of knowledge in the discipline has been very limited. As a result the presence of psychology on the national scene in terms of policy making is drastically being undermined.

Pointing out that "the concepts, categories and models used to teach and conduct research in psychology in Indian institutions and even the tools of investigation employed by Indian psychologists have had little indigenous content and are borrowed from the West", Rao (2011a: 663) says that it "is hardly surprising therefore that Indian contributions to psychology with very few exceptions remain marginal at best. They attracted scanty attention, received hardly any recognition in the world of psychology and also played relatively little role in national development."

Relationship of Culture and Psychology

The relationship between culture and psychology is quite complex. Culture, has a myriad of manifestations at physical, social and psychological levels, and represents the close association of meanings and practices shared by a particular community. The influence of culture tends to persist across different time periods and is passed on to future generations. Cultural diversity in today's world is an obvious aspect of life and culture remains one of the central concerns for many disciplines including anthropology and sociology. Culture's conceptualization, however, has been quite varied in terms of scope (e.g. physical, subjective, symbolic) and level of treatment (e.g. super organic, meta-conceptual). This has led to varied approaches to the study of culture, which are distributed in the polar categories of internal/mind and external/objective environment. It is also viewed as the medium through which humans relate self to the environment. The different approaches toward conceptualizing culture have offered different spaces for undertaking the exploration of psychological issues.

It is interesting to note that while culture provides a context for any scholarly discourse, psychological theorization has remained largely accultural for a long time. Recent analyses of the history of the discipline (Brock 2006; Cole 1996), however, suggest that the interest of psychologists in understanding culture started in many forms beginning with the writings of people like Wilhelm Maxmilian Wundt, Lev S. Vygotsky and Wilhelm Dilthey. The acknowledgement of the explanatory power of evolutionary theory coupled with the acceptance of the natural science model as the prototype of science to be followed, psychological research has assumed a strong quantitative bias. However, such a perspective does not capture the fact that almost all domains of human endeavour exhibit the indelible mark of culture and humans are a "cultural species". In the recent past the cross-cultural, cultural and indigenous psychological movements have critically addressed the issue of the place of culture in psychological sciences in general and in understanding diverse psychological phenomena in particular. Thus, culture is used in the following ways: (a) context for behaviour, (b) complex/composite/unpackaged independent variable or treatment, and (c) as a dynamic meaning system irreducible to either the person or environment. In psychological research, however, scholars often take recourse to culture as an independent variable to explain variation in the behavioural outcomes and processes.

Self in Modern Psychology

The engagement of psychology in the aforementioned developments has largely been framed within the cultural imperative of the ideology of individualism which has shaped a unique conceptualization of selfhood. The self is inescapably localized in the "I". In this framework, "freedom" and "independence" are highly valued ingredients of self. Accordingly, a person's maturity is evaluated in terms of increasing level of individuation and separation from the group and society. This account of self is peculiarly Western in nature and under-represents the views held in many non-Western cultural contexts. There is growing evidence that many non-Western cultures as well as sub-cultures within the Western part of the world subscribe to less individualistic and more comprehensive models of self (Cross & Madson 1997; Enriquez 1992; Heelas & Locke 1981; Hsu 1985; Triandis 1989).

It is heartening to note that after being culturally blind for such a long time, the discipline has started moving towards culturally informed perspectives (Bruner 1990; D'Andrade & Strauss 1992; Kakar 1997; Gergen et al. 1996; Marsella 1998; Marsella et al. 1985; Misra & Gergen 1993). In some ways it is the revival of an old tradition of scholarship going back to Wundt, the author of *Volkerpsychologie.* Recent years have witnessed substantial increase in interest in cultural and indigenous approaches within psychology (Hwang 2012; Kitayama & Cohen 2007; Matthijs et al. 2011; Misra & Mohanty 2002; Rao et al. 2008; Valsiner & Rosa 2007). These approaches view culture either as a moderator or constitutive of psychological processes. Interestingly, this shift is coincided with the diverse happenings outside the academic world (e.g. increasing immigration, globalization, capital and labour flow, identity politics and so on). Also, the meaning of culture has undergone serious transformation. Instead of a "trait" approach, the term "culture" is employed more to connote a chronic social/political/economic situation or a set of circumstances which determines the kind of attributes, life ways and social practices prevalent in a given society (Kitayama & Cohen 2007). As such culture becomes an emergent property of individuals interacting with their environments. Hence it is inter-subjective, shared, and socially established system of meanings and practices. As a rich network of habits and experiences culture performs representational as well as prescriptive functions. Interestingly many of the accepted natural categories of current psychological theory (e.g. emotion and self) owe their existence to the cultural distinctions found in natural language categories and embodied in everyday social practices. In these efforts culture is viewed as a symbolic resource which amasses and gets transmitted across generations.

The Indian Cultural Context

The Indian culture with its rich heritage provides an interesting vantage point to contrast the predominant Western psychological perspective. In particular, it situates interactions and relationships not only in the context of other humans but also encompasses transcendental or spiritual reality. It has, however, yet not received enough attention. Cross & Gore (2005: 557) have remarked:

> Given the overwhelming proportion of North Americans who believe in a god or who practise some form of religion, it is puzzling that spirituality has largely been ignored in research on self and identity. . . . To date, Western researchers have paid little attention to this perspective on self.

The reluctance in attending to this aspect of self indicates that culturally informed research is yet to cover a large ground (Kitayama et al. 2007). It is to the credit of Rao that he courageously championed the cause of spiritual psychology in his edited volume *Towards a Spiritual Psychology* (Rao & Marwaha 2005).

For a long time, mainstream psychologists who believe in empiricism have been aspiring to generalize beyond their samples and advance universal theories. This goal is mired when investigators base research on data from limited and unrepresentative samples of human variety. Upon such critical scrutiny the widely celebrated and projected image of the universality of psychological knowledge becomes untenable on many counts.

First, the database does not furnish such a ground. As Arnett (2008) has shown, in the publications in the prestigious *Journal of Personality and Social Psychology* during 2003 to 2007 a vast majority (94 per cent) of the samples were from Western countries, with 62 per cent coming from the United States of America. Also, 67 per cent of the American samples (and 80 per cent of the non-American samples) were drawn from those enrolled in the undergraduate psychology courses.

Second, the available cross-cultural data tends to indicate that with respect to a number of basic psychological phenomena (1) members of industrialized societies respond differently than those from less industrialized societies; (2) the responses of people from Western industrialized societies evince more prominent responding than those from the non-Western societies; (3) within the Westerners, American participants show more extreme responses than others; and (4) the responses of contemporary American college students are even further different from those of non-college educated American adults. The samples of American college students are often colloquially referred to as "WEIRD samples" (i.e. they are samples of Western, educated, industrialized, rich, and democratic societies) (Henrich et al. 2010).

Third, the cultural variability in psychological phenomena has been documented in several areas including cognition, emotion, motivation, personality and modes of social interaction (Norenzayan & Heine 2005). In general, studies evince an intrinsic association of psychological phenomena with the meanings and practices of a culture. Investigations of cultural psychology suspect the assumption of psychic unity, as though the psychological processes are hardwired in a manner that the outcomes would remain invariant across cultures. There is growing convergence in favour of the position that the biological potentials rooted in evolutionary process get adjusted to the specific cultural meaning systems within which people grow and develop. Also, cultures emerge through engagements directed by the human drive for meaning making and the resources available to that end. It is in this sense that culture and psyche are seen as interdependent and co-constituted (Shweder 1990).

While marked cultural variance has been noticed in basic psychological phenomena including approach-avoidance motivations, formal reasoning (Nisbet et al. 2001) and moral reasoning (Miller & Bersoff 1992), there are indications of different degrees of universality in facial expressions of emotions (Ekman et al. 1969), sex differences in violence (Daly & Wilson 1988) and personality structure (McCrae et al. 2005).

Culture and Self-Understanding

Within the modern discipline of psychology the first serious analysis of self was attempted by William James (1890). Calling it psychology's most "puzzling puzzle" James held that "self is the centre of the psychological universe and is the lens through which other aspects of the world are perceived". Subsequently the psychological study of self was marginalized under the behaviourist anti-mentalistic suppositions. Being a philosophical construct, it was considered less appropriate for objective and empirical investigation. For George Herbart Mead (1934: 173) "self consciousness rather than affective experience . . . provides the core and primary structure of self, which is thus essentially a cognitive rather than an emotional phenomena". His cognitive emphasis was contested by subsequent theorists (Goffman 1967; Hochschild 1979) who held that emotion is a unique dimension, of social interaction. Mead proposed that the self has two primary dimensions, i.e. a reflexive process as well as a structured and internalized set of self-conceptions. While the former allows emergence and change in self, the latter helps in creating a coherent sense of self as an object that provides an anchor to the sense of being. They represent "I" and "Me", respectively. These processes and structural emphases result in positions of multiple situational identities (Blumer 1969; Goffman 1959) and the idea of a trans-situational core self in which social identities are hierarchically arranged in terms of salience and prominence.

While theorists like Charles Cooley, Geroge H. Mead, Herbert Blumer and Erving Goffman, and the Neo Freudians like Alfred Adler, Karen Horney and Harry Stack Sullivan did try to develop various perspectives on self, it was only during the last quarter of twentieth century that self could resurface as a theme. The resurrection of interest in the self in recent past owes to many factors including interest in the role of self-esteem, the cognitive revolution and the publication of several measures of dispositional attributes of self. The current interest in self is following two lines of research focusing on cognitive and motivational–emotional aspects, respectively (Leary & Tangney 2005). In today's psychological literature, there is a proliferation of self-related constructs (e.g. self-schema, self-disclosure, self-esteem, self-determination, self-categorization, self-monitoring, self-worth, self-consciousness, self-reference, self-awareness, self-efficacy). Underlying these constructs is a causally active and somewhat unitary self-structure. It is treated as free, autonomous, conscious, morally responsible, author of action, and holder of rights. To some, self is nothing but continuity of one's memory of mental events while others hold it as a pre-wired feature of human brain. The notions of private, public and collective selves have been differentiated (Triandis 1989). The notion of "possible selves" has also generated considerable interest among the researchers (Markus & Nurius 1986). The self-other differentiation, having an identity, and remembering self are also being studied. In recent years there has been a revival of interest in the study of self-related processes from clinical, developmental, social and cognitive perspectives and it is difficult to have a coherent conceptualization and definition of self.

In contrast to the above analysis the cultural approach attends to those aspects of self that develop through membership in some local cultural community and through a history of symbolically mediated experiences of that group. It assumes that the nature and experience of self depends to a large extent on early socialization, peer interaction and subsequent experiences in one's life. Our perception and experiences of self, therefore, are coloured by the culture(s) that we inhabit. The dialogues, narratives and other social discourses tell us as to how self is described, responded to and evaluated. Thus cultures help in representing and experiencing a self both as an object and as a subject of experience (Nandy 1983). It may however be noted that while culture supplies the scripts of how to conduct oneself and how to participate in a community, people too are active agents and constituents of culture (Oyserman & Markus 1993). People do change culture and the lives of many great leaders of the world substantiate this.

Search for Authentic Self

The self emerges as well as evolves as life progresses. It's a continuous process of "becoming" through "being", that has been the crux of many existential philosophies and the very essence of the Indian thought system. In being one's self, one mostly forgets the "being" aspect. None the less, "being" is the only element that gives a sense of aliveness, a sense of ownership and a sense of satisfaction in whatever one becomes. It's a continuous process of approximating something that is much higher and deeper. The moment this coherent flow of experiences, the stream of consciousness that comprises the being of the self, is frozen into rigid definitions of self-concept or self-esteem or identity or the "me" self, problems start to emerge. This is because of the tension between the dynamic (subject) and the static (object), between the inner and the outer dimensions of self and their unhealthy balance.

As has been discussed in the preceding sections, modern psychology has been overly identified with the notion of self as an object and all its endeavours are predominantly directed towards catering to this sense of self. Well, this may have some advantages, evidenced through the celebration of the behaviourist school of thought. None the less, this view falls short of embracing, explaining and accommodating the complex processes that constitute our social-cultural life.

Think for a moment to answer the question, "Who are you?"

Now, ponder over, "Who am I?"

One can see a difference in responses to both the questions. And a moment of reflection would also reveal a difference in one's inner frame of reference while answering the two questions. This indicates the difference between, what some 120 years ago Father of Psychology Sir William James termed, the "me self" (self as object) and the "I self" (self as subject). A lot of problems in modern living emanate from the self as object. Leary (2004) has written extensively on the curse of having a self. Indian philosopher J. Krishnamurti (1972) has located the source of problems in "self", which is an outcome of the conditioned mind. Erich Fromm (1976) enters into a detailed deliberation over "to have or to be". In fact, Carl Rogers (1961) said that communication breakdowns in relationships happen particularly because of lack of one's ability to talk to one's own self (the self as subject). These writings indicate the importance of both the experiencing "self" and the self which is experienced — the subject and the object. The problem is that in all our processes of socialization, the "objective" self is over-emphasized and the experiencing self, ignored. Happiness is the key to life, and such an outward conceptualization directs us in a way that happiness is searched for in objects, not in the moments of being happy. Due to overemphasis on "objects", the orientation shifts completely towards external existence. So, even when looking out for a life partner external beauty counts more than inner compatibility!

On the contrary, Indian psychology in its various forms has emphasized inner orientation, with the experiencing self as the reference point. Search for true self has been its central concern and authenticity, as the sole criterion of a worthwhile life, has been the cherished ideal. As has already been discussed, the Western view of self holds individuals as separate, autonomous entities constituted of traits, abilities, values, needs and motives (Markus & Kitayama 1991). The Indian perspective, on the other hand, "views human beings as bio-psycho-social-spiritual organisms" (Salagame 2011: 135). In this thought system the notion of "Self" (universal/cosmic Self) as a ground for existence has been widely emphasized. The individual self exists in its entirety in relation to an eco-system that includes the material, social and spiritual worlds (Misra 1999), and not as an ego-system. The person is considered a being, the sense of which is derived from the way one connects with the broader reality/ Self. The idea of broader reality serves as a foundation for one's being in some form. In fact the search of a true or authentic self (*ātmānām viddhi*) is held to be the prime goal of human life.

Rao (2011a: 457-58) addressed these and similar issues. He observes that the "primary and fundamental difference between Western and Indian perspectives [of the self] is that the former tends to view the self as an object whereas in the Indian theories, self is generally seen as the subject. Self can also be seen beyond the subject–object framework", as Advaita does. However, what he considers as specially important is that nearly all major systems of Indian thought, the Hindu as well as Buddhist, hold that the ego-centred self is not the authentic, but a pseudo-self. The search for and realization of the authentic self begin with the deconstruction of the ego. "If this approach is typical of Indian thought, it stands in utter contrast with concerns of psychologists in the West that strive to preserve the ego intact as the centre of the person," says Rao (2011a: 459).

Against this backdrop and aimed towards studying the subjective self, the authors, informed by the cultural approach and Indian psychological perspectives, have explored a very vital aspect of self-experience, i.e. authenticity.

Conceptualization of Authenticity

The concept of authenticity is an integral part of the notion of "being oneself" or "being true to oneself". The *Chambers Concise Dictionary* (1992) defines "authentic" as genuine, authoritative, true, and entitled to acceptance and of established credibility. *Oxford Advanced Learner's Dictionary* (2004) defines the word "authentic" as "known to be real and genuine and not a copy, true and accurate, made to be exactly the same as original". Authenticity has been derived from the Greek word "authentes" meaning author and indicates a person who scripts his own life story, who rules or who is the master, i.e. a person who is in charge of self. This requires living life on one's own terms, being the author of one's own destiny and following a chosen direction in life, guided by one's values and beliefs, rather than passively submitting to the external pressures or blind compliance with the wants and the expectations of others (Harter 2002).

There have been multitudes of perspectives on authenticity which have emphasized different aspects of it. Goldman & Kernis (2002: 294) have defined it as "the unobstructed operation of one's true- or core-self in one's daily enterprise". They have provided a four-component model of authenticity, comprising of awareness, unbiased processing of self-relevant information, behaviour and relational orientation. Their work assumes the essentialist view on self and emphasizes authenticity as the correspondence between inner and outer. The same was underlined by Rogers (1961) in his concept of congruence. Congruence occurs, says Rogers (1969: 228),

> When experiencing of this moment is present in my awareness and when what is present in my awareness is present in my communication, then each of these three levels matches or is congruent.

Another view holds that an important characteristic of authenticity is non-conformance to the prevailing societal and cultural norms. Rousseau (1979) viewed the dominant culture of his society as a powerful threat and obstacle to an authentic existence. Rousseau's authentic individual listens to his own heart, speaking and acting resolutely on its dictates. The existentialist philosophy regards choice as the key element in defining authenticity. For Sartre (1969), each individual is an agent endowed with unlimited freedom. His notion of freedom amounts to making spontaneous choices. In this context, authenticity is good faith wherein people must choose and create meaning in life and accept full responsibility for their actions. For Kierkegaard (1992), choice is the marker of an ethical life and it is what makes the reality of selfhood tangible and possible. An important feature of Kierkegaard's assertion was that authentic functioning reflects subjectivity in choices that involves people's "essential knowing"—knowledge that concerns the deepest meanings of existence. Within the framework of self-determination theory, Sheldon et al. (1997) hold that authenticity is a behaviour that is phenomenally experienced, as being authored by the self (Wild 1965) or internally caused (de Charms 1968; Ryan et al. 1995). People feel most authentic when they act with a full sense of choice and self-expression. Another approach which appears more promising for conceptualizing authenticity is the integrationist view of the self as a complex structure in which all parts are essential. Authenticity involves acknowledging and accepting all parts of the self and the harmonious functioning of all parts together as a whole (Sayers 1999). It is a matter of coherence, harmony, integrity or unity of social and individual elements, of public and private facets, and of seemingly paradoxical aspects of oneself. Burks & Robbins (2011: 96) based on their qualitative study state that

> authenticity involves consciously and mindfully striving for an awareness of one's values, beliefs, thoughts, and feelings, followed by maintaining consistency (or exploring the inconsistency) of those inward concepts with one's outward expressions and behaviours.

The Indian perspective on authenticity is an evolutionary perspective that is most encompassing and holistic for conceptualizing authenticity. If we keep aside the metaphysical differences in the various schools of Indian philosophical thought, there are common themes across these systems which are pertinent to our understanding of authenticity. One of them is the concept of universal, pure consciousness (referred to as *Brahman* in Advaita Vedānta and as *puruṣa* in Sāṁkhya-Yoga), which is at the heart of Indian thought. The other is the description of the person (*jīva*) as a series of five successive sheaths (*koṣas*), comprising of the body, the senses, mind, intellect and *ātman* — a purely and deeply spiritual entity or process that equals *Brahman* (the ubiquitous absolute which has no form or matter) (Bharati 1985; Mascolo et al. 2004). The Indian perspective in general believes that the difference between the embodied self and the highest self is metaphorical, and experienced as differentiated due to layers of ignorance. In reality there is only one absolute Self, the supreme consciousness, the *Brahman*. The goal of all lives is to evolve and become identified with this supreme reality.

> The goal in *yoga* is to transcend sense-bound mental processes to attain a stage of pure consciousness, *kaivalya*. Similarly, Advaita advocates achieving the transcendental state of pure consciousness which is realizing *Brahman* in one's being. — Rao 2010: 19

The realization of *ātman* as one's true self that is indistinguishable from the absolute reality (the *Brahman*) is a lifelong and effortful process. The Indian tradition also charts multitudes of pathways, procedures and practices to reach the true self. This transcendence is attainable as the states of pure consciousness are not merely metaphysical presuppositions, but empirically grounded in the genuine experience of a few persons. It enables the individual "to live authentically (*sat*) to know truth in a pristine fashion (*cit*) and to live in happiness (*ānanda*)" (Rao 2010: 20).

The spiritual interiority of Indian selfhood has significant implications for authenticity. Since at the core of our being, the innermost sheath of our existence lies in the all-pervading *Brahman*, an Absolute that makes us what we are, thus leading an authentic life implies a striving for relationship with one's true Self (*Brahman*) and realizing in reality all potential possibilities of our true nature. It is the process of transforming the empirical self to the true self of pure consciousness, and the realization of the universal oneness (oneness with the cosmic Divine and with all beings). Given that the Indian tradition is based on deep awareness of an implicit underlying unity, the striving "to be authentic" incorporates love and respect for others. An excerpt from Sri Aurobindo's *Synthesis of Yoga* (1970b) surmises what it means to be authentic. It states:

> To arrive at freedom, mastery and perfection we have to get back to the

> real self and soul within and arrive too thereby at our own true relations with our own and with universal nature.
>
> — Sri Aurobindo 1970b: 724-25

Insights from a Qualitative Study on Authenticity

As researchers of authenticity, the challenge was to ascertain how a thorough understanding of this subjective, inner-directed approach can optimally be gathered. Mainstream psychology has equipped us with a positivist lens of objectifying every process, to make it amenable for measurement. However, the experience of self as a multi-layered complex entity (multiple selves as some call it) in an equally complex environment brings forth the picture of dynamic flux and interplay of forces, which makes the reductionist, quantitative approach of studying it quite inadequate. Subjective nuances of inner life are hard to convert to tangible, measurable entities that can acquire scaled values. A viable approach is provided by the qualitative genre of inquiry, particularly the analysis of autobiographies and life stories. They help us engage in deeper explorations of the "subjective" self. An in-depth study of exemplary lives of great Indians can provide insights into the vicissitudes of their inner lives, the choices they made, and what went into the making of their authentic selves.

With this background, the life stories of two great Indians — Sri Aurobindo and Mahatma Gandhi — were studied and analysed to understand the nature and evolution of authenticity in their life trajectories. The focus was on the subjective meanings of authenticity as available in the narratives of their (auto)biographies — an inside–out means of studying these great lives.

> "Great men" . . . are selected because in them, uniquely, are found certain values and crises which have a much wider bearing on the age in which they lived than those of the "common man". — Plummer 1983: 88

It is essentially to share insights from the Indian tradition that we focus on these two modern Indian visionaries. These extraordinary men demonstrated the power of an authentic life in every way. Sri Aurobindo was a spiritual master and Gandhi, a spiritual leader. Both succeeded in transforming themselves in order to achieve a greater, selfless purpose. They were contemporaries and remarkable representatives of Indian culture in their own ways. Their storied lives were analysed qualitatively through the texts from Sri Aurobindo's *On Himself* (1972) and his biography by Nirodbaran (1990) *Sri Aurobindo for All Ages* and from

Gandhiji's autobiography *The Story of My Experiments with Truth* (1927). Overall, it can be seen as an endeavour to identify various facets, processes and challenges related to authenticity in these lives.

Life stories or autobiographies provide first-hand accounts of human experiences (social as well as personal) and reveal the subjective realm of life. Bogdan (1974: 4) says:

> The autobiography is unique in allowing us to view an individual in the context of his whole life, from birth to the point at which we encounter him. . . . It permits us to view the intersection of life history of men with the history of their society, thereby enabling us to understand better the choices, contingencies and options open to the individual.

Journeying into the subjective inner world of authentic persons can yield potent discoveries related to the processes of authentic selfhood, which no other inquiry (except perhaps auto-ethnography) can give. There were common themes that we identified in the lives of Sri Aurobindo and Mahatma Gandhi, which unfolded in different ways. What follows is a discussion on the major themes delineated from the life stories, highlighting certain central themes of authenticity and authentic living.

Metamorphosis: Journey of Self-Transformation

For Sri Aurobindo, it was a transformation from Aurobindo Ackroyd Ghose to Maharshi Sri Aurobindo and for Gandhi, it was from M.K. Gandhi to Mahatma Gandhi.

> I was extremely selfish and then something came upon me and I felt I ought to give up selfishness. I tried in my own way — of course imperfectly — to put it into practice. But that was a sort of turning point in my inner life. — *Sri Aurobindo for All Ages*: 10

An inner orientation characterized Sri Aurobindo's life since the very beginning. His childhood years were spent mostly in reading literature, writing poetry and learning new languages. That Sri Aurobindo's journey was more inwardly than on the outside is reflected in his words,

> . . . neither you nor anyone else knows anything at all of my life; it has not been on the surface for men to see. — *On Himself*: 378

On the other hand, Gandhi lived an active social life. The ordinariness in Gandhi during his early years is reflected in his accounts of what he calls "his failings", "tragedy" and "shame". These include his friendship with a person who instigates him into meat-eating (a taboo for Vaiṣṇavas); his brothel visit; his suspicions about his wife; stealing, smoking, lying; failure to practise sexual restraint, among other issues. However what sets Mahatma Gandhi apart was his "awareness" of these failings. As he mentions at different points in his biography (Gandhi 1927):

> Moreover, I was a coward. — p. 17

> I could not bear to talk to anybody. I was even afraid lest anyone should poke fun at me. —p. 5

> It took me long to get free from the shackles of lust, and I had to pass through many ordeals before I could overcome it. —p. 26

There were many such moments of weakness in Mahatma Gandhi's life. However, after each such experience he was engulfed by guilt, and absorbed in introspection, and the desire for atonement. This capacity — to realize his mistakes and reflect on his experiences — helped Mahatma Gandhi to reposition himself.

For Sri Aurobindo it was his *yoga sādhana* that catalyzed the metamorphosis, which was entirely internal.

> I came away (from politics) because I did not want anything to interfere with my *yoga* and because I got a very distinct *ādeśa* in the matter.
>
> — *On Himself*: 55

> I had no urge toward spirituality in me, I developed spirituality. I was incapable of understanding metaphysics, I developed into a philosopher. I had no eye for painting — I developed it by *yoga*. I transformed my nature from what it was to what it was not. I did it by a special manner, not by a miracle and I did it to show what could be done and how it could be done. I did not do it out of any personal necessity of my own or by a miracle without any process. . . . I also did not do it by myself, if you mean by myself the Aurobindo that was. He did it by the help of Kṛṣṇa and the Divine *Śakti*. I had help from human sources also."
>
> — *On Himself*: 148-49

The above quote helps us visualize as to how authenticity is a process of "transformation". Gandhi too transformed himself from a shy, timid boy to a courageous seeker of truth. His quest for truth was manifested through various experiments that he carried out with non-violence, celibacy, vegetarianism and other principles of conduct, including *satyāgraha*. The experiences and experiments have sustained me and given me great joy (Gandhi 1927: 420).

His decision to come back to South Africa and fight for the cause of Indians there, the Phoenix settlement, his water and earth treatment, experiments in dietetics, self-restraint, fasting, all these activities and experiments are not beyond the purview of human capacity, but they are not something everyone can have the courage to do. Mahatma Gandhi had that courage and aspiration to seek truth and self-purification in whatever he did. "He who would go for novel experiments must begin with himself. That leads to quicker discovery of truth, and God always protects the honest experimenter" (Gandhi 1927: 257). It is also important to note that on the part of both these seekers, transformation was an intentional and effortful process involving extreme rigour and discipline.

Acts of confession too hold great significance in shaping Mahatma Gandhi's life. They seemed to be a move towards being authentic in his life.

> A clear confession, combined with a promise never to commit the sin again, when offered before one who has the right to receive it, is the purest form of repentance. — Gandhi 1927: 24

Confession "is both a communicative and an expressive act, a narrative in which we (re)create ourselves by creating our own narrative, reworking the past, in public, or at least in dialogue with another" (Besley 2005: 370). It can be seen throughout his life that Mahatma Gandhi was fond of making confessions, and did so at many critical junctures in his social and personal life. These may have been his way of accepting parts of him by confessing things in public when he felt that he was not being true to himself or had in some way violated the two great values of *ahiṁsā* (non-violence) and *satya* (truth). Gandhi's protests against the unjust Rowlatt Act passed by the British turned violent at some places, despite his insistence on non-violent resistance. A pained Gandhi accepted the responsibility for misjudging his people's readiness for civil disobedience. He defused this threat by reorienting himself in the service of the higher purpose, without losing faith and composure:

> My confession (Himalayan miscalculation in calling upon people to launch upon civil disobedience prematurely) brought down upon me no small amount of ridicule. But I have never regretted having made that confession. For I have always held that it is only when one sees one's own mistakes with a convex lens and does just the reverse in the case of others, that one is able to arrive at a just relative estimate of the two. . . . With these thoughts filling my mind I reached Bombay, raised a corps of *satyāgrahī* volunteers through the *Satyāgraha Sabhā* there, and with their

> help commenced the work of educating the people with regard to the meaning and inner significance of *satyāgraha*. — Gandhi 1927: 391-92

Mahatma Gandhi's ability to learn from experience and his openness to new experience further fuelled his transformation and growth. The transformation in him was also marked by a change from an outer gaze to an inner orientation. During a short period of his stay in England he was obsessed with becoming an English gentleman and he spent good amount of money on this endeavour: Purchasing new clothes and accessories (like hat, double-watch chain of gold), attempting lessons in dancing, learning French elocution and even pursuing violin. But shortly afterwards, a realization came in and he embarked upon simple and plain living. He thought, "If my character made a gentleman of me, so much the better. Otherwise I should forgo the ambition" (Gandhi 1927: 44). Mahatma Gandhi's reference to the word "character" has an inward bearing.

> Let no one imagine that my experiments in dancing and the like marked a stage of indulgence in my life. The reader will have noticed that even then I had my wits about me. That period of infatuations was not unrelieved by a certain amount of self-introspection on my part.
>
> — Ibid.

This inner reflective gaze incorporated the attitude of accepting one's self as one is. Gandhi accepted his shyness.

> I must say that, beyond occasionally exposing me to laughter, my constitutional shyness has been no disadvantage whatever. — Ibid.: 53

> Thus in the very first battle of the kind, I found myself siding with the losing party. But I had comfort in the thought that the cause was right.
>
> — Ibid.: 51-52

Extraordinariness

The dynamism for both these great men manifested in the form of a continuous questioning of *status quo*. Both, Sri Aurobindo and Mahatma Gandhi were guided by superordinate ideals, rather than being content with the mundane. In this context, Sri Aurobindo's description of India and his call to the people of India to work for her freedom are extremely relevant. He said:

> Other people look upon the country as an inert piece of matter . . . to me She is the Mother. I adore Her, worship Her.
>
> — *Sri Aurobindo for All Ages*: 53

They never shied away from taking risks or moving beyond the comfort/ settled zones of their life.

> Poverty has never had any terror for me nor is it an incentive. . . . I left my very safe and "handsome" Baroda position without any need to do it and then I gave up also the Rupees 150 of National College Principalship leaving myself with nothing to live on . . . — *On Himself*: 357

> The separation from wife and children, the breaking up of a settled establishment, and the going from the certain to the uncertain — all this was for a moment painful, but I had inured myself to an uncertain life. I think it is wrong to expect certainties in this world, where all else but God that is truth is an uncertainty. — Gandhi 1927: 209-10

Mahatma Gandhi's entire life can be seen as an incessant effort to reform not just the society where discrimination and injustice of all sorts reigned, but also his own self.

> I have known only one way of carrying on missionary work, viz., by personal example and discussion with searchers for knowledge.
>
> — Ibid.: 223

Their efforts were constantly directed towards Truth. Their lives bear witness to the infinite possibilities within human beings for self-actualization and self-realization.

> Truth became my sole objective. — Ibid.: 29

> The one aim of [my] *yoga* is an inner self-development by which each one who follows it can in time discover the One Self in all and evolve a higher consciousness than the mental, a spiritual and supramental consciousness which will transform and divinize human nature.
>
> — *On Himself*: 97

In a letter to his wife Mrinalini, dated 30 August 1905, at the age of thirty-three years, Sri Aurobindo wrote:

> My second madness . . . is this: By whatever means I must have the direct vision of God. If God exists, there must be some way to experience His existence, to meet Him face to face. However arduous this path is, I have made up my mind to follow it. — *Sri Aurobindo for All Ages*: 53

> I worship God as Truth only. I have not yet found Him, but I am seeking after Him. I am prepared to sacrifice the things dearest to me in pursuit of this quest. — Gandhi 1927: xi

Dialectics of Life: Living Life in Shared Spaces

Self and other seem to be the anchors of experiencing authenticity. Authenticity involves negotiating the dichotomies of self-society/social roles, public–private and inner–outer. For some people it becomes a struggle, for some a challenge which is resolved with an undaunted sense of faith and conviction in the higher (spiritual) truth (and in themselves), which these two great men embodied.

For Sri Aurobindo and Mahatma Gandhi single-minded focus was none the less not beyond social, cultural influences. Life is a constant negotiation with external forces, at times constraining, in order to honour and safeguard our very selves, and create a sense of harmony in our being. This does not always entail fighting with those external forces, but does involve taming them, so that inner and outer reach a state of harmonious equilibrium. Sri Aurobindo's approach of negotiating inner–outer balance was quite unique and inspirational. First, his life

> exemplifies his insistence that a transformation in consciousness precedes and moulds personal and historical forms . . . inner precedes the outer realization . . . historical and institutional expression.
>
> — McDermott 2001: 14.

> Sri Aurobindo's habit in action was not to devise beforehand and plan but to keep a fixed purpose, watch events, prepare forces and act when he felt to be the right moment. His first organized work in politics . . . was undertaken at an early age, but took a regular shape in or about 1902; two years later he began his practice of *yoga* . . . to find spiritual strength which would support him and enlighten his way. — *On Himself*: 18

Second, his faith that Divine constitutes and inhabits all dissolved any dichotomy of inner and outer.

> My own life and my *yoga* have always been, since my coming to India, both this-worldly and other-worldly without any exclusiveness on either side. . . . For me all is *Brahman* and I find the Divine everywhere.
>
> — Ibid.: 98

Due to his belief that the inner work precedes the outer manifestation, Sri Aurobindo always preferred to remain in the background while participating in the Revolutionary Movement.

> I was never ardent about fame even in my political days; I preferred to remain behind the curtain, push people without their knowing it and get things done. — *Sri Aurobindo for All Ages*: 71

Mahatma Gandhi also followed a similar approach. Further, their actions under crucial circumstances demonstrate how an authentic person's actions are governed by a completely different kind of consciousness (attitude). Outwardly, to a lay person, it might appear as a very simple and average act, at times cowardly too. But such acts have their genesis in deeper layers of our being and are done for higher-order goals. When in Natal/ Durban (South Africa) Mahatma Gandhi was admitted as an advocate in the Supreme Court he was asked to remove his turban and he complied:

> I saw my limitations. The turban that I had insisted on wearing in the district magistrate's court I took off in obedience to the order of the Supreme Court. Not that, if I had resisted the order, the resistance could not have been justified. But I wanted to reserve my strength for fighting bigger battles. I should not exhaust my skill as a fighter insisting on retaining my turban. It was worthy of a better cause . . . this instance (was that) of the applicability of the principle of looking at a thing from different standpoint in different circumstances. But all my life through, the very insistence on truth has taught me to appreciate the beauty of compromise . . . this spirit was an essential part of *satyāgraha*. It has often meant endangering my life and incurring the displeasure of friends. But truth is hard as adamant and tender as a blossom. — Gandhi 1927: 123

This event is significant in attempting to understand authenticity, as initially when Mahatma Gandhi was asked to take off his turban by a district magistrate in Durban he had refused and had left the court. The episode elucidates that judgement of any act as right–wrong or authentic–inauthentic is contextual. His contradictory behaviours in both the situations (i.e. taking off the turban in one and not doing so in another) were authentic, though inconsistent with one another. The above incident shows that sensitivity to the context (its affordances and limitations, assessing the social forces) and awareness of greater good/larger goal are crucial ingredients of authentic living. A stance of detachment is also evident in Mahatma Gandhi's actions. He did not get overly sentimental about certain issues, which could be seen from one standpoint as having considerable potential for hurting his ego.

> I smarted under the insult, but as I had pocketed many such in the past I had become inured to them. I therefore decided to forget this latest one and take what course a dispassionate view of the case might suggest. . . . But even the community will have to pocket insults like these. Have we any alternative . . . I was fully conscious of the limitations of the community. — Ibid. 1927: 217

This stance of detachment was present throughout in the life of Sri Aurobindo:

> I have no special liking for the ideal of Śiva, though something of the Śiva temperament must necessarily be present. I never had any turn for rejection of the money power nor any attachment to it. One has to rise above these things; but it is precisely when one has risen above that one can more easily command them. — *On Himself*: 356

The "turban" instance also conveys that authenticity is not about consistency of behaviour. It is about maintaining a sense of being true to one's self in that very moment. Another instance through which the "beauty of compromise" can be understood is regarding Mahatma Gandhi's becoming a target of colour prejudice in South Africa while travelling in a train. After being thrown out of the train for insisting to travel in his authorized first-class compartment, when next day he continued his journey he complied and sat on coachman's seat instead of his authorized compartment. In his words:

> I knew it was sheer injustice and an insult, but I thought it better to pocket it. I could not have forced myself inside, and if I had raised a protest, the coach could have gone off without me. This would have meant the loss of another day, and heaven only knows what would have happened the next day. So, much as I fretted within myself, I prudently sat next to the coachmen. — Gandhi 1927: 95

What Gandhi did in such circumstances epitomizes responsibility in action. Schmid (2001: 225) recognizes that when a person in need reaches out to another person, "being authentic" means being there in response to another person in need. And "it is this capability of responsiveness from which response-ability evolves". Gandhi's actions of taking insults or behaving inconsistently in similar situations were a part of his "response-ability" to others in need of his services. Thus responsibility is a robust part of authenticity. As members of a collectivist culture, this position of appreciating beauty of a compromise is extremely relevant for living life in shared–relational spaces. These events in Gandhi's life also demonstrate what Parameshwar (2005: 696) refers to as "perspective agility", i.e. transcending one's own predicament and a compassionate noticing of other's suffering. Gandhi shows perspective agility in locating his circumstance in the broader context of racial discrimination. Rather it clearly indicates how an authentic individual struggles with and resolves challenges in the external environment. Sri Aurobindo rightly states:

> Our actual enemy is not any force exterior to ourselves, but our own crying weaknesses, our cowardice, our selfishness, our hypocrisy, our purblind sentimentalism. — *Sri Aurobindo for All Ages*: 40

This is also exemplified in the life of Mahatma Gandhi, who as a lawyer (popularly known as a "liar's profession") "never resorted to untruth in (his) profession" (Gandhi 1927: 302). "In my heart of hearts I always wished that I should win only if my client's case was right" (Ibid.). He had once asked the magistrate to decide a case against his client whom he found to be dishonest and deceiving. And it always had a positive result. Despite being in a profession that according to practical wisdom demands inauthenticity, Gandhi was able to steer through it without an iota of untruth.

> I was delighted . . . and I was confirmed in my conviction that it was not impossible to practise law without compromising truth. — Ibid.: 305

For Gandhi, *satyāgraha* was the primary means for his struggle for truth, with *ahiṁsā* (non-violence) as its soul. It seems to us that one of the most intense and beautiful ways of being authentic is *satyāgraha* (*sat* = truth, *āgraha* = firmness). This mode of authenticity appears as being a potently promising and functional one, as it in no way implies a self-centred way of responding. It is a "truth-centred" way of responding.

> Our creed was devotion to truth, and our business was the search for and insistence on truth. — Ibid.: 330

> I must say that, though these officers were so bad, I had nothing against them personally. I helped them too. . . . This attitude of mine put the officials with whom I came in contact perfectly at ease, and though I had often to fight with their department and use strong language, they remained quite friendly with me. . . . I learnt later that it was an essential part of *satyāgraha* and an attribute of *ahiṁsā*. Man and his deed are two distinct things. Whereas a good deed should call forth approbation and a wicked deed disapprobation, the doer of the deed, whether good or wicked always deserves respect or pity as the case may be. . . . This *ahiṁsā* is the basis of the search for truth. . . . It is quite proper to resist and attack a system, but to resist and attack its author is tantamount to resisting and attacking oneself. For we are all tarred with the same brush, and are children of one and the same Creator, and as such the/divine powers within us are infinite. — Ibid.: 230-31

Gandhi's philosophy integrated both personal and relational aspects of authenticity in his life and connected it to a universal cause (Sarvodaya). He translated this philosophy into action, with non-violence (not violating the being of other) as the relational aspect and Truth as the personal (upholding the principles of one's own being) as well as universal aspect. Rao (2011b) argued plausibly that Gandhian practices of *satyāgraha* and the like are applied spirituality. Rao (2011b: 25) writes:

> *Satyāgraha*, as Gandhi conceived it, is a collective *yoga* which is believed to generate spiritual force that transforms the adversary and the performer alike and brings about what would seem like a magical resolution of the problem. *Satyāgraha* is not merely a secular act mobilizing people and public opinion, but in its essential sense it is a kind of *yoga*, a resource of generating spiritual force.

According to Rao, Gandhi was a *yogin*, and *satyāgraha* is *yoga* of non-violence.

These were the ways through which Gandhi dealt with situations that were mostly overpowering and overwhelming (it should not be forgotten that he waged his struggles and reforms first in a foreign land and later in his own country which was under the clutches of British). They help us understand how deep faith in one's own self brings about fruitful outcomes. The outer circumstances are actually mirrors of our own self.

Context Sensitivity and Flexibility

Related to the above theme are the elements of "sensitivity to the contextual reality" and the "attitude of flexibility" inherent in any authentic position. This was seen in the life of both Mahatma Gandhi and Sri Aurobindo. While deciding about the most authentic way of responding in a given situation, an appraisal of the person, the relationship, the circumstances (its affordances and limitations, assessing the social forces) and an overarching meta-goal are necessary. This involves shaping the expression of one's true self accordingly and could also entail not doing what one's immediate sense of self says keeping in view the higher goals that one strives for. For this, flexibility in self is essential, along with "greater common good/well-being of all/harmony of larger existence" as the benchmark. But the behaviour is such that it keeps alive one's sense of being authentic.

> Self-assertion is not viewed as being authentic, but instead as being immature. Giving in is not a sign of weakness; rather, it reflects tolerance, self-control, flexibility and maturity. — Markus and Kitayama 1991: 229

Context sensitivity has been identified as a necessary quality of an authentic leader (Avolio et al. 2004). It is interesting to note that context sensitivity is also one of the core features of Indian psyche (Sinha & Kanungo 1997). In discussing their ideas on individualism in collectivist cultures like India, Sinha & Tripathi (1994: 199) mentioned that in Indian culture,

> actions are conditioned by the exigencies of situations . . . Though truth has a very high place in the Indian moral code, its practice is bound by context.

Apart from appreciating the beauty of a compromise through context sensitivity and awareness of greater common good, Mahatma Gandhi also steered his arduous path of authenticity with the help of his attitude of reconciling with the situation and making peace with it; and trying to understand the perspective of the other/outer. The very first way of managing a difficult situation is to accept that it is difficult, and then to respond to it in the best possible manner with patience and clarity of goals.

> Critical as my mind was in observing these things, there was enough charity in me, and so I always thought that it might after all be impossible to do better in the circumstances, and that saved me from undervaluing any work.
>
> — Gandhi 1927: 190

In responding to challenging circumstances Gandhi chose higher purpose and moral principles over societal norms and authority structures. He refused/dismissed the notice served on him by the police superintendent asking him to leave Champaran. Upon receiving summons to attend trial for disobeying the court order, he pleads guilty to having disobeyed the governmental order not out of disrespect but in obedience to the higher law of conscience and to give the country its first lesson in civil disobedience.

His attitude of non-resistance helped him overcome many barriers. At times not reacting, not retaliating and not asserting are better ways to maintain one's authenticity. Such acts cannot be regarded as cowardly but prudent. It is also interesting to note that civil disobedience and non-resistance are seemingly opposite to one another, with one entailing reaction/resistance and the other non-reaction. But both can be an authentic way of responding to a given situation. Gandhi made use of both to reconcile with varying situations and uphold his principles of truth and non-violence.

Both Sri Aurobindo and Mahatma Gandhi were at peace with their self and experienced joy in their actions. They had a clear vision of the purpose and meaning of their lives and had compassion for others. Because of their awareness of the divine interiority of self, they were always in a state of receptivity, inner joy, energy, progress, strength and freedom.

> When someone is destined for the path, all circumstances through all the deviations of mind and life help in one way or another to lead him to it. It is his own psychic being within him and Divine Power above that use to that end the vicissitudes both of mind and outward circumstance.
> — Sri Aurobindo (1970a): 550

A striking similarity between these two great Indians was their experienced conviction that action must be disciplined, this conviction being rooted in spirituality. The very title of their autobiographies bears a common theme, that of detachment. The two approaches that were inherent in the way they related to themselves and to others are:

a. Relating to one's self as an "other" (objectively) — This stance of detachment was evident in the lives of Mahatma Gandhi and Sri Aurobindo. In *On Himself*, Sri Aurobindo addresses himself in third person, with objectivity and detachment being inbuilt in such a stance. The phrase "Experiments with Truth" seems to embody an active, playful as well as detached orientation towards life. Detachment gave them the power of freedom to do what probably every Indian aspires for.

b. Relating to the other as incorporated in one's self (extended self) — This view is the most profound one as it holds the spiritual principle of "unity" or "undifferentiated consciousness", the notion of a universal, extended self. Not surprisingly, the lives of Sri Aurobindo and Mahatma Gandhi exemplified this way of living. The strong faith of both modern Indian visionaries that the "Divine constitutes and dwells all" fuelled their untiring efforts towards universal upliftment and well-being. It involves, at a deeper level, transcendence of the self–other dichotomy towards a more complete and whole existence.

The preceding analysis reckons authenticity as the process of "Being to Becoming". This "becoming" is translated as the growth and expansion of one's consciousness towards unity with the absolute Truth or *Brahman* or *ātman*. Parameshwar (2005: 713) emphasizes:

> Although scholars differ in the number of levels of consciousness and the terms used to designate them, there is broad agreement that at the farthest spectrum of consciousness, the individual "I" is fully transcended and the pure consciousness of "Spirit" is all that remains.

Using Smith's (1991) analysis of religions, she posits that the wider the self's identification (one person may identify with their family, while another may identify with humanity), the more one approximates "God's eye-view", and the more one is able to experience the non-dual *Brahman* in everything.

Elaborating on the conception of "person" Schmid (2001) remarks that "person" is comprised of two un-renounceable dimensions of human existence: The individual aspect of being a person and the relational or dialogical aspect of becoming a person. It is only through relationships with others that a person (being) develops and actualizes himself (becoming). Both of these ways of understanding the human being might appear contrary or even conflicting, yet it is precisely this tension of autonomy and interconnectedness (or relationality), which uniquely characterizes the reality of being human. Schmid notes:

> Thus essential elements of the person are both, independence and dependence on relationships, sovereignty and commitment, autonomy and solidarity. Only in the dialectic of both interpretations, not in an "either-or", but in a "both-and" does the mystery of the person become accessible to whoever allows himself or herself to become involved in a relationship from person to person. — 2001: 219

Apart from establishing authenticity as a process of growth (and not as an all-or-none state/trait), the study of these life stories helps in identifying certain processes and attributes which catalyse this growth. They can be presented in terms of four broad categories — motivational, cognitive, behavioural and affective. The motivational aspect covers strong aspiration for truth, quest for growth, continuous questioning of the *status quo* and a deep sense of mission and purpose in life, which is particularly prosocial and for the collective good. The cognitive components comprise of the belief that the Divine constitutes everything and is the only truth of existence, awareness of greater common goals, attitude of non-resistance in certain circumstances, sense of detachment, non-egoist attitude, self acceptance, inter-personal and context sensitivity, and the conviction that inner precedes outer realization. The behavioural components include the efforts one builds up to aid the transformation and consists of discipline (for example the self-restraint practised by Mahatma Gandhi through various experiments), spiritual practice (*sādhanā*), ego transcendence, social service and *satyāgraha*. Stability, equanimity, simplicity, meaningfulness and compassion constitute the affective components.

Thus authentic living implies knowing and accepting the true self and acting with detachment, determination and conviction, rather than being shaped by superficial conventions and whims. Both these men chose higher purpose over societal norms. Sri Aurobindo was groomed to become an Englishman, he instead became an Indian spiritual seeker. Mahatma Gandhi became an extraordinary ordinary man. His life clearly establishes that the spiritual law does not work in a vacuum, but is expressed through the ordinary activities of life. This aspiration to relate the search for spirit/ soul to the problems of everyday life runs like a thread throughout Gandhi's life. Their lives also bear witness to the power of the cultural and social dimensions of our existence, and the necessity of a continuous negotiation with it as integral to living authentically. For freedom and dignity, Sri Aurobindo joined Baroda State Services instead of Indian Civil Services (ICS). He chose to participate in the freedom struggle indirectly or rather implicitly, so that his work would not be hampered. Mahatma Gandhi pocketed insults multiple times in South Africa in order to accomplish his larger mission of helping Indians against discrimination. "My experience has shown me that we win justice quickest by rendering justice to the other party" (Gandhi 1927: 151). His struggles against racial discrimination in South Africa — his untiring efforts in terms of launching campaigns, managing Natal Indian Congress and getting discriminatory legislations changed in favour of the Indians staying in South Africa — were recurring ordeals. With respect to the opposition to the exploitative heavy taxation of indentured Indians by Natal government, which took more than twenty years to be successful, he said:

> But truth triumphed in the end. The sufferings of the Indians were the expression of that truth. Yet it would not have triumphed except for unflinching faith, great patience and incessant effort. Had the community given up the struggle, had the Congress abandoned the campaign and submitted to the tax as inevitable, the hated impost would have continued to be levied from the indentured Indians until this day, to the eternal shame of the Indians in South Africa and of the whole of India.
>
> — Ibid.: 131

Such instances show that an authentic person prefers to struggle with faith, courage and optimism rather than easily succumb to the external conditions.

> In responding to challenging circumstances, the leaders defuse ego threats by transcending their ego and by enlarging their commitment to

> their higher purpose rather than by protecting their ego and shortchanging their higher purpose. — Parameshwar 2005: 703

An authentic person can never negate or disown his true self and has the necessary strength to stand for what he believes to be true. In existentialist thought a person is construed as "Dasein", which indicates the concretely existing human being who is there as part of a world (being-in-the-world). The person and the world are co-constituted, and not separate entities. Hence personal authenticity operates in relation to others. It entails responsibility not only toward one's self, but also toward others, so that a sense of wholeness is experienced with all the paradoxes and complexities, as well as all the simplicities and harmonies.

The analysis also reveals cultural differences in the ways authenticity is experienced and hence conceptualized. The Western conception of authenticity has been limited to certain dimensions like freedom of choice/ self-regulation, self-awareness, self-acceptance, accepting external influence, congruence in behaviour and relational orientation. Issues of connected existence, of responsibility, of shared goals, of concern for other's needs and well-being have not been given due status in conceptualizing authenticity. The lives of Sri Aurobindo and Mahatma Gandhi are important torch bearers in this regard, as means to understand a more holistic conception of authentic living. The finding of the present research is pivotal as the concept of authenticity has evolved from the limits of individualism into a more relational and responsible arena. Extensive literature on the nature of Indian self construal as relational, interdependent and collectivistic exists and throws light on the inadequacies in the Western ways of conceptualizing psychological processes. However, the present analysis of biographies reveals how autonomy as well as compromise, freedom as well as responsibility constitute authenticity. Thus, autonomy/individualism/independence and relatedness/connectedness/interdependence cannot be considered dichotomous extremes that cannot be bridged. The beauty of an authentic existence is how it holds these aspects together without compromising on a sense of being true to the self and others.

In this sense the process of authenticity is intrinsically spiritual and involves self-transcendence. Accentuating the spiritual component further is the picture of authenticity as a journey of finding one's real Self — the Divine or the Soul. This journey towards finding the divine essence of our self is effortful, and has the built-in process of moving beyond the limits of the ego and its selfishness. The effort of the ideology of individualism was for partitioning the self and non-self as two opposite and exclusive categories, which resulted in treating humans as self-sufficient and the *ahaṁkāra* (ego) model of self (Misra 2010). However, in the present analysis authenticity comes across as a spiritual journey. This journey is not just about one's growth, but also the growth of others. Authentic existence involves a clear-sighted recognition that, at the deepest level, being human does not consist of self-encapsulated individuals in unavoidable conflict with others (Guignon 1993: 235), but having a broader existence. The lives of Sri Aurobindo and Mahatma Gandhi substantiate this to a great extent. Both succeeded in transforming themselves into remarkable and inspiring seekers of Truth and the Divine, thereby being able to achieve great, selfless goals. They demystified authenticity and established that the authenticity of a spiritual level is in continuity with the authenticity of everyday life. This analysis of authenticity suggests that the discipline of psychology would become more universal and enriched if it moves towards culture-inclusiveness and openness to ideas from outside the Western tradition.

To conclude, this effort to study the authentic self is inspired by Indian psychological thought, which as Rao sees is rich in conceptual wisdom and methodological resources. During his long career and extensive publications Rao pointed to numerous other areas that would be greatly enriched by studying them from the perspective of Indian psychology. His vision is of a holistic, inclusive psychology with appropriate theories, technologies and techniques. His mission is to spread this message and inspire a new generation of scholars around the world and help "open up new frontiers for serious psychological study and research anchored in Indian conceptual system" (Rao et al. 2008: 8). There is good reason to think that his vision and mission are likely to be realized sooner than he himself has envisaged.

Acknowledgement

Authors are grateful to Dr Preeti Kapur and Ms Ujwalla Bhandari for their comments on a earlier draft of this paper. Part of the work was supported by an R&D Grant from the University of Delhi to the second author.

References

Arnett, J.J. (2008), "The Neglected 95%: Why American Psychology Needs to Become Less American", *American Psychologist*, 63: 602-14.

Aurobindo, Sri (1970a), *Letters on Yoga* (parts 1-4), Pondicherry: Sri Aurobindo Ashram.

——— (1970b), *The Synthesis of Yoga*, Pondicherry: Sri Aurobindo Ashram.

———, (1972), *On Himself*, Pondicherry: Sri Aurobindo Ashram.

Avolio, B.J., W.L. Gardner, F.O. Walumbwa, F. Luthans, and D.R. May (2004), "Unlocking the Mask: A Look at the Process by Which Authentic Leaders Impact Follower Attitudes and Behaviors", *The Leadership Quarterly*, 15: 801-23.

Besley, A.C. (2005), "Self-Denial or Self-Mastery? Foucault's Genealogy of the Confessional Self", *British Journal of Guidance & Counseling*, 33: 365-82.

Bharati, A. (1985), "The Self in Hindu Thought and Action", in G. Marsella, A.J. DeVos and F.L.K. Hsu (eds.) *Culture and Self*, New York: Tavistock, pp. 185-230.

Blumer, H. (1969), *Symbolic Interactionism*, Englewood Cliffs, NJ: Prentice Hall.

Bogdan, R. (1974), *Being Different: The Autobiography of Jane Fry*, Toronto: Wiley.

Brock, A.C. (2006), *Internationalizing the History of Psychology*, New York: New York University Press.

Bruner, J. (1990), *Acts of Meaning*, Cambridge, MA: Harvard University Press.

Burks, D.J. and R. Robbins (2011) "Psychologists' Authenticity: Implications for Work in Professional and Therapeutic Settings", *Journal of Humanistic Psychology*, 52: 75-104.

Cole, M. (1996), *Cultural Psychology: A Once and Future Discipline*, Cambridge, MA: Harvard University Press.

Cross, S.E. and J.S. Gore (2005), "Cultural Models of the Self", in M.R. Leary and J.P. Tangney (eds.) *Handbook of Self and Identity*, New York: Guilford Press, pp. 536-64.

Cross, S.E. and L. Madson (1997), "Models of the Self: Self-Construals and Gender, *Psychological Bulletin*, 122: 5-37.

D'Andrade, R.G. and C. Strauss (eds.) (1992), *Human Motives and Cultural Models*. Cambridge, England: Cambridge University Press.

Daly, M. and M.I. Wilson (1988), "The Darwinian Psychology of Discriminative Parental Solicitude", *Nebraska Symposium on Motivation*, 35: 91-144.

de Charms, R. (1968), *Personal Causation: The Internal Affective Determinants of Behavior*, New York: Academic Press.

Ekman, P., E.R. Sorenson and W.V. Friesen (1969), "Pan-Cultural Elements in Facial Display of Emotions", *Science*, 164: 86-88.

Enriquez, V.G. (1992), *From Colonial to Liberation Psychology*, Quezon City: University of the Philippines Press.

Fromm, E. (1976), *To Have or to Be?*, New York: Harper & Row.

Gandhi, M.K. (1927), *The Story of My Experiments with Truth* (tr. from the Gujarati by Mahadev Desai), Ahmedabad: Navajivan Publishing House.

Gergen, K.J., A. Gulerce, A. Lock and G. Misra (1996), "Psychological Science in Cultural Context", *American Psychologist*, 51: 496-503.

Goffman, E. (1959), *The Presentation of Self in Everyday Life*, Garden City, NY: Doubleday.

——— (1967), *Interaction Ritual: Essays on Face-to-Face Behaviour*, Allen Lane: The Penguin Press.

Goldman, B.M. and M.H. Kernis (2002), "The Role of Authenticity in Healthy Psychological Functioning and Subjective Well-being", *Annals of the American Psychotherapy Association*, 5: 18-20.

Guignon, C.B. (1993), "Authenticity, Moral Values, and Psychotherapy", in C.B. Guignon (ed.) *The Cambridge Companion to Heideggar*, Cambridge (UK): Cambridge University Press.

Harter, S. (2002), "Authenticity", in C.R. Snyder and S.J. Lopez (eds.) *Handbook of Positive Psychology*, Oxford, England: Oxford University Press, pp. 382-94.

Heelas, P. and A. Locke (eds.) (1981), *Indigenous Psychologies*, London: Academic Press.

Henrich, J., S.J. Heine and A. Norenzayan (2010), "The Weirdest People in the World?", *Behavioral and Brain Sciences*, 33: 61-83.

Hochschild, A.R. (1979), "Emotion Work, Feeling Rules, and Social Structure", *American Journal of Sociology*, 85: 551-75.

Hsu, F.L.K. (1985), "The Self in Cross-Cultural Perspective", in A.J. Marsella, G. DeVos and F.L.K. Hsu (eds.) *Culture and Self*, London: Tavistock, pp. 24-55.

Hwang, Kwang-Kuo (2012) *Foundations of Chinese Psychology: Confucian Social Relations*, New York: Springer.

James, W. (1890), *The Principles of Psychology*, New York: Holt.

Kakar, S. (1997), *Culture and Psyche*, Delhi: Oxford University Press.

Kierkegaard, S. (1992/1843), *Either/or: A Fragment of Life*, tr. Alastair Hannay, London: Penguin Books.

Kitayama, S. and D. Cohen (eds.) (2007), *Handbook of Cultural Psychology*, New York: Guilford.

Kitayama, S., S. Duffy and Y. Uchida (2007), "Self as Cultural Mode of Being", in S. Kitayama and D. Cohen (eds.) *Handbook of Cultural Psychology*, New York: Guilford, pp. 136-74.

Krishnamurty, J. (1972), *What Are You Doing with Your Life?*, Chennai: Krishnamurty Foundation India.

Leahey, T.H. (1987), *A History of Psychology: Main Currents in Psychological Thought*, 2nd edn., Englewood Cliffs, NJ: Prentice-Hall.

Leary, M.R. (2004), *The Curse of the Self: Self Awareness, Egotism, and the Quality of Human Life*, New York: Oxford University Press.

Leary, M.R. and J.P. Tangney (eds.) (2005), *Handbook of Self and Identity*, New York: Guilford Press.

Markus, H.R. and S. Kitayama (1991), "Culture and the Self: Implications for Cognition, Emotion and Motivation", *Psychological Review*, 98: 224-53.

Markus, H. and P. Nurius (1986), "Possible Selves", *American Psychologist*, 41: 954-69.

Marsella, A.J. (1998), "Toward a 'Global Community-psychology': Meeting the Needs of a Changing World", *American Psychologist*, 53: 1282-91.

Marsella, A., G. De Vos and F.L.K. Hsu (eds.) (1985), *Culture and Self*, London: Tavistock.

Mascolo, M.F., G. Misra and C. Rapisardi (2004), "Individual and Relational Conceptions of Self in India and the United States", *New Directions for Child and Adolescent Development*, 104: 9-26.

Matthijs, C., G. Misra and S. Varma (eds.) (2011), *Foundations of Indian Psychology*, New Delhi: Pearson.

McCrae, R.R., A. Terracciano, and 79 Members of the Personality Profiles of Cultures Project (2005), "Personality Profiles of Cultures: Aggregate Personality Traits", *Journal of Personality and Social Psychology*, 89: 407-25.

McDermott, R. (ed.) (2001), *The Essential Aurobindo: Writings of Sri Aurobindo*, Great Barrington: Lindinsfarne Books.

Mead, G.H. (1934), *Mind, Self and Society*, Chicago: University of Chicago Press.

Miller, J.G. and D.M. Bersoff (1992), "Culture and Moral Judgment: How Are Conflicts Between Justice and Interpersonal Responsibilities Resolved?", *Journal of Personality and Social Psychology*, 62: 541-54.

Misra, G. (1999), "Cultural Diversity and Control", *Indian Psychological Review*, 53: 180-99.

——— (2010), "Being and Becoming: The Indian Quest for Competence", in D.K. Bhattacharjee, A. Sibia, P.K. Mishra and S. Gulati (eds.) *Psychology and Education: Indian Perspectives*, New Delhi: NCERT, pp. 268-78.

Misra, G. and K.J. Gergen (1993), "Beyond Scientific Colonialism: A Reply to Poortinga and Triandis", *International Journal of Psychology*, 28: 251-54.

Misra, G. and A.K. Mohanty (eds.) (2002), *Perspectives on Indigenous Psychology*, New Delhi: Concept.

Nandy, A. (1983), *The Intimate Enemy: Loss and Recovery of Self Under Colonialism*, Delhi: Oxford University Press.

Nirodbaran (1990), *Sri Aurobindo for All Ages: A Biography*, Pondicherry: Sri Aurobindo Ashram.

Nisbett, R.E., K. Peng, I. Choi and A. Norenzayan (2001), "Culture and Systems of Thought Holistic versus Analytic Cognition", *Psychological Review*, 108: 291-310.

Norenzayan, A. and S.J. Heine (2005), "Psychological Universals: What Are They and How Can We Know?", *Psychological Bulletin*, 131: 763-84.

Oyserman, D. and H.R. Markus (1993), "The Sociocultural Self", in J.M. Suls (ed.) *Psychological Perspectives on the Self*, vol. 4, Hillsdale, NJ: Erlbaum.

Oxford University Press (2004), *Oxford Advanced Learner's Dictionary* (7th edn.). Oxford: Oxford University Press.

Parameshwar, S. (2005), "Spiritual Leadership Through Ego-Transcendence: Exceptional Responses to Challenging Circumstances", *The Leadership Quarterly*, 16: 689-722.

Plummer, K. (1983), *Documents of Life: An Introduction to the Problems and Literature of a Humanistic Method*, London: George Allen and Unwin.

Rao, K. Ramakrishna (2010), "Indian Psychology: Towards a Psychology of the Future, in D.K. Bhattacharjee, A. Sibia, P.K. Mishra and S. Gulati (eds.) *Psychology and Education: Indian Perspectives*, New Delhi: NCERT, pp. 5-33.

——— (2011a), *Cognitive Anomalies, Consciousness and Yoga*, New Delhi: Centre for Studies in Civilizations and Matrix Publishers.

——— (2011b), *Gandhi and Applied Spirituality*, New Delhi: Indian Council of Philosophical Research and Matrix Publishers.

——— (2012), "Indian Psychology Curriculum: Moving Beyond Borrowed Knowledge", in C. Alvarcs and S.S. Faruqi (eds.) *Decolonizing the University: The Emerging Quest for Non-European Paradigms*, Pulan Pinang: Penerbit Universti Sains Malaysia, pp. 255-66.

Rao, K. Ramakrishna and S.B. Marwaha (eds.) (2005), *Towards a Spiritual Psychology: Essays in Indian Psychology*, New Delhi: Samvad India Foundation.

Rao, K. Ramakrishna, A.C. Paranjpe and A.K. Dalal (eds.) (2008), *Handbook of Indian Psychology*, New Delhi: Cambridge University Press.

Rogers, C.R. (1961), *On Becoming a Person: A Therapist's View of Psychotherapy*, Boston: Houghton Mifflin.

——— (1969), *Freedom to Learn*, Ohio: Charles E. Merrill Publishing Co.

Rousseau, Jean-Jacques (1979), *Emile*, United States of America: Basic Books.

Ryan, R.M., E.L. Deci and W.S. Grolnick (1995), "Autonomy, Relatedness, and the Self: Their Relation to Development and Psychopathology", in D. Cicchetti and D.J. Cohen (eds.) *Developmental Psychopathology*: vol. 1: Theory and Methods, New York: Wiley, pp. 618-55.

Salagame, K.K.K. (2011), "Ego and *Ahamkara*: Self and Identity in Modern Psychology and Indian Thought", in R.M.M. Cornelissen, G. Misra and S. Verma (eds.) *Foundations of Indian Psychology: Theories and Concepts*, Delhi: Pearson, pp. 133-45.

Sartre, J.P. (1969), *Being and Nothingness* tr. H.E. Barnes, London: Methuen.

Sayers, S. (1999), "The Concept of Authenticity", retrieved from http://www.kent.ac.uk/secl/philosophy/articles/sayers/authenticity.pdf (accessed on 22 November 2009).

Schmid, P.F. (2001), "Authenticity: The Person as His or Her Own Author: Dialogical and Ethical Perspectives on Therapy as an Encounter Relationship and Beyond", in G. Wyatt (ed.) *Rogers' Therapeutic Conditions Evolution, Theory and Practice*, vol. 1: Congruence, Rosson-Wye: PCCS Books, pp. 217-32.

Sheldon, K.M., R.M. Ryan, L.J. Rawsthorne and B. Ilardi (1997), "Trait Self and True Self: Cross-Role Variation in the Big-Five Personality Traits and Its Relations with Psychological Authenticity and Subjective Well-being", *Journal of Personality and Social Psychology*, 73: 1380-93.

Shweder, R.A. (1990), Cultural Psychology: What Is It?", in J.E. Stigler, R.A. Shweder and G. Herdt (eds.) *Cultural Psychology: Essays on Comparative Human Development*, New York: Cambridge University Press, pp. 1-43.

Sinha, J.B.P. and R.N. Kanungo (1997), "Context Sensitivity and Balancing in Indian Organizational Behaviour", *International Journal of Psychology*, 32(2): 93-105.

Sinha, D. and R.C. Tripathi (1994), "Individualism in a Collectivist Culture: A Case of Coexistence of Opposites", in T.S. Saraswathi (2003) (ed.) *Cross-Cultural Perspectives in Human Development: Theory, Research, and Applications*, New Delhi: Sage, pp. 192-211.

Smith, H. (1991), *The World's Religions: Our Great Wisdom Traditions*, New York: Harper-Collins.

Triandis, H.C. (1989), "The Self and Social Behaviour in Differing Cultural Contexts", *Psychological Review*, 96: 506-20.

Valsiner, J. and A. Rosa (eds.) (2007), *The Cambridge Handbook of Sociocultural Psychology*, New York: Cambridge University Press.

W&R Chambers Ltd. (1992), *Chambers Concise Dictionary*, New Delhi: Allied Chambers India.

Wild, J. (1965), "Authentic Existence: A New Approach to 'Value Theory'", in J.M. Edie (ed.) *An Invitation to Phenomenology: Studies in the Philosophy of Experience*, Chicago: Quadrangle Books, pp. 59-78.

Wundt, W.M. (1904), *Vökerpsychologie: eine Untersuchung der Entwicklungsgesetze von Sprache, Mythus und Sitte*, Leipzig: Wilhelm Engelmann.

7

K. Ramakrishna Rao's Mission to Link the Wisdom of East and West

Jean L. Kristeller

I FIRST met Dr Ramakrishna Rao when we both presented at a conference on spirituality and health sponsored by the Metanexus Institute in 2003 at Villanova University near Philadelphia, Pennsylvania. He had invited me to breakfast to ask me more about a talk I had given the day before on a multi-domain model of meditation practice, in which I had emphasized the importance of considering the spiritual aspects of meditative experience as much (or more so) than the physiological or cognitive effects. During breakfast, he also opened my eyes to his life's work. In doing so, he helped me to deepen my appreciation even further of the contributions of Indian psychology to understanding meditation practice and to developing current dialogues between the East and the West. I am particularly honoured to be asked to contribute to this book because, in a sense, he pushed me to expand my own thinking regarding the psychology of meditation, from being primarily focused on Buddhist psychology, to re-engaging the profound contribution of Indian psychology to both the dissemination and the substance of the growing practice of meditation in the United States over the last 100 or more years.

He shared with me at that breakfast that he was compiling a textbook on Indian psychology (Rao et al. 2008) which was to be the first in many decades pulling together the breadth and depth of Indian perspectives on understanding human functioning. I recall being quite surprised that such a substantive gap existed in India. I am now aware how hard he has worked his entire career at both a national and international level, to address this gap.

In my talk, I had also spoken to the commonalities among the different meditative traditions as they are being recognized within the major religious traditions of the world. Apparently, these conceptual perspectives, which are also reflected in my own research and teaching of meditation, resonated with him, and by the end of our conversation, I was immensely honoured to be asked to contribute the chapter on meditation to that textbook (Kristeller & Rikhye 2008). Thus began our professional relationship, one which has now extended to a valuable friendship.

I am now doubly pleased to be asked to contribute to this volume. However, I am also somewhat challenged as to how to proceed, for I have had little opportunity to work with Rao, other than noted above and as his host for a visit to my university. I then presumed I would read through his writings in preparation — until it became very quickly apparent that to do so would be a truly daunting task, given the sheer quantity and sophisticated thinking reflected therein. I am therefore limited to reflecting on those aspects of his body of work which most clearly interface with my own areas of research and professional perspectives. These include his astute observations in three areas: (1) exploring from a psychological perspective both the breadth and the depth of meditation practice; (2) the role of spirituality as a valid and core aspect of human experience; and (3) the contributions of Eastern or Asian perspectives to investigating the fullest range of human functioning (Rao 2002).

Perhaps I will reflect first on the value of cross-cultural perspectives in appreciating the range of human experience. It is apparent in reading Rao's work how deeply and profoundly he has engaged this question, from the very beginning of his career, and more recently as described in his book *Consciousness Studies: Cross-cultural Perspectives*. He has taken on as his life's work promoting ways to integrate wisdom arising from Indian culture, scholarship and epistemology not only into the Westernized psychology that had become dominant in India, but also into arenas within Western psychology that have called for a broader framework of methodology and openness to wider questions, including the controversial arena of parapsychology, and subsequently, meditation research and spirituality.

Until Rao shared with me the background and inspiration for developing his *Handbook of Indian Psychology* (Rao et al. 2008), I had had little awareness of the enormous gap that had developed in India between the dominant Westernized perspectives and traditional Indian approaches to understanding human consciousness. Over the years, in the context of my own research, I had certainly kept abreast of the empirical literature coming out of India on meditation practice (at least that which is accessible to me in English-language journals), and I had presumed that such research represented just a small portion of ongoing psychological research in India relevant to Indian perspectives on human functioning. Rao addresses this in his excellent review of the meditation literature (Rao 2011a), by identifying the very small proportion of such research that has been carried out in India or by Indians. But I had thought otherwise. I also have had Indian colleagues, including an Indian doctoral student, Kobita Rikhye, in our programme in clinical psychology at Indiana State University, and I had presumed that Indian psychology, both infused by Western thought (my student had an excellent foundation in contemporary Western psychological perspectives) and by traditional perspectives, was alive and well, and had been part of her own background of study. Unfortunately, I have never had the opportunity to travel to India, so was more familiar with the state of psychological research in other parts of Asia, where I had spent time, notably in Japan, China and Thailand.

At the same time, my first exposure to meditation and to Indian psychology was through Transcendental Meditation (TM), in 1971. TM was taking the US by storm; I was an undergraduate at Swarthmore College, and had already made the decision to become a psychologist. The concept of mind–body medicine was not yet being widely taught, and it was deemed somewhat odd that I had an interest both in physiological psychology and in clinical psychology. Given these interests, however, I resonated to the posters promoting TM that were evident around campus and that focused primarily on the effects of meditation on producing physical relaxation effects, such as heart rate and blood pressure reductions.

I was also intrigued because I was planning to head for the first time to Japan for a two-year stay. Classmates were reading Alan Watts' notable book *The Way of Zen* (Watts 1957, 1999) and I had been asked several times if I was going to Japan to study Zen meditation. I sought out Watts' book to read myself, and in truth, found aspects of it quite puzzling. The sound of "one hand clapping"? I was a committed logical positivist and empiricist, intending to go into psychology as a scientist, and I had little openness or patience for such perspectives. My interests in going to Japan were fuelled by both personal reasons (my parents had lived there for a number of years) and by a strong interest in cross-cultural studies on psychological functioning of a more ordinary type. Yet I was attracted by the concept of meditation, particularly in the context of physiological self-regulation, so I decided to take advantage of attending an introductory talk on TM in nearby Philadelphia, which was also far easier than finding a Zen monastery to visit.

The lecture proved to be quite fascinating. The evidence being shared, on the early research being carried out on TM, was compelling. Astoundingly, the first paper published on TM by Wallace (1970) had been published in *Science*, one of the premier American journals, so it carried substantial weight. I was more bemused than drawn in by the pictures of Mahesh Maharishi Yogi, with his flowing beard and robes. It was the data that pulled me through to signing up for the actual initiation — and the desire to have some personal experience of "meditation", mostly from a position of curiosity than from any desire for a "life-changing" experience.

But a life-changing experience was what happened. I received a "personal" secret *mantra* (kept "secret" because, as I've been told since, every other twenty-year-old female in the US received the same one), and was instructed by a sincere, young male TM teacher. In the following twenty minutes of sitting quietly, I experienced a shift in my inner awareness and state of consciousness that had never happened before. My "chattering" mind/analytic thinking paused for much of that time, and I was able to connect to a quality of open experience that was quite new to me. At the same time, I was a novice and realized that this experience was akin to taking a first airplane ride — a totally different way of looking at reality, but certainly not one that made me a pilot, simply someone eager to have the experience again.

I also appreciated opening this door to meditation from the perspective of my growing interest in cross-cultural psychology. I was intrigued by TM's use of the term "transcendental", in contrast to the rather mundane focus of virtually all the marketing of TM toward its value in lowering blood pressure and producing "relaxation". Like most other Americans, I probably would have been put off by a presentation that emphasized "transcendence", but was drawn in by the focus on relaxation and health. I also knew little of the meaning or implication of the term "transcendental". Although I was somewhat aware of the "transcendentalist" movement in the US in the late 1800s, I had no basis for linking what TM was teaching with the work and messages of the great works of Ralph Waldo Emerson, Henry David Thoreau, and others (nor was I yet aware that they had been influenced by Indian thought). An appreciation for that would come much later. However, I knew that what I had experienced was not readily available to me through any other Western resource at that time, nor had it been something I had accessed through my own Protestant religious background, except at perhaps the most minimal level. Even as a student at a Quaker College, one of the few Christian groups respectful of silent "meditative" practice in the service of spiritual engagement, attendance at several of those services had never provided me with this type of experience. I was, of course, also familiar with the counter-culture movement, and now had more of an appreciation for public media showing the Beatles in the presence of the Maharishi. Drug use was rampant at the time, though not particularly on our campus, and research on altered states related to LSD and marijuana was widely publicized and read. The difference was that TM was legal, safe and altered consciousness only in ways that were easily incorporated into daily life, improving well-being rather than challenging it.

Rao, in his introduction to *Consciousness Studies: Cross-cultural Perspectives* (2002: 5), observes:

> The difference in the relative emphasis on the inward or the outward focus is the starting point of divergence between Eastern and Western traditions. In the Western tradition . . . the approach is rational and intellectual. Consequently, the preferred method is scientific and outward focused . . . and may be traced to the Greek notion that the essence of humanness consists in reason and that man is a rational being. Different from this, the central focus in the Eastern tradition is on the inward. [Reason] is seen as secondary to the inner experience. The two traditions . . . may not be seen as incompatible and conflicting. Rather they are complementary and distinct. Together they may constitute a more comprehensive and holistic approach, giving both breadth and depth to our understanding of who we are and what our place in the universe is.
>
> There is no denying the fact that the dominant scientific notions about consciousness in the Western tradition are clearly alien to the core assumptions underlying the Eastern tradition. In the East, consciousness is regarded as an autonomous principle grounded in spiritual foundations. In the West, any such spiritual association is suspect.

I left shortly after my initiation into TM for my studies in Japan, but I believe it was with that first meditation experience that I began to question the limitations of the assumptions with which I had grown up, and which were certainly dominating my intellectual growth as a scientist. Yet I was not fully cognizant of this until almost near the end of my two-year stay in Japan. I had continued to practise TM, but I found myself increasingly drawn to expressions of Buddhism in Japanese culture, and in ways that

I suspect would not have occurred without my own personal shifts in consciousness. I've written about this in an essay entitled, "Finding the Buddha, Finding the Self: Seeing with the Third Eye" (2003). "Finding the self" is purposefully ironic given the Buddhist perspective of no-self, but is also intended to convey that this journey, while perhaps on the road to uncovering the ineffable, was still very much grounded in conscious experience. However, the journey was also very much about learning to uncover/discover the spiritual side of self, which had been lying dormant.

Still, this sense of personal growth had not permeated my scientific conscientious or "self" as psychologist at all until I had the unusual opportunity (I was still an undergraduate) to attend the International Congress of Psychology, held in Tokyo in 1972, in the middle of my stay there. It was indeed terrifically exciting to be at my first professional conference and hear the presentations of psychologists from around the world. Slowly, though, I found myself growing frustrated by the rigid "scientism" of the American presenters, while being drawn in by the richer, more conceptually complex presentations being offered by the Japanese. Gently, quietly, over the year, I had grown to appreciate the weaving of ideas, the willingness to extend meaning by tangents, the comfort with leaving possible implications hanging, rather than needing to circle back and complete all arguments in a linear manner. The contrast between this style within the Western presentations and the looser evocative style of the Japanese began to become clearer as the meetings progressed. It absolutely crystallized when an American member of the audience stood up to challenge the value and reasoning of a Japanese presentation, in an argumentative and condescending way. Not only was this painfully bad manners in Japan, but I realized that in contrast I had judged the presentation as one of the best I had heard, delivered by a professor from one of the top Japanese universities, who was highly regarded as a scientist and psychologist. I believe, in that moment, I ceased being a logical positivist, and began to take more seriously the power, from an intellectual perspective, that could come from being open to a wider range of styles of observing the world as a scientist of human experience and behaviour.

Back in the states, I was, however, casting around for a focus for my future work. Again, I resonate to the challenges that Rao has so systematically and thoroughly engaged throughout his illustrious career. Returning to Swarthmore, I registered for a course on Theravāda

Buddhism being offered by a senior scholar in the field, Donald Swearer (1970, 1971) and the following semester for his course on contemplative practices across religious traditions. In the first course, I found myself drawing deeply on my experience in Japan and travels through the other Pacific-rim countries, especially Indonesia, where I was first exposed to Hinduism (in Bali), and Thailand. In the second course, I became appreciative for the first time of the richness of meditative traditions across many cultures, and the commonalities in practice and experience expressed in the religious literature. Equally important in support of identifying my own professional directions was that credible meditation research was beginning to be published by two different research groups at Harvard University. These were Herbert Benson's group in the medical school on his secularized version of TM (Benson 1975) and Gary Schwartz' group in the Department of Psychology, including his doctoral students, Daniel Goleman and Richard Davidson who have gone on to make many substantial contributions to addressing the value of meditation practice (Davidson 2002; Goleman 1981, 2003; Lutz et al. 2008, 2009; Schwartz et al. 1978). Goleman's first book, *The Meditative Mind: The Varieties of Meditative Experience* (Goleman 1988), still in print, honoured all meditative traditions.

In my own work, my first research endeavour in the meditation area was my Master's thesis at the University of Wisconsin-Madison (Cuthbert et al. 1981); without Benson's research secularizing the approach and further legitimizing the psycho-physiological effects of *mantra*-based practice, I would not have been permitted to undertake such a study. At the same time, I was continuing to explore Indian meditative traditions at a more personal level, having the opportunity in Madison to link in with Swami Ajaya, an American psychologist and early protégé of Swami Rama, who founded the Himalayan Institute. This group of Swami Rama's followers in Madison provided a richer, more complex perspective on the Hindu meditative traditions than had my limited experience with TM. I received a new *mantra* (which did not need to be kept *secret*, along with an explanation of its meaning) and training in *yoga*. At the same time, I was supported in exploring the parallels between meditation effects and the growing interest in biofeedback (Kristeller 1977), in that both of them can be used in the service of relaxation, to promote interoceptive awareness, and to facilitate self-control of physiological processes.

Despite the support for this work in Madison, I found myself increasingly struggling with a hard-core empiricist/logical positivist perspective that characterized the faculty there. Gary Schwartz had, in the meantime, left Harvard for Yale University, and I was able to shift the remainder of my graduate work to that programme. The increase in intellectual flexibility proved compelling; I had made the right choice, and I was able to begin my own work developing the use of meditation-based practices as components of treatment for individuals struggling with a range of eating disorders. Over the years that work has grown from its initial focus on interoceptive awareness to engaging a full range of mindfulness experiences, including helping individuals draw on their own spiritual strengths for finding inner wisdom (Kristeller & Wolever 2011).

Nevertheless, out of both these personal and professional experiences, I also resonate with Rao's concerns that much of Western psychology and science has been overly focused on the more easily identified and studied aspects of meditative practice, as he lays out in several chapters, most recently in an impressively substantive review of meditation in his book *Cognitive Anomalies, Consciousness and Yoga* (2011a). As Rao points out, with relatively limited exceptions, the research on meditation from 1971 through the early 1980s focused almost exclusively on the physiological benefits of meditative practice, along with a few studies on emotional regulation and cognitive shifts. This focus on the "relaxation" effects of meditation created somewhat of a scientific backlash within the clinical application arena. By the early 1980s, several studies had compared the physiological effects of meditation to other "relaxation" interventions, such as Progressive Muscle Relaxation (PMR), and found no differences on physical outcome responses in novice meditators. David Holmes (1984), published a very widely read paper, which Rao summarizes well (2011a: 729), that was highly critical of meditation-based approaches, essentially dismissing any claims of the uniqueness of these practices in regard to reducing somatic arousal, and also criticizing them for lack of methodological sophistication. That paper had significant impact on the field; initially it discouraged funding for more substantial research trials focused on meditation, but in a more positive way, it forced researchers, including myself, to move their focus away from the "relaxation" effects of meditation to considering a wider range of possible values.

However, in defence of the focus on the "relaxation" effects of meditation, the strategy of the TM organization to emphasize this aspect of meditation practice likely made a critical difference in the acceptance of meditation practice in the United States and in the West in general. Meditation practice has almost become "mainstream", and as Rao summarizes, the numbers of publications have been steadily increasing, albeit with a much broader and more sophisticated focus on both underlying neurological processes and effects of psychological self-regulation. Meditation research, both my own and that of many others, is being funded by the National Institutes of Health; meditation-based interventions are being integrated into programmes at major health centres, including Veteran Administration hospitals and university teaching hospitals; and participants from virtually every walk of life and religious orientation sign up for meditation-based treatment programmes. Notably, rather than "relaxation", the terminology has shifted somewhat to being more inclusive, more generally using the term "stress reduction", another widely acceptable concept, in that people generally recognize that a wide range of experiences, from cognitive to behavioural to interpersonal relations can be affected by "stress".

Jon Kabat-Zinn, whose Mindfulness-Based Stress Reduction (MBSR) (Kabat-Zinn 1990) programme has supplanted TM and Benson's "Relaxation Response" programme as the most widely taught in the US, emphasizes all of these valuable aspects, defining "mindfulness" as "paying attention in a particular way, on purpose, in the present moment and non-judgmentally" (Kabat-Zinn 1994: 4). When shift in attention is defined as the core mediator of meditation effects, particularly early in practice, then it becomes more apparent how a wider range of effects than simply "relaxation" may follow from an apparently simple process, consistent with a multi-domain model of meditation effects (Kristeller 2007). Rao identifies mindfulness as corresponding with the fifth limb in Patañjali *yoga*, *pratyāhāra*, a passive attentive state "designed to understand the workings of the psyche or bare perceptions" (Rao 2011a: 701) which is the stage following cultivating the physical exercises of an appropriate sitting posture (*āsana*) and breath control (*prāṇāyāma*). He makes the point that traditionally the term "meditation" is reserved for the sixth through eighth stages: *dhāraṇā* (concentration), *dhyāna* (meditation), and *samādhi*, a standstill state of psyche. Yet he argues, and I would agree, that the developing body of research suggests that many individuals may benefit substantially from engaging the earlier stages of this process, heightening an ability to concentrate, increasing interoceptive awareness, and engaging a sense of inner calm that appears almost to be unique to these processes of meditation more broadly defined.

Consistent with this has been the substantial broadening of research focus on these other aspects of meditative effects over the last fifteen years. Somewhat less mainstream, but growing, has been more systematic attention to the spiritual or transpersonal effects, as called for by Rao in numerous publications. This is in parallel to the upsurge in research on spiritual aspects of human experience that began in the late 1990s in the United States. Although there is a long history of research on religion in the US, and an identification of these topics as viable aspects of psychological investigation going back to William James's book *Varieties of Religious Experience* (James 1902/1968), such work has, until relatively recently, focused on psychological aspects of religious identification and beliefs and/or on their role in psychological or physical health. As Rao aptly points out, William James, often identified as the father of American psychology, engaged both the empiricist perspective modelled on the natural sciences that was informing the newly-founded American Psychological Association (APA), and the role of alternative ontological foundations that he saw as underlying psychic or spiritual experience. Although most psychologists at that time began to distance themselves and the field of psychology from the spiritualist perspectives of the late 1800s and early 1900s, William James remained a member of both the APA and the Society for Psychical Research (Hood 2013). The Jamesian scholar, Eugene Taylor, in his intriguing chapter on William James in Rao's *Handbook of Indian Psychology*, makes a compelling argument that James's thought evolved with ongoing influence from Hindu perspectives (Taylor 2008).

Little, if any research, was conducted on the nature of spiritual experience, in contrast to religious engagement, for another fifty years. Freudian theory had cast a negative pall over most religious experience, becoming dominant in the US over the more receptive perspectives expressed by C.G. Jung. Jung, who was substantially influenced by his travels in India, wove his perspectives on both religious belief and experience of transcendence into his theories of personality (Jung 1970). Other influences from the East were also evident, now coming for the first time directly to America from Asia rather than through England and Europe, largely through the continuing influence of the 1894 World Congress of Religions held in Chicago as part of the World's Fair. For example, RoshiSoyenShaku, a Rinzai Zen monk who spoke at the Congress, then sent D.T. Suzuki to represent Zen Buddhism. Suzuki made numerous trips to the US, also mentoring Americans who went to Japan. Appealing notably to the general public was Yogananda, who continued the spiritualist teachings of Swami Vivekananda, drawing huge audiences, particularly after the publication of his book *The Autobiography of a Yogi* (Yogananda 1946).

Without question, the rapid development of transpersonal and humanistic psychology in the US in the 1960s and 1970s, particularly on the west coast, spurred appreciation for Eastern thought, transcendent aspects of experience, and the value of these in the human potential movement. A hallmark shift within psychoanalytic thinking in respect for the positive effects of meditation practice occurred with the recognition in the 1960s by several respected psychoanalysts, notably Erich Fromm, Karen Horney and Albert Stunkard, of the value of Zen meditation, largely through Suzuki's influence (DeMartino 1991; Fromm et al. 1970; Horney 1945; Horney and Ingram 1987; Stunkard 2004), still influencing contemporary work within this area (Jones 2003; Rubin 1999). Nevertheless, the split continued between these approaches to engaging Eastern spiritual practices and empirical psychology.

Both reflecting this split and maintaining it was the lack of viable measurement tools, in particular in regard to spiritual experience. The psychology of religion received an enormous revival through the work of Gordon Allport (1950), professor of psychology at Harvard University, and one of the most important social psychologists of his time. Allport is associated with two important developments within the psychology of religion. The first was acknowledging and addressing the strong relationship between what he considered the negative aspects of religious beliefs and racial–ethnic prejudice. The second was development of the most widely used measurement tool between the 1960s and 1990s, the Religious Orientation Scale (Allport & Ross 1967). That measure contains two factors: "intrinsic" religious experience and "extrinsic" religious experience. The "intrinsic" religious domain, however, was not necessarily "spiritual" but focused on how individuals drew value from prastising religion and being a member of a congregation. Allport was, however, well aware and respectful of the Eastern religious traditions, including recognition of the importance of transcendent experience. This is reflected in his writing the Introduction to Swami Akhilinanda's 1948 volume, *Hindu Psychology: Its Meaning for the West*, published as part of the International Library of Psychology. Although expressing doubts concerning the "occult" aspects of Hinduism referred to at points in the volume, he shares a more open mind by stating:

> Does the . . . psychology action and behaviour so characteristic of America treat adequately all the capacities of the human mind? Are the powers of meditation revealed through *yoga* illusory and slightly absurd? Is it conceivable that the energies released through mental discipline are of no potential use to men who live in the West?

Allport's answer to these questions is clearly "no".

It took until 1975 until a well-validated measure of mystical or transcendent experience was published, by Ralph Hood as a way to capture a model of mystical experience relevant to the general public and he had continued to lead in this area (Hood & Francis 2013). Beginning in the 1980s, additional measures that attempted to capture both religious engagement and spiritual experience began to appear (Hill & Edwards, 2013; Hill et al. 1998, 2000). In my own work, I have made use of the FACIT-SP, a measure developed as part of a systematic project to understand the key factors affecting adjustment to cancer (Peterman et al. 2002). Consistent with Rao's concerns of the failure to recognize the importance of this aspect of human experience, the research group had not initially included any component assessing Religious or Spiritual (R/S) issues (Cella 1993). However, they began to receive feedback from research participants that they were "missing something", namely, the core value of their religious and spiritual resources in coping with their cancer. In fact, this feedback was also consistent with other emerging data suggesting that R/S resources are the most important factor in adjustment to cancer, even for individuals who are neither particularly religious nor believe in a transcendent God. To their credit, these investigators responded to this feedback. Not finding an acceptable measure to use, particularly one that was viable for both those who had strong religious beliefs and for those who do not, they initiated state-of-the-art measurement development: Qualitative interviewing, generation of a large item pool, multiple administrations to a wide sample, using psychometric guidelines to reduce the item set to the core key items. The language of the items was also adapted to make them usable for individuals regardless of religious belief. Although the focus was on milder to moderate levels of spiritual engagement, rather than on more unusual transcendent or mystical experience, marrying state-of-the-art psychometric approaches to addressing what had been, for many decades, considered ineffable aspects of human experience, would address Rao's assertion that such aspects of human experience deserve or even demand this level of consideration and exploration.

The results of this by Cella and his team were dramatic. Two factors were identified: religious involvement (Faith) and spiritual well-being (Meaning and Peace). Even after adjusting for depression, spiritual well-being accounted for very substantial proportions of the variance in adjustment to cancer, despite high levels of physical pain (Brady et al. 1999). Furthermore, in our work, we have found that "Meaning and Peace" consistently shows up as a factor distinct from religious involvement in multiple populations (Johnson et al. 2008a). We have been able to show that this factor protects against developing alcohol-related problems in students (Johnson et al. 2008b), and serves as an indicator of positive response to a very brief patient-centred exploration of spiritual concerns by oncologists (Kristeller et al. 2005).

Of perhaps most relevance to Rao's interests and contributions to the field, I became very motivated to explore how this indicator of spiritual well-being might respond to meditation practice. Drawing on my earlier collaborations with the research team at the University of Massachusetts Center for Mindfulness (Kabat-Zinn et al. 1992), we included the FACIT-SP as part of the assessment package for individuals enrolled in several cohorts of the MBSR programme (Kabat-Zinn 2005). Not only did we find significant increases on "Meaning and Peace" after only two months of meditation practice, but we found that such improvement was highly correlated with other measures of improved sense of health and well-being (Carmody et al. 2008).

Research on spirituality as a valid — and powerful aspect of human experience — is growing increasingly sophisticated. A number of other measures of spirituality have become available that are becoming increasingly widely used and that are contributing to the development of psychometrically more sophisticated investigation of the role of both religious and spiritual factors in psychological health and well-being (Hill & Edwards 2013). Also important, particularly in relation to meditative practice, has been the development of far more sophisticated neuro-imaging techniques. This work has focused on meditative practices from a variety of religious traditions, including Hinduism, Buddhism (Lutz et al. 2007; Newberg & D'Aquili 1998) and Christianity (Beauregard & O'Leary 2007). Again, this body of work is compatible with Rao's call for a linkage between the ordinary and the transcendent, and the articulated and the ineffable.

The concept of spiritual intelligence has been put forth as a way to further encapsulate this aspect of human experience (Emmons 2000a, b).

I would like to propose that this construct resonates very well with many aspects of spiritual engagement that Rao raises, perhaps most profoundly so in his beautiful reflections on Mahatma Gandhi (Rao 2011b). I have heard arguments that the concept of spiritual intelligence does disservice to the meaningfulness of the transcendent experience, yet to me, it captures much of what Rao proposes: That some level of this experience is available to all; that it can be cultivated, through disciplines such as meditation; that its functions are discernible in the human brain; and yet, that there are "spiritual geniuses" whose teachings inspire, even if they can rarely be matched. I would propose that Rao himself is one of these rare individuals whose words and endeavours have placed him at the forefront of the revolution in thinking in these areas over the last fifty years.

References

Allport, G.W. (1950), *The Individual and His Religion*, New York: Macmillan.

Allport, G.W. and J.M. Ross (1967), "Personal Religious Orientation and Prejudice", *Journal of Personality and Social Psychology*, 5: 432-43.

Beauregard, M. and D. O'Leary (2007), *The Spiritual Brain*, New York: Harper One.

Benson, H. (1975), *The Relaxation Response*, New York: William Morrow.

Brady, M.J., A.H. Peterman, G. Fitchett, M. Mo and D. Cella (1999), "A Case for Including Spirituality in Quality of Life Measurement in Oncology", *Psycho-oncology*, 8: 417-28.

Carmody, J., G. Reed, J. Kristeller and P. Merriam (2008), "Mindfulness, Spirituality, and Health-related Symptoms", *Journal of Psychosomatic Research*, 64: 393-403.

Cella, D.E.A. (1993), "The Functional Assessment of Cancer Therapy Scale: Development and Validation of the General Measure", *Journal of Clinical Oncology*, 11: 570-79.

Cuthbert, B., J. Kristeller, R. Simons, R. Hodes and P.J. Lang (1981), "Strategies of Arousal Control: Biofeedback, Meditation, and Motivation", *Journal of Experimental Psychology: General*, 110(4): 518-46.

Davidson, R.J.H. (ed.) (2002), *Visions of Compassion: Western Scientists and Tibetan Buddhists Examine Human Nature*, London: Oxford University Press.

DeMartino, R.J. (1991), "Karen Horney, Daisetz T. Suzuki, and Zen Buddhism", *American Journal of Psychoanalysis*, 51(3): 267-83.

Emmons, R.A. (2000a), "Is Spirituality an Intelligence?: Motivation, Cognition, and the Psychology of Ultimate Concern", *International Journal for the Psychology of Religion*, 10(1): 3-26.

——— (2000b), "Spirituality and Intelligence: Problems and Prospects", *International Journal for the Psychology of Religion*, 10(1): 57-64.

Fromm, E., D.T. Suzuki and R. DeMartino (1970), *Zen Buddhism and Psychoanalysis*,

New York: Harper and Row.

Goleman, D. (1981), "Buddhist and Western Psychology: Some Commonalities and Differences", *Journal of Transpersonal Psychology*, 13(2): 125-36.

Goleman, D. (1988), *The Meditative Mind: The Varieties of Meditative Experience*, New York: G.P. Putnam & Sons.

——— (2003), *Destructive Emotions: How Can We Overcome Them?: A Scientific Dialogue with the Dalai Lama*, New York: Bantam Books.

Hill, P.C. and E. Edwards (2013), "Measurement in the Psychology of Religiousness and Spirituality: Existing Measures and New Frontiers", in K.I. Pargament (ed.) *APA Handbook of Psychology, Religion and Spirituality*, Washington, DC: American Psychological Association.

Hill, P.C., K.I. Pargament, J.P. Swyers, R.L. Gorsuch, M.E. McCullough, R.W. Hood and R.F. Baumeister (eds.) (1998), *Definitions of Religion and Spirituality*, Philadelphia, PA: John M. Templeton Foundation.

Hill, P.C., K.I. Pargament, Jr. R.W. Hood, M.E. McCullough, J.P. Swyers, D.B. Larson et al. (2000), "Conceptualizing Religion and Spirituality: Points of Commonality, Points of Departure", *Journal for the Theory of Social Behaviour*, 30(1): 51-77.

Holmes, D.S. (1984), "Meditation and Somatic Arousal reduction: A Review of the Experimental Evidence", *The American Psychologist*, 39(1): 1-10.

Hood, R.W. (2013), "Methodological Diversity in the Psychology of Religion and Spirituality", in K.I. Pargament (ed.) *APA Handbook of Psychology, Religion and Spirituality*, Washington, DC: American Psychological Association.

Hood, R.W. and L.J. Francis (2013), "Mystical Experience: Conceptualizations, Measurement, and Correlates", in K.I. Pargament (ed.) *APA Handbook of Psychology, Religion and Spirituality*, Washington, DC: American Psychological Association.

Horney, K. (1945), *Our Inner Conflicts*, New York: Norton.

Horney, K. and D.H. Ingram (1987), *Final Lectures*, New York: WW Norton & Co.

James, W. (1902/1968), *Varieties of Religious Experience*, New York: Fontana Library.

Johnson, T.J., V.L. Sheets and J. Kristeller (2008a), "Empirical Identification of Dimensions of Religiousness and Spirituality", *Mental Health, Religion & Culture*, 11(8): 745-67.

——— (2008b), "Identifying Mediators of the Relationship Between Religiousness/Spirituality and Alcohol Use", *Journal of Studies on Alcohol and Drugs*, 69(1): 160-70.

Jones, J.W. (2003), *The Mirror of God: Christian Faith as Spiritual Practice — Lessons from Buddhism and Psychotherapy*, New York: Palgrave Macmillan.

Jung, C.G. (1970), "Psychology and Religion: West and East", in G. Adler and R.F.C. Hull (eds. and trs.) *The Collected Works of C.G.* Jung, vol. 1, Princeton, NJ: Princeton University Press/Bollingen Foundation.

Kabat-Zinn, J. (1990), *Full Catastrophe Living*, New York: Delacorte Press.

——— (1994), *Wherever You Go, There You Are*, New York: Hyperion.

——— (2005), *Full Catastrophe Living: Using the Wisdom of Your Body and Mind to Face Stress, Pain, and Illness: Fifteenth Anniversary Edition*, New York: Delta Trade Paperback/Bantam Dell.

Kabat-Zinn, J., A.O. Massion, J. Kristeller, L.G. Peterson, K.E. Fletcher, L. Pbert et al. (1992), "Effectiveness of a Meditation-based Stress Reduction Program in the Treatment of Anxiety Disorders", *The American Journal of Psychiatry*, 149(7): 936-43.

Kristeller, J. (1977), "Meditation and Biofeedback in the Regulation of Internal States", in S. Ajaya (ed.) *Meditational Therapy*, Glenview, IL: Himalayan International Institute Press.

——— (2003), "Finding the Buddha/Finding the Self: Seeing with the Third Eye", in S. Segal (ed.) *Encountering Buddhism*, Albany, NY: SUNY Press, pp. 109-30.

——— (2007), "Mindfulness Meditation", in P.M. Lehrer, R.L. Woolfolk and W.E. Sime (eds.) *Principles and Practice of Stress Management* (3rd edn.), New York: Guilford Press, pp. 393-427.

Kristeller, J. and K. Rikhye (2008), "Meditative Traditions and Contemporary Psychology", in K.R. Rao, A.C. Paranjpe and A.K. Dalal (eds.) *Handbook of Indian Psychology*, New Delhi: Cambridge University Press.

Kristeller, J. and R.Q. Wolever (2011), "Mindfulness-based Eating Awareness Training for Treating Binge Eating Disorder: The Conceptual Foundation", *Eating Disorders: The Journal of Treatment & Prevention*, 19(1): 49-61.

Kristeller, J., M. Rhodes, L.D. Cripe and V. Sheets (2005), "Oncologist Assisted Spiritual Intervention Study (OASIS): Patient Acceptability and Initial Evidence of Effects", *International Journal of Psychiatry in Medicine*, 35(4): 329-47.

Lutz, A., J.D. Dunne, R.J. Davidson, P.D. Zelazo, M. Moscovitch and E. Thompson (2007), "Meditation and the Neuroscience of Consciousness: An Introduction", *The Cambridge Handbook of Consciousness*, New York: Cambridge University Press, pp. 499-551.

Lutz, A., L.L. Greischar, D.M. Perlman and R.J. Davidson (2009), "Bold Signal in Insula is Differentially Related to Cardiac Function During Compassion Meditation in Experts vs. Novices", *Neuro Image*, 47(3): 1038-46.

Lutz, A., H.A. Slagter, J.D. Dunne and R.J. Davidson (2008), "Attention Regulation and Monitoring in Meditation", *Trends in Cognitive Sciences*, 12(4): 163-69.

Newberg, A.B. and E.G. D'Aquili (1998), "The Neuropsychology of Spiritual Experience", in H.G. Koenig (ed.) *Handbook of Religion and Mental Health*, San Diego, CA: Academic Press, pp. 75-94.

Peterman, A.H., G. Fitchett, M.J. Brady, L. Hernandez and D. Cella (2002), "Measuring Spiritual Well-being in People with Cancer: The Functional Assessment of Chronic Illness Therapy-spiritual Well-being Scale (FACIT-SP)", *Annals of Behavioral Medicine*, 24(1): 49-58.

Rao, K. Ramakrishna (2002), *Consciousness Studies: Cross-cultural Perspectives*, Jefferson, NC: McFarland.

——— (2011a), *Cognitive Anomalies, Consciousness and Yoga*, New Delhi: Matrix Publishers.

——— (2011b), *Gandhi and Applied Spirituality*, New Delhi: Matrix.

Rao, K. Ramakrishna, A.C. Paranjpe and A.K. Dalal (2008), *Handbook of Indian Psychology*, New Delhi: Cambridge University Press.

Rubin, J.B. (1999), "Close Encounters of a New Kind: Toward an Integration of Psychoanalysis and Buddhism", in R. Segall (ed.) *Encountering Buddhism*, Albany, NY: State University of New York Press, pp. 31-60.

Schwartz, G.E., R.J. Davidson and D.J. Goleman (1978), "Patterning of Cognitive and Somatic Processes in the Self-regulation of Anxiety: Effects of Meditation Versus Exercise", *Psychosomatic Medicine*, 40(4): 321-28.

Stunkard, A.J. (2004), "Daisetz Suzuki: A Buddhist Philosopher", *The Eastern Buddhist*, 36(1-2): 192-228.

Swearer, D. (1970), *Buddhism in Transition*, Philadelphia, PA: Westminster Press.

——— (ed.) (1971), *Secrets of the Lotus*, New York: Macmillan Company.

Taylor, E. (2008), "William James on Pure Experience and Samadhi in Samkhya-yoga", in K.R. Rao, A.C. Paranjpe and A.K. Dalal (eds.), *Handbook of Indian Psychology*, New Delhi: Cambridge University Press.

Wallace, R.K. (1970), "Physiological Effects of Transcendental Meditation", *Science* (New York), 167(3926): 1751-54.

Watts, A. (1957, 1999), *The Way of Zen*, New York: Vintage Books.

Yogananda, P. (1946), *Autobiography of a Yogi*, Los Angeles: Self-Realization Fellowship.

8

Perspectives on Nature of Consciousness

Contributions of Prof. K. Ramakrishna Rao

Janak Pandey

It is a privilege for me to contribute to this Festschrift volume reviewing the work of Prof. K. Ramakrishna Rao during the past sixty years. Rao's contributions in the areas of parapsychology, meditation and *yoga*, cross-cultural studies of mind and consciousness, and Indian psychology and social identity are internationally recognized and provide refreshing perspectives to understand human consciousness, mind and behaviour and, in short, human nature. His academic leadership and initiatives in building science of consciousness and parapsychology are equally important.

At the end of the nineteenth century, William James articulated the classical theory of consciousness, and elaborated a sequence of conscious mental states, each state being experience with some content. According to James, consciousness is continuous with an evolutionary purpose for our survival. James argued that thinking is useful for our survival just like eating and mating.

The twentieth century witnessed tremendous progress in science. Rise of Watsonian behaviourism led to downgrading study of consciousness on the ground of considering it as a subjective phenomenon which cannot be studied objectively. Rao as a young scholar in the 1950s did not get carried away by the storm of behaviourism. His thinking was firmly grounded in classical Indian thought and he dedicated himself to the study of human consciousness for a true understanding of human nature. Rao, whose research career is now sixty years old, and his academic work came into focus with his first book published in 1957 under the title *Psi Cognition*. The book discusses the importance of the study of parapsychological phenomena from Western as well as Eastern perspectives. As a young scholar, he dedicated himself to systematic and scientific study of difficult and complex mental phenomena using innovative paradigms of research.

The most perplexing fact about consciousness, rightly stated by Rao, is that "it is too familiar and intimate to ignore and yet too complex and elusive to understand and explain" (Rao 2002:3). Consciousness is most familiar, but yet most mysterious. We all experience consciousness; and it is basic to all our knowing. Still, we cannot say what exactly it is. It would seem that its subjectivity required innovative approach and creative scientific enquiry from an extraordinary scholar like Rao.

Cultural and intellectual traditions of scholars influence their approach in studying any phenomenon; and consciousness studies are not an exception to it. Rao has systematized varied knowledge traditions defining and understating consciousness; and he has further enriched the consciousness discourse by identifying two bipolar dimensions. The first one is subject–object dimension with one extreme, "phenomenal awareness of concrete objects, memories and images, and other extreme of pure consciousness". The second one is implicit–explicit dimension which ranges from focal awareness "readily available for introspection" (ibid.: 27).

Rao writes:

> On the one hand, their awareness is directed outward towards objects and events, fellow beings, their appearances and actions. On the other hand, the awareness is sometimes focused inward, to one's own thoughts, feelings and being. The two-dimensional activities go undistinguished in the early stages of cognitive development, but they are differentiated as such with maturation. — Ibid.: 4

Thus subjective is personal, whereas objective is independent of cognizing person and publicly verifiable. The two could be conceptually distinguished, but they blend harmoniously in human experience.

Recognizing limitations of Western scientific methods in study of inward experiences, it is argued that Western rational and intellectual tradition is good for the study of outward and objective events. In his book on *Consciousness Studies: Cross-cultural Perspectives*, Rao argues:

> In the East, consciousness is regarded as an autonomous principle grounded in spiritual foundations. In the West, any such spiritual association is suspect. — Rao 2002: 5

Many others like Watson (1928) and Skinner (1974) in particular rejected consciousness as a subject for scientific enquiry. Rao argues that "consciousness has a capacity of its own and is involved not only in ability to know the world but also in effecting changes in it" (Rao 2002: 5). So consciousness is dynamic and it brings about internal as well as external changes. In the Western tradition, consciousness has been considered as a state, a structure, as a function with levels and degrees of consciousness. Rao in his comparative analysis has tried to develop clarity for a focused discussion on consciousness. Due to decline in cortical functions, conscious awareness at human level also declines. Massive evidences of all kinds connect consciousness to brain but subjectivity in conscious experiences like feeling of "warmth and intimacy" as explained by William James cannot be fully translated into neurobiological processes. Therefore, consciousness cannot be treated completely as a product of human brain. Consciousness is much more than simple physiological process of the brain. Rao (2002) writes: "Individuals have intentions, goals and objectives that may not be reduced to brain states." He rightly argues against machine model and physical laws for fuller understanding of human thoughts, affects and behaviour.

The work of Rao and others on paranormal phenomena like Extra-Sensory Perception (ESP) and Psychokinesis (PK), even at the cost of marginalization, challenges the mainstream dominant scientific research tradition of the West. They make "a prima-facie case for the primacy of consciousness in our being and behaviour". In his cross-cultural and comparative studies of consciousness, Rao recognizes universality across cultures, such as the need to experience spiritual growth and of mystical religious experiences and "incompatibility between what we think we are and the conception of man as an entirely brain-driven machine" (2002: 7). Conscious experiences, though dependent on neurological process, are not identical to such processes because such an approach excludes "awareness that goes beyond categories of sense and understanding".

Rao subtly analyses awareness and states of knowing based on "the nature of relationship between the knowing agent and the object of knowledge" (2002: 28). Awareness according to him falls into four broad categories, and he calls them as four Ps of awareness:

1. Primary awareness (subjective acts of perception, thought, feeling and volition).
2. Paradoxical awareness (knowing without awareness as in subliminal perception).

3. Pathological awareness (aberrant and dysfunctional awareness).
4. Paranormal awareness (non-conventional knowing such as extra-senory awareness and knowing without representation).

In states of paranormal awareness, the relationship between the knower and the known is one of identity. Thus, paranormal awareness in a sense, according to Rao, extends the range of awareness beyond sensory and representational knowledge that may manifest in a form similar to primary awareness, paradoxical awareness, or pathological awareness. Rao has elaborately explained paranormal awareness. It has no causal link between the subject and the object of awareness and such experience may occur in the form of hallucination and may also be misleading (psi-missing). He argues that it may be a manifestation of contentless state of "pure consciousness experience".

The Western scientific model, thus, yields incomplete knowledge about the nature of human consciousness and mind. Rao, therefore, emphasizes alternate models. The one he prefers is the Sāṁkhya-Yoga system, a heuristic model of Indian philosophy that deals meaningfully with complexities of consciousness. Unlike the Western approaches, the Indian approach makes a basic distinction between consciousness and mind. Accordingly, existence of pure non-intentional states of consciousness and mental phenomenon with intentions are accepted. Western perspective emphasizes on the manifestation, the contest of consciousness, whereas from the Indian perspective, the emphasis is on understanding pure consciousness so as to prepare the person to realize and participate in transcendental aspects of consciousness.

Rao sees strength in both Eastern and Western approaches of consciousness and therefore he takes a position to avoid the "either–or" option. He, as a true believer in the Gandhian inclusive philosophy, has adopted the same inclusiveness of interdisciplinary approach. Integrating the knowledge systems of the West and East and highlighting the strength of India's indigenous knowledge system, Rao relates them to nature of consciousness, mind and brain. Thus, he has ably reviewed the works of philosophers, psychologists, physiologists and physcists, and with great ease integrated his own position by stating the main features of consciousness at primary levels that include (a) subjectivity, (b) change, (c) continuity, and stream-like nature, (d) intentionality, and (e) selectivity.

Rao further recognizes cognitive-science approach in consciousness studies as cognitive science unravels many mysteries of consciousness, especially in understanding various functions of consciousness and cortical process involved in them. In the last two decades, cognitive science has emerged as a front-runner discipline of mind but still is little investigated in India. Largely, on the initiatives of Rao, the Department of Science and Technology, Government of India, recognized cognitive science as one of the four pillars of knowledge along with nano, bio and information technologies. Cognitive science is the science of cognition and mind, and Rao recognizes that there would be no cognition without consciousness and, therefore, studies of consciousness and mind have acquired special significance today.

Consciousness is a natural phenomenon like all natural phenomena. Therefore, there must be laws to explain it. Strangely, still many consider consciousness as an elusive phenomenon. Strength of Rao's work lies in the fact that he has been successful in minimizing elusiveness in understanding consciousness and in enhancing our scientific knowledge of human nature.

References

Rao, K.R. (1957), *Psi Cognition,* Tenali (AP): Tagore Publishing House.

Rao, K.R. (2002), *Consciousness Studies: Cross-cultural Prespectives*, Jefferson, NC: McFarland.

Skinner, B.F. (1974), *About Behaviourism*, New York: A.A. Knopf.

Watson, J.B. (1928), The Unconscious of the Behaviorist, in C.M. Child, K. Koffka and J.E. Anderson (eds.) *The Unconscious: A Symposium*, pp. 91-113, New York: A.A. Knopf.

9

Striving to Connect with the Roots
A Mentor Makes the Difference

Ajit K. Dalal

As a young psychology faculty at the Allahabad University in early 1980s I was somewhat familiar with Prof. Ramakrishna Rao's work in the area of parapsychology. In fact, as an Indian I was proud of the fact that Prof. J.B. Rhine chose Rao as a worthy inheritor to head his world-famous Institute of Parapsychology after his retirement from Duke University, North Carolina. I was excitedly searching for the experimental work being conducted at the Institute. By that time Rao's (1982) book *J.B. Rhine: On the Frontiers of Science* was just published. I was quite intrigued by the possibility of knowing without any known medium. Those were the days when there was no e-mail, no internet; and information about such research was available only through colleagues, libraries and personal communication.

Since my student days I was fascinated with parapsychology and reading popular books in the areas of premonition, psychokinesis, clairvoyance, and similar phenomenon. I was also charmed by Uri Geller's live demonstrations of psychokinesis in different parts of the world which I watched on TV. I wondered whether it is real or some trickery! Can anyone learn to do it by one's own psychic power? The idea that one can read other's mind clicked my imagination. I bought books on research in this area, particularly experimental studies, like the *New Soviet Psychic Discoveries* (Gris & William 1978), *Psychic Discoveries Behind the Iron Curtain* (Ostrander & Schroeder 1970), *Paranormal Foreknowledge: Problems and Perplexities* (Eisnbud 1982), *Learning to Use Extrasensory Perception* (Tart 1976), etc. I was wondering if such research can be conducted with the governmental support in the communist Russia, why such research is not promoted in a spiritual country like India, where such phenomena are largely believed and practised. I, myself, wanted some training in this field and wondered why parapsychology is not part of psychology course curriculum? It was during my doctoral work in the area of experimental cognitive psychology at the Indian Institute of Technology, Kanpur, I understood the reasons. Scientific psychology considers paranormal phenomena as subjective, and thus, hard to replicate using established research methods. Such phenomena were held as mystical and esoteric by those who were somewhat sympathetic, whereas the vast majority of psychology faculty considered it pseudoscience and fraudulent. Academic courses in psychology, therefore, kept a distance from the study of paranormal phenomena. I was, however, not much convinced with such arguments. To me it was not a problem of subject field but that of not having proper research methodology.

In between I left Allahabad for a major surgery, and then to join at the Udaipur University as a faculty. Two years later when I returned back to rejoin the University of Allahabad in 1986 parapsychology was still in my mind. Rao's earlier publication *Experimental Parapsychology* (1966) was there in the Departmental Library. His recent publication *The Basic Experiments in Parapsychology* (1984) was also available in India by that time.

In 1986-87, I was teaching basic experiments in Psychology Practical Course to the first year Bachelor students. Inspired by Rao's work, me and one other colleague designed an experiment in parapsychology and introduced as a part of the training in basic psychology experiments. In that experiment undergraduate students were asked to identify two category of research participants — those who believed in precognition, in foreknowledge (called them as "sheep"), and those who did not (called them as "goats"), as Gertrude Schmeidler did in some of her experiments to examine the effect of believing and non-believing on precognition. We took a pack of playing cards and the blind-folded research participants were asked by the experimenters to guess the type of the card (spade, heart, diamond or club) it was, placed upside down before them on the table. The card was shown to them later. Similar way, each participant was given twenty trials and it was calculated in how many trials his/her guesses were correct. Since one can be correct in 25 per cent of the cases by chance factor, to show evidence for precognition one should be correct in more than five trials. After pooling data of the whole class we made a comparison between the sheep and the goats. I do not remember what students actually found about pre-cognition phenomenon, probably the findings were inconclusive. This experiment, however, became very popular. So much so that many of the parents and family members of our students wanted to participate in this experiment to get their paranormal powers tested. Anyway, we continued this experiment in the BA class for few batches and had to abandon it later for various reasons. Many years later when I met Rao and told him about this basic experiment, he just smiled.

Once back to India and settled in Vashakhapatnam in 1995, Rao was a regular visitor to our Department. His lectures and participation in other academic activities used to be major highlights of the academic calendar of the Department. Though, in between, he would go off to the US for long durations. When the Centre of Cognitive and Behavioural Science, a new stream of psychology was established at the University of Allahabad in 2002, he was a regular visitor there also. This Centre was adjacent to the Psychology Building and thus we had more opportunities to listen and interact with him. He was a model of serious academic scholarship for we young faculty. As the Vice-Chancellor of Andhra University and later as the Director of the Institute of Yoga and Consciousness in Andhra his work was by now widely known in India. The journal which he started around that time, the *Journal of Indian Psychology*, was the first effort to bring out the essence and relevance of classical Indian knowledge system in dealing with the contemporary world problems. This journal and his other writings offered exciting research possibilities to many of my generations, who were primarily extending Western work in India, to establish our scientific and academic credentials. By that time Prof. Anand Paranjpe's first book *Theoretical Psychology* (1984) was already in print, which I was extensively using in teaching my Master's course on Psychology in the Indian Context, along with articles from the *Journal of Indian Psychology*. That was the time when Rao had contributed 150-page long chapter on Consciousness to the Fourth ICSSR Survey in Psychology brought out by Janak Pandey (Rao 2000a). This chapter was a comprehensive exposition of the core Indian concept of consciousness. His own book in this area *Consciousness Studies: Cross-Cultural Perspectives* was also published in the very same year. These two publications of Rao and another book by Paranjpe around the same time, *Self and Identity in Modern Psychology and Indian Thought* (1998) firmly established consciousness as an important field of teaching and research in India. These publications, in a way, gave a strong impetus to the movement for indigenous psychology of Indian origin.

I had a chance to invite Rao in the early years of this millennium to a conference on Social-psychology of Health and Well-being, which I organized at Allahabad. I remember he gave his keynote address on *yoga*, meditation and parapsychology. Later, when the Chairperson of that session, Prof. Manas Mukul Das, raised some objections about the methodology of parapsychology research, he did not contest, rather agreed with most of the criticism. He agreed that the experimental method which was used in parapsychology research was not yielding consistent results, and that parapsychology was going nowhere for want of appropriate methodology. I was much impressed by his humility, openness and undogmatic approach to scientific research. Later, he contributed a chapter to my and Subha Ray's volume on the *Social Dimensions of Health* (Rao 2005), based on the conference proceedings.

That was the time when he was seriously working on his Indian psychology project and striving to develop it as an alternative non-Western psychology. Rao took the position that the Indian psychology should be defined as the scientific study of consciousness. It was a logical transition for him to move from parapsychology to research on *yoga* and consciousness, and then on to Indian psychology. Rao did not imply consciousness as a state of wakefulness, or as opposite to unconsciousness, often understood in the Western psychology. Consistent with the Indian perspective, he considered consciousness as a reality of the Being, that which manifests itself in various forms and quality. In the Preface to his edited volume *Yoga and Parapsychology: Empirical Research and Theoretical Essays*, Rao has clearly stated why he believes *yoga* and parapsychology need to be studied together:

> A serious and scientific study of the two and the resultant synergy of their confluence could result in resolving many of the riddles that puzzle parapsychology today and be the harbinger of a vibrant science opening to new frontiers. Further, it could be seen as a productive East–West meet in a profound sense. — Rao 2010: xv

The goal of *yoga* is to transcend sensory mind and its products to attain the state of pure consciousness, which is the authentic and true state of being. At the level of sensory mind, empirical knowledge is bound by the context, perspective and perceptual distortions. At the transcendental level of pure consciousness, knowledge is not mediated through sense-organs but is direct and immediate. In the state of transcendence subjective–objective dichotomy ceases, and our experience and knowledge is not limited by space–time barrier, or by our senses. Such an explanatory model of Indian psychology can account for all — normal, abnormal and paranormal behaviour (Rao 2003).

As an inquisitive new entrant in this area, I have been trying to closely watch these developments in psychology. During my initial years as faculty at Allahabad I had gone to the University of California, Los Angeles (UCLA) in 1982 as a Fulbright Fellow to work with Bernard Weiner and Harold Kelley on attribution theory. I realized that the faculty and students in the Psychology Department there were more interested to know about what psychology we are doing back in India. I was a total naïve and felt ashamed that I did not know much about psychology in my own country, and had to cut a sorry figure. I started frequenting the library to learn about psychology back home. Ironically, I read more about psychology back in India there than on attribution theory during my later stay at UCLA. I gave a talk in the Department there on psychology in India, and also at few other American universities. On returning back to India, I was more preoccupied about changing the job due to health and other reasons.

But when I returned back to Allahabad in 1986, as the chance would have it, the Unesco asked to write a country status report on psychology in India. Prof. D. Sinha's book *Psychology in a Third World Country* (1986) had come by that time, and I realized what I write should be different from his perspective and content. Though I also started with historical development my coverage and critique were more from the contemporary perspective. In writing about psychology in India the primary discussion is about the beginning, growth and development of Western psychology in India, in contrast to the Indian psychology, which refers to the psychology of Indian origin. This report was published later along with the other country status reports of Asia and Pacific region (1990). Few years later I wrote another comprehensive article "A Science in Search of its Identity" (1996), in which I also discussed at length the growth of a new movement of "Indian Psychology", with Rao as one of the major pioneers. That was the beginning of a series of other articles which I wrote on the history of psychology in India. Writing these articles helped me in perusing Rao's work more closely. As a result of my readings of the work of Rao and Paranjpe, I was slowly gravitating toward Indian psychology. Coming from experimental cognitive psychology tradition, Indian psychology was mostly an unknown territory for me. Still I was convinced that Indian psychology holds the potential to offer a new psychology which this world needs. This psychology is needed to survive the onslaught of brute consumerism and to save the humanity from suffering and destruction. In the last one decade I had many opportunities to meet him in conferences and workshops on Indian psychology at different places. Every time I came back with renewed vigour and resolve to engage in serious academic research in this field. Later, Prof. Girishwar Misra and I brought out our first volume on *New Directions in Indian Psychology* in 2002, to cover Indian research in social psychology. When we brought out our other volume *New Directions in Health Psychology* (2011), as a mark of our gratitude, we dedicated this volume to Rao. This was only symbolic. It was, indeed, difficult for us to appraise and articulate how much he has contributed to our academic growth.

It is also amazing to realize how much one can contribute to the growth of a discipline with all other administrative and official engagements. His books, monographs and research articles, published in the last two decades have helped in giving the new and growing discipline of Indian psychology a firm ground and identity. To expand the reach of Indian psychology in different geographical regions, he was instrumental in organizing many of such conferences, since the beginning of this millennium. As the Chairman of the Indian Council of Philosophical Research (ICPR) he supported many of these conferences, workshops and symposia with generous grants. The increasing participation and publications in the area of Indian psychology has resulted in an intense debate in the academic portals for the acceptance of Indian psychology as a viable scientific discipline. As Rao's work shows, Indian psychology is never envisaged as a psychology of the Indian region and people. He viewed it as a universal science that transcends narrow geographical and cultural boundaries and focus on the essential meaning of human existence. These efforts have culminated in the establishment of new centres and courses on Indian psychology in different parts of the country.

Within the broader canvas of Indian psychology, Rao's main thrust was on *yoga* and consciousness. His work can be viewed as belonging to the *śāstrīya paramparā* (classical tradition) in Indian psychology. The famous anthropologist, Mariott (1955) talks about two types of traditions — the great tradition and the little tradition. The great tradition is characterized by the practices based on classical and philosophical texts like Vedas, Upaniṣads, *Gītā*; and by *yoga* and consciousness. On the other hand, *loka* (folk) practices are considered within the little tradition, i.e. the beliefs and practices of the masses. Shamans, spirits, local deities are all part of it. I am of the view that the psychology of *yoga* and consciousness should be complemented by the *loka* (folk or the little) tradition in defining the subject field of Indian psychology. These two traditions have their own concepts and theories, which may or may not overlap. Taken together, these two traditions cover the whole range of explanations for human behaviour. In both of these traditions the notion of the universality of human behaviour is inherent. There was never an occasion for me to discuss with Rao and know his views about the complementarity of the two traditions from the Indian perspective. I, though, always found him supportive of my work on Indian folk health and healing practices. As a true scholar and a *guru* he let us explore the Indian tradition in our own ways, in our own areas of interest. He was also not antithetical to Western psychology and respected its contribution to our understanding of human behaviour. I do not think he ever had any rigid views about what comprises Indian psychology. He probably preferred an organic growth of the discipline.

I had an opportunity to work with Rao as a co-editor of the *Handbook of Indian Psychology* (2008). Working with two stalwarts, Rao and Paranjpe, on this project was a lifetime opportunity for me. In completing this project, though we all three worked as a team, I always felt that my contribution in preparing this volume was marginal, though they never gave me such a feeling. Most of the hard work was done by Rao and Paranjpe whose commitment to bring out this volume in time was exemplary. This *Handbook* was the first comprehensive volume in the area of Indian psychology. It fulfilled a basic need to have sufficient study material to teach Indian psychology in universities and colleges. The volume was well received by the academic community and all copies of the book were sold out. We are presently working to bring out its second international edition.

For all these years as the founder Director of the Institute for Human Science and Services and as the Chancellor of GITAM University, Rao has been prolific in his writings. He is still very actively pursuing his academic projects. He is participating in conferences and organizing activities to promote Indian psychology. Like a true Indian *ṛṣi* he is always accessible to his students and colleagues. We always expectantly look forward to his new publications and the words of wisdom.

References

Dalal, A.K. (1990), "India", in G. Shouksmith and E. Shouksmith (eds.) *Psychology in Asia and Pacific: Status Reports on Teaching Research in Eleven Countries*, Bangkok: Unesco Publications.

——— (1996), "A Science in Search of Its Identity: Twentieth Century Psychology in India", *Indian Psychological Abstracts and Reviews*, 4: 1-41.

Dalal, A.K. and G. Misra (2002), *New Directions in Indian Psychology*, vol. 1: *Social Psychology*, New Delhi: Sage.

——— (2011), *New Direction in Health Psychology*, New Delhi: Sage.

Eisnbud, J. (1982), *Paranormal Foreknowledge: Problems and Perplexities*, New York: Human Science Press.

Gris, H. and D. William (1978), *The New Soviet Psychic Discoveries*, Englewood Cliffs, NJ: Prentice-Hall.

Mariott, M. (1955), *Village India: Studies in the Little Community*, Chicago: University of Chicago Press.

Ostrander, S. and L. Schroeder (1970), *Psychic Discoveries Behind the Iron Curtain*, Englewood Cliffs, NJ: Prentice-Hall.

Paranjpe, A.C. (1984), *Theoretical Psychology: The Meeting of East and West*, New York: Plenum Press.

Paranjpe, A.C. (1998), *Self and Identity in Modern Psychology and Indian Thought*, New York: Plenum.

Rao, K. Ramakrishna (1966), *Experimental Parapsychology*, Springfield, IIL: Charles C. Thomas.

——— (ed.) (1982), *J.B. Rhine: On the Frontiers of Science*, Jefferson, NC: McFarland.

——— (1984), *The Basic Experiments in Parapsychology*, Jefferson, NC: McFarland.

——— (2002a), "Consciousness Studies: A Survey of Perspectives and Research", in J. Pandey (ed.) *Psychology in India Revisited*, vol. 2, New Delhi: Sage, pp. 19-162.

——— (2002b), *Consciousness Studies: Cross-cultural Perspectives*, Jefferson, NC: McFarland.

——— (2003), *Self and Personality in Yoga and Indian Psychology*, Vishakhapatnam: Institute for Human Science and Services.

——— (2005), "Religiosity and Sense of Well-being: Spiritual Dimensions of Health", in A.K. Dalal and S. Ray (eds.) *Social Dimensions of Health*, Jaipur: Rawat Publications, pp. 69-88.

——— (ed.) (2010), *Yoga and Parapsychology: Empirical Research and Theoretical Essays*, New Delhi: Motilal Banarsidass.

Rao, K. Ramakrishna, A.C. Paranjpe and A.K. Dalal (eds.) (2008), *Handbook of Indian Psychology*, New Delhi: Cambridge University Press.

Sinha, D. (1986), *Psychology in a Third World Country: An Indian Experience*, New Delhi: Sage.

Tart, C. (1976), *Learning to Use Extrasensory Perception*, Chicago: Chicago University Press.

10

Gandhi, Rao and Applied Spirituality

R.C. Pradhan

In this paper I will give an account of Prof. Ramakrishna Rao's philosophy of applied spirituality in the light of his interpretation of the spiritual philosophy of Mahatma Gandhi and the entire Indian spiritual tradition.[1] Rao's unique approach to the philosophy of spirituality is marked by his deep understanding of human psychology both Indian and Western, especially of the Indian *yoga* psychology. He is well versed in Indian and Western philosophies which gives the added advantage of providing a philosophical foundation to spirituality as a way of life. Rao is both a pragmatist and realist in his basic philosophical thinking. For him, as for Gandhi, spirituality is a matter of man's pragmatic interest in the transformation of life, and, at the same time, it is not a matter of policy or strategy for making life more meaningful but is rooted in the realm of the spiritual consciousness which far surpasses the mundane life of desires and propensities. Therefore both Gandhi and Rao call for the spiritualization of life including the mundane life so that man can attain a higher level of consciousness. Gandhi calls the spiritual man the *satyāgrahī* and Rao calls him the man of practical wisdom, the *yogī*.

The Need of a Philosophy of Spirituality

Gandhi stumbles upon spirituality as a philosophy of life in his personal encounter with the existential situations of life both in his private life as well as public life. To solve the myriad problems of life, he discovers the philosophy of spirituality in the Indian and Western religions, especially in the *Bhagavad-Gītā* and the Bible.[2] These two texts had deep impact on

---

[1] K. Ramakrishna Rao (2011), *Gandhi and Applied Spirituality*, New Delhi: ICPR and Matrix Publishers.

[2] M.K. Gandhi (1961), *My Philosophy of Life*, (ed.) Anand T. Hingorani, Bombay: Pearl Publication.

his mind because both are spiritual texts aiming at solving the existential problems of life. The *Gītā* gives the message of disinterested action or *karma-yoga*, while the Bible teaches the philosophy of love and compassion. Both texts ask us to surrender to the Divine and to carry out the Divine Will in our life.[3] Thus Gandhi meets his spiritual destiny in the crucible of social and political, life, and carried out the message of the *Gītā* and Bible while fighting the battles of life. This we can call, in the words of Rao, the philosophy of applied spirituality, because this made Gandhi apply the tenets of the spiritual philosophy in the field of life in the world. For Gandhi, spirituality is not a matter of philosophical contemplation alone but of practice and application in the world. It is not meant for those who have renounced the world but for those who are in the world and fighting for their rights and freedoms against the forces of inhumanity, evil and immorality. For the Gandhian *satyāgrahī* all life is dedicated to "truth" and "non-violence" because life is a journey towards spiritual realization. Outlining his philosophy of spiritual life, Gandhi writes:

> I hold that non-violence is not merely a personal virtue. It is also a social virtue to be cultivated like other virtues. Surely, society is largely regulated by the expression of non-violence in its mutual dealings. What I ask for is an extension of it on a larger, national and international life. . . . The love that Jesus taught and practised was not a mere personal virtue, but that it was essentially a social and collective virtue. Buddha taught and practised the same thing six hundred years before Jesus.[4]

For Gandhi, truth and non-violence are the corner-stones of spiritual life. To be spiritual, according to him, is to follow the principles of truth and non-violence in one's personal as well as social life.

The Gandhian spirituality is applied spirituality because the spiritual ideals of life have to be practised in the realm of practical life. Though spirituality is concerned with the inner development of the person, it has wider application in the society the way Gandhi has indicated above. Spirituality also includes the practice of virtues like love and compassion such that they make man more and more developed inwardly. So it may appear as if spirituality is something personal and private. But Gandhi has made it universal by taking it out of the personal life. He writes:

> Non-violence is not a cloistered virtue, confined only to the *ṛṣi*s and cave-dwellers. It is capable of being practised by the millions, not with

[3] *Bhagavad-Gītā*, XVIII.66.

[4] Gandhi, *My Philosophy of Life*, p. 69.

> full knowledge of its implications, but because it is the law of our species.[5]

That is, spiritual life is open to all because every human being is capable of practising virtues like truth, non-violence, love and compassion such that we become morally and spiritually developed persons.

Rao has adopted the Gandhian approach in his philosophy of applied spirituality. He also believes that spirituality is not a matter of personal virtue but of universal application in the collective life. Spirituality is basically transformational not only at the individual level but also at the collective level. He writes:

> Gandhi's philosophy, as I see it, is contextual and transformational with a spiritual slant. Non-violence is seen as transforming the individual as well as society. Classical Indian philosophy in general is transformational. Reaching *kaivalya, mokṣa* or *nirvāṇa* is essentially a transformational experience.[6]

For Rao, spirituality basically transforms man in the sense that man leads a virtuous life and changes his or her self according to the principles of truth and non-violence. The spirit of practicality is important in this context because man's moral and spiritual way of life applies to the practical field of life in the society. There is no conflict between our inner life and the outer life in the world. He says:

> Gandhi's thoughts are an excellent example of contextual and transformational philosophy, which is essentially spiritual. The change brought about in the other (the opponent) by *satyāgraha* of the strong practising non-violence is truly anomalous in that it does not fit into basic rational principles relating to adversarial transformation. The transformation is almost "magical".[7]

This magical transformation is beyond our rational understanding and so it can be called spiritual. Anything that cannot be encapsulated within our rational and logical understanding can be spiritual because it indicates the presence in man of a higher capacity.

Rao takes the Gandhian idea of *satyāgraha* as a kind of *yoga* because the *satyāgrahī* has learnt the art of practising truth and non-violence in all circumstances including the most difficult adversarial conditions. As he says:

> This is precisely how *satyāgraha* is supposed to work on the adversary transforming him to eschew violence, see the truth and help in resolving

[5] Gandhi, *My Philosophy of Life*, p. 69.

[6] Cf., Ibid., p. 26.

[7] Ibid.

> conflict. In Gandhi, spirituality is thus extended and becomes the social force beyond personal transformation.[8]

This is how Rao takes the Gandhian model of spirituality to the heart of the world in resolving conflicts and bringing about a social transformation through the spiritual principles of truth and non-violence.

Spirituality and the Practical World

The crux of spirituality is its application in the practical world where man is engaged with the world in various ways. Man's actions fall within the world where there is possibility of his becoming violent in the process of living in the world. Not only individuals but also societies enter into conflict for various reasons, personal, social and political. There are violent responses regarding identity of race and culture but also violent responses due to violation of one's rights. Thus there is a whole gamut of real-life situations which breed violence within an individual and also within a society. Tracing the roots of violence in human nature, Rao investigates the genesis of violence[9] in the evolutionary biology of man which includes human evolution in the process of history. Violent behaviour has appeared at different stages in the process of evolution at the early stage of man's hunting and gathering of food, at the level of community formation and then at the level of organization of state. So there are not only individual cases of violence, but also group violence, and also communal and political violence. In all the cases of violence, there are manifestations of the aggressive instinct in man in different situations. Rao writes:

> Violence has been around humankind for as long as we can remember; but the forms of violence, causes for violence and functions of violence varied over time. We have come to understand and to a degree live with criminal violence as in rape and murder, political violence as in war and social unrest, and economic and social violence as seen in exploitation and exclusion of certain segments of society.[10]

Thus violence is multifaceted and multi-dimensional and is rooted in human aggressive behaviour. As a psychologist, Rao has done extensive research on violence and found that though violence is endemic in the human world, he does not think that violence is original to man and that man can never overcome his violent nature. As a philosopher of man he agrees

---

[8] Cf. Gandhi, *My Philosophy of Life*, p. 26.

[9] Ibid., chap. 2.

[10] Ibid., p. 35.

with Gandhi that man is basically inclined towards love and non-violence and that only under negative conditions he falls into the trap of violence. He rejects the idea that man is primarily violent and only secondarily non-violent because he believes that man adopted violence as a method only to protect himself and his family. Rao writes:

> It would be fair to say that violence is in our nature no more than lying is in our nature. Violence, however, has had instrumental value to protect and defend oneself from predators and to enable one to pursue her interests.[11]

Violence has instrumental value for man because of the practical necessity of protecting life as such against the predators. However, it is undeniable that some of the individuals engage in criminal violence out of frustration of some kind or other. Such individuals are always in a minority. Society is by and large prone towards non-violence because of the necessity of survival and the social conditioning. The fact that the human species has survived so long is the evidence of the fact that man's violent nature can be controlled and transformed by the practice of non-violence. Rao unveils the most important side of the human nature when he says:

> What would seem to be the saving feature, which often goes unnoticed and little appreciated, is the dimension of love, compassion, benevolence and altruism. They emanate from the spiritual side of human nature. Cultivating them would have the salutary effect of preventing the outbreaks of violence. Spirituality is thus the natural antidote to contain violence.[12]

It is this spiritual and positive side of human nature which is the foundation of the principle of non-violence.

Man has to choose between violence and non-violence if he has to remain true to his own spiritual nature. He cannot choose to be violent because that negates his interest in survival as a social being. To live in the society is to develop the social instinct which negates aggressive behaviour on the part of man. Society promotes non-aggressive behaviour and lays the foundations of a non-violent social order. That is the right environment for man to grow spiritually by developing the instinct of love, compassion and fellow-feeling. The spiritual life which Rao envisions is based on the philosophical assumption that there is a "spiritual side to human nature and that it can be cultivated by practising non-violence".[13]

---

[11] Cf. Gandhi, *My Philosophy of Life*, p. 46.

[12] Ibid., p. 71.

[13] Ibid.

Thus spirituality emerges as a principle in man's engagement with the world. Therefore spirituality cannot be the ideal of an abstract life. It is very much needed in the practical world.

Non-violence and Human Actions

The spiritual man's engagement with the world is very different from the ordinary person's involvement with the world. In the Indian spiritual tradition, especially in the *Gītā*, there has been a lot of debate on the kind of actions a spiritual man is supposed to perform. Actions are an essential part of any man's life in the world, because without actions man's life is empty. But all actions are not ethically permitted, nor are all actions spiritually conducive. For example, the actions like killing, stealing, deceiving, cheating, etc., are not morally permitted and so are called immoral actions. Neither morality nor spirituality permits these actions because they are against our moral and spiritual values. Morality accepts some eternal values which bind the human beings together; they also bind us with the entire universe. Spirituality pursues these eternal values and conducts human life according to the values and principles accepted by morality. Gandhi has emphasized two important eternal values such as truth and non-violence as the foundations of moral and spiritual life. Human actions are performed according to these values when the person pursues the path of morality and spirituality. Rao, following Gandhi, emphasizes the eternal values in human life for, according to him, no human society can thrive without following these values which are characterized as *dharma* in Indian moral and spiritual tradition.

The concept of *satyāgraha* embodies the philosophy of moral and spiritual actions in the form of non-violent actions. Non-violent actions, for both Gandhi and Rao, are the genuine moral and spiritual actions because they issue from the good will of the agent who performs the actions. A non-violent agent is led by his good will to perform the acts of love and compassion for all. He has no ill-will towards his enemy. The moral agent transforms the enemy by his acts of love and charity. Gandhi writes:

> *Ahiṁsā* in us ought to soften and not to stiffen our opponents' attitude to us; it ought to melt him; it ought to strike a responsive chord in his heart.[14]

[14] Gandhi, *My Philosophy of Life*, p. 72.

Such is the faith of Gandhi in the efficacy of *ahiṁsā* that he thinks the acts of love can change the heart of the opponent. This is how he thinks that if we do acts of non-violence we can conquer the earth. For him:

> Non-violence is not a mere passive quality; it is the mightiest force God has endowed man with. Indeed, possession of non-violence distinguishes man from the brute creation. It is inherent in every human being, but in most it lies dormant.[15]

Rao, on the basis of his analysis of the genesis of violence, has come to the conclusion that man is not inherently violent but becomes violent under circumstances which are beyond his control. In that sense, for him, as for Gandhi, non-violence is natural to mankind and given an opportunity man will demonstrate his instinct of love and compassion to others. Rao writes:

> Violence begets violence; and newer generations of violence are more potent with more devastating effects. In the final analysis, violence is self-destructive. We have now come to a point of helplessness to control violence. The survival of human species, nay life itself on this planet, may depend on what we do to control the spread of violence.[16]

Rao agrees with Gandhi on that the future of mankind depends on how effectively we control the spread of violence by the acts of non-violence. That is to say, how much non-violent techniques we evolve to check violence at all levels — individual, social, national and international. Rao is particularly interested in the analysis of non-violent social actions which include all forms of actions including the political and the economic actions. He considers *satyāgraha* as the right method of solving the social problems arising out of economic disparity, social exclusion of the marginalized groups and the religious conflict-situations. Rao wants to extend the sphere of non-violence actions to include all forms of social action. That is the reason, why, according to him, the Gandhian method of *satyāgraha* is the best method to tackle not only national problems but also the international problems. According to him, "*satyāgraha* is superior to any other method of conflict resolution known to human kind".[17]

Thus human actions performed in the spirit of non-violence and love can be the right way to make the world safe from violence and ill-will. The moral agency of man grounded in the will to resist evil and

[15] Gandhi, *My Philosophy of Life*, p. 71.

[16] Rao, *Gandhi and Applied Spirituality*, pp. 100-01.

[17] Ibid., p. 90.

demonstrate the greater will to love one another can resolve the conflicts in the spirit of brotherhood and co-operation.

Satyagraha as Yoga: Spirituality in Action

Gandhi has developed his philosophy *of satyāgraha* to solve all human problems by applying the method of non-violent actions without injuring anyone in word, thought and deed. That is, *satyāgraha* is an all-comprehensive way of acting in accordance with the principles of non-violence and truth at all levels — from personal to international. This philosophy of non-violent action is not just a technique or method of solving problems but a way of spiritually transforming man. It is a philosophy of action and life with a goal of transforming man. This Gandhi calls the philosophy of soul-force in the efficacy of which he had the deepest faith. He writes:

> The force of love is the same as the force of the soul or truth. We have evidence of its working at every step. The universe would disappear without the existence of that force.[18]

The soul force or truth-force which is the basis of *satyāgraha* is the foundation of life in the universe and in that sense *satyāgraha* is not merely a political weapon as it has been so often misunderstood. Gandhi has so much faith in the soul-force which is evident from the following passage:

> There have been cataclysmic changes in the world. Do I still adhere to my faith in truth and non-violence? Has not the atom bomb exploded that faith? Not only has it not done so, but it has clearly demonstrated to me that the twins constitute the mightiest force in the world. Before it, the atom bomb is of no effect.[19]

The force of spirituality for Gandhi is the force of truth and non-violence and of *satyāgraha* such that nothing can defeat it in the ultimate analysis.

Rao takes the Gandhian *satyāgraha* as applied spirituality for the reason that he thinks that *satyāgraha* is no less a form of *yoga* because it transforms man and society. He emphasizes the transformational aspects of *satyāgraha* because he thinks that it makes man and society spiritually changed if truth and non-violence are followed in letter and spirit. He compares Gandhi's *satyāgraha* with Patañjali's *yoga*:

---

[18] M.K. Gandhi (1938), *Hind Swaraj or Indian Home Rule,* Ahmedabad: Navajivan Publishing House, p. 67.

[19] Gandhi, *My Philosophy of Life*, p. 75.

> The similarities between Gandhi's *satyāgraha* and Patañjali's *yoga* are remarkably striking. Non-violence is Gandhi's *yoga*. What *samādhi* is in Patañjali's *yoga*, *satyāgraha* is in Gandhi's *yoga* of non-violence. *Satyāgraha* is not a mere set of practices, but a state of mind achieved by certain practices of non-violence.[20]

By this Rao gives a certain depth to the Gandhian concept of *satyāgraha* by making it a spiritual way of life without, at the same time, making it other-worldly. Spirituality for him is always a matter of practical life and not a way of life of the socially recluse. The comparison between *samādhi* and *satyāgraha* is very apt because it makes *satyāgraha* itself a spiritual activity leading to the realization of a spiritual harmony in life in the face of difficulties and hardships. *Samādhi* is a state of equanimity of the mind that is realized through the spiritual practices or *sādhanā*. So is the case with *satyāgraha* which also needs *sādhanā*. Rao writes:

> Practice of non-violence is more than suppression of violence in one's behaviour in that it is more than cognitively apprehended appreciation of virtues of non-violence. It is non-violence in thought and action that is built into the mindset of the person and therefore has become a way of life for her. It is a state of *samādhi* where subject and object, knowing and being blend harmoniously. It seems to presuppose, as mentioned earlier, the development of a certain level of spiritual maturity on the part of the person practising non-violence as appears to be the case with a practising yogin endowed with miraculous powers (*siddhis*).[21]

Thus *satyāgraha* has assumed a yogic status in Rao's thought because he finds that the *satyāgrahī* is no less a spiritually evolved person than the *yogī*. In this sense, he suggests one could formulate the principles of *satyāgraha* in the form of treatise like *Satyāgraha-Sūtra*[22] in the way Patañjali wrote his *Yoga-Sūtra*.

Science and Spirituality

In view of the fact that spirituality is fundamental to life and society as such, there is a need for evaluating its importance *vis-à-vis* religion on the one hand and science on the other. Spirituality is a distinct mode of human existence which cannot be reduced to any other mode of existence for the reason that spirituality encompasses the entire life of man including his moral and social life. To be spiritual is not to exclude any aspect of life

---

[20] Rao, *Gandhi and Applied Spirituality*, pp. 141-42.

[21] Ibid., p. 142.

[22] Cf., Ibid., p. 142.

such as the social and the moral life. Besides, to be spiritual is not to be necessarily religious in the traditional sense of the term, because spirituality and religion are not the same. Spirituality pertains to the inner life of man, whereas religion mostly pertains to the adoption of a particular set of beliefs and attitudes. However, religion and spirituality can meet because a religious person can become spiritual by transforming his inner life. Rao holds that both religion and spirituality have the idea of transcendence which is the basis of man's evolution in his spiritual journey. For him, "spiritual pursuit is an exercise for transformation of the human condition to achieve states of transcendence. Such transcendence provides for resolution of problems in ways which appear almost magical."[23] Further, he observes:

> . . . Spirituality is the quest and religions are the tools and technologies, first, to aid the person in the quest and, second, to apply the discoveries of the spiritual quest to life and living. . . . *Spirituality is to religion what science is to technology.*[24] (Italics original)

In this sense, spirituality is the core to the religious life and therefore religions can be more or less the technologies which help the seekers in attaining spirituality. Without spirituality, a religion may become empty.

However, the greatest challenge to spirituality comes from science, because science due to its naturalistic method and orientation does not take spirituality seriously. Either it rejects spirituality outright or makes spirituality a mere matter of aberrational psychology. For science everything other than the pursuit of objective truth is a matter of emotional blindness which has no worth of any kind. This antagonism towards spirituality on the part of science is unfounded and wrong. Rao rejects the view that science and spirituality are antagonistic to each other. He finds a great deal of complementarity between these two pursuits. He writes:

> Seen in this light, science and spirituality are two truth-seeking activities that seem to run parallel to each other. One is experimental and objective, and the other experiential and subjective.[25]

Both science and spirituality are pursuits of man though they relate to different aspects of the human life. Science is concerned with the truth about the physical universe including man's own life from the objective

[23] Cf., Rao, *Gandhi and Applied Spirituality*, p. 216.

[24] Ibid.

[25] Ibid.

point of view. Therefore, it is limited to the knowledge of the physical laws which operate in the universe. Science has no method of understanding the human condition from the subjective point of view. Spirituality looks into the truth regarding the inner subjective life of man. Its truth is subjective and phenomenological, and so pertains to the inner life of man, his sufferings, and trials and tribulations within his subjective life. Spirituality is always about the removal of suffering and bringing peace and harmony into the mind. As Rao puts it:

> At its best, spirituality is known to free humans from all kinds of suffering born out of dysfunctional egos with insatiable desires, and consequent personal frustration and externally directed aggression. *Spirituality could be the soothing syrup to congested minds that cough conflict and abuse.*[26] (Italics original)

That is to say, spirituality is a practical science of transforming man and bringing liberation to his suffering soul. In that sense, spirituality is concerned with the welfare of the inner being of man and making man a better human being as an individual as well as the social being.

The domain of science is altogether different as it discovers the truth about man from the outside and as part of the universal causal order. Its truths are verifiable in experience and are subject to external scrutiny. But for that, however, science and spirituality do not exclude each other but are parallel to each other and so can co-exist. In both Gandhi's and Rao's scheme of things, they can co-exist and can influence each other. Gandhi holds that modern science has been anti-spiritual and therefore it has not understood the human condition. Gandhi therefore condemns modern science as negating spirituality.[27] Rao, however, takes a more positive view of science because he believes that science liberates man from hunger and other inhuman conditions. Science has helped mankind develop technology in order to eliminate poverty, hunger and other ills in society. Therefore, according to him, science is a great boon for mankind and so must be pursued for its positive contributions. But at the same time, according to Rao, science without spirituality is blind and must therefore keep spirituality as a co-partner in the discovery of truth.

> On its part, spirituality helps science to find meaning in life and to set goals that enhance human potential and happiness by adding an ethical

[26] Cf., Rao, *Gandhi and Applied Spirituality*, p. 218.

[27] Cf., Gandhi, *Hind Swaraj*, p. 55.

> dimension to its pursuits. Spiritually balanced science will add value to its pursuits.[28]

Rao, however, is of the opinion that science alone cannot solve the problems of man. Science because of its methodological limitations does not recognize the paranormal experiences of man which include man's religious or spiritual experiences. The latter are such that they cannot be fully justified according to the available scientific methods. The objective methods of science emphasize the empirical observability of all phenomena and therefore do not allow the paranormal stream of experiences which are subjective and personal to a great extent. The scientific observations are from the third-person point of view and so they allow for the possibility of the first-person experiences. That is the reason why the Western sciences have been dismissive of the spiritual experiences. "Spirituality is one of those areas that are inherently resistant to scientific investigation and therefore it is considered an inappropriate subject matter of science."[29] Rao goes against this prevalent opinion of the Western sciences because he believes that it is possible to reconcile science and spirituality because science can accept the experiences of the mystics and religious thinkers for study, especially in psychology and other human sciences. Both science and spirituality can co-exist provided we enlarge the scope of science itself to include man's paranormal experiences.

Spirituality and the Paranormal Yogic Experiences

Rao is a defender of parapsychology which opens the way to a phenomenological study of the paranormal experiences relating to the non-physical realm of reality. Influenced by Joseph Banks Rhine and other pioneers in the field, Rao has been involved in research in parapsychology and has arrived at significant results in this science applying it to religious and other spiritual experiences. He writes:

> The Eastern traditions, especially the Hindu and the Buddhist, recognize that psychic (paranormal) abilities are a natural outcome as one progresses on the path to achieve states of transcendence and has religious experience.[30]

These experiences are so fundamental to human existence that we can neglect them only at our own peril. These experiences are found in all

[28] Rao, *Gandhi and Applied Spirituality*, p. 218.

[29] Ibid., p. 226.

[30] Ibid., p. 235.

religions and cultures from the ancient times to the modern. Therefore it is unscientific to reject these experiences as illusory and based on abnormality. Rao writes:

> I am persuaded that a systematic and descriptive study of such experiences would reveal something more basic to religious experiences than do the contents of these experiences translated to us in common language forms. Religious experience, we are told, is essentially ineffable. . . . Religious experience, the mystic experience, the peak experience, and all paranormal experiences may have one thing in common. They are the encounters with consciousness as-such, pure consciousness in which there is no subject–object distinction, no content, but a transformational process that often results in remarkable behavioural changes and beliefs and sometimes translates itself into informational content.[31]

Thus we can assert that religious experiences are no less important for human life than other normal experience based on sense-contact with the world. These experiences reveal to us the many dimensions of man's consciousness.

The yogic experiences are the rich sources of knowledge so far as the inner world is concerned. *Yoga* psychology and philosophy have revealed the higher dimensions of human consciousness. *Yoga* is itself a science of consciousness in the sense that it has revealed to mankind new depths of the human mind and consciousness. According to Rao, the *Yoga* psychology has opened up new vistas in the realm of consciousness research because it has unfolded the new levels of consciousness beyond the sensory and cognitive experiences. He hints at a third level of experience beyond the sensory awareness and rational thinking.

> The level of excellence involves total transcendence from sensory awareness and rational thinking. At this level, knowing becomes being. For this reason, this level may be called transcendental being, which involves the transformation of the person to realize truth in her own being and thus become perfect.[32]

Yoga attempts at reaching the highest stage of human consciousness which is the same as the attainment of perfection. *Yoga* marks the highest level of spirituality.

For Rao, though *yoga* and spirituality are one, the former can be treated

---

[31] Rao, *Gandhi and Applied Spirituality*, pp. 235-36.

[32] Ibid., p. 306.

as the means to the way of spirituality because it is always concerned with the methods of control of the mind and other allied mental functions. Spirituality is the transformational process while *yoga* tells us how to actually accomplish this transformation. Spirituality is always a practical matter and can have no concern with the intellectual matters alone regarding spirituality. As regards the applied aspects of spirituality, it goes without saying that it has wider ramification for the society and mankind as a whole in that the spiritual persons are the beacon lights for their respective society. Buddha, Jesus and Gandhi are the burning examples of such beacon lights which have guided mankind in the hour of spiritual crisis.

Conclusion

Gandhi and Rao are both defenders of applied spirituality because both see its importance in the life of man both at the individual and social level. While Gandhi has taken the philosophy of spirituality from the traditional religious sources, Rao has taken his philosophy from his encounter with Indian tradition and also from his own psychological research in the domain of both normal and paranormal consciousness. Rao is a philosopher and psychologist of spirituality in the academic sense of the term, while Gandhi got his spiritual experience from his own life as a political leader and thinker. Though both differ from each other in their specific areas of action, both agree on the fundamentals of the philosophy of spirituality. It is the belief in the applied spirituality which brings Rao closer to Gandhi. In Rao's interpretation, Gandhi has emerged live and relevant to our contemporary times which need the healing touch of the applied spirituality.

11

Prof. K. Ramakrishna Rao's Conception of Philosophy and His Contribution to It

G. Vedaparayana

THIS paper is an attempt to bring out Prof. K. Ramakrishna Rao's conception of philosophy and his contribution to it, as found in his recently published book, *Gandhi and Applied Spirituality*.[1] Rao here identifies classical Indian conception of philosophy as philosophy "proper" and seeks to contribute significantly to it by discussing and deciphering some of the complex issues embodying it. His contribution also consists in giving an emphasis to the spiritual and practical side of the ancient Indian wisdom which forms its nucleus. The book is of seminal philosophic importance as it is pregnant with several issues dealt with, in detail, in the light of the Indian conception of philosophy. It is also an attempt to explore Gandhian thought which Rao regards as an illustration of the Indian conception of philosophy comprising profound spiritual insights and practices. The book consists of a thorough discussion of the topics like identity, national integration, violence, science and spirituality, parapsychology and *yoga*. It also deals with Buddhist psychology and consciousness, Indianness, Nehru and Ambedkar. The variety of the philosophical issues and the insightful way Rao has dealt with them are a testimony to his philosophic depth and understanding of the intricate problems with conceptual clarity and a clear perspective of their practical applicability and relevance to the present Indian and global context. In this paper, I propose to bring forth Rao's conception of philosophy in brief and then highlight his contribution to it by presenting his elucidation of the three important issues — the question of identity, the Buddhist theories of the person and the phenomenology of the Buddhist consciousness.

Introduction to Rao's Conception of Philosophy

To Rao, philosophy is predominantly a pursuit to discover "wisdom aimed at transforming the person and the society" (p. 12).* Philosophy is the discipline intimately connected with the understanding and resolution of the problems of life. The wisdom that philosophical reflection aims at is both contemplative and practical in character. It is both spiritual and secular in the sense that the "self" or the "spirit" that it embodies has profound implications for a meaningful social praxis. To Rao, philosophy is not merely an activity of conceptual clarification but an art of living by the resolving existential problems of life. Disputing Daya Krishna's conception of philosophy as the clarification of conceptual confusions in which the philosopher finds himself or herself involved when thinking about certain problems, Rao holds that "there is more to philosophy than finding oneself in the cocoons of conceptual confusions and trying to come out of them" (p. 9). He does not like to delimit philosophy to the mundane realm of the conceptual confusions that arise in thinking about any subject and the attempt at the clarification of those confusions. He does not subscribe to the idea of regarding logic and reason as the sole arbitrators in settling the genuine confusions. Reason is not necessarily the only route to know the truth of any problem and logic is not the sufficient means to clear confusions, conceptual or otherwise. Rao contends that philosophical conflict and real-life confusions are not limited to concepts. There are other kinds of conflicts and confusions which warrant an understanding that is more than semantic, logical or intellectual.

Espousing the philosophy of pragmatism as advocated by G.S. Peirce and John Dewey, Rao says that philosophy is not a search for the eternal, the "really real" but a problem-oriented and context-relevant inquiry. Philosophy seeks of intimate relation of thought to action and understands concepts in terms of the purpose of their having a bearing on our conduct. It fixes our beliefs not merely by elaborating them by reason and logic but by relating them to the facts and purposes of lived experience. Philosophy ascertains the meaning of an intellectual conception by considering the practical consequences resulting from the truth of that conception. The meaning of the conception in question is constituted by the sum of these consequences. That is, philosophy should be practical in the sense of being "apt to affect conduct" (p. 11). Problems are not merely

* All page numbers given in the brackets are from Prof. K. Ramakrishna Rao's book *Gandhi and Applied Spirituality* (2011).

intellectual but experimental and contextual. Their resolution therefore is neither in vacuum nor limited to their analysis. The ideas and beliefs need to be studied in relation to the context in which they arise, besides logically analysing them. The profound task of philosophy therefore consists in dealing with ideas and their impact on ourselves and our place in the universe. It consists "in learning the existential conditions that give rise to particular thought systems, philosophical problems and their resolution" (ibid.). Following Dewey, Rao says that the problems and the subject matter of philosophy grow out of stresses and strains in the community life in which a given form of philosophy arises. Further, he adds to the Deweyian stresses and strains the spiritual dimension encompassing the emotional, the moral and the aesthetic. Man is a complex being embodying several dimensions — the physical, the vital, the mental, and the spiritual, each influencing the other. It is lopsided to understand man just as a rational being. Rao boserves:

> Man does not live by reason alone. One's thirst is not quenched by a rational understanding of its causes. A man is not relieved of his grief by syllogistic reasoning but by comforting counsel and empathy. The existential conditions not only precipitate problems, philosophic or otherwise, but they also provide their plausible solutions. — p. 9

In the light of his conception of philosophy as mentioned above, Rao proposes to reconstruct philosophy on the Gandhian thought which, to him, is the epitome of the harmonious blend of reason and spirit, science and spirituality. He considers Gandhian thought as a clarion call for a fresh reconstruction in philosophy which has lost its way and finds itself in a disarray. Gandhi's philosophy is becoming more and more relevant in the present context of the strife of humankind confronted with weapons of mass destruction. It addresses the spiritual side of the person transcending the physical, emotional and mental. It aims at the attainment of the Deweyian "intelligent happiness" by appealing to the spiritual and altruistic side of the person. Rao argues that moral issues go beyond the purely physical and mental, and call for a spiritual understanding which ultimately triumphs in restoring happiness to humanity. He considers this as the central claim of Gandhian thought and calls for a philosophical reconstruction developing a philosophy around it, which, according to Rao, will be far more profound than what Dewey had envisaged. Gandhi's experiments are the attempts to test the implications of the spiritual and moral dimensions for transforming the world. The experiments involve clarifying moral ideas and the spiritual truths through experimental methods. They seek to demonstrate their relevance in practice through ingeniously conceived experiments. "In doing so, Gandhi showed a way to bridge the gap between the secular and the sacred, science and spirituality, the mundane and the moral" (p. 7).

As mentioned, Rao's vision of reconstructing philosophy by developing a philosophy around the Gandhian conception of applied spirituality has its roots in the classical Indian philosophical tradition which is more than a theory about the human condition. Indian philosophy is concerned with the wisdom of applying knowledge to enhance the potential of the humans to transform their condition. It is holistic rather than merely analytical and takes a synthetic approach to combine facts from different aspects of life and generates wisdom aimed at transforming the person and society. Rao argues that philosophy in India has been culturally contextual, interdisciplinary and practical. As distinguished from simple knowledge, philosophical wisdom is the running thread that weaves the Indian cultural fabric. Indian philosophy tended to be applied to a large extent since the Vedic times up until the colonial period. It has the unique identity of having an avowed connection with life and grew along with religion, science and other human endeavours. The Hindu scriptures like the Vedas, Upaniṣads, *Yogavāsiṣṭha, Rāmāyaṇa, Bhagavad-Gītā, Arthaśāstra, Caraka Saṁhitā, Nāṭyasāstra,* Dharmaśāstra, *Kāma-Sūtra* and *Yoga-Sūtras* are a clear testimony to the fact that Indian philosophy has been as much practical as theoretical. In fact, it may also be said that here practice takes precedence over theory and wisdom rules over knowledge. It secures freedom and perfection to the person and welfare to the society at large. "Philosophy in India has been truly a wisdom discipline. Wisdom is knowledge applied to life" (p. 12).

Indian Identity and Integration

Rao here deals with the problem of identity and in particular with Indian identity as being pluralistic, inclusive and synthetic. He argues that the Indian value of detachment enables the person to surmount the compulsions of the ego and to move in the direction of non-paradoxicality of the multiple identities. The spirituality of the Indian philosophic tradition and Gandhi's thought in particular comprising the Indianness of pluralism, inclusiveness and unity in diversity form a firm ground for harmonious co-existence of multiple identities that are contrary to each other.

CONCEPT OF IDENTITY

In his search for an authentic Indian identity, Rao undertakes a conceptual analysis of the notion of identity and the related issues such as politics of identity, national and global identity, identity reduction, identity crisis and national integration *vis-à-vis* multiple identities. Rao defines identity as the sense of self-sameness in the person which makes one a discrete individual and gives her historical continuity; the concept of identity is paradoxical in that the sameness it refers to is the opposite of change which can be seen in our speaking of the distinctiveness of the individuals and holding them to be responsible for what they believe and do, despite the fact that there is no one who is unchanging and remain to be the same from birth to death; the paradox is that despite being apparently the same we are an unending continuum of multiple manifestations in every aspect of our being; this paradox "is not a simple intellectual puzzle but has important psycho-social and ethical ramifications", says Rao (p. 149).

Distinguishing between individual and social identity, Rao considers the former as referring to the psychological image one has of oneself, and the latter as signifying the categorization of the individual as belonging to particular groups such as caste, gender, religion, region, employment, nationality and so on. Accordingly, each one of us, Rao opines, enjoys multiple identities of being a father, husband, philosopher, an environmentalist, a Hindu, an Indian, and so on. Yet, one is a unique person, a mosaic of varied identities merged into a distinctive identity. Rao maintains that the different identities need not necessarily entail any proneness to conflict but can be organized hierarchically to function smoothly (p. 150). Identity politics, according to Rao, is a concerted political effort to push the social identity forward beyond self-determination based on religion, language or ethnicity; it often provides a body of thought which forms the basis for uniting people and forge them as a political force; identity politics may be built around a race, religion, gender or even disability; and practised by the minority groups like the Dalits, or the majority community espousing the Hindutva ideology; Rao observes that identity politics, besides serving some useful social purposes, has a potential for devastating and disruptive effects (p. 150).

Rao sees national identity as the way the citizens of a particular nation differentiate and distinguish themselves from others; it involves an emotional attachment, a sense of semi-sacred belonging arising from some kind of moral identification with cultural, political or ideological distinctiveness and attribution of superiority to it. Rao at the same time contends that given the multiplicity of groups prevalent in many nations, it would be wrong to characterize a nation on the presumption that there is a single distinctive way of life in it; each nation must define its identity by taking the interests and values of its multiple groups. A nation may choose to either assimilate, as in France, or subordinate, as in Germany, its minority groups or accept the diversity as real and provide them appropriate place. In the case of countries like India and Sweden with their variety of cultures, multiculturalism is a natural choice in defining their identity, argues Rao (p. 151).

Holding that national identity is not ultimate and inclusiveness does not stop with the nation state, Rao calls for a reassessment of the sociology of nationalism. As the forces of globalization, namely, migration of people across the continents with attendant cultural, linguistic and ethnic diversity, the web of multinational economic structures and international media networks, have led to an identity crisis in a nation state, and caused the emergence of supra-national entities, there is a need for resorting to non-solitarist understanding of human identities. Following Amartya Sen, Rao asserts that the contemporary world demands a global sense of belonging besides our national allegiances and local loyalties. An overarching global identity, Rao affirms, is possible only through "a common universal value line and shared ethics which permits ethical pluralism but rejects ethical relativism". This calls for a free debate which in itself may be the ultimate value, says Rao (p. 155).

He further argues that reduction of our multiple identities to a single identity creates a solitarist illusion that divides people into hardened categories and foment devastating intergroup strife as in the case of Islamic single-minded advocacy of a belligerent religious identity and exclusiveness. Inclusiveness of identities without reducing them to a single dominant identity resolves identity crisis arising out of confusion and conflict of multiple identities. Our identities have to be inclusive not in the sense of absorption or assimilation of the many by the one but in the spirit of coexisting mosaic of multiple identities each with its distinctiveness but contributing to a gestalt configuration. For instance, children with dual ethnicity or as members of more than one cultural group have demonstrated greater flexibility, adaptability and creativity, as adults. Therefore, it is important to realize, Rao maintains, that preservation of multiple social identities is a precondition for national solidarity and integrity of the nation state and global peace. This calls for education and upbringing of the children that allows them to have multiple group affiliations and identities and be able to shift them constantly without conflict, dissension, negative stereotyping or prejudice against out groups. Education should enable them to amicably resolve identity crises by perceiving similarities rather than differences between one's own identities and those of others (p. 152).

INDIANNESS

In his quest for the quintessence of the Indianness of Indians, Rao examines the views expressed by some scholars like Sudhir Kakar, Alan Roland and Agehānanda Bhāratī, and relegates them to the background. He disputes Kakar's view that the meta-reality of the *puruṣārtha*s constitutes the Indian "psyche" on the ground that millions of non-Hindu Indians do not possesses the same psyche; but, Rao subscribes to Kakar's later formulation of the Indian identity as exemplified in the joint family system, the context-sensitivity seen in the relativity of value, the context-relatedness of virtues and the less marked perception of differences between man and woman (p. 156). Rao objects to Alan Roland's notion of Indianness as the striving of Indians for the realization of the spiritual self through a complex structure of gods and goddess, through rituals and meditation; he contends that Roland's view is at best a theoretical speculation for which there is some basis in the Hindu texts but it hardly touches the action and behaviour of the average Indian; the urge for spiritual realization of one's identity with the *Brahman* is not relevant to the existential context of the Indian identity (p. 157). Rao seems to agree with Agehānanda Bhāratī who characterizes Indian identity as the permanent self, the *ātman*, the cynosure of Indian cognition and action and also as the empirical or the "dividual" self which is systematically marginalized and undergoing constant change in a wide range of social transactions (pp. 157-8). Rao subscribes to a certain extent the views of J.B.P. Sinha who sees Indian identity as the product of the intrapsychic structures based on the Hindu religio-philosophical ideas, familial and social relationships as well as the existential conditions of contemporary India like the threat of economic poverty that forces people to engage in power struggles to gain risk-free ingratiation. But at the same time, Rao does not agree with Sinha's equation of Indian identity with the Hindu identity (p. 158). He maintains that attempts to find Indian identity in the Hindu ethos are misplaced and temptations to stereotype the Indian character. In a multicultural country like India, it is wrong to associate Indian identity with the Hindu identity, for it will invoke a suspicion among the minorities that their distinct identities would be assimilated into the mainstream. Alluding Shahabuddin's view, Rao also objects to the proponents of Indianization who equate India with Hinduism, Indianization with Hinduization, and expect the Indian Muslims to join the mainstream (p. 158).

Rao contends that in the current socio-political climate, reducing Indian identity to Hindu identity proves to be more divisive than cohesive and finds fault with Vinayak Savarkar's attempt to reconstruct the Indian national identity through Hindutva ideology which equates the Hindu with one who is living in India instead of with one who is practising the Hindu religion, and reiterates the traditional belief that Indianness is a natural phenomenon that existed since antiquity, the view subscribed by B.G. Tilak and Swami Vivekananda as against the liberal nationalists — Govinda Ranade, Surendranath Benerjee and Gopal Krishna Gokhale — view that the nationhood of India is not given but something to be constructed voluntarily through democratic political institutions. Prof. Rao also subscribes to the view that Indianness is a consciously cultivated idea that is also reflected in the notion of "India in the making" enshrined in the Indian Constitution (p. 160). He argues that India, the mother of multiculturalism, a country of several contrasting identities, has endured the birth pangs of emerging new identities and the horrors of identity conflicts. It is a fertile soil for the growth of communal harmony and for harvesting of cultural synthesis which is not an amalgamation of multiple identities coalesced into a hybrid identity but a mosaic of picturesque shades and shapes coexisting as a grand colourful mix of many faiths, multiple tongues, varied tastes and lifestyles. The fact that some of our presidents, vice-presidents, prime ministers, chief ministers and many other top political figures have come from the minority, the dalit and women categories shows that India is the only country which accommodates a diversity of caste, creed, class and gender in the higher echelons of political power. Multiculturalism in India is not an accidental coincidence but a natural phenomenon which has been there all through its history.

Following Nehru, Rao says that the tremendous impress of oneness had held Indians together for ages past whatever political fate or misfortune had befallen them (p. 146). But Rao expresses concern over the increasing polarization of identities in terms of language, religion, region and caste and a frightening feeling of virulent divisiveness born of exploitation of these identities for electoral gains in contemporary India. He reminds us of the grim spectacle of alarming divisiveness, growing economic and social inequalities and the consequent tensions that undermine the stability of the country. He finds hope saying that the identity conflicts are not deeply inlaid but only a thin outer veneer of the Indian culture. He suggests that revolutionary developments in communication and transport, easy access to weapons and technologies of destruction with increased potential for collective violence, glaring disparities in income, lack of access to good education and health services, and the exclusion of significant number of people from the process of growth and development of the nation are the contributory factors to the precipitation of identity crisis.

Rao maintains that a conceptual analysis of the notion of identity, its operationalization and differentiation of identities poses a difficult challenge. It is more so in the case of the Indian identity which is embedded in the vast socio-cultural matrix of a long history. It warrants an approach that is radically different from that of the West, for, the Indian identity is unique in the sense that it is formed predominantly on the basis of caste and community. The approach should be multidisciplinary aimed at an in-depth understanding of all the factors associated with identity formations. Theoretical models and social theories have to be generated by bringing together the intellectuals belonging to different disciplines. The models and theories thus generated can contribute for enlightened political discussion, public policy and administrative action (p. 149).

Having analysed the concept of identity and the related issues such as identity politics, multiple identities, national and global identity, identity crisis and its resolution, and having examined the views of some scholars expressed on Indianness, Rao maintains that Indianness consists neither in being a Hindu, a spiritual seeker, nor in subscribing to *varṇāśrama dharma*, nor in following a behaviourial stereotype. Even the religion, the language, the culture or the community in which one grew up singly or collectively cannot define one's identity as an Indian. He holds that genuine Indianness or *bhāratīyatā* consists "in my categorization and self-definition as an Indian and the consequent emotional bonding and sharing certain sentiments and feelings with fellow Indians". It manifests, in essence, as the overpowering emotional experience of my being an Indian, an experience which is not an intellectual conception but has a primitive origin in our collective mind. It is embedded in my categorization and self-definition as an Indian and the consequent emotional bonding and sharing of certain sentiments and feelings with fellow Indians. It also consists in the extent of identification one subjectively feels for India and other Indians and by which one achieves a sense of self-enhancement. Rao says:

> My Indian identity is manifest in the joys and sorrows I experience when good or bad things happen to India and Indians. It is the jubilation I have when India wins an international sports event and when Sachin Tendulkar breaks a world record. It is the pain I feel when I read about the Bombay blasts, the Bhopal tragedy, the Ayodhyā demolitions. It is in the pride I have for Ajantā caves, the Taj Mahal and the Telugu literature.
> —p. 160

Rao maintains that *bhāratīyatā* is a naturally given quintessence of the Indian psyche and a continually evolving cultural complex that defies any particularization as this or that. He calls it an archetype, the central *saṁskāra*, the cultural bond of Indians, which holds men and women together; the archetype is not merely "the exclusive and identifying 'meme' of Indianness alone but a particularized form of general bonding magic that manifests in all natural groups, beginning with family and extending to nationality and beyond" (p. 161). As an archetype, *bhāratīyatā* is not a doctrine of ideas but a nucleus of psychological force buried in the unconscious with the power to generate powerful images, motives and beliefs of far-reaching consequences. Admitting that in identifying *bhāratīyatā* with archetype, he is following in part the Jungian concept of archetype, Rao describes it as a collective unconscious, a shared, a "racially"-based inherited universal which is different from personal unconscious formed of the present life experiences (p. 161). Arguing that *bhāratīyatā* as an archetypal disposition may culminate in a full-blown system of ideas in a cognitively developed mind or precipitate itself as a massive collective belief and behaviourial pattern in a religion, Rao sees Indianness as being associated with certain characteristic ways of life and living, a set of dispositions to believe and act. In this, he likens it to a *maṇḍala* in the unfolding of which lies Indianness as expressed in our culture and consciousness (p. 161).

Rao associates the disposition of Indianness with the following five characteristics, which he calls the unfolding petals of the lotus of *bhāratīyatā* as *maṇḍala*. They are: pluralism, inclusiveness, unification, non-paradoxicality and detachment. Rao calls them the five minds of India, which are integral to the spiritual perspective that binds reason with value, links the "self" and the "other", individual and society, observation and experience.

Rao holds that **pluralism**, the quintessence of Indianness embodying multitude of identities, has been the way of life of Indians for long as it did not melt away under the sway of any common cause or culture, including nationalism. Pluralism is the adroitness or the tact in dealing with persons and circumstances; the law of subscribing to reason and dialogue as the means of knowing and promoting the truth; the acknowledgement that it is mind, not might, that is the arbitrator in settling the differences; it is also the recognition of the fallibility of the intellect to give us truth and so the need for tolerance for divergent perceptions and interpretation. On its philosophical level, Rao traces pluralism in India back to the Sāṁkhya-Yoga conception of the multiplicity of *puruṣa*s and the Advaita concept of *jīva*s (p. 163).

Inclusiveness of Indianness, according to Rao, lies in its spirit of inclusion of Indus Valley Civilization, the Āryan settlements, the Draviḍians and other groups into Hinduism; it can be seen in the Indians' disposition of adopting to polytheism, pantheism and even animism; Indians' reverence for the Buddha, who is said to have saught to replace the Hindu religion, as one of the incarnations of the Lord Viṣṇu, and the light-skinned Āryans' worshipping of Rāma and Kṛṣṇa, the dark-skinned gods resembling the natives of south India, according to Rao, constitute the inclusiveness of Indians with divergent identities; he regards the phrase *vasudhaika kuṭumbakam* as representing an overarching idea of the inclusiveness of India (pp. 163-4).

Unification, a natural corollary to pluralism and inclusiveness, can be seen in the coexistence of Indians with a multitude of identities and their remarkable resilience to tremulous crises and conflicts. This is because, as Rao says, the unity of Indians is not an ad hoc and a loose tying together, not a simple mixture of colours, shapes and texture but a mosaic representing greater binding together of commonalities and complimentaries to the avoidance of distinctions and differences. In this, Rao rejects the Western metaphors of "the melting pot", "the salad bowl" and "the floral bouquet" as being inadequate to truly and fully represent the unitary and synthetic disposition of Indians (p. 164).

Non-paradoxicality, according to Rao, is the disposition of allowing the contraries to co-exist, having a high threshold of tolerance for ambiguity and giving little room for dissonance arising from the perception of differences; in India, as Rao rightly observes, differences are seen but not taken to heart or acted upon; this attitude of non-paradoxicality is due to the fact that Indian thinkers have made little of the distinctions between the subject and object, individual and society, natural and supernatural, science and religion; it is not because they were insensitive to differences and tried to gloss them over for fear of compartmentalization or balkanization but because they clearly recognized the fallibility of knowing and reason and the strength of the belief in the ultimate synthesis and unity that underlies existence. He holds that the non-paradoxicality can be seen manifesting in the mystic of magical synthesis of differences in Indian life and thought ranging from the popular Advaita philosophy to the Constitution of India which provides for caste-based reservations for establishing a casteless society. Rao calls this aspect of the Indian constitution "a Houdini feat to abolish caste by recognizing caste" (p. 165); the non-paradoxicality, the magical synthesis of the opposites, can also be seen, as Rao maintains, even in the mixed economy of India, in its pursuance of capitalist goals with socialist policies and socialist goals with capitalist policies. These programmes and policies of the government of India, "are not merely consistent with but driven by the Indian mindset of non-paradoxicality" (p. 165),

Detachment, which means self-denial (*vairāgya*), the prized virtue to be cultivated, is an important characteristic of the Indianness; as advocated by the Yoga and Buddhist philosophies, detachment works as an antidote to the sense of ego (*ahaṁkāra*) which tends to give an exclusive identity to the person and promotes the spirit of inclusiveness among Indians; paradoxically, in the Indian tradition, self-denial is not only regarded as a means of self-realization but a method of overcoming exclusions. Rao says:

> This may appear as a paradox, but to me it is a profound message of inclusiveness, a recipe for turning economic disparities and social exclusions on their head, to merge the opposites and promote common good. —p. 165

GANDHI AND INDIANNESS

Rao holds that there is a profound articulation of Indianness as *maṇḍala* in Mahatma Gandhi's thought and action. Gandhiji's pragmatic pluralism is a great hermeneutic exercise and a "beautiful expression of the five minds with their socio-economic implications and application" (p. 166). As a clear and creative interpretation of the Indian tradition, Gandhian heuristic hermeneutics withstood the test of time in making a significant contribution to understanding the identity issues of India. Based on the principle of individualism, Gandhi's pluralism treats the individual as supremely important and envisages a society of "enlightened anarchy" wherein "everyone is his own ruler and rules in such manner that he is never a hindrance to his neighbour" (p. 166). It also includes a political system, namely, the village *pañcāyat*, a decentralized small local community which functions like a self-sufficient free individual. Composed of numerous villages, a *pañcāyat*, is an ever widening but never ascending circle, "not a pyramid with the apex sustained by the bottom but an oceanic circle whose centre is the individual" (p. 166). Rao regards the *pañcāyat* as the best representative of an ideal community with multiple identities and Gandhi's social, religious thought and action and his struggle against all kinds of exclusion in our society as second only to his struggle for freedom from the foreign rule. Despite being a devout Hindu, Gandhi adopted the principle of inclusiveness in according respect to other religious persuasions and in declaring that essentially all religions are equal. Rao holds that Gandhiji's adherence to inclusiveness is all too evident when he says:

> If you read the Quran you must read with the eye of the Muslim, if you read the Bible, you must read it with the eye of Christian and if you read the *Gītā*, you must read it with the eye of a Hindu. —p. 166

Gandhi strongly opposed industrialization and corporatization since they usurp the power of the individual and he would also have opposed with similar vehemence the so-called "globalization", for, it too eclipses the individual, maintains Rao. Justifying Gandhi's opposition to globalization, he makes a significant observation that "globalization in business is what solitarist reduction of identities is to religious fundamentalism" (p. 166). Thus Gandhism, to Rao,

> is an epitome of individualism, pluralism, inclusiveness, openness, and tolerance, the key ingredients of multiculturalism built on the recognition of the inevitable plurality of identities and ideas in almost every sphere.
> — p. 166

Then Rao speaks of the paradoxical character of Gandhiji's personality, ideas and actions. As a person, Gandhi was not a leader, his ideas of non-violence were alleged to be Utopian, and his actions like "Salt *Satyāgraha*" appeared to be a joke, but the world knows today that he was the leader *par excellence*, his non-violence the best means of conquering violence and *satyāgraha* the moral equivalent of war; a powerful symbolism is embedded in them. Rao sees Gandhi's sense of detachment as another instance of the paradox. In Gandhi, detachment takes the form of love which is attachment, the opposite of detachment, as "the magical synthesis which consists in resolving in one's mind the paradox of the coexistence of contraries" (p. 167); love is paradoxical in another sense that it warrants less of self-love and more of love for the other; one who loves herself more cannot truly love another, and exclusiveness of the self is a hindrance to inclusiveness; pure love is paradoxical in yet another sense that it presupposes complete selflessness and freedom from passion; as *vairāgya* in its best sense, pure love implies self-suffering as the way for happiness. To Gandhi, love is both the strongest and the most humblest force of self-suffering which alone can secure us the things of fundamental importance. Thus, Gandhism stands for pluralism rooted in spiritualism transcending reason as the way to nurturing of Indian identity and national unity encompassing multiple identities and subscribing to a few overarching principles that help bind identities in a hierarchical system of salience, avers Rao (p. 168).

Rao strongly asserts as he did long ago in his earlier works that the faithful practice of the Gandhian pragmatic pluralism will be the only hope for human survival; when nationalism appears to have lost its unifying magic and religious faith is fast failing to bind people in harmony, Gandhian pluralism is the only way out of the morass of moral morbidity and failing of bonding among humans; Gandhism alone can resolve the identity crisis that is likely to unleash an array of social aberrations, precipitate disharmony, cause communal conflict and flare up social conflagration. He writes:

> Gandhian pluralism with its altruist slant, I believe, is essentially an interesting, pragmatic articulation of the primary archetype of human identity, which in the final analysis has the potential to bridge the identity divides. All his life, Gandhi sought to bring down the divides, whether they be between rich and the poor, the upper and the lower castes, Hindus and Muslims. The last years saw him, strive relentlessly seeking Hindu–Muslim unity and prevent identity conflicts. — p. 145

The Buddhist Concept of the Person

The matters of identity crop up in Buddhist discussions of the self. Rao here discusses the concept of the person as it has been dealt within different schools of Indian Buddhism. He brings out in detail the concept of the person as understood by the *pudgalavādin*s, Vasubandhu and Candrakīrti. He is of the view that the Buddhist concept of the person founded on the doctrine of no-self (*anātma*) has profound implications for understanding and resolving the problems of identity.

Self and Identity

Before explicating the Buddhist way of relating the unique identities and liberties of the individual to the identity of the community founded on inclusiveness and universal brotherhood, Rao attempts to examine the conundrum of self and identity. Since person's sense of the self determines the goals one seeks and the way they are pursued, the self-concept has profound implications for the person's behaviour and the way one experiences the world and participates in it. Identity is what makes a person unique, a discrete and distinctive individual. Identity, according to Rao, is not the same as character, personality, attitude or belief, although these factors have a bearing on the felt identity in a given context. Identity has two dimensions — personal and social with two influential theories — one is clinical and the other anthropological. The former is associated with the clinical psychologists like Erik H. Erikson, and the latter with the social psychologists like Henri Tajfel. Following Erikson, Rao says that individual identity development involves a synthesis of prior identifications in the process of socialization; yet it is more than the sum of prior identifications as it emerges from the influence of social group in which the development takes place; the identity of an individual consists of the "sense of self-sameness and continuity in time and space" (p. 179). As there are several variations on this *theme*, Rao admits that the notion of a stable and unified individual identity is problematic, for it involves the inescapable plurality of identities experienced by individuals. Referring to identity crisis, Rao says that it is not only the individuals but groups and even nations undergo crisis of identity. In the process of seeking identities, the groups, like individuals, face problems of social cohesiveness and value conflicts which may trigger an identity crisis calling for significant re-evaluation and search for new identity; identities, whether individual or group are relatively stable and there could be just one salient identity in a normal and healthy situation, but that identity may get blurred or become dysfunctional because of changed circumstances leading to a search for new identity which may ultimately emerge (p. 179).

And, according to social identity theory, identity is not in vacuum but socially situated, not fixed but changes in relation to the context; the self-concept is the product of a hierarchical organization of the multiple identities in terms of their salience; just as there are multiple group identities there are also multiple social identities, which may be ascribed and involuntary or acquired and deliberately chosen. One may identity oneself as an Indian, an Andhrite, a Hindu, a philosopher and so on. Often these identities are not problematic and one may shift identities constantly with ease and without conflict; but conflict does arise between the competing identities and the individuals have to negotiate their way as unified persons without creating a situation of conflict, play their roles at personal and social levels shifting identities with ease, and navigate through personal space discharging multiple social responsibilities. What is required is the permeability of identities and their hierarchical ordering of the multiple identities not as a hotchpotch of disparate images but a coherent, coexisting and consistent assemblage. This depends upon the concept of individual identity and the relationship between the individual and society regarding which Buddhist philosophy and Ambedkar have something significant to offer, which Rao discusses in an elaborate manner.

Buddhist Theories of Person

Rao holds that the Buddha's metaphysics of impermanence and his axiological postulation of overcoming ubiquitous suffering is relevant to Buddhist social theory which is intimately linked to Buddha's no-soul theory. There can be no permanent, enduring, and eternal self in a world of impermanence; suffering is caused by attachment, grasping and clinging to the dictates of the mind and body; the mistaken view of changeless and permanent self is the ground of attachment and clinging; eradication of suffering therefore requires the realization that there is no enduring self anywhere either in the mind, in the body, in their combination or outside them. This warrants primarily a correct understanding of the Buddhist notion of no-self and as to how it accounts for personal identity. Although all the Buddhists subscribe to the non-existence of a permanent self, the problem has taken different forms in the hands of the Buddhist thinkers.

Rao deals with the three prominent Buddhist theories of the self — the *pudgalavāda*, Vasubhandu's theory and that of Candrakīrti. According to *pudgalavādin*s there is no such thing as the enduring and changeless self. What they admit is the person who is a changing and yet a continuous entity; the person is real but without an independent and distinctive identity; the individual is only a composition of changing physical and mental aggregates (*skandha*s), neither the same nor different from the aggregates. *Pudgalavādin*s subscribe to two kinds of reality — substantive and conventional. Substantive reality is that which does not lose its identity even when it is broken or analysed into its elements; conventional reality is the conception of the entities as established and dependent on the substances which are ultimately real; conventionally, real objects do not possess an identity of their own, for instance, a jar possesses only a conventional reality, since it loses its identity when broken or analysed into the ultimate elements that constitute it. *Pudgalavādin*s call the conventional reality the substantially established reality, and they subscribe to another kind of conventional reality, which refers to the inexplicable nature of objects as to whether they are the same or different from the substances on which their conception is based. Vasubandhu illustrates this reality through the examples of milk and fire. Milk is substantially established conventional reality in so far as its reality depends on the elements constituting milk; it loses its identity when it becomes curd or when it is chemically analysed into its constituent elements but it can be expressed in terms of the elements constituting it. But fire cannot be expressed in terms of the fuel from which it arises in the manner milk can be explained by its elements. Fire is neither the same nor different from the fuel; if fire were other than fuel, fuel would not be hot; and if fire were not other than fuel, what is burned would be the same as what burns it. So we cannot explain whether fire is the same or different from fuel, and so fire is an inexpressible reality.

Pudgalavādins hold that the reality of the person is analogous to the inexpressible reality of fire and since the ultimate existence of the individual is inexpressible, they call it the inexpressible conventional reality; the reality of the person is inexpressible in the sense that it is neither the same nor different from the five aggregates that constitute the body–mind complex. Following Pxriestley (1999), Rao says that although inexpressible, persons (*pudgala*) are ultimately and substantially real entities, both conventional and substantive entities; conventional in so far as they are conceived and their reality is dependent on the *skandhas*; substantive in so far as they exist independently of the aggregates, although without separate identities. Following Duerlinger (2003), Rao clarifies that the notion that persons have self-perceptions even though they do not have separate identities is central to *pudgalavāda* theory of the person.

According Vasubandhu, the author of *Abhidhammakoṣabhāṣyam,* who belonged to no specific school or sect of Buddhists, but was greatly influenced by *yogācāras*, especially his brother, Asaṅga, and had sympathies for Sautrāntikas, the "self" is a continuum of aggregates; there is no self as a separately identifiable entity because we have no direct perception or valid inference of it. When we conceive of self, we only refer to one or more of the aggregates which are the causal basis of its conception; on examination of any of these aggregates either individually or in association with each other, we find no self. Vasubandhu accepts *pudgalavādins*' thesis that it is persons and not selves that ultimately exist, but rejects their view that persons are inexpressible phenomena. He admits the existence of two kinds of entities — substantial and conceptual — the former is substantially established and dependent on the substances constituting it. Persons are both conceptually real and substantially existent; they are ultimately real because their conception is based on the collection of their bodily and mental states (*skandhas*) which exist by themselves and have their identities. At the conceptual level, the reality of persons is intrinsic and first-person based; at the same time, persons can also be considered from third-person extrinsic perspective as objectively real in so far as they are conceived and their identities are construed in dependence on externally real events and entities. Rao holds that Vasubandhu's thesis of the self is opposed to the self as a substantive and changeless entity as conceived by the Hindu thinkers of the Nyāya-Vaiśeṣika and Vedānta. It is the middle way between the transcendental conception of a permanent self and the nihilism of no self of any kind, says Rao (p. 185).

Candrakīrti, the author of *Mādhyamakāvatāra*, and who came 500 years after Nāgārjuna, offers the most explicit exposition of the Mādhyamika theory of self or person. According to him suffering is due to the false belief that there exists a permanent self. Therefore, proper knowledge as to the non-existence of unchanging self is the necessary condition for the cessation of suffering. And he also contends that the conception of the person as posited by other Buddhist schools does not really contribute to the negation of the false notion of the self and total cessation of suffering; he maintains that the notion of self as either substantially real, real as substantially established, or only conceptually real, cannot liberate the person from the web of his thoughts that bind him to the sense of "I", "me" and "mine" which distort true knowledge and perpetuate ignorance and suffering. Freedom from suffering is possible only by realizing that the self has no substantial existence. The self as a concrete and an independently existing entity, not caused by another substance as held by the Sāṁkhya system, is self-contradictory and so utterly unreal and a conceptual figment like the barren woman's baby. Candrakīrti rejects even the notion of the person as the aggregates of the *skandhas*, and argues that if the person is the same as the aggregates, then like them, there would be a multiplicity of persons which should be substantial and visible like the aggregates; further, the aggregates are continually changing and totally disappear in the state of *nirvāṇa*, then where does the self go, or what is its status? If the self continually is changing or would totally disappear then who is the agent to whom the kārmic fruits relate? (p.

130). Candrakīrti thus refutes the Theravāda notion of the self as an aggregate of the five *skandhas*. He also refutes that the self is an indescribable entity, which is neither the same nor different from the aggregates but yet a substantial person, and argues thus: nothing exists that does not have its own distinctive identity; a thing that is existent cannot be regarded as beyond expression; and if one could show that the self is an existent thing, it would be real like mind and not at all ineffable (p. 147).

According to the Mādhyamika system, Prof. Rao says, phenomena have no intrinsic reality, the aggregates, physical mental or together, are inherently empty and *nirvāṇa* itself is "voidness of the ultimate" (6.189). Candrakīrti admits of the conventionally existent person but objects to the ascription of ultimate existence to it; he accepts the self as constituted by the aggregates but rejects the idea that the aggregates are substances, and agrees with *pudgalavādins* that persons are neither the same nor different from the aggregates; he also seems to agree with Vasubandhu in arguing that the self is devoid of its own identity since it cannot be substantially or ultimately existent (p. 186).

Rao maintains that in rejecting the self as an enduring entity and in focusing their attention on the empirical self, the Buddha and his followers were concerned with existential questions and their solutions, and not interested in finding ultimate answers to metaphysical issues relating to God or soul. Rao here makes a significant observation that the self the Buddha rejects is not the metaphysical but the psychological self with the primary functions of the ego which harbours desires and causes craving, clinging and suffering. Buddhist discourse on the self or the person is aimed at the deconstruction of the ego and against the ego-driven identity which is exclusive and the source of suffering (p. 187).

Buddhism as Interpreted by Ambedkar

Rao enunciates the following as the salient features of Buddhism as interpreted by B.R. Ambedkar: (1) identities are changing and multiple, and pluralism is the law here; (2) the particular identities are not necessarily exclusive but inclusive; (3) inclusiveness is not absorption or assimilation but compatible coexistence; (4) inclusiveness is value mandated and ethically driven; and (5) individual and society are reflexive of one another, neither of them claiming primacy. Ambedkar's Buddhism recognizes identities as person-centred, situation-specific and socially relevant; they are value-laden and motivators of thought and action; anchored in shared values of universal relevance, they are inclusive in a significant sense. Although, it is arguable whether Ambedkar's social philosophy centre's around the core of Buddhist ideas, Rao says, that it is fairly obvious that it is consistent with Buddhism. Scholars of Ambedkar have hailed his social philosophy as the best representation of the true import and spirit of the teachings of the Buddha (Ahir 1993). At same time, Rao says that some of the orthodox Buddhists like Jīvika has denounced Ambedkar's work, *The Buddha and His Dhamma*, as being unfaithful to the Buddha.

Reviewing the book, Jīvika wrote, Rao quotes:

> The title should be changed from the misleading one of *The Buddha and His Dhamma* to *Ambedkar and His Dhamma*, for he preaches non-*dhamma* as *dhamma* for motives of political ambition and social reform.
>
> — *Mahābodhi* 1959

Rao contends that although the reviewer is right in some sense, "it does not undermine the contribution of Ambedkar to the development of Buddhist social philosophy" (p. 180) and he defends Ambedkar's interpretation of Buddhism on the grounds that even the leading lights of Buddhist thought like Nāgārjuna, Vasubandhu and Dharmakīrti departed from the Buddha's original teachings. In view of the fact that the Buddha's sayings gave rise to irreconcilable trends like the Theravāda realism and the Vijñānavāda idealism, Ambedkar's espousal of Buddhist social philosophy can be taken as a creative development of the seminal thoughts of the Buddha. Rao further argues that nobody can disagree with Ambedkar's characterization of *dhamma* as maintaining purity, giving up craving, living in *nibbāna*, believing that all compounded things are impermanent and *karma* the instrument of moral order.

Rao maintains that Ambedkar, the architect of Indian Constitution and the most outstanding leader of the dalits, is the most influential personality since India's Independence; Ambedkar's relevance is not limited to the awakening of the dalits and the downtrodden but extends to Indian social reality as a whole; his heuristic and context-relevant interpretations of Buddhist social philosophy prove to be valuable to the reconstruction of contemporary India; attracted by the Buddhist notion of inclusiveness, he tried to counter the growing divisiveness and exclusionist tendencies prevailing in the Hindu society, and contended that the Hindu social thought based on the Sāṁkhyan and the *Gītā* theory of *guṇa* as postulating not only "graded inequality" among humans but also their relative permanence; *guṇa* theory is the rationale behind the caste system which perpetuated social inequality indefinitely and an impediment for creating an inclusive society. Ambedkar maintained that caste creation is inconsistent not only with the Buddhist *dharma* but also with the Hindu *guṇa* theory, since the *prakṛti* of an individual is always changing because the relative position of the *guṇa*s is also changing; so there can be no permanent and fixed classification of people into *varṇa*s and no fixed assignment of occupations. Buddhist *dharma* preaches that persons are a process of ever-changing aggregates and not permanent entities or embodied souls; the process, the ever-changing flux is both unique and universal but not permanent or eternal; so the individuals in a society play changing roles with varying responsibilities and obligations; thus the principle of change and impermanence gives rise to an inescapable and a pervasive pluralism. Rao says that Ambedkar's social philosophy is enshrined in three principles — liberty, equality and fraternity — which he borrowed not from the French Revolution but from the teachings of the Buddha; they refer to the three Buddhist refuges — *buddham, dharmam* and *saṅgham*; liberty is freedom to seek perfection; equality is the *dharma* to uphold and perform; it is not pre-ordained, not intrinsic to humankind, and not even limited to the idea of opportunity accorded by the society; as excellence in morality, equality defines one's duties; and fraternity is the sacred *saṅgha*, the ideal inclusive community.

In his *magnum opus*, *The Buddha and His Dhamma*, Ambedkar argues that the Buddhist *dharma* is *saddhamma*, since it seeks to bridge the gap between knowing and being, cognition and conduct; *saddhamma* is more than *prajñā*, mere knowing what is right and what is wrong; right thinking must be accompanied by *śīla*, right action, *karuṇā* and *maitrī*; *dhamma* becomes *saddhamma* only when it is open to all, breaks down barriers between people, regards worth and not birth as the measure of the individual, and promotes equality in society. Ambedkar's interpretation of Buddhist *dhamma* as *saddhamma*, as Rao puts it, "spells out succinctly the different tenets of his social philosophy with its basic concepts of inclusiveness, correct insight (*prajñā*), right conduct (*śīla*) and love and compassion (*karuṇā*)". The *saddhamma* aspect of the Buddhist *dhamma* is contained in the Buddha's refusal to claim any divine origin, supernatural powers or authority for himself or for his teaching. Unlike the prophets of other religions who proclaimed themselves to be the messengers of God, Buddha remained content to be a common man and exhorted his followers not to treat his teachings as infallible and sacrosanct but to doubt them and follow them only after they stood to the test of reason and experience; proclaimed that just as he became the Buddha by his own effort, others too can attain *nirvāṇa* following the path shown by him, which is not the privilege of a few but open to all, the high and low, even to women and the destitutes. The fact that King Bimbisāra, the brāhmaṇa Sāriputta, the barber Upāli and the sweeper Sunīta followed the middle path speaks of its spirit of inclusiveness; it is because the Buddha gave us freedom to modify or even abandon any of his teachings if found to be irrelevant to given circumstances that Ambedkar could "interpret Buddhism as a context relevant philosophy that is necessarily relativist and not absolutist" (p. 177), says Rao.

Rao argues that it is wrong to call Buddhism pessimistic, since it takes removal of suffering as its prime concern; Buddhism indeed is a positive philosophy, since pursuit of happiness is its primary goal; it seeks to achieve *nirvāṇa* or *ānanda* by inquiring into the physical, psychological and spiritual dimension of the person; happiness that it seeks is not the one that is brought about by the satisfaction of physical needs, which are necessary but not sufficient to ensure happiness, since the causes of suffering are precisely the constraints to happiness. So to the Buddha, Rao maintains, freedom from suffering is the quintessential aspect of happiness; insatiable desire is the most potent cause of suffering; desires are harboured in the ego which is engendered by the illusion of identity and imagined self-sameness in the midst of continuous and incessant change in our being, the physical and mental states; the identities that we assume are the shadows that envelop and shroud us in suffering; the assumption of the self is an attempt at achieving unity and coherence to the manifold manifestation of the person; the ego gives rise to identity and the resultant attachment which generates desires; desires cause action and volition gets intertwined with thoughts; actions lead to accumulation of *karma* which gives rise to formation of *saṁskāra*s; as a result, the person becomes conditioned, loses inherent freedom and gets caught in suffering.

Rao says that suffering is caused by the existential dilemma confronting the person; the dilemma consists in perceiving change and impermanence in and around him and at the same time craving for permanence, stability and continuity. This leads the person to identify the ego experience with the so-called unchanging self-sameness of the self; but the ego itself is subject to change and instability which gives rise to existential despair, the root cause of identity crisis and the search for new identities. Rao argues that true solution to the problem of suffering "is not to search for new identities but to raise the person to higher level of awareness and achievement by cultivating consummate values of love and compassion that bind identities together than individuate them to conflict" (p. 174). Deconstruction of the ego is the key to transforming the person, for it is the ego which obscures truth and values and creates false identities; the notion of no-soul is the medicine to cure the ego of its attachments and cravings that condition one's outlook and rule the conduct.

Ambedkar and Gandhi: A Meeting of Buddhism and Hinduism

In this essay Rao discusses the potential relevance the Indian thought has for twenty-first century and he explicates the implications that Hinduism in the form of the Gandhian thought, and Buddhism as interpreted by Ambedkar, have for contemporary human concerns. Rao holds that both Gandhi and Ambedkar sought the same goals but travelled different paths which appear to ultimately merge; Ambedkar attempted to reconstruct the Indian social reality on the basis of Buddhist denial of the self and *ātman*; he wanted to construct a new social philosophy which would go beyond the caste stratified Hindu society but espouse a new ethic that transcends selfish interest of the dominant castes. He felt that the concept of enduring self tended to drive people to be exclusive rather than inclusive; he saw in the Buddhistic *dharma* the natural justice that does not discriminate among people. Ambedkar, like the Buddha, was interested in the psychological and ethical aspects of the self and not in its metaphysical aspects; it is the worldly aspects of the Buddhist *dharma* and its place in society that appealed to Ambedkar; he clearly saw that the remedy for psychological and social problems lies in the deconstruction of the ego through love and compassion; he loved the Buddha's idea that it is not to please God but for one's own good that one has to love another; morality arises from the direct necessity for people to love one another. Ambedkar therefore found in Buddhism ample scope for an inclusive society and universal values of humankind; although born a Hindu, he converted to Buddhism toward the end of his life and found his identity in it (p. 188).

Unlike Ambedkar, who was a rebel, Gandhi, according to Rao, attempted to reform the Indian social order by reforming Hinduism; belonging to the dominant group of caste Hindus, Gandhi pleaded for reform and assimilation of the untouchables; accepting the *varṇāśrama* in principle and denouncing caste system in practice, he pleaded for assimilation of all sections of Hindus within a single salient identity by removing negative attributions of low-caste Hindus; he regarded the caste system in *practice* as the antithesis of *varṇāśrama*, a monstrous parody of the original. According to Gandhi, caste is an extension of the principle of the family governed by blood and heredity; he saw in the caste system the best possible means of maintaining social stability, economic progress, and a step toward inclusive community. Following Gandhi, Rao says that just as family is inclusive of those who love each other and are wedded to each other by ties of blood and relation, "caste also tries to include families of a particular way of purity of life" (p. 190). Gandhi thus embarked on a social mission of removing disparities without demolishing the *varṇāśrama dharma*.

Rao maintains that both Gandhi and Ambedkar were social activists who fought against social injustice and structural violence; both of them espoused the cause of dalits but differed in their perspectives of it. Anchored in Hindu ethos and representing the tradition and establishment, Gandhi attempted to transform it in unimaginable ways to cope with current challenges. As a rebel, Ambedkar attempted to awaken millions from their age-old cultural slumber and gave them new identity and self-respect. Rao says that in important ways the ideological stance and practical actions undertaken by Gandhi and Ambedkar are mutually complementary, since both equally abhorred social exclusion and economic exploitation. As the cultural icons of the country, they constitute the two sides of the cultural coin of Indian identity: Gandhi's image is displayed on the head side of the coin, representing the upper caste Hindu tradition; and Ambedkar's spirit is characterized by the tail that stands for the dalits and the downtrodden, the lower bottom of the Indian society. Both were seeking the same goals but travelled different paths. The goal is establishing an inclusive community in which everyone can participate with full potential to bring about an egalitarian society devoid of any structural violence and social injustice. Rao says that the philosophies of Gandhi and Ambedkar can work together and in tandem as the right means to include those who are excluded and bring them into the mainstream and make them equals. According to him the main concern of Gandhi's and Ambedkar's social thought and action is to resolve the paradox of identity and inclusiveness. It centred round the idea of merging the multiple identities, which are necessarily plural, into an inclusive community for common good. Both found the resolution of this paradox in universally shared values.

Although they were contemporaries who lived in the same country, the main concern of their thought and action differed. Gandhi's mission was political liberation of Indians from foreign rule. Ambedkar's principal endeavour was to socially emancipate the depressed class of Indians from their exploiters. Nevertheless, the primacy of their distinct commitments is the establishment of inclusive community governed by the values of love and compassion, says Rao. Although Gandhi and Ambedkar came from two different backgrounds, as social reformers they abhorred the prevailing caste practices and prejudices and the built-in inequalities in the system. The perceived inequalities in identities had different impacts on them: for Gandhi, it was a crisis of conscience that prompted him to fight for inclusive society; and, it was a crisis of identity that prompted Ambedkar to fight against exploitation and degradation of his community. Crisis of conscience led Gandhi to denounce untouchability as the sin of Hindus but without denouncing his Hindu identity; the crisis of identity led Ambedkar to fight against untouchability but by renouncing Hinduism rather than reforming it, argues Rao.

Rao holds that Gandhi's Hindu practical idealism and Ambedkar's Buddhist realism are closely related to each other. Truth and non-violence are the twin principles of Gandhi's social action. To Gandhi, truth is the same as morality, non-violence is synonymous with love, and religion is allegiance to moral law. Gandhi found truth and non-violence as the force that bind people together in an inclusive community. And Ambedkar found the similar force in the Buddha's *dharma* embodying the principles of liberty, equality and fraternity which contribute to the emergence of universal value of love that binds humanity together in an inclusive community. Buddhist *dharma* is not limited to the *saṅgham* of *bhikkhus* but applies to the entire human community. Rao says that Ambedkar's equation of *dharma* with religion is analogous to Gandhi's equation of God with truth.

Rao maintains that it is not surprising that both Gandhi and Ambedkar stood for an inclusive Indian society given the fact that Hinduism and Buddhism, which they represent, are essentially philosophies of inclusiveness. Founded on the Advaita Vedānta conception of the absolute identity between the individual soul (*ātman*) and the universal soul (*Brahman*), the Hindu philosophy advocates that the individual identity merges with the most superordinate identity of all, with the being in its most widest and pristine sense. Rao sees in the monist and absolutist philosophy of Advaita "an exemplary form of pluralism and an extraordinary way of relating individual identities with more inclusive identities" (p. 192). Thus the Advaita ontology admits pluralism, consistent with the notion of unity in diversity at the empirical level. Rao holds that

Buddhism also subscribes to a superordinate human identity over and above personal identity. Buddha's denial of the substantial self and his conception of the *saṅgha* as creatively interpreted by Ambedkar have profound implications for an inclusive community of the humankind (p. 192).

CONTEMPORARY RELEVANCE OF THE BUDDHA

Rao holds that the Buddha's teachings have profound relevance to contemporary global scenario wherein identities based on nationalism, religion and language are becoming salient with disastrous consequences. Humanity is being fast divided and disturbed by the politics of conflicting identities with a potential of violence capable of wiping out life on this planet. The world is fast shrinking into a global village, humanity is getting fragmented and polarized with growing alienation among groups. The regional, caste, religious, ethnic and linguistic identities are gaining salience at the cost of human identity. Rao says that identity concerns and matters of alienation among people are not merely immense intellectual challenges but are issues of policy making. So there is an urgent need to recognize the inevitable plurality of identities and reinforce the global human identity as the salient, superordinate and unifying identity. There is a need to foster the global human identity by promoting universally shared values of love, trust and altruism (p. 192).

Referring to the contemporary India, Rao observes that India is poised to take a big leap forward in economic growth and development in the coming decades; as a knowledge society India is far ahead of most of the developing countries and competing with confidence with the developed nations; but at the same time, India is getting more and more divided and polarized into smaller and smaller groups of self-interest; forces of exclusion, conflict and violence have been raising their ugly head in several parts of India; politics of divisiveness have been thwarting the sense of national integrity and inclusiveness; the country is going through an identity crisis, as the superordinate identities are becoming less and less salient ones, resulting in role confusion at various levels and hampering national development. Rao maintains that when the society is fragmented and fractured, its polity is unlikely to perform at the peak of its potential; it slowsdown the onward march to grow economically and realize the goals of sharing what we have, experience equality in every sphere and fulfil the values enshrined in the constitution. Let me quote a significant statement Rao makes in this context:

> In order that a sense of national unity and a philosophy of inclusiveness may prevail, we need to have in place a policy framework and necessary intellectual tools that address all sorts of alienations afflicting our people, distorting the sane image and the sacred persona of the nation. All developmental issues are not economical. Even economical matters are profoundly affected by ontological considerations, ethical issues and cultural and psycho-social factors. — p. 193

Rao regards Buddha's middle path as relevant to the resolution of identity crisis which is at the root of the national and global conflicts. The middle path is the best means of negotiating between individual and global identity within the matrix of altruistic ethics; methodologically, the robust tool to handle the disasters of conflict that ensue from dichotomies that place one in opposition to the other. Rao maintains that in the face of opposing dichotomies between first-person subjectivity and third-person objectivity, there is a need for second-person mediation; the dialectic of being and nothing should be replaced by becoming that unites the two; thus the "I" and the "other" are conjoined in the conception of "we". Buddha says that the world is accustomed to look at everything in terms of duality that "everything is" or "everything is not", but the truth is the middle way between the extremes of "it is" and "it is not"; the middle path works like a golden mean to resolve the division and conflict that arise from the ignorance of placing one identity in opposition to the other says, Rao (p. 194).

Further, Rao maintains that in the event of admitting the necessity of the plurality of identities, it necessarily warrants a mechanism to bring about unity in plurality, but the unity that we envisage cannot be reduced to nationalism, religion, regional or ethnic loyalties, for they preclude the overarching global identity. The only avenue for establishing a super-ordinate human identity cutting across national, religious and other identities, according to Rao, is "the value matrix, common ethics and agreed morality" (p. 194). And, he envisages love in its celestial sense as the only value which is universally relevant as the binding force of collective being; love in its purity can function as the universally shared ethic; love in the sense of compassion, the core of the Buddhist ethics, is the healing aid of humans ailing from ego-centred ignorance and suffering. It is not only a fine emotion that binds people but also a sure means of spiritual upliftment.

Rao regards the Buddhist practice of detachment as another value that has special relevance to the Indian society, with profound implications to human identity issues. Detachment implies ego-transcendence and good action which is unselfish and non-exclusive; it is not ceremonies and rituals but good conduct that leads us to salvation; Buddha exhorted us to pay homage to the person grounded in *dharma*. The legacy of Buddha's teachings embody *śīla* based on *dharma* which is defended by reason directed at common good. Rao says that in an age of growing alienation across the globe, and in a nation of growing superstitions, and in a society divided by narrow identities, the relevance of Buddha's teachings is indeed paramount.

Buddhist Phenomenology of Consciousness

Rao here explicates the issue of consciousness in the light of the Buddhist thought. He is of the view that the Buddhist phenomenology of consciousness has profound theoretical and practical implications. The Buddhist metapsychology of consciousness is pregnant with possibilities for a shift in our conception of human nature with a potential for a radical transformation of the human condition.

INDIAN PSYCHOLOGY

Rao says that Indian psychology is a distinct tradition rooted in the classical Indian thought and manifest in the multitude of practices prevailing for centuries in the subcontinent; it is not an ad hoc mix of varied ideas on the nature and destiny of humans but a theory with a paradigmatic shift from the currently dominant reductionist and neurobiological theorizing in psychology, and with consciousness as the defining attribute of the human condition. Rao clarifies that Indian psychology stands for classical Indian thought which is not exclusively Hindu but includes non-Hindu traditions such as Buddhism and Jainism. Notwithstanding fundamental differences at the ontological level between the different classical philosophical systems, Indian psychology includes all the major Indian thought systems that have contributed to understanding consciousness. Indian psychology, according to Rao, refers not to psychology that is confined to a specific region or country, but to the one that is pan-human and to which even the non-Indian thinkers have made significant contributions. The perennial global interest in *yoga* and meditative practices is a further evidence for the universal relevance of Indian psychology. In the phrase "Indian psychology", the emphasis is not on geography but on the Indian ethos which is a complex mix of thought and practices, and provides a new psychological model developed in different directions by different schools within and outside the Vedic tradition. Indian psychology is inclusive of the different and distinctive shades and shapes of classical Indian thought in one fold for a unified mosaic of colourful, common and coherent psychological ground in terms of some general principles, says Rao (p. 257).

According to Rao, consciousness is the central concept of Indian psychology, the person is the subject of its focus, the mind is the main instrument of its study and its goal is the freedom of the person. He therefore considers consciousness, person, mind and freedom as the conceptual building blocks of the edifice of Indian psychology. He gives twenty-six general principles of Indian psychology in the form of the following aphorisms: (1) psychology is the study of the person; (2) the person is consciousness embodied; (3) embodied, consciousness becomes conditioned; (4) conditioned, consciousness loses its spontaneity and freedom and is embellished by biases, presuppositions and sensory colouring. Let me give the gist of the remaining principles without venturing to enumerating them: they sketch the way the person gets caught in the net of *saṁsāra* and ultimately attains enlightenment by following the path of meditation. In presenting these principles, Rao gives a clear picture of the nature and purpose of Indian psychology; he says that the twenty-six principles which he has expanded into 333 in his book, *Cognitive Anamolies, Consciousness and Yoga* (2011) are equally applicable to the heterodox systems like Buddhism and Jainism as they do to *yoga* and Vedānta; utilizing the same or similar principles, each system has advanced Indian psychology with a special emphasis on some areas and making significant contributions to them.

BUDDHIST PSYCHOLOGY

Rao says that Buddhist psychology is one of the main strands of Indian psychology and it has excelled in giving a well articulated and explicitly stated analysis of consciousness; it conceives the person as essentially a flow of consciousness which constitutes the content as well as continuity of the person; consciousness as the person is the subject of focus in Buddhist psychology; the Buddhist thinkers have classified consciousness at various levels: (1) at the first level, consciousness is classified as the conscious and subconscious mentation; (2) at the second level, it is classified into its different planes; (3) at the third, it is classified as the awareness of objects and also as the affective and conative aspects of thought; and (4) at the fourth level, consciousness is analysed into its basic elements.

CONSCIOUS AND THE UNCONSCIOUS

In Buddhism, consciousness is equivalent to thought which is a relation between subject and object, which are relative to each other and mutually dependent, and impermanent; only the relation between them is constant and it is precisely this relation the Buddhists call consciousness which is not static but a dynamic process like a flowing river, having subliminal and supra-liminal forms. In Theravāda Buddhism, the subliminal stream of consciousness is called *bhavaṅga*, the ground condition for all conscious experiences. Following S.Z. Aung, Rao says that as the subconscious state of mind below the threshold of consciousness, *bhavaṅga* works as the condition for the continuous subjective existence; as the continuous unconscious medium subsisting in our subjective existence, *bhavaṅga* resembles the state of dreamless sleep, and is endowed with the potentiality to guide, influence and cause our thoughts, passions and actions, and works as the carrier of *karma*, the merits and demerits of one's actions. *Bhavaṅga* also aids the process of our cognition thus: when an external stimulus or internal sensation arises, the thought process starts with a reference to an object, then *bhavaṅga,* the unconscious stream is momentarily interrupted, the mind acts in the form of attention (*manodhātu*) giving rise to sensory awareness, which is followed by a succession of cognitive acts (*manovijñāna*) resulting in the cognition of the perceptual object. There are four kinds of perceptions as envisaged by the Buddhist thinkers. First is the bare perception of the perceptual object, the registering of the sensation resulting from the processing of the sensory inputs; second is the mental apprehension of perception (*manovijñāna*); third is self-consciousness (*sva-saṁvedana*); and fourth is the paranormal awareness (*yogī-pratyakṣa*) to be attained by intense practice of meditation (p. 261).

Rao says that in Buddhist psychology, the concept of *bhavaṅga* first appears in *Milindapañha* wherein Nāgasena says that when a man is in deep sleep the mind "goes into *bhavaṅga*", but here the concept has not been developed further beyond the notion that it is one where the mind takes recluse during states of sleep. *Milindapañha* describes the person as a series of mental states (*dhamma-santati*) in the waking state, and *bhavaṅga* as the subconscious state into which the mind retreats during deep sleep. Prof. Rao says that after the *Milindapañha*, it was Buddhaghoṣa, the Theravāda thinker, who has made use of the *bhavaṅga* concept to explain not only sleep states but also higher forms of consciousness and the cycle of births in the person's march towards *nirvāṇa* (pp. 262-63).

Bhavaṅga gives an unbroken continuity to the different states of mind and the identity of the person in this life, and in the past and future lives; it accounts for the Buddhists' doctrine of rebirth and moral responsibility of the person for his actions; it is based on the notion of *bhavaṅga* that Buddhaghoṣa accounts for the continuity of the same person across different births. The *bhavaṅga*-consciousness in the new birth is caused by the *bhavaṅga* thoughts of the person at the time of death. According to Buddhaghoṣa, *bhavaṅga* is the mind that is unconscious and passive, free from the usual thought processes and impurities caused by external influences, and shines by its own radiance and luster, says Rao.

He holds that there are a varied interpretations of *bhavaṅga* and different opinions have been expressed as to what it actually refers to. Following Aung (1929), Rao says that *bhavaṅga* is not the same as the cognitive consciousness that arises from moment to moment; the two are mutually exclusive processes, and the latter is not a modified manifestation of the former. Following Cousins (1981) and Nyanatiloka (1983), Rao considers *bhavaṅga* as the carrier of accumulated *karma*, an unconscious storehouse of the past impressions and experiences concealed to full consciousness, but occasionally emerge and approach the threshold of full consciousness. Following William Waldron (2003), Rao says that the *bhavaṅga-citta* carries the essential features of the individual which are fixed for a particular lifetime at the time of conception, and it is intermittent and occurs occasionally when other cognitive processes are inactive.

Rao says that although *bhavaṅga* has traces of the psychoanalytic unconscious as well as of the Jungian collective unconscious, it is necessary to be circumspect in comparing it with the Freudian unconscious. He also holds that *bhavaṅga* is not the same as the *ātman* of the Hindu philosophy, the self-conscious and permanent soul, but only a phenomenon of moments that change from moment to moment and is continuous and causally connected; *bhavaṅga* is "a non-substantial ground condition of consciousness, a condition without which no cognition is possible". *Bhavaṅga* is not a cognition which is noetic but a non-noetic consciousness, which is non-intentional; it is a being consciousness, pure consciousness, consciousness as-such as distinguished from knowing consciousness (p. 265).

Rao compares the Theravāda conception of *bhavaṅga* consciousness with the *yogācāra* conception of *ālayavijñāna*, the unconscious ground of our thoughts and feelings, the continually changing stream or the mother-sea of consciousness, out of which things arise and into which they return. *Ālaya*-consciousness is pure in and of itself but gets blemished in human minds which makes subject–object distinctions. *Ālaya* is the non-conscious universal that is potentially conscious, the source of the individual consciousness. Rao says that besides these similarities, there are some differences between the *bhavaṅga* and *ālaya* consciousness. First, *ālaya* is the memory bank, a depository of persons' thoughts, deeds and their consequences, a storehouse of *saṁskāras* (conditioned impressions) and *vāsanās* (innate dispositions). But Buddhaghoṣa does not regard *bhavaṅga* as the storehouse of memory. Second, *ālaya* is the ground of the manifestation of the cognitive consciousness, but Buddhaghoṣa makes a sharp distinction between *bhavaṅga* and cognitive consciousness. Following Saratchandra (1958) and S. Radhakrishnan (1923/1989), Rao says that *ālaya* is very much like the Upaniṣadic soul, the permanent entity but carrying with it impressions and memories (p. 266).

Elements of Consciousness (Cetasikas)

In Buddhism, consciousness is a process of thought consisting of various physical and mental elements (*cetasika*s), which are classified into fifty-two different kinds which are grouped into four classes. The first group consists of seven elements — (1) contact (*phassa*), (2) feeling (*vedana*), (3) volition (*cetana*), (4) perception (*sanna*), (5) individuation (*ekaggata*), (6) psychic life (*jīvitindriya*), and (7) attention (*manasikara*); these are the universal elements which seem to relate to the basic psychological process. Rao gives a very detailed and intricate analysis of these elements which I do not mention here for the paucity of space. The second group comprises of six particular elements — (1) initial application of the mind (*vitakka*), (2) continued application of the mind (*vicāra*), (3) decision or resolution (*abhimokkha*), (4) effort (*vīrya*), (5) joy (*piti*), and (6) intention or resolution (*chanda*); these are called particular elements and they may not accompany all thoughts, unlike universal elements. For instance, joy is present in meditative states only and not in other states; resolution is absent in thought where there is doubt. The third group consists of fourteen immoral elements (*akusala cetasika*s) — (1) delusion (*moha*), (2) impudence (*śirika*), (3) carelessness (*anottappa*), (4) distraction (*uddacca*), (5) greed (*lobha*), (6) error (*ditthi*), (7) conceit (*māna*), (8) hate (*doṣa*), (9) jealousy (*issa*), (10) selfishness (*maccharīya*), (11) worry (*kukucca*), (12) sloth (*thina*), (13) lethargy (*middha*), and (14) doubt (*vicikiccha*). These are the motivating factors leading to evil acts. They are interrelated influencing one another. And, the fourth group embodies twenty-five moral elements (*kusala cetasika*s). Of them nineteen are common to all moral thoughts and six are present only in some of them. The common elements in moral thoughts are: (1) confidence, (2) mindfulness, (3) equanimity, and (4) non-attachment. And the particular elements of moral thought are: right speech, right action, right livelihood, pity, rejoicing in the happiness of others and wisdom. As there are ten moral thoughts, there are also ten moral actions corresponding to them.

FOUR STATES OF CONSCIOUSNESS

Buddhists describe consciousness as belonging to four different realms depending on the state of the person in his or her psychological development. They are: (1) the empirical realm known through the senses and driven by desire; (2) the meditative realm with form; (3) the meditative realm without form; and (4) the realm of the transcendence. These four realms are respectively called: (1) *Kāmaloka,* (2) *Rūpaloka,* (3) *Arūpaloka,* and (4) *Lokottara.*

1. **Forms of Consciousness in Kāmaloka:** The Buddhists distinguish between fifty-four forms of consciousness in the empirical world which is common to all humans (*kāmaloka*) and it is known cognitively and driven by desires; of the fifty-four states, eight are moral states, twelve immoral states, thirty-four morally indifferent states which are again classified into eleven inoperative and twenty-three resultant states.
2. **Forms of Consciousness in Rūpaloka:** This realm constitutes the first of the three higher states of consciousness, to which the practitioner progresses step by step in the state of concentration; with the initial application, the mind enters the meditative world of *rūpa;* in this meditative plane, the meditator experiences fifteen thought forms that are not only intentional but also moral, despite being subtle.
3. **Forms of Consciousness in Arūpaloka:** Here thoughts are devoid of form and the objects thereof are too abstract; the meditator at this level of concentration, meditates on non-material things like infinite space, infinite thought, nothingness and on awareness which is neither perception nor non-perception; having attained *arūpāvacāra citta,* the meditator in this state of mind attains the twelve thought forms.
4. **Forms of Consciousness in Lokottara:** In this final realm, consciousness is non-intentional and pure, the attainment of which transforms the practitioner into a saint and leads her to attain *nirvāṇa.* Having transcended the empirical world, consciousness here

goes beyond the subject–object duality and the mind is no more a succession of thoughts but unconditioned, non-relational, without a cause, symbol or object. Knowledge here is not a knowing by sensing but realization by being (p. 274). Rao mentions that consciousness at this level can be seen in eight forms each of which is subdivided into five classes, totalling forty forms of consciousness; thereby we can notice a total of 121 forms of consciousness in Buddhism. Rao says that this division is very similar to the fourfold division of consciousness found in the Upaniṣads and elaborated in Advaita, namely, the waking, dream, deep sleep and *turīya*. But the difference between the two, says Rao, is that the Buddhists divide the fourth state, namely, *turīya*, into three separate states; whereas the Buddhistic empirical consciousness of *kāmaloka* appears as the three different states of waking, dream and deep sleep of the Vedānta. In addition to the four, the Buddhists further divide consciousness based on the moral and motivational nature of thoughts. However, as Rao notes, there is a major difference between the Buddhist and the Hindu accounts of consciousness. Buddhist psychology does not make an explicit distinction between consciousness and mind in the empirical realm and it treats intentionality as the defining characteristic of mind and consciousness. In all other systems of Indian philosophy, a clear-cut distinction is made between the mind and consciousness. Sāṁkhya-Yoga and Advaita systems explicitly attribute intentionality to mind and not to consciousness.

Rao contends that the Buddhist thinkers have gone far beyond their Hindu counterparts in their classification of consciousness into a myriad forms. In their analysis of consciousness, they have paid attention to different elements of consciousness such as the cognitive, conative, emotive and ethical aspects that determine it at a given time; they have taken cognizance of the states of consciousness that are automatic, spontaneous or involuntary as well as desired, voluntary or self-willed; they have also examined the true and false cognitive states of consciousness, states of consciousness accompanied by feeling or devoid of it, the feeling accompanying it as wholesome or not. Rao says:

> Permutation and combination of these and other associated factors give Buddhists a variety of forms of consciousness, a variety broader and comprehensive than anything we find in Hindu or any other psychological literature. —p. 270

BUDDHISM AND WILLIAM JAMES ON CONSCIOUSNESS

Rao says that Buddhist psychology comes very close to the Western psychological tradition, William James in particular, in equating consciousness with mind and treating intentionality as the defining characteristic of consciousness. James' shift in focus and perspective, and the consequent understanding of consciousness from his *Principles of Psychology* (1890) to the *Varieties of Religious Experience* (1902) have an uncanny resemblance to the Buddhist shift in the description of consciousness from the *kāmaloka* to *lokottara* state. Rao wonders if the Buddha were to be a systematic thinker instead of being a religious reformer, he would have said as James said, "the hour is ripe for consciousness to be openly and universally discarded" (*Essays on Radical Empiricism*).

James' discussion of consciousness in his *Principles* resembles the Buddhist analysis of consciousness in the realm of *kāmaloka*; here James, like the Buddhists, deals with the empirical nature of consciousness with the help of the metaphor of the stream and describes it as personal, changing and yet continuous, selective, noetic and unified; he also describes consciousness in its non-rational forms through the metaphors of "mother-sea", which is similar to the Buddhist notion of *bhavaṅga* and *ālaya*. Here he describes consciousness in its subliminal, the multiple subterrain streams that lack unity and cohesion and James regards those states of consciousness which transcend reason and defy logic as real facts of experience which psychologists cannot afford to ignore.

Rao observes that in rejecting the concept of "consciousness" in his *Essays on Radical Empiricism*, James did not do away with consciousness all together. What he was attempting to discard was not consciousness *per se* but only consciousness as an entity or substance, a notion which is repugnant to his radical empiricism. In this, he is again close to the Buddhists who opposed the idea of consciousness as a substantial and eternal entity, such the *Ātman* or *Brahman* in Hindu thought.

The Buddhists make no clear distinction between mind and consciousness in the realm of *kāmaloka* and endow the mind with content and intentionality; but in the realms of *rūpa* and *arūpa* planes, they make a distinction between the mind and consciousness; in these *lokas*, the mind is restrained in a state of *samādhi* and consciousness takes a different form; and in the *lokottara* plane, the mind gets completely annihilated, and consciousness attains *nirvāṇa* and manifests in its most sublime form. Rao therefore says that the Buddhists' account of consciousness at different levels of being is as consistent as James' discussion of consciousness in different contexts of his career (p. 276).

Although, the Buddhist conception of consciousness is similar to that of James who also uses the terms "thought" and "consciousness" indiscriminately, Rao differentiates between the two by saying that the Buddhist *bhavaṅga* is more an unconscious stream than the cognitive consciousness of James; *bhavaṅga* is like the "fringe" as distinguished from the "focus" of consciousness in James; the fringe, according to James (1890/1952), is what surrounds every conscious thought and gives it "psychic overtures" or "halos", which provides the context and the network of past experiences and future expectations that render the contents and the network of present awareness. *Bhavaṅga* has a different and an enlarged role and function in the Buddhist psychology as it is closer to the "transitive" states as distinguished from the "substantive" states of consciousness in James; the substantive states are the "resting places" whereas the transitive states are those that give the unbroken continuity between thoughts despite the intervening periods of no awareness such as in sleep (p. 262).

RELEVANCE OF BUDDHIST PSYCHOLOGY

Rao says that although James' writings are often considered to be foundational for developing a science of consciousness in the West, Buddhist psychology is more encompassing and inclusive than James' theory of consciousness. Buddhism provides a highly developed conceptual framework for the science of consciousness which goes beyond the rudiments contained in the *Principles of Psychology*. Buddhist psychology encompasses a variety of conscious states that James later on referred to in his *Varieties of Religious Experience*, and it also deals with practical methods to develop and study these states of consciousness. Rao argues that much of Buddhist psychology is more a kind of metapsychology than an empirical science of consciousness; concepts like *bhavaṅga* and *ālaya-vijñāna* are admittedly metaphysical but yet less mysterious than the Freudian unconscious and the Jungian archetypes. The explanatory models of the Buddhist psychology extend psychology's scope to account for abnormal and paranormal behaviours. They deal in clear terms with the states of transcendence in which new cognitive relationships are established, subject–object dichotomies cease to be, and experience and knowing transcend the barriers of space and time.

Rao maintains that the Buddhist theory of consciousness fits well with several of the psychodynamic factors studied by the depth psychologists and some aspects of it have test implications and permit empirical verification. Rao, therefore, says:

> I believe Buddhist texts and practices contain the architectonic and blue print for erecting a comprehensive edifice of the science of consciousness.
> —p. 276

Obviating the objection that the Buddhist psychology cannot be given the status of the science of consciousness as it mixes up empirical issues with axiological matters, Rao says that the strength of Buddhism lies in its conjoining of facts with value. In this sense, Buddhism is holistic in the profound sense of holism and comprehensive of human existence comprising thought, passion and action. It takes into account the cognitive, affective and emotive aspects of life, and places a high premium on moral development of the person. Rao further says that the *abhidhamma* tradition of the Buddhist psychology has profound implications for a comprehensive cognitive science and in it we find a detailed map of the mind sketching the contours of consciousness which has been acknowledged by the Western psychologists like Varala, Thomson and Rosch (1991).

Rao affirms that the Buddhist psychology has a great relevance to behaviour modification; application of mindfulness techniques in a variety of psychotherapeutic practices has proved effective as a counter conditioning strategy to overcome undesirable emotions, neurotic fears and anxieties. Further, meditation-based interventions appear to have beneficial effects on some secular matters like eating disorders, physical ailments, besides producing spiritual experience. Psychotherapeutic and meditational procedures of the Buddhist psychology are not only widely appreciated but currently in vogue all over the world, says Rao. Buddhist psychology is all the more relevant in the strife-torn world of *dukkha*, since it seeks to rescue the humans from suffering and establish a world of peace and plenty by striking at the root of the problem of identity crisis and ideological hegemony by asserting unequivocally that there is no permanent and enduring self.

Conclusion

It is interesting to note that Rao long ago conjectured that more than the ideological divides, identity conflicts would pose new threat for peaceful survival of human species. He wrote that more than the threat of Cold War that loomed large between the erstwhile superpowers, the emerging new configurations of identity would become hardened categories precipitating inter-group divides fomenting strife in the world in an unprecedented manner. He also said, in particular reference to India that we would face the challenge of increasing polarization and divisiveness born of the exploitation of identities for political gains. And as a solution to the national and global problems of identity crises and conflicts, Rao suggests adoption of "a common universal value line and shared ethics" (p. 155). He says that the need of the hour is a global sense of belonging and a non-solitarist understanding of human identity without sacrificing national allegiances and local loyalties. He holds that the contemporary world demands an overarching human identity that would bind people in a more stable and inclusive manner than the narrow identity groupings.

My contention in this context is that the superordinate human identity with global or cosmic proportions that Rao advocates would be an actuality only when the individual becomes "one with" the inward truth of his or her being which is "nothingness". Nothingness, not-being-a-thing, is the ultimate and absolute truth of our being, the realization of which awakens "intelligence" that can negotiate with sanity the identities at the personal and social levels. Realization of the inner vastness, the infinite space without a centre or circumference constitutes the core of spirituality in its true sense, devoid of which identities are bound to confound confusion and conflict. No amount of research and theorization at the psychological and social levels ignoring the spiritual depths of the individual can resolve the crisis arising out of multiple identities. It is wrong to think that whole of one's being lies in a particular identity or in a group of identities. When one's being is unlimited, it is ignorance to limit it to an ego, a group, a religion or a nation.

It is through tradition, prejudice or imitation that one identifies oneself with a sect, language or religion. It is also out of habit or laziness that one conforms to an ideology, belief or symbol. Identification of any kind puts an end to creative understanding, makes for insensitivity and destroys the supreme love, the highest form of sensitivity which is receptive and inclusive. Identification is essentially a thought process by which the mind seeks to safeguard and expand itself and create constant conflict between various identifications. Identification destroys freedom to discover for oneself the truth of one's being, namely, the inward being of nothing, which is beyond the accretion of all identities. Nothingness is the source of supreme love that unites all by resolving division and conflict and it establishes peace and stability on the planet. It calls for the cultivation of the art of living on the ground-of-being-anonymous rather than traversing the slippery path of identification. It warrants a radically different kind of education.

Rao's book is a reflection of his commendable commitment to applied spirituality and especially to Gandhiji's application of it to the resolution of the problems of identity at the national and global level. But my contention is that Gandhiji's spirituality is predominantly a Hindu spirituality rooted in the *Sanātana Dharma* which has often been attacked as being the source of the hardened structural identities of caste and colour justifying the evils of social injustice and inequality. That is why the thinkers like Swami Vivekananda held that Buddhism came as the fulfilment of Hinduism which lacked in compassion. Swami maintained that the wonderful intellect of the brāhmaṇa should be joined with the noble heart and the humanizing power of the great master, the Buddha. And Ambedkar outrightly rejected Hinduism, the religion of his birth, and embraced Buddhism attacking the former as the antithesis of the principles of liberty, equality and fraternity which form the core of Buddhism. He extolled Buddhism as *saddhamma* of all *dharma*s and decried Hinduism as no *dharma* at all. Rao in his book has subscribed to the superiority of Buddhism to Hinduism and has argued for the supreme relevance of Buddhism to the contemporary India. However, Gandhi–Ambedkar controversy *vis-à-vis* the reformation of the Indian social reality remains to be enigmatic as they approached it from two backgrounds of spirituality which Ambedkar considered to be diametrically opposed.

I would like to mention the relevance of spirituality devoid of all identity that transcends all religions in their institutionalized sense. Spirituality that directly enlightens us by revealing our true being is the need of the hour. The essence of it lies in the religiosity that has nothing to do with religion as an organization. One may call it the one religion, the universal religion of humanity. It may also be called a truly secular spirituality, secular not in the sense of being non-religious or anti-religious, not even in the sense of treating all religious as being essentially the same and equal. The secular spirituality is that which preaches that Truth is one and the same for all and thus brings together people belonging to all religions by making them spiritually autonomous and authentic as advocated by the father of existentialism, Soren Kierkegaard in the West and the unique spiritual master Jiddu Krishnamurti in the East. This is the spirituality that we find even in the ancient texts that are not amenable to religious labels. This is the spirituality that has been taught by the sages past and present who shunned all identifications and chose to be anonymous.

Rao has clearly explicated that the Buddhist theory of consciousness or the person devoid of the intrinsic self-being is far superior to the William James' conception of consciousness. James' essay "Does Consciousness Exist?" shocked even the realists like Russell and Moore when James declared that consciousness does not exist as a substantial entity but flows like a stream, a process of thought. But this discovery was made by the Buddha nearly 3,000 years ago. Buddha's doctrine of no-soul embedded in dependent origination has profound implications for understanding the reality of the person and society in their right perspective which Rao has clearly brought out in his book. But what I would like to point out here is that the Buddhist conception of consciousness is far more superior even to that of the phenomenologists. It is deeper and more comprehensive than Husserl's and Sartre's conceptions of consciousness. Husserl confined his consciousness to the epistemological realm and his notion of the transcendentally reduced consciousness serves only as the subjective principle of knowledge. Although a pure subjectivity, a pure ego and independent of the "object", Husserl's notion of consciousness is that which is essentially intentional and in immediate relation with its object. Buddhist notion of consciousness is more profound than even that of Sartre who characterizes consciousness as being essentially divisive and conflicting. To Sartre, although a non-substantial absolute and the principle of freedom and autonomous choice, consciousness is condemned to anguish and unhappiness. But the Buddhists have delved into the depths of consciousness and thrown light on all its dimensions — ontological, psychological, social and spiritual. They have uncovered the potentials of the human mind for attaining the sublime states of bliss in the higher meditative realms of *nirvāṇa* with profound implications for the order and peace in *saṁsāra*.

I conclude with a sincere appreciative note that Rao's work in general and his book *Gandhi and Spirituality* in particular is undoubtedly a powerful vindication of the contemporary relevance of Indian philosophy as a whole, Indian psychology and spirituality in particular, and Gandhiji's practice of it in personal life and his application of it to resolution of vexatious social and political problems at the national and global level. In bringing out this book Rao has done immense service to the academic community and humanity as a whole, for it has brought to centrestage the spirituality that has largely been marginalized, misunderstood as being impractical and often misused too. The book is dense with ideas of perennial and topical interest and importance ranging from the Buddhist phenomenology of consciousness to the current problems of identity. The discussions are thorough and threadbare, arguments are incisive and persuasive, and conclusions are insightful and quite revealing. The book as a whole and the topics that have been dealt with here speak of Rao's significant contribution to philosophy in general and to Indian philosophy in particular.

References

Ahir, D.C. (1993), Dr. Ambedkar's "The Buddha and His Damma: An Assessment", in K.N. Kadam (ed.) *Dr. B.R. Ambedkar: The Emancipator of the Oppressed*, Bombay: Popular Prakashan.

Aung, S.Z. (1929), A Compendium of Philosophy, London: Oxford University Press.

Cousins, L.S. (1981), "The Path and the Development of the Theravadin Abhidhamma", *Journal of the Pali Text Society*, Saranath.

James, William (1890/1952), *The Principles of Psychology*, New York: Henry Holt and Co.

Nyanatiloka, M. (1983), *Guide Through the Abhidhamma-pitaka* (4th edn.), Kandy, Sri Lanka: Buddhist Publication Society.

Radhakrishnan, S. (1923/1989), *Indian Philosophy* (Centenary edn.), 2 vols., Delhi: Oxford University Press.

Rao, K. Ramakrishna (2011), *Gandhi and Applied Spirituality*, New Delhi: Matrix Publishers.

Saratchandra, E.R. (1958), *The Buddhist Psychology of Perception*, Colombo: The University of Ceylon Press.

Waldron, William, S. (2003), *The Buddhist Unconscious: The Alaya-vijana in the Context of Indian Buddhist Thought*, London: Routledge and Curzon.

Varala, F.J., E. Thomson and E. Rosch (1991), *The Embodied Mind*, Cambridge, MA: MIT Press.

12

Spirituality
The Essence of Gandhi's Thought and Action

Ashok Vohra

"WHAT is the predominant characteristic of the personality of Mohandas Karamchand Gandhi? What is the essence of Gandhi's perception of the issues dealt by him? What is the underlying principle of the possible solutions offered by him to the diverse problems faced by him? What is the archetype of the Gandhian methods and techniques when applied to the contemporary issues faced by all of us, irrespective of our spatial location? What is the secret of the success of the doctrine of sustainable development preached and practised by Gandhi?" In short, "What is the quintessence of Gandhi's life, teachings, thought and practices?" If these questions were to be put to Prof. Ramakrishna Rao,[1] his answer in his

---

[1] I first met Prof. K. Ramakrishna Rao in the late 1980s in Delhi in Prof. K. Satchidananda Murty's office. Murty was his teacher and later his colleague in the Department of Philosophy, Andhra University. I had gone to Murty's office to finalize our manuscript on Radhakrishnan (later published as *Radhakrishnan: His Life and Ideas,* New York: SUNY Press).

I saw a well-dressed, tall, very fair and extremely handsome man with receding hairline enter the office around its closing time. After introductions, we started talking on several academic issues. I was struck by the depth and breadth of his knowledge. In the ensuing discussion, I gathered that he left teaching philosophy and developed a deep interest in psychology and was recognized as a leading psychologist not only in India but abroad also — a position that he has maintained throughout.

After that meeting, I met him only after he was appointed the chairperson of Indian Council of Philosophical Research (ICPR) in 2006. During his first three-year tenure as chairman of the ICPR I had very few occasions to meet him though I heard from my friends who were Council members during that period about his objective, democratic and impartial ways of running the Council. He set right many wrongs done in the past in six years and put the Council on the right track.

→

latest book *Gandhi and Applied Spirituality*[2] would be in just one word — spirituality. Rather, he prefers to call it "pragmatic spirituality" (p. xv). By the term "spirituality", he means:

> . . . a hypothetical level of human functioning that transcends reason and logic. It is an area where rational explanations appear inadequate to elucidate the observed events and call for assumptions involving "non-rational" forms of knowing and non-physical forms of being
>
> —p. xiii

By pragmatic spirituality he understands "practical application of spirituality" which *inter alia* includes

> Gandhian practices of non-violence, such as *satyāgraha*, *siddhis* arising from practice of *yoga*, studies of psychic phenomena by parapsychologists

---

→ During the years 2009-12, the Government of India appointed me as the member of the Council. I was also appointed a member of its governing body. It gave me an opportunity to watch Rao's way of functioning closely. I was the most vocal member. I severely criticized him for some of his decisions. So much so that once, despite the request of my other friends on the governing body, I even registered my vote of dissent. However, he never took it personally. He always did his homework before the meetings and never came to a meeting with a pre-set mind. I found him always open to discussion and abide by the consensus. Once the decisions were arrived, he struck to them even if they were not savoury for the concerned persons. There were times when some persons approached him for appointing their favourites on the bodies/committees of the Council. He firmly refused them even at the cost of making them his enemies. Because of his firm attitude, many persons, including those who had benefitted from him, mischievously and erroneously called him a dictator or *zamīndār*. He had an inclusive approach and took the members of the different bodies with him. That is why he successfully implemented the ongoing programmes of the Council and added many more to them.

Despite the heavy administrative work, Rao kept on participating in conferences, seminars, Congresses in not only the field of philosophy but in psychology and other allied disciplines in India and abroad. He published several research papers and three books titled *Violence, Identity and Gandhi* (2010); *Gandhi and Applied Spirituality* (2011); *Cognitive Anomalies, Consciousness and Yoga* (2011). He co-edited *Handbook of Indian Psychology* (2008) and *Yoga and Parapsychology* (2010). The second edition of *Yoga and Parapsychology* has been recently published.

I am happy to be a part of this felicitation volume to celebrate Rao's eightieth birthday. I wish him a long, active and healthy life — *jivem śāradaḥ śatam.*

[2] Indian Council of Philosophical Research and Matrix, New Delhi, 2011. All page numbers shown as reference are from this book.

> and the results of epidemiological researches into religiosity and spirituality. —p. xiii

He goes on to include in the list the "studies of the paranormal by parapsychologists and the researches into health benefits of religiosity and spirituality" (p. xiv). According to him:

> Gandhi's life may be seen as a modern man's spiritual search to find solutions to secular problems. His experiments are explorations into the application of spirituality in the practical, secular world.
>
> —p. xiv

So much so that his doctrine of *satyāgraha* yields fruits in the practical arenas of all lifestyles as in the words of Rao, "it is believed to generate spiritual force, which he (Gandhi) termed the "truth force". It results from practice of non-violence and can be applied for "just conflict resolution in different situations, at the level of the individual or groups" (p. xiii).

Rao justifies the inclusion of spirituality as well as pragmatic spirituality as a part of "serious philosophy" in Gandhi's thought because of his (Rao's) own conception of philosophy. He upholds the view that "philosophy deals with ideas and their legitimacy" (p. 9). However, he insists:

> There are several criteria by which the legitimacy (of philosophical themes) may be assessed. What is "agreeable to reason" is just one of them. Others include those that are (a) aesthetically appealing, (b) emotionally satisfying, and (c) morally imperative. All these are driven crucially by cultural factors and not given a priori as unalterable and absolute rules dictated by reason and logic. —p. 9

Rationality, rational satisfaction and conformity to logic though are a necessary precondition of all philosophy, it is not a sufficient condition. It is not sufficient because there is no one or absolute criterion of rationality or reasonableness. There are varieties of rationality.

Those who uphold that "rationality" has just one or unique connotation mistakenly believe that there is just one model of rationality and that is the one presented by either mathematics or the empirical sciences. They also presume that the model of rationality that they have in their mind is universal, final, all comprehensive and perfect. However, this is not so. The fact that even mathematics is not a complete system was proved by Kurt Gödel. Gödel's first incompleteness theorem proved that in mathematics as well as in any other consistent system, there have to be certain statements which cannot be proved. In his second theorem, he conclusively proved that no system including mathematics could prove its own consistency. Therefore, it is not a complete and comprehensive system. As far as the issue of completeness is concerned, the Einstein–Podolsk–Rosen thought experiment established that the quantum mechanical description of physical reality is not complete. Bell's interconnectedness theorem also shows that any local model of reality leaves aside many unexplained brute facts.

Broadly speaking, even in the empirical sciences there are two models of explanation or rationality. These are the Newtonian model and the Einsteinian model. While the former insists that it is possible for us to give a completely deterministic account of the phenomenon around us, the latter upholds that our account of reality cannot be the fully determined final account. Which one of these models of explanation or rationality one should choose is very difficult to decide. The difficulty is confounded by the fact that even Newton believed in the existence of some forces other than the mechanical ones for which no explanation could be given. Newton confessed in his book *Principia* that how "mere mechanical causes could give birth to so many regular motions" is beyond explanation. He goes on to add that he has "not been able to discover the causes" of several such phenomena.

In philosophy, it was David Hume who, taking the clue from Newton, showed that science, scientific method and the rationality embedded in these, serve only a limited purpose. He argued that the events in nature are in themselves "loose and separate". Chance is quite apparent and chaos very normal throughout Nature. All that scientific investigation can ever do is to place the events of nature into law-like orders and patterns. The law-like generalizations in science and our workaday life are also nothing but habits of the mind.

Whether one is rational or not depends on the context of discourse. In a film when the unarmed hero beats the hell out of more than a dozen well-armed opponents and emerges victorious, no one ever says that it is irrational. One in fact always enjoys such things. When asked how we could enjoy such an irrational act, we do reply by saying that it is perfectly rational in the context of the make-believe world of cinema.

Looking at different systems of medicine, one can see that there are varieties of rationality. The rationality governing the Allopathic system of medicine is curing the illness in isolation by the administration of chemical compounds; that of Homoeopathy is based on holistic treatment taking into account the total nature of the person, his background, etc. and administration of chemical compounds based on the above. The rationality underlying Āyurveda is the imbalance of *vāta, pitta* and *kapha* and administration of natural herbs to restore balance. Naturopathy is based only on natural living. Can we regard anyone of these competing models or paradigms of rationality to be higher than all the others?

Once the rationalist realizes that there can be, and in fact there are, different notions of rationality, and each one of them depends on the context, he would stop questioning the logic of the spiritual discourse. He would refrain from judging it with the kind of paradigm of rationality which is typical of a very narrow view of science which is completely alien to all forms of spiritual discourse.

Though Rao does not argue for the principle of varieties of rationality, he asserts what following Wittgenstein has come to be known as "Context Principle". Second, he argues:

> Man does not live by reason alone. One's thirst is not quenched by a dose of logic, but a glass of water. Hunger is not overcome by a rational understanding of its causes. A man is not relieved of his grief by syllogistic reasoning but by comforting counsel and empathy. The existential conditions not only precipitate problems, philosophical or otherwise, but also provide their plausible solutions. —p. 9

In the pragmatic use of reason Rao is supported by Jonardan Ganeri[3] when he says:

> Reason is the instrument of all philosophers, but conceptions of the nature and function of reason vary along with varying ideas about the work for which reason is properly employed. Manu, the lawmaker, said that those whose only guide is reason should be banished from the company of the virtuous. That is the view too of the great narrators of the Indian epics. Reason unchecked was seen as a threat to the stability of Brāhmanical social order, as the tool of heretics and troublemakers. But the epic horror of pure reason was a disdain not for reason itself, but only for its capricious use, to undermine belief rather than to support it, to criticize and not to defend.

However, Rao seems to reach the limit of his conviction when he asserts without any argument or even empirical evidence, "Reason we use to establish our relationships appears to divide us; spirituality may unite us" (p. 27). He forgets that blind spirituality or blind following of spiritual leaders can and in fact divide us; it is rational spirituality which alone

[3] *Philosophy in Classical India: The Proper Work of Reason*, London and New York: Routledge, 2001, p. 1.

unites us. His "pragmatic spirituality" to my mind is nothing else but rational spirituality. After all, it is an agreed fact that there is no one or unique notion of rationality. There are varieties of rationality.

Moreover, Rao after discussing and analysing various other philosophers' conception of philosophy upholds:

> There is more to philosophy than finding oneself in the cocoons of conceptual confusions and trying to come out of them. Reason is not necessarily the only route either to know what is "really real" or to clear confusions, conceptual or otherwise. Philosophical conflicts and confusions are not limited to concepts. There are other kinds of conflict between ideas. Their clarification is more than semantic. —p. 9

His rejection of the view that philosophy is essentially concerned with the logical and linguistic clarification of thoughts, concepts and notions and that its sole aim is to get rid of the conceptual confusions reminds one of H.D. Lewis' book *Clarity Is Not Enough*,[4] and H.H. Price's essay by the same title. Both of them present a critique of analytic philosophy.

In the Western philosophy, especially modern Western philosophy after Descartes, a hiatus has been maintained between science, scientific method, philosophy and spirituality. In general, it is argued that scientific temper has nothing in common with spirituality. Nevertheless, Rao argues:

> Science and spirituality may not be seen as one opposing the other. They are not necessarily two disparate and mutually exclusive areas that are not to be clubbed together but compartmentalized in hermeneutically sealed separate hemispheres. Any conflict seen between the two, scientific search for truth and spiritual pursuit, I believe, arises from the misunderstanding of one or both. —p. 17

Relying on Tart's findings in the psi research which establishes the existence of a trance-cognitive state which in turn leads to the view that though "we are in some ways electro-chemical machines, often acting like materialist animals, we are also spiritual beings with enormous potential", Rao concludes that we are "the agent(s) of science as well as spirituality" (p. 238). Thus, he concludes, "in human condition there is no value-empty endeavour" (p. 237). While upholding the thesis that Gandhi's philosophy is a symbiosis of science and spirituality, Rao is cautious in making a distinction between "spiritualism" and "spirituality". Likewise, he makes a distinction between science and scientism — the use of the scientific method of acquiring knowledge, whether in the traditional sciences or in

[4] Allen and Unwin, 1962.

other fields of inquiry. Whereas "scientism" — a doctrine or dogma is like spiritualism, "spiritual refers to non-physical aspects of being. It is overruled a priori by science in its doctrinaire sense and not in its true sense. It is possible to study spiritual phenomena scientifically" (p. 28).

Explaining the notion of spirituality further Rao says:

> Spirituality bestows on one the ability to interact with others and the environment and influence them in ways that appear anomalous from the perspective of the ordinary. The usual constraints that limit one's thoughts and action appear irrelevant at the spiritual level. Spirituality, according to *yoga*, for example may be promoted by cultivating the habit of dispassionateness (*vairāgya*) and the practice of detachment from the ego drives by focused attention. Inasmuch as spirituality is an intrinsic aspect of human nature, people manifest altruism by their love and compassion to others and they also respond positively to love and compassion shown to them by others. —p. 32

In fact, Gandhi's practical or pragmatic spiritualism, according to Rao, "starts with an ideal that would be an instance where the dichotomies like the individual and society can be related not as parts of a whole but as reflexive of each other" (p. 77). Nevertheless, this according to many of the contemporaries of Gandhi was an Utopian thought. That is why very often Gandhi's spiritualism was seen as a threat by nationalists like B.G. Tilak who said that politics was a game for worldly people not *sādhus*. It is interesting that some saw Gandhi's spiritualism as a deft move to defer any kind of revolution while for others it was truly revolutionary. Rao apparently belongs to the later category. Like a faithful follower of Gandhi, Rao has not reflected on the fact that Gandhi's spirituality implies a version of society which is egalitarian, and distrustful of the state like the anarchists and the socialists.

Gandhi's philosophy is holistic as it caters to the "inner" as well as the "outworldly" or what Rao prefers to call "secular" or what I would like to call the "worldly" needs of man — the requisites of the lived life. It combines the *preyas* with the *śreyas*. The success of Gandhi's philosophy shows "how science and spirituality may work in tandem and how the two may be applied together in the life of the individual as well as for social well-being of all people" (p. 17). It is by a synthesis of the two that philosophy becomes a comprehensive rather than a fragmented branch of learning and acquires the status of "truly wisdom discipline. Wisdom is knowledge applied to life" (p. 12).

Philosophy is directly concerned with our lived life. It takes into account not only bare facts, factual information but also the cultural, social and economic conditions of life. Its doctrines are based on the real, lived human conditions. It is *not* what many wrongly think a second order activity. According to Rao:

> Cultural relevance is an inherent aspect of philosophical excellence. From the factual perspective, philosophy is the binding discipline that weaves facts together and brings out a meaningful pattern, order and understanding. All intellectual issues of relevance should be ultimately addressed at the level of philosophy and they cannot be completely resolved at a narrowly circumscribed disciplinary level, however important their theories may be. Indeed, they were addressed in the past in exceedingly interesting ways by philosophers. All this makes philosophical pursuit necessarily interdisciplinary, contextual, culture-relevant and problem-oriented. —p. 14

He reasserts the same when rejecting the notion of "universal philosophy". He says:

> Philosophy, like most other social disciplines, is contextual. I share the view that philosophies are characteristic ways of reacting to the problems of the world confronting and agitating the human mind. —p. 21

Philosophy, therefore, is like the warp and weft which make the cloth. Just as cloth is nothing over and above the warp and weft, philosophy is nothing over and above life — it is embedded in our lived life. The term "philosophy and life" bewitches us of our intelligence in the same way as "language and reality" does by creating the illusion that they are two when they are in reality just one. This bewitchment is because of our limiting ourselves, and our quest to the surface grammar of language. The moment we delve into the depth grammar, we get rid of the chimera and see the two as one.

Gandhi's philosophy is a paradigm of the blending of the doctrines of pragmatism and idealism. It is perennial because

> His ideas are possibly the most relevant for current socio-economic and political crises confronting the world at large. His philosophy is practical, person-centred and action-oriented. At the same time it is focused on the collectivity embedded in the person and it is infused with idealism, common good and altruism. —p. 24

Gandhi is an enigma not only for the philosophers for such a blending of abstract ideas, but is also so for the political scientists as he synthesizes utilitarian, result-oriented practical politics with spiritual pursuits in his private as well as public life. What makes him more mysterious is he "was an idealist and a pragmatist, a saint and a scientist, at the same time" (p. 139).

Rao once again takes the example of *satyāgraha* to show how Gandhi was able to achieve this marvellous feat. According to him.

> *Satyāgraha,* as Gandhi conceived and practised, encompasses scientific and spiritual dimensions. Its understanding is incomplete from any single perspective. So are Gandhian politics. Gandhi added a spiritual dimension to politics while participating in public life with scientific objectivity and precision. Gandhi's work is not *politics of spirituality.* Rather he helped to *spiritualize politics.* Practising politics of spirituality, leaders put up a spiritual façade to achieve political success. Gandhi's political practices are spiritual and they help to sanitize power politics contaminated by self-centredness. They are believed to evoke altruism all around and generate *spiritual force* to transform the world. In Gandhi, we find no cleavage between but a consummate synthesis of the spiritual and secular perspectives. —p. 17

That is why his "thought and practices continue to be relevant to the current complex problems in today's troubled world" (p. 16). Rao through his analysis is successful in tracing the uniqueness and underlying principle of Gandhian method which makes its application both universal and universalizable. According to him Gandhi's technique of spiritualizing politics lies in "locating an ideal in a traditional value concept in a spiritual mode and transforming it pragmatically to be subservient to existential conditions, secular as well as sacred" (p. 124). He shows how Gandhi's methods are as relevant and practical today as they were in the times of Gandhi by hypothetically applying them to the contemporary issues raised by the fundamentalists, terrorists, Naxals and supporters/opposers of Telangana issue.

Recognizing the fact that human nature is "a combined product of nature and nurture, learning and instinct" (p. 45), Rao believes that both violence and conflict are natural in a human society. They are ubiquitous and part of human existential predicament. They like co-operation and competition, love and hatred are part of evolutionary characteristics of human beings. According to him:

> There are a variety of conditions that trigger violence. They occur at different levels — (a) physical, (b) biological, and (c) psycho-social. At the physical level, for example, as we noted, temperature and exposure

> to lead fumes could be factors contributing to the outbreak of violence. In general, any threats to one's physical needs could provoke violence. At the biological level, we know that gender is related to violence. So are neurological and other abnormalities. Again, we could say that threats to one's survival and frustrations to satisfy one's biological needs could trigger violence. The physical and biological conditions could provoke psychological states that prompt violent behaviour. There is significant evidence that frustration, anger, sense of insecurity and perceived threat of different kinds could lead to violence. From a holistic perspective, taking all the three levels together, we could say that experience of suffering, and even the very thought and fear of suffering, is the root cause for triggering violence at the level of the person. Many of these factors are also relevant to group violence. —p. 70

Gandhi goes a step further and upholds that "there are degrees of violence as of non-violence" (*Harijan*, 30 September 1939). One can conclude that state of violence and conflict is a natural state of man. A perfectly peaceful and co-operative state without any conflict and violence is at the most Utopia based on ignorance of the real nature of man.

Though one tends to agree with Rao when he says that "manifest violence is a manifold product of the threat/need-generating situation, psychological factors associated with the person affected by the situation and the accessible forms of violence and available victims" (p. 55), one fails to agree with his conclusion that violence has its own fruits — benefits or shall we call it advantages. According to him, it "serves as a vent providing emotional catharsis and some kind of stress reducing sublimation" (p. 55). In addition, "violence . . . may also have the value of enhancing one's self-image and esteem". Likewise, Rao argues that conflicts, especially group conflicts, are also not "a bad thing". He says:

> Even group conflicts are not evil. Conflicts could lead to bonding and greater cohesion not only for the members of the in-group but also between groups. —p. 65

Whatever may be considered to be the advantages of violence, or the beneficial role of conflicts in group consolidation in the wayward self of Rao, and whatever may be his reasons for upholding these advantages even he has to agree that.

> it is . . . becoming increasingly irrelevant and obsolete as an instrument for conflict resolution. Its self-perpetuating propensity, its tendency to incrementally increase and its enormous destructive potential make us fear violence as the ultimate curse of human kind. —p. 71

Gandhi and his principles based on spirituality are an attempt to bring this fact to the notice of humankind and suggest alternate sustainable ways of existence and survival. In the alternative ways of survival and existence he discards the ideas which cannot be translated into action, abandons the beliefs which cannot be practised and rejects the values which cannot be shared with fellow men. Therefore, in Gandhi, there is no chasm between thought and practice — the two coalesce into one. His thought and practice thereof can never be Utopian. According to Rao, Gandhi was able to achieve this oneness in thought and action because "his philosophy is person-centred but focused on the collectiveness embedded in the person. It appears best suited to contain violence in all its forms, because it addresses the different dimensions of human nature" (p. 72). "The collectiveness embedded in the person" is nothing else but spirit — the human spirit. Spirituality is common to all men.

Though Gandhi like the Indian seers recognized that man essentially is *nitya-śuddha-buddha-mukta-svabhāva-parmātman* — the eternally pure, awakened and free self, he being a realist also recognized that man has to fight against all odds, natural and otherwise, for his day-to-day survival. Man is an outgoing individual searching for ways to satisfy his organic needs. To meet these needs he has to live in a world full of fierce, cut-throat competition. Man's lived world is full of struggle. In it only the fittest are able to satisfy their desires and fulfil their needs. As the *Kaṭha Upaniṣad* says: *nāyam ātma balahīnena labhyaḥ* — perfection cannot be achieved by the weak.

Therefore, the realist in Gandhi in the words of Rao "had no illusions that we can totally wipe out violence. Violence cannot be simply obliterated because it is a part of the repository of human response system" (p. 107). That is why

> Gandhiji also acknowledged that violence is not a sporadic and occasional occurrence. Rather it is a common and ever-present phenomenon, born out of our instinctive nature and something that we must learn to grow out of. Violence is "the law of the beast in us".
>
> — p. 103

One may not agree with Rao when he says "indeed it (violence) may have some useful role to play in an imperfect society to set things right" yet one would agree with him when he asserts "even assuming that aggression is instinctive, what differentiates humans from the rest of the animal kingdom is the fact that humans are endowed with reason and moral sense that help to check and control aggression and channel it in less destructive and harmful ways" (p. 107). Rao is fully supported in this conclusion by Gandhi when he says:

> As humans we need to strive to overcome this natural tendency (to indulge in violence) and respond to it by self-suffering, which is "the law of the man in us".
> — Gandhi, 2001, vol. 18, p. 305

Rao traces the origin of violence in the human existential situation itself. He analyses the given human condition and after analysing the multiple criteria of identity and individuation he concludes that

> In the human condition, identities are multiple; therefore, conflicts are inevitable. As long as violence is an option, identity-violence exists. That option can only be closed by cultivating compassionate love. — p. 106

Depending on the criteria adopted by us in identifying and individuating ourselves, Rao says:

> There are four different levels of controlling violence — (1) physical, (2) biological, (3) psychological, and (4) spiritual. At the physical level, in addition to the security networks such as police, we need to ensure that the physical and biological factors contributing to violence need to be addressed. For example, deprivations and discriminations of all kinds are significant contributory factors for the outburst of violence at the level of the individual as well as group. However, taking care of them though necessary will not be sufficient to control violence.
> — p. 107

For Gandhi violence includes violence in thought, word and deed. That is why his method of dealing with violence aims at eliminating it at all these levels. Gandhi is also fully aware that violence exists at both an individual and societal, and what Rao prefers to call "structural" level, or self-directed and other-directed, individual and collective levels. It exists at moral and mundane, ideological and contextual planes. Essentially Gandhi upholds that any act or thought that is conflict-prone is an instance of violence. However, Rao is certainly mistaken in thinking that "Gandhi conceived violence essentially at the level of the person" (p. 141). This is mistaken because Gandhi's *satyāgraha*, *sarvodaya* and trusteeship, which have been discussed by Rao in considerable details throughout the book, are the methods of eliminating social evils including slavery.

Violence does not lead to a solution to any issue confronting an individual, a society, or a state because as Rao says, "dispassionate pursuit of truth is not possible in an atmosphere of violence, coercive agitations, emotional upheavals, and campaigns of hate and anger" (p. 114). Moreover, violence generates more of its kind. It breeds more violence in an ever-widening cycle of conflict. Violence, therefore, instead of ending conflict situations generates more conflicts of a more intense and severe kind than before. It grows in geometric progression. Therefore, it is *not* and it *cannot* be a solution to the resolution of any kind of conflict. Any kind of violence has to be met with non-violence. Gandhi put it very forcefully when he said, "an eye for an eye will make the whole world blind". Rao like Gandhi believes:

> Spiritualization of the human condition is the ultimate solution for containing violence. Spiritualization involves not only developing values antithetical to violence but also transforming the person to bridge the deep divide between beliefs and behaviour, between what one professes and what is practised. Spiritualization means raising humans to a different level of being. —p. 108

As opposed to violence, non-violence, which by its very nature is conflict containing and not conflict generating, is seen by Gandhi as a spiritual force. According to Rao, non-violence "is also the moral imperative engendering conflict-containing behaviour . . .".

Therefore, necessarily non-violence is the ideal means for conflict resolution. In addition, Gandhi's moral stance makes violence in all its forms a vice to be avoided. Non-violence is not merely a virtue to be cultivated but it is also a practice that generates spiritual force to bring about necessary transformation in the person as well as the society" (p. 140). Once cultivated

> The Gandhian way of non-violent conflict resolution by its very nature is something that would be ultimately satisfying to all those involved in the conflict. —p. 117

While reading Rao's *Gandhi and Applied Spirituality* one must remember that Gandhi is polysemic, meaning different things to different people with many of these perceptions divergent or even radically different from each other. The different interpretations may even be severely polemical. However, for Rao,

> Gandhism is essentially an approach and a method that combines reason and intuition and uses the force of reason and the strength of spirituality to resolve all kinds of conflicts, personal and social. At the bottom of all this is the deep conviction that the person at the core is a spiritual being, altruistic and not an ego-driven selfish machine. Gandhian hermeneutics helped to relate tradition with modernity; and his emphasis on the experimental habit of mind gave us new tools for resolving human

> problems. Without disturbing the social equilibrium, Gandhi added a new dimension of co-operative participation in social action based on individual freedom; and this gave a new insight into the emerging values. Gandhi sought to clarify his ideas in action. — pp. 138-39

Rao, by surveying the philosophical assumptions, the application of these abstract and abstruse principles, has shown that all of Gandhi's philosophy and actions are essentially spiritual in nature. Despite this extensive and indepth study it must be the humility of Rao which makes him say:

> No attempt is made to systematically develop the thesis of pragmatic spirituality in this book. What we have here is only a suggestive reasoning, and we barely touch the fringes. — p. xv

He unassumingly calls his study and analysis "a modest attempt". Like the Dalai Lama, I hope and wish "that this book . . . will inspire readers to develop practical ways in which children and adults can be educated in the paths of non-violence, kindness and compassion, if we can do that, I believe we will aptly fulfil Gandhi's legacy to us."

13

Science and Spirituality

Complementary Thesis of Prof. Rao Re-examined

Alok Tandon

PROF. K. Ramakrishna Rao's book *Gandhi and Applied Spirituality* is inspired by the pragmatic spirituality of Gandhi, though, as he himself admits, "no attempt is made to systematically develop the thesis of pragmatic spirituality". By pragmatic spirituality he simply means practical applications of spirituality. Spirituality, for him, "is a hypothetical level of human functioning that transcends reason and logic". And to explain such events one needs to assume "non-rational" forms of knowing and non-physical forms of being. Further he assumes a conceptual unity of science and spirituality and pleads for a synthesis, sanitizing science with spirituality and enriching spirituality with science. The effort is laudable, especially in an era of massive commercialization and politicalization of spirituality with the threat of terrorist violence and nuclear war looming large over the horizon. The book with twelve chapters (377 pages) has a large canvas, covering Gandhi, Nehru, Buddha, science, spirituality, parapsychology, cognitive science, hypnosis, *yoga* and psychic phenomenon under single framework. It is a daunting task for a single person to review the whole book. Therefore, I shall restrict myself to three chapters: "Nehru and Gandhian Legacy", "Science and Spirituality: A Search for Common Ground", and "Cognitive Science and Classical Indian Philosophies of Mind".

Nehru and Gandhian Legacy

"Jawaharlal Nehru's impact on India is too great not to be re-examined periodically. As an Indian writer, I am conscious that his legacy is ours, whether we agree with everything he stood or not. What India is today, both for good and for ill, we owe in great measure to one man."[1]

[1] Shashi Tharoor (2003), *Nehru: The Invention of India*, United States: Arcade Publishing, p. xi.

There can be no better justification than the above for the re-appraisal of Nehru, attempted in the sixth chapter of the book by Rao. His central thesis, in his own words,

> . . . is that, pulled from one side by the contextual idealism to which he was constantly exposed at home during the course of the freedom movement and by his close association with Mahatma Gandhi and by the remarkable industrial and political revolutions in the Western world he came to appreciate and admire from the other side Nehru attempted to an alternative political and economic posture that would give benefits of both to Indian people. Towards this end he chose the Buddhist middle path and ended up with mixed results.[2]

Elaborating his thesis further, Rao points out the middle ground Nehru chose between Western capitalism and Soviet socialism, between Gandhian commitment to individual freedom as a personal virtue and the Western notion of freedom as socially given, and between the emphasis on inner transformation advocated by both Gandhi and the Indian tradition and Western commitment for exploiting the external world for common welfare.[3]

However, Rao castigates Nehru, not so much for deviation from Gandhi in choosing the middle path but for neglecting spirituality and consequent overemphasis on secularism. For him, Gandhian idealism which Nehru shared, "is rooted in spirituality which indeed is the connecting and transformational link between the practical and the ideal, the individual and society, personal interest and common good, reason and experience and indeed between the ego and the true self (*ātman*)".[4] But, Nehru as Rao asserts, "stops with practical idealism" and it gives an impression of Nehru's idealism being rootless without spirituality. This overstatement seems contestable on both, theoretical and factual grounds. Foundation of moral behaviour may be traced to one's religious/spiritual or secular beliefs/attitudes. Superiority between the two may be debatable but not the capacity to provide the roots. And, factually too, Nehru himself admitted the influence of Marxism[5] on his thinking, though he was not

---

[2] K.R. Rao (2011), *Gandhi and Applied Spirituality*, New Delhi: ICPR and Matrix Publishers, p. 197.

[3] Ibid., p. 207.

[4] Ibid., p. 207.

[5] In *The Discovery of India*, Nehru wrote, "Russia apart, the theory and philosophy of Marxism lighted up many a dark corner of my mind. History came to have a new meaning frame. The Marxist interpretation threw a flood →

happy with many Soviet practices of implementing it. His emphasis on the unity of means and ends and consequent ideology of democratic socialism bear testimony to his deep moral concerns. In fact, in his autobiography, he quoted Romain Rolland saying that those who fearlessly search for the truth — whether they are nationalists, humanists, socialists, communists or rationalists — can be called spiritual as they accept faith in a purpose which they consider higher than present-day life of the humanity. Nehru has no objection to such spirituality, he himself said that he was not bound to any religion or sect but had full faith in inherent spirituality of man that gives dignity to him. Then, one may say that the practical idealism of Nehru was rooted in his own synthesis of scientific temper, Gandhism, Marxism and agnosticism. The emphasis on secularism was a natural result of it. Going by a definition of spirituality given by Rao himself, "spirituality may be seen as that aspect of human behaviour that enables the person to go beyond 'I' and the ego and to identify herself with others",[6] one cannot deny Nehru having spiritual roots as his identification with the Indian nation and its people was beyond doubt. At its best, it can be called secular spirituality of a skeptic agnostic. Judging Nehru from Gandhian perspective only may do injustice to him.

Rao's central thesis, quoted in the beginning can be accepted but his overemphasis of the influence Buddhist middle path had on Nehru is unwarranted. Nehru did try to resolve the tension arising out of various theoretical influences on him with his experience and understanding of changing Indian and social reality, not having much to do with the Buddha. His concept of *pañcaśīla* governing the relations between nation states does show Buddhist influence but that is marginal and moreover does not make him a follower of Gautama Buddha rather than Gandhi. *Ahiṁsā* is common to both but it is the Gandhian version which appeals to Nehru more. Calling it Buddist middle path seems rather unnecessary. At best, it can be called the third path.

Rao has invoked the pragmatism of Charles Sanders Peirce to argue that (a) Nehru's contributions are indeed in the realm of philosophy, (b) he brings a pragmatic dimension to Gandhian contextual idealism, and thus (c) makes a distinct contribution to contemporary thought. One can

---

→ of light on it, and it became an unfolding drama with some order and purpose, however unconscious, behind it. It was the essential freedom, from dogmas and the scientific outlook of Marxism that appealed to me".

6. Rao, op. cit., p. 32.

hardly disagree with Rao while keeping his understanding of philosophy in mind.

> Philosophy, for him, is an inquiry in thought concerning the modes of resolution of problems encountered in experience or anticipated in future. . . . There is no sharp dichotomy between theory and practice in so far as both are concerned with solution of problems, since the solution of problems in practice depends upon coming to agreement through communication and discussion.[7]

Accordingly, he concludes that "Nehru like Gandhi is a pragmatic idealist".

In his discussion of the "practicality" of any given philosophy, Rao points out two problems:

(a) to what extent and in which ways have the present circumstances influenced thought, and

(b) what are the consequences of his philosophy in influencing a change in or gaining control over the present circumstances.

This calls for, in my opinion, not only a deep understanding, in this case, of Nehru's legacy to India but also the evaluation of its achievements and failures to deliver the results it sought for. Rao, in this chapter of the book, has successfully clarified the ideas of Nehru, though at times judging them harshly for their lack of spiritual content. But Rao's analysis falls short of critical evaluation of Nehru's achievements and failures. Perhaps he leaves this for some other occasion or to some other person so that one may evaluate what is living and what is dead in Nehru's legacy. I can only add to say that the principle pillars of Nehru's legacy to India — democratic — institution building, staunch pan-Indian secularism, socialist economics at home and foreign policy of non-alignment all of which were integral to his vision of India, are contested today. There can be no better words, than those of Shashi Tharoor, to depict the present situation: ". . . democracy endures, secularism is besieged, non-alignment is all but forgotten and socialism barely clings on." Nehru seems "curiously dated, a relic of another era". His goal of creating "a just state by just means" has been undermined by the centrifugal forces of Indian religious and cultural divisiveness.

Finally, to the questions as to where lies Nehru's success, one cannot but agree with Sunil Khilnani what he says in his book *The Idea of India*:

---

[7] Rao, op. cit., p. 209.

> Yet the true historic success of Nehru's rule lay not in dissemination of democratic idealism but in its establishment of the state at the core of Indian society. The state was enlarged, its ambitions inflated, and it was transformed from a distant, alien object into one that aspired to infiltrate the everyday lives of Indians, proclaiming itself responsible for everything they could desire: jobs, ration cards, educational places, security, cultural recognition. The state thus itched itself into the imagination of Indians in a way that no previous agency had ever done. This was enduring legacy of the Nehru period. [8]

Science and Spirituality: A Search for Common Ground

The title of the seventh chapter, "Science and Spirituality: A Search for Common Ground" is very clear in its intent, what follows afterwards is the forceful argumentation to attain that objective. Before commenting on the success or failure of the exercise, let us summarize what he has to say about, perhaps, the most important issue discussed in the book. For him, twofold task of sanitizing science and energizing spirituality is facilitated by finding the common ground between science and spirituality. He starts with making a distinction between religion and spirituality on the one hand and spirituality and "spiritualism" on the other. The latter, like "scientism", is a doctrinaire belief system. Science and spirituality, both are dedicated to search for truth, one from mundane and the other from transcendental perspective. They seem to run parallel to each other. One is experimental and objective, and the other is experiential and subjective. The necessary dialogue between the two requires a meta-theory aimed at the unification of science and spirituality. The basic postulates of which are, first, science and spirituality are two knowledge streams that spring from the human mind; second, the objective of both is to attain happiness and well-being; third, there is no intrinsic opposition between the two, though, there are epistemic differences between them, and fourth, both seek truth, science is more reliable to understand the physical world while spirituality is more appropriate in dealing with non-physical matters such as values.

Elaborating his thesis further Rao states:

> Science and spirituality involve two distinct epistemic modes. Science draws from the rational mode. Observed data constitute its territory; and one rides on reason. Spirituality is linked to the intuitive mode, where

[8] Sunil Khilnani (1998), *The Idea of India*, New Delhi, Penguin Books, p. 41.

> experience is the ground, and revelation is the vehicle. The validity of spiritual claims is predicated on the truth value of the revelations just as the validity of the scientific claims is contingent on the truth of its observations. The two suggest that there are rational as well as non-rational pathways to truth.[9]

Again,

> Their relationship is not one of interaction, but of complementarity. Science supplies what is needed when spiritual practices go astray and fall into the trap of superstition and dysfunctional attitudes and beliefs. On its part, spirituality helps science to find meaning in life and set goals that enhance human potential and happiness by adding ethical dimension to its pursuits.[10]

In order to bring them closer, Rao tries to find out the main reasons for insulating science from spirituality and suggests what he considers to be priority strategies for bringing the two together. The main culprit in his eyes is the outdated understanding of what constitute legitimacy in science. He argues that

(1) the notion that these are objective criteria that distinguish genuine science in absolute and logically compelling terms from other knowledge claims is a pious myth,

(2) the legitimacy in science is what we attribute to, rather than discover in an area of study,

(3) science is a fascinating mixture of thought, action and passion, and

(4) a scientist's passion is no small determinant of legitimacy in science.

However, Rao contends further that anything does not go in science. Though there is no pure method in science and no perfect knowledge, we have a body of knowledge which we have little reason to question and that works pretty well in practice. But the present practice of science has few glaring pitfalls. While the emphasis on third-person observation appears appropriate in the domain of physical sciences, its indiscriminate extension to include all areas, especially human sciences, is not warranted. Often, science goes beyond its method and includes a worldview of essential materialism. This "scientism" is a dogmatic belief, rather than authentic science that undermines spirituality. Science is considered to be value free. Values are supposed to be in the domain of religion and

[9] Rao, op. cit., p. 218.

[10] Ibid.

spirituality. The divorce between science and spirituality leads to ethical vacuum.

Rao admits that there can be two broad strategies for reconciliation between science and spirituality. One is secularizing the sacred; and the other is to challenge the view, by collecting data, that humans are "materialist animals" and suggest a spiritual view of the world. For the purpose, Rao quotes and examines the results of recent epidemiological research which suggests significant relationship between religious practices taken as indices of spirituality and human health. But Rao rightly observes that beneficial health outcomes can be explained by the psychological effects brought about by religious beliefs and practices in reducing stress and anxiety. This may provide for legitimacy of religious lifestyle without addressing the basic questions whether there is any scientific validity for spirituality phenomenon. Rao also examines a number of studies that gave positive evidence linking intercessory prayer with beneficial health outcomes and found them inconclusive. In the end, Rao cites massive database collected in parapsychological research to reject essential materialism, what he calls doctrinal twin of methodological scientism. He calls for the parapsychology of religion to undertake the systematic study of the religious beliefs, practices and experience to provide empirical grounds in place of doctrinal philosophies and theologies as their veridicality can be attested by observation and actual experience. Only then, the chasm between the religion and science may be bridged. His conclusion is:

> We are in some ways electrochemical machines, often acting like materialist animals, but we are also spiritual beings with enormous potential. The person is thus the agent of science as well as spirituality. Parapsychological phenomenon prominently displays the common ground covered by science and spirituality. In a meaningful sense, parapsychology may be seen as a spiritual science.[11]

I have quoted at length from Rao's book not only to do justice to his views on this very controversial subject but also keeping in view its importance in the life of vast majority of Indians who believe in some sort of spiritualism. In my opinion, Rao's major thesis hinges on there being a non-physical side of our being, the validity of which he wants to establish by the results of parapsychological research. Let us take the bull by its horns and find out what is the current state of affairs in

[11] Rao, op. cit., p. 238.

parapsychological research and findings. We need to answer three very simple, direct questions:

1. Is there conclusive experimental evidence of psi?
2. Would the existence of psi contradict established science?
3. Is parapsychology a science or a pseudo-science?

The fact of the matter is that, for well over a century, the debate is going on and there have been strongly divided opinions about the existence of psychic phenomenon such as telepathy, clairvoyance and psychokinesis. Despite the overwhelming evidence of psychic phenomena, as they claim, provided by the researches since at least 1950s, the skeptics are not convinced. Given the long history of war between science and religion in the West, they are suspicious and associate parapsychology as part of efforts to bring back religious superstitions in the garb of respectable science. For them, the evidence is neither enough nor conclusive. On their part, the supporters of parapsychology assert that the question of the reality of psi phenomenon is not primary about evidence, but about the interpretation of evidence; it is about frameworks of understanding,[12] what Thomas Kuhn called paradigms. For the skeptics, with their assumptions and preconceptions, these sort of phenomena don't make any sense and challenge their worldview, and they are compelled to deny its existence. But I think, in the end, the question of whether or not psi phenomenon occur, and how they might be explained, depends on evidence and research. So, there is a strong case for scientific inquiry of psi phenomenon as well as that of religious experience and following the data wherever it leads to, regardless of the spiritual implications. Classical science may have no room for psi, but we no longer live in the seventeenth century. Modern science is no longer mechanistic. There is nothing in quantum mechanics that would be compromised by the existence of psi phenomenon. As very well brought about by Rao, the understanding of what constitutes the legitimacy in science has also undergone change and we must be beware of degeneration of science into scientism. We in the East, need not defend an outmoded philosophy of science to oppose an open investigation of the psychic phenomenon. Let us not sacrifice the spirit of free inquiry at the altar of our belief systems, either materialism or spiritualism.

Once it is settled, as very well pleaded by Rao, that spiritual experience could be a proper topic of scientific inquiry, the relationship between the

[12] Chris Carter (2007), *Parapsychology and the Skeptics*, Sterling.

two may be left to the outcome of the research. It may be only interactive or complementary, as suggested by Rao. The question, which is yet to be answered, is whether spiritual experiencing is more than hallucination and self-entertainment of a complex neuronal system left to play with itself. Mere consensus of persons experiencing the same "reality" does not guarantee that what is experienced is indeed reality or has anything to do with it. It might simply be a consensual hallucination. But, if what the mind is and experiences, namely consciousness, is not only an emerging property of the brain as a complex system but a complementary aspect of reality, then consciousness would touch reality not in its material but in its complementary manifestation. In that case, spiritual experience and its scientific study could help us understand consciousness and its relation to brain. Thus, science and spirituality could well be complementary modes of knowing and understanding reality.

Cognitive Science and Classical Indian Philosophies of Mind

As we have discussed above, no discussion about the relation between science and spirituality is complete without throwing light on the nature of human consciousness. Aptly, Rao, in the eighth chapter of his book, tries to evaluate the contributions of cognitive science and Indian philosophies of mind in this regard. He is very hopeful about Indian thought making a valid contribution for developing an "indigenous and yet inclusive cognitive science with pan-human relevance". Let us see how he proposes to do it.

Overviewing research done in cognitive neuro-science, Rao finds behaviourist theory of mind outdated, computational theory of mind inadequate due to its inability to solve basic issues such as problem solving and pattern recognition, and biological naturalist model as inappropriate in dealing with genius, mystical experiences and the notion of free will. He does accept the role of the brain as a structure involved in our cognitive functioning but what precisely that role is and what its limits are, are the matters he considers as yet to be ascertained, not to be assumed a priori. Extensively relying on the excellent work of Kelly et al. (2007),[13] he points out certain cognitive anomalies and a category of mental phenomenon arguably resistant to biological naturalism. These include exceptional skills exhibited by some in an altered state of consciousness such as automatic writing, memory of past experience, unity of conscious experience and

[13] Rao, op. cit., p. 244.

the so-called binding problem especially in the visual experience, near-death experiences, extraordinary ability of a genius and mystical experiences reported in major religions of the world. And the final argument in his own words states:

> It is consciousness itself that may be in principle irreducible to brain states. The "subjectivity", an inherent aspect of consciousness, is what makes it special, first person event, and sets it apart from the observable physiological events and processes. Consciousness appears to give an inward dimension to our being. If the mind were without consciousness, if our knowing abilities were limited to what we perceive through our senses, and if one's freedom of will and choice were no more than chimerical attributes of human condition, then perhaps we could ungrudgingly settle for a mechanistic and reductionist conception of the mind as a complex computing machine. However, the intrinsic subjectivity of consciousness . . . suggests that perhaps we are not merely brain-driven machines and there may be something beyond the neurological configurations that is essential for understanding the nature of human mind.[14]

Thus, after rejecting biological naturalism, Rao looks towards Indian tradition to provide a new and viable paradigm to cognitive science. Actually, he strongly advocates the marriage of cognitive science with classical Indian philosophies of the mind. The central thesis of Indian theories of consciousness, according to him, "is that brain does not generate consciousness. The brain in some ways embellishes consciousness. This point has enormous implications to research in cognitive science."[15] Indian tradition allows for non-intentional consciousness, a pure conscious state devoid of any content. A distinction is made between consciousness and the mind. The mind is connected as an interface between consciousness and the brain. As such, he is of the view "that the Indian thought has much to offer to creatively untangle the Cartesian web in which the Western attempts to scientifically study consciousness are cripplingly caught".[16] Finally, he pleads for a top–down approach instead of bottom-up inclusive of anomalies and exceptional states, and indigenous to involve Indian theories of mind, to develop an inclusive, indigenous cognitive science. He also suggests some potential areas of research in this regard.

---

[14] Rao, op. cit., p. 245.

[15] Ibid., p. 248.

[16] Ibid., p. 253.

John Searle, in his recent book, *Freedom and Neurobiology: Reflections on Free Will, Language and Political Power*, addresses the putative incompatibility between the doctrine of freedom of the will and contemporary neurobiology by suggesting an account of free will that allows for scientific solution. For first person freedom (psychological) he asserts, indeterminism at the neuro-level is necessary[17] because the absence of causally sufficient conditions at the psychological level must be matched by the absence of such conditions at the neurophysiological level. Since, all indeterminism in nature is quantum indeterminism and consciousness is a feature of nature that manifests indeterminism, he concludes that consciousness manifests quantum indeterminism. Searle's proposal takes the possibility of quantum neural indeterminism as seriously as epiphenomenalism. I am not sure how Rao will respond to this move of biological naturalists like Searle who himself admits that we have not made much progress in solving the free-will riddle so far. Therefore, testable hypotheses from classical Indian models of mind, which assume that the brain is not the generator of consciousness but merely a "filter" or "transmitter" that constraints and moulds consciousness, could give Indian touch to the ongoing debate by adding insights arrived by first-person experience of exceptionally evolved persons and, in turn, testing them scientifically too. Brain mapping of exceptional states of mind and other such studies may certainly open exciting possibilities for resolution of the problem. We need, for the purpose, an open, unbiased approach of the researchers as well as co-operation of authentic persons with exceptional abilities.

Conclusion

In the end, I can say that the three chapters under review, though written at different times with different purposes, seem to be very well interconnected by the focal theme of the book. On a very interesting yet controversial issue of conceptual unity of science and spirituality, they provide thought-provoking remarks by the author in a very lucid prose, to be easily understood by a layman like me. I think, the merit of Rao's endeavour lies in successfully presenting the arguments of both sides of the issue, keeping his own assumptions clear and explicit. Thus, he is successful in inviting all of us not only to join the debate but also to support future research in neuroscience with an open mind with the

[17] John Searle (2007), *Freedom and Neurobiology: Reflections on Free Will, Language and Political Power*, New York: Columbia University Press, pp. 74-75.

possibility to revise our standpoints in the light of its findings. His agenda is futuristic and he is very optimistic about the synthesis of science and spirituality to solve the problems of mankind. He might not have succeeded fully but bringing the two warring camps, from outright dismissal to a respectable dialogue is no mean achievement.

14

Yoga, Parapsychology and Gandhi
Some Reflections

B. Sambasiva Prasad

I HAVE known Prof. K. Ramakrishna Rao since a long time as a distinguished philosopher/psychologist and an educationist, but it was from a distance until 2010 when I joined GITAM Centre for Gandhian Studies as its director. During my tenure at GITAM, I came in close contact with Rao. I found in him a man of hard work, sincerity and punctuality, and doing things faster with utmost accuracy. I received considerable guidance and suggestions to develop the GITAM Centre for Gandhian Studies and bring out the *GITAM Journal of Gandhian Studies*, which is an international and interdisciplinary bi-annual journal of Gandhian thought and practices, peace and non-violence.

When I first read his book *Consciousness Studies: Cross-Cultural Perspectives,* I was wonderstruck on his amazing art of writing, vast knowledge on the subject and moreover his lucid expressive skills. His attempt of bridging the gulf between the Eastern and Western theories of consciousness attracted me. In that book Rao showed how the Eastern and Western theories of consciousness are not contradictory, but complementary. Being convinced with his argument, I felt that both S. Radhakrishnan and Rao dispelled the misnomer: "East is East and West is West, and never the twain shall meet" — while Radhakrishnan dispelled it from the point of comparative religion, Rao dispelled it from his studies of consciousness.

In this paper I confine my discussions on Rao's views on *yoga*, hypnosis, psychic phenomena and Gandhi as contained in his thought-provoking book, *Gandhi and Applied Spirituality*.

Hypnosis, Yoga and Psychic Phenomena

While analysing the relation between "hypnosis, *yoga* and psychic phenomena" Rao opines that they "appear to belong to a common family"

(p. 279).[1] He views that "all the three subject areas had their origin in prevalent practices" and that they struggled all along for an acceptable theoretical niche" (ibid.). Apart from their historic commonalities, Rao feels that "yoga, psychic phenomena and hypnosis may be seen to share a common ground in human condition that is at once the chilling source of controversies as well as the challenging potential and promise for a full understanding of human nature" (ibid.). By analysing the relation between hypnosis, *yoga* and psychic phenomena, Rao attempts to cover the ground, which, he thinks, is the meeting point of the mind and consciousness on the one side, and the mind and brain on the other. The implication of this common ground, Rao feels, "goes beyond the individual disciplines to impact on our understanding the very basics of human nature" (ibid.).

Rao observes that the essence of *yoga* is meditation. "If *yoga* helps to gain access to paranormal abilities, then practice of meditation may be psi conducive" (p. 294). He observes that there are unquestionable similarities between hypnosis and meditation. "In both the general cerebral activity can be suppressed at will. In both the attention can be focused on the desired object to a degree that is definitely superior to the waking state" (pp. 294-95). He thinks that the yogic concentration in its early phases generates hallucinatory imagery similar to that obtained under hypnosis. The point of Rao is that even if we conclude from these similarities that yogic concentration produces a state similar to hypnotic state, *yoga* does more. *Yoga* involves further training to which claims of paranormality could be attributed. "It is in this context", says Rao, "we may refer to the similarities between *yoga* and Ryzl's technique" (p. 295). Describing the state of mind favourable for the manifestation of psi cognition in Ryzl's experimental studies, Rao observes that it is a particular state of consciousness, defying adequate description, between sleep and waking. This is "precisely what *yoga* claims to do by means of physical exercises and concentration" (p. 295).

The one clear underlying state characterizing both hypnosis and meditation, Rao feels, is relaxation. He thus remarks: "Relaxed state of the mind and loosening of sensory controls appear to be the basic hallmark or the ground condition of hypnosis as well as meditation" (p. 295). They are also the conductive conditions for the manifestations of psychic phenomena such as Extrasensory Perception (ESP) (p. 295). The thesis of

---

[1] The page numbers given in the brackets refer to Prof. K. Ramakrishna Rao's book *Gandhi and Applied Spirituality*, New Delhi: ICPR and Matrix Publishers, 2011.

Rao is that "hypnosis, *yoga* and psychic phenomena have several interesting commonalities that indicate some interconnectedness among them. Perhaps they belong to a common family and follow a common rationale" (p. 296).

Rao is aware of the fact that scholars of Indian psychology may not agree to his suggestion of commonality between *yoga* and hypnosis, on the pretext that such a suggestion may lead to the danger of reducing the state of *samādhi* to the state of sleep or a dissociated state of mind. Reacting upon such a misconception, Rao says that such a fear arises only when value considerations dominate. He observes that there is a justification for his suggestion of commonality between *yoga* and hypnosis. His justification is fourfold:

1. hypnosis and psychical research share the same roots and have similar developmental histories;
2. the two disciplines seen in a broader and holistic context may fit into a model that may have more wholesome implications for theory and testing in both;
3. the possibility of receiving necessary recognition and support is likely to be greater in a combined effort rather than by a fragmented approach; and
4. the commonalities outlined are the ground conditions of a model closely akin to *yoga* psychology (pp. 296-97).

Rao argues that hypnosis, ESP and meditation (*yoga*) are interconnected links in the chain of human science. The three basic parts that constitute the person are the gross body, mind and consciousness. "The person is consciousness embodied" (p. 294). The body has two dimensions — the gross and the subtle. The gross body includes the brain. The subtle body refers to the mind in its multiple functions. Thus "the person", argues Rao, "is a continuum with body at one end, consciousness at the other and the mind in the middle". After thus analysing the relation among body, mind and consciousness of man, Rao explains that while hypnosis is primarily concerned with the link between the brain and the mind (gross and subtle forms of the body), *yoga* goes beyond to explore the link between mind and consciousness. Psychic phenomena are the by-products that emerge out of the cultivation of the mind and its transactions, following its interconnectedness with the gross body on the one side and consciousness on the other. Thus Rao suggests that "hypnosis, *yoga* and psychic phenomena" together provide solid evidence against the cerebro-centric model. They prove that man is more than a brain-driven machine.

"The mind influences the processes in the brain. Consciousness is beyond the mind connecting it with extraordinary resources for personal transformation" (p. 297).

Centrality of consciousness, says Rao, "is the single most important characteristic of Indian psychology" (ibid.). The chief concern is the person. The person is consciousness embodied. To Rao "mind and consciousness are qualitatively different. Mind is the interfacing instrumentality that is connected with consciousness at one end and with the brain at the other. Therefore, mind influences and is influenced by brain processes and at the same time holds a special relationship with consciousness" (ibid.). By consciousness, Rao means pure consciousness. It could be identified either with *Brahman* (Advaita) or *puruṣa* (Sāṁkhya-Yoga) or *nirvāṇa* (Buddhism). Thus Rao does not stop his inquiry with body–mind complex of man. He pursues beyond mind and discusses the significance of consciousness (pure consciousness). In this regard he took cue from the Indian philosophical tradition.

Rao, though attempts to explain the close relationship among hypnosis, *yoga* (meditation) and psychic phenomena, he opines that *yoga* goes beyond the realms of hypnosis and psychic phenomena. Therefore he argues that the researches in the area of hypnosis as well as psychic phenomena have something to learn from the Indian model, i.e. *yoga* (ibid.).

Parapsychology and Yoga Psychology

While explaining the significant challenges of parapsychology and *yoga* psychology, Rao expounds several issues. To start with, he discusses the "challenges of psi". He observes that the chief problem of parapsychology is that "its research methods by and large are designated to test what psi is not rather than what it is" (p. 301). While parapsychologists are reluctant to speculatively draw the implications of their results, their critics freely speculate and suggest that parapsychological research is more a search for the soul (p. 301). Rao feels that if parapsychological researches do suggest some non-ordinary forms of knowing, which in turn imply some non-physical aspects of being; this should not be taken as a discredit. "Rather, it should be taken as a profound challenge for science itself" (p. 301).

Rao feels that there are two challenges thrown up by psi research. "One is directed at parapsychology itself; and the other is the challenge for science in general" (p. 303). The twin challenges, opines Rao, "must be taken seriously" (p. 304). The psi researches should be prepared to go to wherever the evidence leads. Parapsychologists, says Rao, are not searching for the soul. If the results do lead them, however, to discover the soul they should not shirk of drawing the conclusion warranted by the evidence. "This could be the single most important discovery ever made in science. Similar lessons hold for parapsychologists as well" (p. 304).

Rao compares parapsychology with that of *yoga* psychology with an objective to focus upon the need for incorporating the unique features of *yoga* psychology into the researches of parapsychology.

While discussing the relevance of *yoga* psychology, Rao makes a distinction between knowing and being. He observes that knowing is cognitive. It is sensorially processed and is not merely coloured by the cognitive apparatus but also biased by the person's beliefs, attitudes and past experiences. For this reason the person learns to dissociate knowing from being so that we often find a person not acting on his beliefs and living the life suggested by knowledge. According to Rao, "The *yogin*'s journey is of bridging this divide so as to realize truth in her being, which is considered a state of perfection and bliss" (p. 304).

"The *yogin*'s journey", says Rao, "consists in systematically sharpening her mind by exercising control over its functions so as to overcome biases and thus come progressively closer to perfection and truth. This is accompanied by practising concentration (*abhyāsa*) and cultivating the mindset of detachment and dispassionateness (*vairāgya*)" (p. 305). The practice of *abhyāsa* and *vairāgya* leads to "excellence in sensory knowing and rational thinking" (ibid.).

By continued practice of concentration (*abhyāsa*), the *yogin* not only understands how the mind works, but also gains control over its functions. Under this impact, there arises in the *yogin*, the intuitive realization of truth, "which may be seen as accessing consciousness as such. Accessing consciousness as such involves direct participation in reality, which is realizing truth in one's being. Reaching excellence in that state makes one a transcendental being . . ." (p. 305). This is called self-realization and it is the goal of the *yogin*. "In this process", says Rao, "the person is transformed into a 'saint', the one in whom there is no divide between knowing and being" (p. 305). In contrast to a saint, the scholar-scientist exhibits only cognitive excellence, but not necessarily "excellence in being" (p. 305). The very embodiment of truth in one's being is considered as the state of absolute bliss (*ānanda*). It is a state where to know *Brahman* is to become *Brahman*. While the person in the state of *ānanda* enjoys absolute bliss and total freedom from all constraints and becomes perfect, he/she does not go through the ordinary states of sensory pleasure mediated by the mind–body complex.

Rao writes that in the practice of *yoga*, the *siddhis* are obtained by *saṁyama*, which consists in the conjoint practice of *dhāraṇā, dhyāna* and *samādhi*. *Dhāraṇā* is making the *citta* steadfast by fixing it on the same object; continuation of *dhāraṇā* is *dhyāna*; when *dhyāna* becomes continuous and the person is fully absorbed in it, it is called *samādhi*. When *dhāraṇā, dhyāna* and *samādhi* are applied to one and the same object then it is called *saṁyama*, perfect meditation (p. 309). By mastering of *saṁyama, prajñā* is generated. *Prajñā* is clarity of insight (*viveka khyāti*) (ibid.). It is the real knowledge.

Demarcating between sensuous and real knowledge, Rao writes that there is a fundamental difference between the two. While the first is for another's sake, the second is for the sake of itself. Knowledge, which is called experience, exists for the fulfilment of our purposes and is not a living reality, but only an idea. On the contrary, knowledge of the self is living knowledge; it is "knowledge which knows itself as knowledge".

Yogic practice, says Rao, enables the *yogin* to attain *siddhis*. There are *siddhis* that give one excellence in developing clairvoyant abilities and know the distant, hidden and subtle objects, gain knowledge of anatomy, etc. Patañjali mentions under *siddhis* the abilities to walk on water and move in space and so on.

Rao draws to our attention the basic distinction between *yoga* psychology and parapsychology. He observes that for Western psychologists (J.B. Rhine) psi cognition is ESP. It is going out of sense-organs. However for the *yoga* psychologists, psi cognition is possible not by going beyond senses, but by controlling the internal sense-organ — the mind. Therefore for the *yoga* psychology, psi cognition is "not extrasensory", but "extraordinary". The difference between Western model and the Indian thinkers is that the former thinks that the senses do not play any part in psi, and that it is "going out" of the mind which achieves this. "From the point of Indian thinkers it may be argued that, if mind itself is considered to be a sense-organ, psi cognition can still be sensory" (p. 314). Again what appears to be significant in Indian thought is the view that gaining access to extrasensory abilities is accessible not by "going out" or transcendence of the mind, but by controlling the mind through one-pointed concentration and focused attention (ibid.).

Rao attempts not only to highlight the unique features of Indian psychology, but also Indian epistemology. Comparing Indian epistemology with that of Western epistemology, he holds that Indian epistemology, like that of the Western model, acknowledges the importance of perceptual knowledge, logic and reasoning as important tools of inquiry in search of Truth. However, Indian epistemology provides scope for intuitive knowing and extraordinary perceptual experience, which are significantly absent in Western epistemology. "In the Western tradition", says Rao, "mysticism had long been discarded by philosophers. In classical Indian tradition, which continues to hold sway among the public as well as philosophers, there is room for nonsensory sources of knowing" (p. 313). While demarcating between classical Indian thought and Western epistemology, Rao writes that "the former has room for extraordinary human abilities like psi. Indeed classical Indian thought provides for a way of knowing that appears to be of an altogether different kind. Here we have a new kind of epistemology backed by reported psychological observations" (pp. 314-15).

The point of Rao is that according to *yoga* psychology, psi cognition is extraordinary, but not extrasensory (p. 314). This point is reinforced in the focused discussion of this topic by Rao. He observes that in the *samādhi* state there is an identity experience of the knower and the known, the blending of knowing and being. "This point", he says, "deserves to be considered carefully by parapsychologists for incorporating it into their research designs" (p. 318).

From the perspective of *yoga* psychology psychic abilities admit development by training. Rao feels that Western model needs to take note of this and "search for methods for psi training, whether hypnosis, meditation or other techniques to shut sensory noise and shield the subject from ego involvement and to allow psi intuitions to manifest in terms of observable effects" (p. 318). In addition to *abhyāsa*, the *yogin* needs *vairāgya*, which is cultivating a detached state of mind. According to Rao, this is what is lacking in parapsychological research and is possibly responsible for less than replicable effects. He feels that there is a need to operationalize *vairāgya* in a manner that yogic concentration is operationalized by the ESP Ganzfeld experiments (p. 319).

What Rao explains here are also focused in his works like *Consciousness Studies: Cross-Cultural Perspectives* (2002) and *Cognitive Anomalies, Consciousness and Yoga* (2011). In these works, one of the objectives of Rao is to reach a holistic understanding of consciousness. According to him, in the Western tradition, the concern is chiefly with the mind defined in behavioural terms whereas in the East it is "consciousness as-such" stated in ontological terms. To put it in his words, "while the Western mind represents the knowing side, the Eastern 'consciousness' refers to being itself". Together, they adequately explain human condition, in which knowing and being are intertwined. According to Rao, *yoga theory* and practices have deep implications for understanding *parapsychological phenomena* and *consciousness*. The three are interconnected in multiple ways. Together they could constitute "a three-pronged weapon, *triśūla*, to win the mind–body battle". Rao's theory in this context is the "Trilogy of Body–Mind–Consciousness (BMC)". He holds the view that the person is the composite of body–mind complex, capable of reflecting consciousness.

It is obvious that Rao shows an inclination towards Indian psychology over that of parapsychological researches as he strongly feels that the former has certain edge over the latter. He thus writes that *abhyāsa* and *vairāgya*, which are the hallmarks of a *yogin*, are missing in extrasensory perceptual research of parapsychology and is possibly responsible for less than replicable effects. He therefore argues that "there is a need to operationalize *vairāgya* in a manner that yogic concentration is operationalized by the ganzfeld procedure in ESP experiments" (p. 319).

Rao rejects the view that *yoga* psychology and parapsychology are contradictory. On the contrary, he considers that they are complementary. For him, together, they offer a holistic picture of psychological research of ESP. His point is that parapsychological research needs to incorporate the merits of *yoga* psychology.

Consciousness in Indian Psychology and the BMC Model

According to Rao the central concern of Indian psychology is consciousness. Consciousness as studied in Indian psychology is basically different from that of the Western psychology in certain important respects. The difference consists in the emphasis on the inward or the outward focus. In the Western tradition, emphasis is primarily outward. The approach is rational and intellectual. Consequently, the preferred method is scientific and observational. On the contrary the central focus in the Eastern tradition is inward. Here reason is considered as secondary to the inner experience. This is the starting point of divergence between Western and Indian psychological traditions. The two traditions, according to Rao, with their differences in emphasis on the outward and the inward, are not incompatible, but are complementary. Together they give a holistic view of consciousness. To put it in the language of Rao, while in the

Western tradition the objective aspect of consciousness is focused, in the Indian tradition the subjective aspect of consciousness is highlighted.

Another major difference between Indian psychology and Western psychology is that in the Western tradition, consciousness and mind are identified. On the contrary, in the Indian tradition, a primary distinction is made between "consciousness" and "mind" and a secondary distinction between "mind" and "brain". Thus in the Indian tradition we find a place for pure consciousness, which is conspicuously absent in the Western tradition. It is through pure consciousness that one could realize truth. The significance of pure consciousness or consciousness as-such, Rao explains in his BMC model that which he developed through the metatheoretical, postulates of *yoga* and Vedānta.

Yoga, says Rao, "is the foundational base of Indian psychology" (p. 320). He holds that while Indian psychology "has its roots in *yoga,* whose origins possibly date back to the times of Haṛappan Civilization, which is older than the Vedic, it had grown fully in the *yoga* system of Patañjali and was later incorporated into other systems." (p. 320). The *yoga,* feels Rao, "is the bedrock of Indian psychology" (p. 321).

In *yoga* theory, reality has two essential ingredients — the subjective and the objective. They are *puruṣa* and *prakṛti.* While *prakṛti* is the quintessential state of undifferentiated physical being, *puruṣa* is the quintessential state of undifferentiated subjectivity (p. 323). The person is the composite of body, mind and consciousness (p. 325). In *yoga* consciousness is called *puruṣa.* "Consciousness has neither a beginning nor an end. It does not grow or diminish. Consciousness as-such is ineffable, non-intentional and non-relational. It has no form or appearance" (p. 325). Knowing, feeling and being are not differentiated in consciousness. It is self-luminous and the source of illumination to all minds. According to *yoga,* consciousness is different from mind. While mind is the active instrument of thought, feeling and action in the person, consciousness has a secondary role. It is more like that of "witness" and plays the role of an observer (*śakṣin*) rather than an active participant. The mind is physical and evolves out of *prakṛti.* However, it is different from the body. It is subtle and a highly evolved matter. The mind does not generate consciousness. On the other hand, it simply reflects it. In the mind knowing, feeling and being are seen as distinct. With its qualities of thinking, willing and feeling, the mind becomes the knower, doer and enjoyer.

The relationship among consciousness, mind and body, says Rao, is not triangular but linear. "The mind is connected with the bodily process at the one end and with consciousness at the other. Thus the mind is the interfacing instrumentality and the connecting link between consciousness, and body. It is the instrument that connects the physical and the psychical in the person" (p. 326). This, Rao calls as the B(ody) + M(ind) + C(onsciousness) Trident model of the person.

Rao holds the view that the paradox of the psychological system is that on the one hand it embellishes one's perceptions and distorts the truth, while on the other hand, it is also an instrument that could help remove the biases and distortions and enables one to know the truth. Quoting the *Brahmabindu Upaniṣad*, Rao observes that the "*manas* is the cause of bondage and liberation to us". His point is that at the level of mind, the psychological system is attached to perceptual knowledge and is restless, ever drifting and unsteady; it cannot go beyond it. Mind is merely an instrument of knowing; it is also the seat of desires, emotions and hopes. As Patañjali says, the mind is burdened by false knowledge (*avidyā*) and egoness (*asmitā*). It is engendered by the *ahaṁkāra* and promoted by false identities and the consequent attachment (*rāga*), aversion (*dveṣa*) and the will-to-live (*abhiniveśa*). All these hindrances obstruct in the realization of Truth. To put it in the language of Rao they "are the sources that continually colour, cloud and condition one's perception, thoughts and actions. To know and grasp Truth, one should be free from these constraints" (p. 327). In order to achieve this, one should control and master the mind. First, the wandering of the mind needs to be controlled by focused attention (*ekāgratā*). It makes the mind steady. Second, the ego-involvement needs to be checked. Then *vairāgya*, the quality of detachment, is recommended. In *yoga* psychology, the practice of *ekāgratā* and cultivation of *vairāgya* not only help to make the mind steady and focused, but they also lead the mind into the stage of *samādhi*. This is the stage of Truth-realization and becoming one with it. *Dhāraṇā*, *dhyāna* and *samādhi* that constitute the *antaraṅga yoga* — collectively called *saṁyama* — would help in Truth realization. While *dhārnaṇā* gives observational excellence, *dhyāna* leads to excellence in understanding and *samādhi* involves excellence in transformational learning (p. 331).

In Vedānta tradition, these stages are put in the language of *śravaṇa*, *manana* and *nididhyāsana*. *Śravaṇa* is observation, *manana* is understanding and *nididhyāsana* is transformation. The knower becomes the known here (p. 331).

Yogic excellence, says Rao, has three tiers — the first tier is observational knowing, the second is intellectual understanding, and the third is transformational realization of intuitive truth obtained by meditation. Rao prefers to interpret the three legs of *saṁyama* — *dhāraṇā*, *dhyāna* and *samādhi* — in *yoga* on par with the three tiers of cognitive excellence of Vedānta — *śravaṇa*, *manana* and *nididhyāsana* (p. 331).

Rao writes:

> The goal of Indian psychology is transforming the conditioned person to the unconditioned state to enable her to experience freedom and perfection by participating in the discovery and realization of truth in her being. Thus the BMC model provides for an inclusive psychology with consciousness at the centre. It has profound practical implications; subscribes secular and sublime purposes; and bridges the gap between science and spirituality, personal happiness and common good.
>
> — p. 334

Rao is aware of the fact that *yoga* and Advaita systems from which the BMC model is derived uphold different and diametrically opposite metaphysical positions. While the *yoga* subscribes to the dualist metaphysics, Advaita advocates non-dualistic philosophy. In *yoga*, *puruṣa* and *prakṛti* are accepted as two ultimate realities. On the contrary, in Advaita, *Brahman* (consciousness) alone is real, the body, the mind and the rest of the world are illusory manifestations of the *Brahman* (p. 335). Though thus, the metaphysical standpoints of *yoga* and Advaita are opposed, Rao argues, it does not hinder the common BMC model. At the psychological level the metaphysical differences between *yoga* and Advaita are not significant. In both *yoga* and Advaita, body, mind and consciousness are experientially different and are therefore psychologically distinct (p. 337).

In the BMC model, it is argued that one has to surpass the stage of mind and reach to the stage of pure consciousness, because it is pure consciousness or consciousness as-such alone that would help in the realization of the Absolute Truth. The point of Rao is that mind or intellect is insufficient to grasp the Truth because it gives only partial truths and is endowed with attachments and aversions. Therefore one should surpass this stage and must reach a higher stage — the stage of pure consciousness — to grasp the holistic Truth.

The term "consciousness" of the BMC model can be compared to the Supermind of Sri Aurobindo or Intuition of Henri Bergson. In the philosophy of Sri Aurobindo, Supermind is Truth-Consciousness. It is the spiritual principle having complete knowledge of *Satcidānanda*. It is the ideal and the culmination of mind. Similarly, in his celebrated work *Creative Evolution,* Henri Bergson makes a distinction between intellect and intuition and said that while the intellect analyses, discriminates between things, it is intuition that gives a synthetic and holistic understanding and enables the man to realize the ultimate reality. According to Bergson, intellect no doubt is superior to instinct, but it is inadequate to grasp the reality, which he calls *elan-vital.* Therefore he suggests the need for intuition, beyond intellect.

It is quite interesting to note that Rao culminates his discussions of BMC model, with the philosophy of Gandhi. He observes:

> The Mahatma is a mature illustration of the BMC Trident model. Gandhi's life is a spiritual flowering of consciousness in the person. *Satyāgraha* is the sweet fruit of spirituality. Central to spirituality is *sarvodaya* which literally means rise of all. The "rise of all", the goal of *sarvodaya,* is accompanied by the fall of the personal ego. *Sarvodaya* is none other than altruism and all-round happiness. It involves transcending the ego and extending the "self" to include others.
>
> —p. 337

Rao believes that studies of Gandhi, *yoga* and parapsychology must be pursued together for a "wholesome understanding of human nature" (p. 338).

If we carefully study Rao's discussions on *yoga,* Indian psychology, Western psychology, parapsychology and Gandhi we find that they are not isolated compartments. On the contrary, we find in them an integrated approach with a holistic vision.

15

Prof. K. Ramakrishna Rao
A Philosopher–Psychologist Extraordinaire

T.S. Devadoss

I HAVE the privilege of knowing Prof. Dr K. Ramakrishna Rao, through my most esteemed friend, philosopher and guide, the late Prof. K. Satchidananda Murty. Murty described Rao as a "world renowned philosopher–psychologist" — a view similarly shared by another eminent scholar. Prof. Dr C.T. Krishnamachari who considered Rao as a "para-psychologist par-excellence". There can be no greater testimony to Rao than these. I feel privileged to contribute to the K. Ramakrishna Rao's Festschrift being brought out to commemorate his 80th Birthday.

In the galaxy of eminent scholars who have made significant contribution to the enrichment of philosophical knowledge combining with psychological insights to the world of thought, Rao stands tall.

He is an outstanding scholar, incisive thinker, a writer with great clarity, precision and logical reasoning who harmonizes modernity with tradition, science with spirituality and theory with praxis.

What inspired Rao towards Gandhi? To this question, Rao replies:

> Gandhi has been an icon that continues to inspire me. However, he is not an idol that I worship. Rather I find him relevant in many ways when I think of myself and the world we live in . . . whenever I begin to reflect on the problems of the world, the images of Gandhi are a powerful influence.
> — Rao 2012: 131

The core aspects of Gandhian thought that influenced Rao are best expressed by him thus:

> Gandhi's philosophy is inclusive in that it overcomes such dichotomies as "I" and the "other", secular and sacred, ruler and the ruled. In Gandhi's thought, subjectivism and objectivity, tradition and modernity, competition and co-operation, science and religion, and the moral and

> the mundane coexist without conflict giving us an uncanny holistic perspective. In it, we find a magical synthesis of ideas often considered mutually negating. It appears to contain the necessary ingredients to nurture sustainable pluralism worldwide. — Ibid.: 132

In essence, Rao lays emphasis on the holistic aspect of Gandhi's philosophy which culminates in his philosophy of Sarvodaya. Rao's recent works on Mahatma Gandhi speak eloquently of his personal involvement and commitment to translate Gandhian ideals into the alphabets of human conduct. Rao's noble vision would positively leave an indelible mark in the minds of those who march forward in the quest of peace and truth.

I would rank Rao's recent book *Gandhi and Applied Spirituality* (2011) as an outstanding work which would be a perennial source of inspiration and guidance to young scholars in understanding Gandhi in the true perspective applicable to the present-day society.

Rao's framework of his philosophical reasoning is based on "pragmatic spirituality". By spirituality, Rao means "a hypothetical level of human functioning that transcends reason and logic" (Rao 2011: xiii). In this category, Rao includes Gandhian practices of non-violence such as *satyāgraha*. Rao equates this with "*siddhi*'s arising from the practice of *yoga*, studies of psychic phenomena by parapsychologists and the results of epidemiological researches into religiosity and spirituality" (ibid.: xiii). This approach is an eye-opener to one and all.

To the question what is spirituality, Rao holds the view that "spirituality is one of the levels of being". He clarifies further thus:

> The centrality of spirituality (*ādhyātmika*) is *sarvodaya*, ultruism. . . . In the human condition, being is like a pyramid with a large base of materiality at the bottom. The apex, the peak point, is spiritual being. In between we have the "sensate" being and the "rational being". Human beings are typically driven by sensate observations and appetites in their actions and are generally guided by reason and logic in their thought. Sensory observations are building blocks of knowing and reason and logic are tools of understanding. In addition, humans are also spiritual beings. Spirituality may be seen as that aspect of human nature that enables the person to go beyond "I" and the ego and to identify herself with others. Whereas at the sensate and rational levels of being, the ego takes the centrestage, at the spiritual level the distinction between "I" and the "other" not only gets blurred but is ultimately obliterated. Therefore, a spiritual person tends to be altruistic. Altruism is indeed the *sine quo non* of spiritual development. — Ibid.: 32

In the process of reconstructing philosophy, Rao foresees a bright future as "philosophy moves its emphasis from ideas to problems, from thought to practice". Rao observes:

> A practical philosophy is one which would seek its problems and principles in practical action. The supremacy of the practical is indicated in the efforts to reduce thought or the conditions under which it operates to some form of action. As pragmatism would have it, the test of hypothesis consists in its successful operation in action. Actions have consequences and what is significant in thought is reducible to these consequences and their meaning. — Ibid.: 209

Rao calls it "pragmatic spirituality" (Ibid.: xv).

Another concept which Rao formulates that draws our pointed attention is "pluralism" in Gandhian thought. In this context, Rao analyses his view point:

> There is in a sense a momentum toward an identity crisis that is likely to unleash an array of social aberrations, precipitate disharmony, cause communal conflict and flare up social conflagration. — Ibid.: 145

He cautions us that a new threat for peaceful survival of human species is "identity conflicts" rather than "ideological differences". To confront this threatening situation Rao sees

> Gandhian pluralism as the best hope out of the morass of moral morbidity and the failing of bonding among humans. Gandhian pluralism with its altruistic slant, I believe, is essentially an interacting pragmatic articulation of the primary archetype of human identity, which alone in the final analysis has the potential to bridge the identity divides.
>
> — Ibid.: 145

Rao pins his hope that India possesses "a fertile soil to grow communal harmony and harvest cultural synthesis" (Ibid.: 145).

Rao draws the conclusion very rightly that "pluralism is the quintessence of Indianness" (Ibid.: 162). He justifies his standpoint by elucidating the political philosophy of Gandhi, which lays emphasis on the supremacy of the individual and a perfect society — enlightened anarchy which Rao equates with "pluralism at its best". The core idea of Gandhi is that there is no dichotomy between the individual and the society in the structure of village panchayats. Thus Gandhian conception of Indian society is "primordially pluralistic", if only the individuals cultivate and live by values of detachment, love, compassion and altruism as envisaged by Gandhi.

Rao projects Gandhi as a "consummate philosopher who sought to build a holistic interdisciplinary system of thought that has enormous potential for transformation of human condition" (Ibid.: 33). If one is to be true to the Gandhian tradition of thought and action, Rao contends that there is an imperative need for a wholesome reconstruction in philosophy in the Gandhian way.

Let us remember that although "Gandhi was not a philosophical system builder, he was a synoptic, consistent and integrated thinker, with a definite worldview (*weltanschauung*), representing an amazing unity of thought and action" as Prof. K.L. Seshagiri Rao puts it (Mathai 2000, cover page).

Jayaprakash Narayan, the veteran Sarvodaya leader and one of the foremost followers of Gandhi, observed:

> Gandhi's political, economic and other ideas are parts of a whole, integrated philosophy of life. Yet Gandhi was not a philosopher, in the accepted sense of the word, nor has he left behind him a systematic statement of his thought. He was essentially a man of action, and it was through the adventure of living, his "experiments" with truth, that he came to formulate ideas that are strewn over thousands of pages of writings, speeches and correspondences. That meant, among other things, that he was learning and evolving and in the process, ever refining and restating his thoughts. . . . The essentials of his philosophy do offer a basis for discussion; and a dynamic understanding of them might even help one to relate them to contemporary society.
>
> — Jayaprakash Narayan 1970: 226

It is an undeniable fact that we cannot forget, except at our peril, the life and teachings of Gandhi, which are in essence, so fundamental, so noble and so basic to our way of life. Gandhi was unique in that he dealt with matters of the spirit, soul and conscience together with social and political affairs in the most natural and unconscious manner.

It is true that Gandhi wrote profusely, writing was not a mental exercise for him. It was only a corollary to action. His life, his way of living, his programme of action to meet a situation or a challenge, those were his true expressions. They were inextricably related to what he was engaged in doing. In that context they do fall into the proper perspective and become meaningful.

Rao belongs to that rare class of thinkers who command equal respect in the East and the West. His profound knowledge in the realm of parapsychology has drawn the attention of both critics and admirers for his in-depth analysis and perception of current issues of academic interest.

Rao infuses in us a strong optimism about the future of man as envisaged by Mahatma's philosophy based on practical application of spiritual view of life. It is universally acknowledged that the core of Gandhian philosophy is derived from the principles of spiritual unity. To quote Gandhi:

> I do not believe that spiritual law works on a field of its own. On the contrary, it expresses itself only through the ordinary activities of life. It thus affects the economic, the social and the political fields.
>
> — *Young India*, 3 September 1925, p. 304

Gandhi's acceptance of spiritual determination, as I understand gave him supreme faith in the inevitable emergence of the non-violent society in the future. The notion of inevitability is a consequence of Gandhi's faith in the redeeming power of the spirit. His theory of ethicization of politics certainly represents a great landmark in the direction of political idealism.

What we need to do, is to develop a framework and perspective rendered by a philosophical analyses for the interpretation and evaluation of the technique of *satyāgraha* more as an instrument of enduring conflict resolution and bringing about social change in the present-day society.

The realization of Gandhian ideals depends on the ethical level of the people in actual practice. As long as morality has any relevance to human life, so long will Gandhi's teachings be relevant.

Gandhi as one of the epoch-making figures in India combined both moral idealism and political success. He is a unique figure because of the simple and straightforward views which he preached and practised without swerving from truth at any moment during his long career as a social reformer, a political teacher, a saint, a true lover of humanity and an apostle of non-violence, truth, love, goodness and peace. Gandhi was not bound to any practical "ism" or "ideology" as such, though he was committed to ideals of practising truth and non-violence.

Today, there seems to be a moral bankruptcy in us. A world that has lost its love, which is the motivation of creation, is turning to Gandhi, whose philosophy anticipates the future.

Gandhi has left his footprints on the sands of time. His message is a beacon of light to guide us forward in our universal quest for truth and peace. Gandhi's whole life was but a saga of spiritual action. He sharpened the weapon of *satyāgraha* and demonstrated to the world its potency.

Rao has done signal service to the world at large through his scholarly contribution to Gandhian literature and his *magnum opus Gandhi and Applied Spirituality* is a revelation to the present generation of Gandhian scholars in understanding, interpreting and application of Gandhian values of life in the context of the emerging scenario of the global society.

References

Mathai, M.P., 2000, *Mahatma Gandhi's World View*, New Delhi: Gandhi Peace Foundation.

Narayan, Jayaprakash, 1970, "Gandhi and the Politics of Decentralization", in Sibnarayan Ray (ed.) *Gandhi, India and the World: An International Symposium*, Bombay: Nachiketa Publications.

Rao, K. Ramakrishna, 2011, *Gandhi and Applied Spirituality*, New Delhi: Matrix Publishers.

———, 2012, "Violence and Non-violence in Gandhi's Philosophy of Life", *GITAM Journal of Gandhian Studies*, **1(1)**: 131-47.

16

Prof. K. Ramakrishna Rao
An Outstanding Person and Scholar

V.V. Raman

It is well known that we live in a world of global economy. The nations of the world are intertwined not just by trade but by banks and monetary interdependence as well. But ours is also a world of interpenetrating cultures and scientific internationalism. In every country there are individuals who proclaim and propagate our differences, and also those who bridge national and cultural differences. They participate in activities and write books on themes that transcend race and religion. In this process some abandon their particular cultural roots while others expand beyond their ethnic confines without uprooting themselves. Prof. Dr. Koneru Ramakrishna Rao belongs to this category.

It has been my privilege to have met and interacted with this eminent scholar, thinker, and scientist from India on a number of occasions: in meetings in Philadelphia at Metanexus conferences, and once in Visakhapatnam. During the last occasion he showed me the fertile lands of Andhra and the hard-working farmers who harvest the grains that feed us in distant cities. In them and in Rao I saw in one grand sweep the wide range of India's richness that feeds our bodies as well as our minds. In all my interactions with Rao, he invariably impressed me as a balanced thinker, a man of wit and wisdom, and a perfect gentleman. His deep understanding of cultures was evident in our conversations.

Rao's contributions to psychology are well recognized by fellow experts in the field. His work on the theoretical and experimental dimensions of parapsychology is regarded as significant. The book he edited on *Basic Research in Parapsychology* contains several experimental reports and meta-analyses of psi-research results. This book has been described as the only source-book of its kind.

Another book he edited is a treasure-chest of breakthroughs and insights on consciousness. It is entitled *Cultivating Consciousness: Enhancing Human Potential, Wellness, and Healing*. Here we find discussions by thoughtful philosophers, knowledgeable psychologists, and keen scientists on the nature, mystery and metaphysics of consciousness. Some of the most recent advances in the emerging field of consciousness-studies are presented here.

One of his major works is *Consciousness Studies: Cross-cultural Perspectives*. Here we find a thorough analysis of consciousness as understood in Western thought, by a respected Indian scholar. Enriched as he was by close association with a premier centre of parapsychology in USA, Rao acquired a thorough grasp of modern scientific methodology as well as of Western philosophical and scientific traditions on consciousness. In this work he also presented in depth the spiritual traditions of the East, especially of India, and their relevance in the modern world. His discussions are uniformly balanced with neither cultural chauvinism nor denigration of the other — two not uncommon failings in commentaries on science by some Indian authors. More importantly, Rao suggests in this book ways by which the two approaches — Eastern and Western — complement each other, and can collaborate to deepen our understanding of this greatest of all mysteries: human consciousness.

Rao is the author of numerous other works and papers. Most recently he published a very timely and important work: *Gandhi and Applied Spirituality*. Science, technology and medicine have made enormous strides, and yet humanity is still facing crises on virtually every plane. There are deep divisions within and among nations, cultures and religions. Something seems to have gone wildly astray. In this context he recalls Gandhi's unrelenting adherence to non-violence and *satyāgraha* which have deep roots in the visions of ancient India. As with ecology and economy, ideals and what may be good in the long run come in direct conflict with the exigencies of current pressures and immediate concerns.

It is a sad irony that because of many historical divisive forces, Gandhi is becoming the victim of derision and denigration by a growing number of people in India.

If humanity can learn anything from history, it is that none of our inter-cultural, inter-religious, and international problems can be resolved in a stable way with a mindset that currently prompts actions and reactions in millions all over the world. But when all the dirt and dust of present conflicts settles down and there emerges peace, harmony, and planetary social and economic justice, then the name and worldviews of Gandhi will shine in the firmament of human ideals. The Gandhian framework, like that of the Buddha, the Upaniṣadic seers, and Christ, belongs not to this race or that religion, to this political party or that nation, but to enlightened humanity everywhere.

Rao's book is an eloquent elaboration of the thesis that Gandhi's message is not simply a strategy for achieving political ends, though it could also serve that purpose; rather that it is based on an internalization of the spiritual dimension of being fully human. Armed with impressive erudition, deep understanding of the human mind arising from years of technical work in psychology, a full grasp of philosophy Eastern and Western, and great wisdom, Rao has written a most timely book that should shake the Indian mind into a recognition of what is genuinely great and glorious in India's ancient roots. This is fittingly one of his climactic works.

His analysis of the distinctions between modern human rights and *dharma* is exceptionally clear and revealing. In this context, he points out that "there would be no human rights problems if one's desires and actions did not come into conflict with those of others". We are reminded of Gandhi's emphasis on *dharma*, truth and non-violence "as pervasive values". He recalls that *satyāgraha* is "a means of direct social action" and as such "is of paramount importance to human rights".

Rao offers interesting reflections on religion and morality. Without explicitly referring to Arjuna in the Kurukṣetra battle-field, he summarizes the roots of ethical problems succinctly. "Ethical problems arise when conventional values do not satisfy demands or when two or more conflicting demands arise at the same time."

His thoughts on modern science are from the perspective of a psychologist who is at home with the most recent advances in the field, and also of a philosopher steeped in Indic wisdom, physicists inquire into the natural world in fascinating and productive ways. Their efforts yield on the practical plane materially useful non-trivial gadgets on which modern technological society survives.

But the deeper questions of human knowledge and consciousness are far more challenging. These are the ones that Rao explores. He says pithily in his most recent book: "Spirituality is to religion what science is to technology". This book is an eminently significant tome on Indian culture.

Psychology and philosophy are interwoven with Gandhi's principles. Rao's books are uniformly solid contributions to fresh perspectives on traditional Hindu thought, making the latter very appropriate and valuable in the modern world.

So here Rao may well be counted among India's intellectual and philosophical luminaries. His life work has been to elucidate India's rich insights in the fields of psychology and consciousness, but equally to explore uncharted domains and to bridge East and West. He has carefully avoided posturing cultures on a plane of antagonism and conflict. He has been able to do this because of his mature understanding of whatever is best both in India's own traditions and in the West's. Rather than energizing the current conflagrations with rage and rancor, the life and work of a person like Rao serves the cause of global peace and understanding.

It is a pleasure and honour for me to join others in congratulating him on the auspicious occasion of his eightieth birthday, and to wish him many more years of good health and productivity.

17

Large Strides
A Short Note from His Younger Brother

Matthijs Cornelissen

PROF. K. Ramakrishna Rao, or rather Ram, as he is known amongst his friends, belongs to the small company of exceptional people who walk through life with larger strides than most of their contemporaries. They are built, as it were, on a larger plan, and use their wider perspective and larger capacities to build bridges between fields that to others seem disparate and unconnected. Not only does Ram's work cover a wide range of academic disciplines and areas of social involvement, but within each field of endeavour, Ram has shown both, exceptional intellectual gifts and exceptional leadership, a combination that, again, is rare.

On the occasion of this Festschrift it may be appropriate to go back to the first time Ram and I met. It was during a wonderful, path-breaking symposium organized by Prof. Girishwar Misra at University of Delhi. As a prelude for things to come much later, the "National Workshop on Puzzles of Perception" had come about with support from the Indian Council of Philosophical Research (ICPR), and it was an interdisciplinary symposium in the best sense of the word: Misra had brought together experts from fields as far apart as Indian philosophy, social psychology, mathematics, cognitive science, medicine, and even plastic surgery, and everybody present was passionate about the particular piece of the puzzle they knew about.

Towards the end of the programme there was a session on "rationality in the Indian culture". The idea was to showcase how the rational mind with all its possibilities and limitations is both a pan-human, and a pan-historic phenomenon, with interesting cultural differences in the way this rational faculty is used. The session featured four philosophers, representing four major schools of classical Indian thought — Advaita, Mīmāṁsā, Śaivāgama and Nyāya.

Prof. Jha gave a brilliant and admirably clear and simple exposition of the Nyāya theory of perception. One of the things he highlighted was that according to tradition, if and only if an act of cognition is verbalizable, it leads to desire, which leads to a mental inclination, which leads to an action, and then the results of the action can be either consistent or inconsistent, according to which the original cognition should be considered true or false. The classical example of this sequence is a piece of mother of pearl which looks like silver, but turns out to be otherwise when you try to melt it or try to make an ornament out of it. He showed how this is a purely pragmatic approach to truth — it is true if it works; false if it doesn't — and that the early American pragmatists would have felt entirely at home with it.

The philosophers then entered into an elaborate discussion of the subtle differences and similarities between the different *darśana*s regarding perception and cognition. After this had gone on for quite some time, Ram came in between and related how modern research had shown conclusively that "subliminal" perceptions, which last too short to be noticed and that as such are not verbalizable, actually do effect subsequent responses to ambiguous stimuli. In other words, these experiments show that, in contrast to what the various Indian cognitive traditions claim, non-verbalizable perceptions too can lead to action. After a short, somewhat painful silence, one of the philosophers then cried out that this was of no interest to him, as he was not at all concerned about the kind of reality psychologists study, but only about the philosophical methods with which the ancients worked out their logical arguments, irrespective of the initial presumptions they had accepted. As the other philosophers enthusiastically concurred, it became clear that they were not bothered about the actual processes that take place in the minds of actual people: They were interested in the perfect execution of the fixed mental moves of their tradition. Their greatest joy came whenever they found that a seemingly new argument turned out to be the repeat of an argument already made hundreds of years ago, and even more so, if they also remembered the exact text in which it had been countered at that remote moment in time.

What is so remarkable about this is that they differed in this respect fundamentally from the ancient scholars they tried to emulate. The original masters took whatever information about reality was available to them, and then built upon those data a sophisticated system of reasoning in order to arrive at the best insight in reality they could manage. In that sense their basic aims and methods were very similar to those of the modern cognitive scientist. But the aims and methods of their descendants are quite different. They are interested in the old system of reasoning for its own sake, and not any longer for the sake of the reality it was supposed to explain. In that sense they are more like performing artists than like scientists. They are like musicians in the classical Western tradition, or like painters in the Tibetan or the Tanjore schools: They are not interested in creating or finding anything new, but only in executing as perfectly and beautifully as possible a pre-existing and already well-known composition, an interest that is as completely different from that of the modern scientist as it is of that of the ancient masters!

By his intervention Ram made clear that this — unfortunately rather common — approach to Indian philosophy and Sanskrit has only a limited value for us moderns: It helps to preserve the outer form of the tradition but not the inner meaning. It looks, in what social anthropologists call an "etic" manner, at the Indian tradition as a frozen art form, as something solidly belonging to the past, while what the world needs is the Indian tradition as a living force for the future.

Of course, not all philosophers look at the Indian traditions in this manner. Another great example of the more helpful attitude that takes psychology and philosophy as allies in a common search for truth, is Prof. S.R. Bhatt, who recently retired as head of the Philosophy Department of University of Delhi. He made once a passionate plea to a group of psychologists gathered in Bangalore for a seminar on Indian psychology, to see if modern research could not help resolve a whole series of issues that according to him had remained unresolved in classical Indian philosophy. But such interdisciplinary humility is rare.

For Ram, the ability to bring insights from different disciplines together and then to confront the established order with courage and respect, is just one of many special gifts that enabled him to make his considerable contribution to science. But for me personally, it is still something else that makes me grateful to have met him on that fateful day, a little over ten years ago. It is his warmth and generosity of spirit. Ram has a completely unique way of showering love and affection on all those around him, and, though hard to describe, it is this that inescapably endears him to everyone who knows him. It has not always been easy for me to live and work in a culture not my own by birth, and the way Ram has consistently treated me as his well-loved younger brother, is something I will always cherish in the depths of my heart.

Literary Works by Prof. K. Ramakrishna Rao

THIS is a bibliography of Prof. K. Ramakrishna Rao's professional publications in English and some of their translations in foreign languages such as German, Italian and Spanish. It does not include numerous articles published by him in national dailies such as *The Hindu, Indian Express, Deccan Chronicle,* and *Newstime* and regional newspapers like *Eenadu.* Not included also are his writings in his native language, Telugu. Prof. Rao has written several short stories, plays and poems in Telugu. His poems are included in *An Anthology of Contemporary Telugu Poetry* and translated into Hindi. His musical ballet *Champaka* was successfully staged in several parts of Andhra Pradesh. His writings are listed below chronologically from 1955 to 2012 in two sections — books and papers.

Books

1957 *Psi Cognition,* Tenali: Tagore Publishing House.

1958 *Pre-University Logic,* Tenali: Tagore Book House.

1966 *Experimental Parapsychology: A Review and Interpretation,* Springfield: Charles C. Thomas.

1967 *Parapsicologia Sperimentale: Esposizione & Interpretazione,* Rome: Astrolobio.

1968 *Gandhi and Pragmatism: An Intercultural Study,* Calcutta: Oxford and IBH Publishing.

1972 *Current Trends in Indian Philosophy* (ed. with K.S. Murthy), Visakhapatnam: Andhra University Press.

- *Mystic Awareness: Four Lectures on the Paranormal,* Mysore: Mysore University Press.

1973 *Experimental Studies of the Differential Effect in Life Setting* (with P. Sailaja) (Parapsychological Monographs, No. 13), New York: Parapsychology Foundation.

1982 *J.B. Rhine: On the Frontiers of Science* (ed.), Jefferson, NC: McFarland.

1984 *Basic Experiments in Parapsychology* (ed.), Jefferson, NC: McFarland.

1986 *Case Studies in Parapsychology* (ed.), Jefferson, NC: McFarland.

1993 *Cultivating Consciousness: Enhancing Human Potential, Wellness, and Healing* (ed.), Westport, CT: Praeger.

1994 *Charles Honorton and the Impoverished State of Skepticism: Essays on a Parapsychological Pioneer* (ed.), Jefferson, NC: McFarland.

2001 *Basic Research in Parapsychology* (ed.), Jefferson, NC: McFarland.

2002 *Consciousness Studies: Cross-cultural Perspectives,* Jefferson, NC: McFarland.

2005 *Towards a Spiritual Psychology* (ed. with S.B. Marwaha), New Delhi: Samvad (India).

2008 *Handbook of Indian Psychology* (ed. with A.C. Paranjpe and A.K. Dalal), Delhi: Foundation Books (Cambridge University Press).

2010 *Yoga and Parapsychology* (ed.), New Delhi: Motilal Banarsidass.

- *Violence, Identity and Gandhi,* Visakhapatnam: Centre for Gandhian Studies, GITAM University.

2011 *Cognitive Anomalies, Consciousness and Yoga,* New Delhi: Centre for Studies of Civilizations and Matrix Publishers.

- *Gandhi and Applied Spirituality,* New Delhi: Indian Council of Philosophical Research and Matrix Publishers.

Papers and Presentations

1955 "Paranormal Cognition: An Essay in Survey of Evidence and Theories", MA (Hons.) dissertation, Visakhapatnam: Andhra University.

- "Vedanta and the *Modus Operandi* of Paranormal Cognition", *The Philosophical Quarterly,* vol. 5.

1956 "A Note on Jung's Conception of Psyche", *Proceedings of the Indian Philosophical Congress.*

1959 "Towards a New Hypothesis" (The Second Annual Convention of the Parapsychological Association), *Journal of Parapsychology,* 23: 288 [Abstract].

1961 "A Note on the Report of the Library Committee to the University Grants Commission and the UGC Revision of Salary Scale of

Librarians in Universities and Colleges", *Indian Librarian,* 16: 69-72.

- "Consideration of Some Theories in Parapsychology", *Journal of Parapsychology,* 25: 32-54.
- "ESP Response to Preferred Targets as Compared to ESP Symbols" (The Fourth Annual Convention of the Parapsychological Association), *Journal of Parapsychology,* 25: 279 [Abstract].
- "Library Development in India", *Library Quarterly,* 31: 135-53 [also published in *Indian Librarian,* 16: 73-97].
- "Philosophy of Librarianship", *Indian Librarian,* 16: 69-72.
- "Pragmatism and Practical Idealism", PhD dissertation, Visakhapatnam: Andhra University.

1962 "A Report of a GESP Experiment Carried Out in an Indian Ashram with the Experimenter in the Role of 'Sender' and Two Swamis as 'Receivers', the Target Material Being Religious Pictures" (The Fifth Annual Convention of the Parapsychological Association), *Journal of Parapsychology,* 26: 264 (Note).

- "Library Co-operation in the United States", *Indian Librarian,* 17: 19-21.
- "The Preferential Effect in ESP", *Journal of Parapsychology,* 26: 252-59.
- "The Story of the Nation and the New Republic", *Triveni,* July, pp. 136-48.

1963 "Studies in the Preferential Effect I: Target Preference with Types of Targets Unknown", *Journal of Parapsychology,* 27: 23-32.

- "Studies in the Preferential Effect II: A Language ESP Test Involving Precognition and 'Intervention'", *Journal of Parapsychology,* 27: 147-60.
- "Studies in the Preferential Effect III: The Reversal Effect in Psi Preference", *Journal of Parapsychology,* 27: 242-51.
- "The Psychological Picture of Psi", *Research Journal of Philosophy and Social Sciences,* 1: 1-28.

1964 "Studies in the Preferential Effect IV: The Role of Key Cards in Preferential Response Situations", *Journal of Parapsychology,* 28: 28-41.

- "The Differential Response in Three New Situations", *Journal of Parapsychology,* 28: 81-92.

- Book Review (*Five Years of Report of Seth Sohan Lal Memorial Institute of Parapsychology*, by S.C. Mukherjee, Sri Ganganagar (India), SSLMI Institute, 1962), *Journal of Parapsychology*, 28: 59-62.
- Book Review (*Mind and Consciousness in Experimental Parapsychology*, by R.H. Thouless, Cambridge: Cambridge University Press, 1963), *Journal of Parapsychology*, 28: 136-38.

1965 "ESP and the Manifest Anxiety Scale", *Journal of Parapsychology*, 29: 12-18.

- "Social Psychology of Psi: Differential Response in a Competitive Situation", *Journal of Parapsychology*, 29: 295-96 [Abstract].
- "The Bidirectionality of Psi", *Journal of Parapsychology*, 29: 230-50 (Presidential Address to the Eighth Annual Convention of the Parapsychological Association). Also published in the *Proceedings of the Parapsychological Association*, 2: 37-59.
- Book Review (*Time Devoured: A Materialistic Discussion of Duration*, by E. Parsons, London: Allen and Unwin, 1964), *Journal of Parapsychology*, 29: 54-56.
- Book Review (*Biographical Dictionary of Parapsychology*, ed. H. Pleasants, New York: Helix, 1964), *Journal of Parapsychology*, 29: 57-58.
- Book Review (*Philosophy, Theosophy, Parapsychology: Some Essays on Diverse Subjects*, by J.J. Portman, Leyden: Sythott, 1965), *Journal of Parapsychology*, 29: 129-30.

1966 "Die theorie", in J.B. Rhine's *Sonderubruck aus Parapsichologie*, Sieten, pp. 742-44, Darmstadt: Wissenschaftliche Buchgesellschaft.

1967 "Dissonance Hypothesis and Some Incongruent ESP Results" (with B.K. Kanthamani and P. Sailaja), *International Journal of Parapsychology*, 9: 128-33.

- "Worldviews: A Psychological Analysis of the Problem of One and Many", *Journal of the Indian Academy of Applied Psychology*, 4: 63-67.
- Book Review (*ESP in Life and Lab: Tracing Hidden Channels*, by L.E. Rhine, New York: Macmillan, 1967), *Journal of Parapsychology*, 31: 302-06.

1968 "ESP and HSPQ Scores on Neuroticism" (with B.K. Kanthamani and P. Sailaja), *Proceedings of the Parapsychological Association*, 5: 59-60.

- "ESP Scores Before and After a Scheduled Interview" (with B.K. Kanthamani and P. Sailaja), *Proceedings of the Parapsychological Association,* 5: 57-59.
- "Psi in Communities and Other Interpersonal Situations in the Eastern World", in R. Cavanna (ed.) *Psi and Favorable States of Consciousness. Proceedings of an International Conference on Methodology in Psi Research* (pp. 74-83), New York: Parapsychology Foundation.
- "Spontaneous ESP in Laboratory Tests: The Error Phenomena", *Journal of the American Society for Psychical Research,* 62: 63-72.
- "The Bearing of Yoga Practice on Psi Research", in R. Cavanna and M. Ullman (eds.) *Psi and Altered States of Consciousness: Proceedings of an International Conference on Hypnosis, Drugs, Dreams, and Psi* (pp. 132-44), New York: Parapsychology Foundation.

1970 Book Review (*Extrasensory Perception,* by G. Schmeidler, New York: Atherton Press, 1969), *Journal of the American Society for Psychical Research,* 64: 443-49.

1971 "Humanities and the University", *Proceedings of the Symposium on Teaching of Humanities,* Waltair: Andhra University Press, pp. 9-23.

- "Personality Characteristics of ESP Subjects I: Primary Personality Characteristics and ESP" (with B.K. Kanthamani), *Journal of Parapsychology,* 35: 189-207.
- "Teaching of Psychology in Indian Universities", *Proceedings of the Symposium on Teaching of Social Sciences,* Visakhapatnam: Andhra University Press, pp. 62-77.
- Book Review (*Dream Studies and Telepathy: An Experimental Approach,* by M. Ullman and S. Krippner (Parapsychological Monographs No. 12), New York: Parapsychology Foundation, 1970), *Journal of the American Society for Psychical Research,* 364-68.

1972 "Alpha Rhythm and ESP in a Free-response Situation" (with Jose Feola), in W.G. Roll, R.L. Morris and J.D. Morris (eds.) *Research in Parapsychology 1971* (pp. 141-44), Metuchen, NJ: Scarecrow Press.

- "Consciousness in Indian Psychology", Paper presented at the Third International Conference on Humanistic Psychology, Tokyo.
- *Education for Living and Learning* (First Convocation Address given at V.S.R. College), Tenali: V.S.R. College.

- "Personality Characteristics of ESP Subjects II: The Combined Personality Measure (CPM) and ESP" (with H. Kanthamani), *Journal of Parapsychology,* 36: 56-70.
- "Personality Characteristics of ESP Subjects III: Extraversion and ESP" (with H. Kanthamani), *Journal of Parapsychology,* 36: 198-212.
- "Practicalistic Approach to Philosophy", in K.S. Murthy and K.R. Rao (eds.), *Current Trends in Indian Philosophy* (pp. 259-68), Waltair: Andhra University Press.

1973 "Beyond the Five Senses", *Science Today,* June, pp. 27-34.

- "Meditation and ESP Scoring (with Hamlyn Dukhan), in W.G. Roll, R.L. Morris and J.D. Morris (eds.) *Research in Parapsychology 1972* (pp. 148-51), Metuchen, NJ: Scarecrow Press.
- "Modernization: An Adaptation Process", Paper presented at the seminar on "The Ethos of Development and the Role of Religion", Visakhapatnam: Andhra University.
- "Personality Characteristics of ESP Subjects IV: Neuroticism and ESP" (with H. Kanthamani), *Journal of Parapsychology,* **37:** 37-50.
- "Personality Characteristics of ESP Subjects V: Graphic Expansiveness and ESP" (with H. Kanthamani), *Journal of Parapsychology,* 37: 119-29.
- "Psi, Science and Society: A Change in Methodology Is Needed", in W.G. Roll, R.L. Morris and J.D. Morris (eds.) *Research in Parapsychology 1972* (pp. 107-10), Metuchen, NJ: Scarecrow Press.
- "Some Reflections on Examinations", Paper presented at the seminar on "Examinations in Higher Education", The State Council of Educational Research and Training, Hyderabad.
- "The Role of Test Preparedness in Psi Experiments" (with P. Sailaja), in W.G. Roll, R.L. Morris and J.D. Morris (eds.) *Research in Parapsychology 1972* (pp. 151-53), Metuchen, NJ: Scarecrow Press.

1974 "Concerning Man and Modernity" (Second Convocation Address given at Bapatla College of Arts and Science on 2 February), Bapatla: Bapatla College of Arts and Science.

- "Indian Psychology: Dreaming", *Proceedings of the Fifth Annual Conference on Humanistic Psychology,* Visakhapatnam: Andhra University, Department of Psychology and Parapsychology, 37 [Abstract].

- "Psi and Personality", in John Beloff (ed.) *New Directions in Parapsychology* (pp. 60-76), London: Elek Science.
- "Social Conflict: Some Crucial Issues" (Paper presented at the Fifteenth All-India Seminar on Philosophy and Social Conflict), Centre for the Advanced Study in Philosophy, University of Madras.
- "Whither Examinations?" (Convocation Address given at Government College on 17 April), Srikakulam: Government College.
- Book Review (*Parapsychology: Sources of Information,* by R.A. White and L.A. Dale, Metuchen, NJ: Scarecrow Press, 1973), *Journal of Parapsychology,* 38: 247-49.

1975 "Consciousness in Indian Psychology" (Paper presented at the Eighteenth All-India Seminar on the Concept of Consciousness), Centre for the Advanced Study in Philosophy, University of Madras.

- "Introduction", in S. Krippner *Song of the Siren: A Parapsychological Odyssey,* New York: Harper & Row, pp. xv-xvii.
- "Psi and Yoga Psychology", *ASPR Newsletter,* 27 (autumn).
- "The Psyche and Soma in Indian Psychology", in L. Pozzi (ed.) *Proceedings of the Third International Congress on Therapy in Psychosomatic Medicine,* Rome: International College of Psychosomatic Medicine.
- Book Review (*Reincarnation and Science,* by R. Reyna, New Delhi: Sterling Publishers, 1973), *Journal of Parapsychology,* 39: 262-64.
- Book Review (*Transpersonal Psychologies,* by C.T. Tart ed., New York: Harper and Row, 1975), *Journal of Parapsychology,* 39: 339-41.

1976 "Interview (with Alan Vaughan)", *Psychic,* 7(4): 48-54.

- "Teaching of Parapsychology in India and the Andhra Experiment", in B. Shapin and L. Coly (eds.) *Proceedings of the Twenty-Fourth International Conference* on *Education in Parapsychology,* New York: Parapsychology Foundation; also in *Parapsychology Review,* 7: 1-8.

1977 "ESP in Life Situations: An Attempted Replication" (with D.H. Weiner), *Journal of Parapsychology,* 41: 157-58 [Abstract].

- "ESP Testing in Life Situations: A Cross-cultural Study of Psi in Academic Examinations" (with J.T. Obrien), *Journal of Parapsychology*, 41: 1-9.
- "Mental Imagery and ESP as Measured by Rao's Subsensory Psi Test (SPT)" (with R. Vindhya Rao and P.V. Krishna Rao), in J.D. Morris, W.G. Roll and R.L. Morris (eds.) *Research in Parapsychology 1976* (pp. 105-07), Metuchen, NJ: Scarecrow Press.
- "Some Frustrations and Challenges in Parapsychology", *Journal of Parapsychology*, 41: 119-35.
- "Subsensory Perception (SSP), Extrasensory Perception (ESP) and Meditation" (with I. Puri), in J.D. Morris, W.G. Roll and R.L. Morries (eds.) *Research in Parapsychology 1976* (pp. 7-9). Metuchen, NJ: Scarecrow Press.
- "The Role of Association in Memory-recall and ESP" (with M. Morrison, J.W. Davis and J.A. Freeman), *Journal of Parapsychology*, 41: 190-97.
- Book Review (*The Philosophy of Parapsychology*, ed. B. Shapin and L. Coly, New York: Parapsychology Foundation, 1977), *Journal of Parapsychology*, 41: 215-19.
- Book Review (*Handbook of Parapsychology*, ed. B.B. Wolman, New York: Van Nostrand and Reinhold, 1977), *Journal of Parapsychology*, 41: 352-58.

1978 "Electrical Activity of the Brain and the ESP: An Exploratory Study" (with J. Feola), *Journal of Indian Psychology*, 2: 118-33.

- "Expectancy Effects, ESP Effects and Replicability", *The Behavioral and Brain Sciences*, 3: 403-04.
- "Further Studies of Memory and ESP", *Journal of Parapsychology*, 42: 167-78.
- "Psi and Its Place in Nature" (Presidential Address, 21st Annual Convention of the Parapsychological Association), *Journal of Parapsychology*, 42: 276-303; also in W.G. Roll (ed.) *Research in Parapsychology 1978* (pp. 159-83), Metuchen, NJ: Scarecrow Press.
- "Psychology of Transcendence: A Study in Early Buddhistic Psychology", *Journal of Indian Psychology*, 1: 1-21.
- "Review of Recent Books on Hypnosis", *Journal of Indian Psychology*, 1: 221-24.

- "Subsensory Perception, ESP and Transcendental Meditation" (with I. Puri), *Journal of Indian Psychology,* 1(2): 69-74.
- "The Differential Effect and Experimenter Effects in Intentional and Non-intentional Psi Tests" (with J.W. Davis), *Journal of Parapsychology,* 42: 1-19.
- "The Role of Association in Memory-recall and ESP" (with M. Morrison, J.W. Davis and J.A. Freeman), in W.G. Roll (ed.) *Research in Parapsychology 1977* (pp. 84-90), Metuchen, NJ: Scarecrow Press.
- Book Review (*Philosophical Dimensions of Parapsychology,* ed. J.M.O. Wheatley and H. Edge, Springfield: Charles C. Thomas, 1976), *Journal of Indian Psychology,* 1: 81-82.
- Book Review (*Philosophy and Parapsychology,* ed. J. Ludwig, Buffalo: Prometheus, 1978), *Journal of Parapsychology,* 42: 319-21.
- Book Review (*Philosophy and Psychical Research,* ed. S.C. Thakur, New York: Humanities Press, 1976), *Journal of Indian Psychology,* 1: 69-74.

1979 "Imagery, Concreteness, and Meaningfulness of Target Words in Relation to Psi Scoring: A Preliminary Experiment" (with H. Kanthamani), *Journal of Parapsychology,* 43: 46-47 [Abstract].

- "Language ESP Tests with a Single Subject Under Normal and Relaxed Conditions", in W.G. Roll (ed.) *Research in Parapsychology 1978* (pp. 90-91), Metuchen, NJ: Scarecrow Press.
- "Language ESP Tests Under Normal and Relaxed Conditions", *Journal of Parapsychology,* 43: 1-15.
- "On 'The Scientific Credibility of ESP' ", *Perceptual and Motor Skills,* 49: 415-29.
- "Psi and Volitional Activity: An Experimental Study of Psi in a Competitive Situation" (with H. Kanthamani and S.R. Krishna), *Journal of Parapsychology,* 43: 101-12.
- "Seven Evidential Experiments: A Commentary on Dr. Beloff's Paper", *Zetetic Scholar,* 6: 107-09.
- "Where Have We Gone Wrong?", *Journal of Parapsychology,* 43: 48-49 [Abstract].
- Book Review (*The Reception of Unconventional Science,* by S.H. Mauskopf, AAAS Selected Symposium 25, Boulder, CO: Westview Press, 1979), *Journal of Parapsychology,* 43: 241-43.

1980 "ESP Tests with Competition Set: Further Explorations of Volitional Influence on Psi" (with H. Kanthamani), *Journal of Parapsychology,* 44: 341-52.

- "Exploratory Free-response Studies with Maimonides Slides" (with R.J. Munson), *Journal of Parapsychology,* 44: 78 [Abstract].
- "Further Studies of Psi and Volitional Activity" (with H. Kanthamani), in W.G. Roll (ed.) *Research in Parapsychology 1979,* (pp. 110-12) Metuchen, NJ: Scarecrow Press.
- " 'Signs of Psi' in Two Series of Long-distance Experiments with a Single Subject" (with H. Kanthamani), *Journal of Parapsychology,* 44: 63-64 [Abstract].
- "The Case for Less Subjectivism Among Skeptics of Psi", *Zetetic Scholar,* 6: 107-09.

1981 "A Tribute to J.B. Rhine", *Journal of the American Society for Psychical Research,* 75: 71-72.

- "Hume's Fallacy", *Journal of Parapsychology,* 45: 147-52.
- "On the Question of Replication", *Journal of Parapsychology,* 45: 311-20.
- "Personality and 'Belief' in Relation to Language ESP Scores" (with S.R. Krishna), in W.G. Roll and J. Beloff (eds.) *Research in Parapsychology 1980* (pp. 61-63), Metuchen, NJ: Scarecrow Press.
- "Possible Sex Related Differences in ESP Scoring of the Same and Opposite Sex Pairs in Competition/Co-operation Situations", *Journal of Indian Psychology,* 3(2): 41-51.
- "Subliminal Perception and Extrasensory Perception in a Learning Paradigm" (with R.J. Munson), in W.G. Roll and J. Beloff (eds.) *Research in Parapsychology 1980* (pp. 96-98), Metuchen, NJ: Scarecrow Press.
- "The Volitional Effect in Competition and Co-operation Situations" (with S.R. Krishna and H. Kanthamani), *Journal of Indian Psychology,* 3(1): 47-56.

1982 "An Attempted Replication of Sex Differences in Volitional Studies" (with B. Norwood), in W.G. Roll, J. Beloff and R.A. White (eds.) *Research in Parapsychology 1981* (pp. 200-01), Metuchen, NJ: Scarecrow Press.

- "J.B. Rhine and His Critics", in K.R. Rao (ed.) *J.B. Rhine: On the Frontiers of Science: The Life and Work of J.B. Rhine* (pp. 192-212), Jefferson, NC: McFarland.
- "Memory and ESP: An Attempted Replication" (with D. Weiner), *Journal of Parapsychology,* 46: 56 [Abstract].
- "Possible Sex-related Differences in ESP Scoring of Same- and Opposite-sex Pairs in Competition/Co-operation Experiments", in W.G. Roll, R.L. Morris and R.A. White (eds.), *Research in Parapsychology 1981* (pp. 154-65), Metuchen, NJ: Scarecrow Press.
- "Science and the Legitimacy of Psi", in B. Shapin and L. Coly (eds.) *Parapsychology and the Experimental Method* (pp. 100-12), New York: Parapsychology Foundation.
- "The a Priori and Theoretical Objections to Psi", *Journal of Indian Psychology,* 4: 3-12.
- "Two Studies of ESP and Subliminal Perception" (with P.V. Krishna Rao), *Journal of Parapsychology,* 46: 185-208.

1983 "From Proof to Acceptance", *Parapsychology Review,* 14(2): 1-3.

- "ESP and SP in TM and non-TM Groups" (with P.V.K. Rao), in W.G. Roll, J. Beloff and R.A. White (eds.) *Research in Parapsychology 1982* (pp. 189-90), Metuchen, NJ: Scarecrow Press.
- "L.E. Rhine on Psi and Its Place", *Journal of Parapsychology,* 47: 347-60.
- "On the Question of Application", in W.G. Roll, J. Beloff and R.A. White (eds.) *Research in Parapsychology 1982* (pp. 263-64), Metuchen, NJ: Scarecrow Press.
- "Sex-related Differential Scoring in Two Volitional Studies" (with H. Kanthamani and B. Norwood), *Journal of Parapsychology,* 43: 7-22.
- "The Volitional Effect in Blind-matching ESP Tests" (with S.R. Krishna), *Journal of Parapsychology,* 47: 51-52 [Abstract].
- "Two Series of Volitional Studies with Competition Set" (with C. Sargent and M.J. Schlitz), in W.G. Roll, J. Beloff, and R.A. White (eds.) *Research in Parapsychology 1982* (pp. 190-93), Metuchen, NJ: Scarecrow Press.
- Book Review (*Psychical Research: A Guide to Its History, Principles and Practices,* ed. I. Grattan-Guiness, Wellingborough: Aquarian Press, 1982), *Journal of the Society for Psychical Research,* 52: 135-37.

- Book Review: (*Psychology's Occult Doubles: Psychology and the Problem of Pseudoscience*, by T.H. Leahey, and G.E. Leahey, Chicago: Nelson-Hall, 1983), *Journal of Parapsychology*, 47: 254-57.

1984 "Introduction", in K.R. Rao (ed.), *The Basic Experiments in Parapsychology* (pp. 1-11), Jefferson, NC: McFarland.

- "Parapsychology", in R.J. Corsini (ed.) *Encyclopedia of Psychology* (vol. 2, pp. 478-82), New York: John Wiley.
- *Parapsychology: Implications for Religion and Science*, Dallas: Isthmus Institute.
- "Rhine, Joseph Banks (1895–1980)", in R.J. Corsini (ed.) *Encyclopedia of Psychology* (vol. 3, p. 239), New York: John Wiley.
- "The Ganzfeld Debate: Introduction", *Journal of Parapsychology*, 49: 1-2.
- Book Review (*The Encyclopedic Dictionary of Psychology*, ed. R. Harre and R. Lamb, Cambridge MA: MIT Press, 1983), *Journal of Parapsychology*, 48: 234-35.
- Book Review (*Test Your ESP Potential*, by J. Randi), *Journal of Parapsychology*, 48: 353-55.

1985 "Replications in Conventional and Controversial Sciences", in B. Shapin and L. Coly (eds.) *The Repeatability Problem in Parapsychology* (pp. 22-27), New York: Parapsychology Foundation.

1986 "L.E. Rhine on Psi and Its Place", in K.R. Rao (ed.) *Case Studies in Parapsychology* (pp. 52-62), Jefferson, NC: McFarland.

- "Louisa E. Rhine: 1891–1983", in K.R. Rao (ed.) *Case Studies in Parapsychology* (pp. 1-5), Jefferson, NC: McFarland.
- *Toward Reorganizing Higher Education in the State* (with others), Hyderabad: Government of Andhra Pradesh.

1987 *India's Heritage: A Philosophical Rendezvous*, Nagarjuna Nagar, AP: Acharya Nagarjuna University.

- The First and the Next Fifty Years", *Journal of Parapsychology*, 51: 1-8.
- "Parapsychology", in Raymond Corsini (ed.) *Concise Encyclopedia of Psychology* (pp. 800-02), New York: John Wiley.
- "Rhine, J.B.", in Raymond Corsini (ed.) *Concise Encyclopedia of Psychology* (p. 985), New York: John Wiley.

- "The Anomaly Called Psi: Recent Research and Criticism" (with J. Palmer), *Behavioral and Brain Sciences,* 10: 539-51.
- The Institute for Professional Studies (with others), Hyderabad: Government of Andhra Pradesh.
- "Where Lies the Bias?" (with J. Palmer), *Behavioral and Brain Sciences,* 10: 618-27.
- Book Review (*Foundations of Parapsychology: Exploring the Boundaries of Human Capability,* by H.L. Edge, R.L. Morris, J.H. Rush and J.A. Palmer, Boston, MA: Routledge and Kegan Paul, 1986", *Journal of Parapsychology,* 51: 353-57.

1988 "Are We Throwing the Baby Out with the Bath Water?" in L. Coly D.S. Joanne and M.C. Mahon (eds.) *Psi Research Methodology,* New York: Parapsychology Foundation.

- "Editorial: Joseph Greenwood", *Journal of Parapsychology,* 52: 95-97.
- "Psychology of Transcendence: A Study in Early Buddhistic Psychology", in A.C. Paranjpe, D.G.F. Ho and R.W. Riebu (eds.) *Asian Contributions to Psychology* (pp. 123-48), New York: Praeger.
- *Report of the Committee on Establishing a Rural University in the State* (with others), Hyderabad: Government of Andhra Pradesh.
- "What Is Indian Psychology?", *Journal of Indian Psychology,* 7: 37-57.
- Book Review (*Concise Encyclopedia of Psychology,* ed. R.J. Corsini, New York: John Wiley, 1987), *Journal of Parapsychology,* 52: 83-84.
- Book Review (*Jung: A Biography,* by G. Wehr, Boston, MA: Shambala, 1987), *Journal of Parapsychology,* 52: 82-83.
- "Books in Brief", *Journal of Parapsychology,* 52: 82-85.
- "Books in Brief", *Journal of Parapsychology,* 52: 241-45.

1989 "Meditation Secular and Sacred", *Journal of Indian Academy of Applied Psychology,* 5(2): 51-75.

1990 "Exploring Normal–Paranormal Interaction within a Memory–ESP Testing Paradigm" (with H. Kanthamani), in A. Henkel and J. Palmer (eds.) *Research in Parapsychology 1989* (pp. 62-67), NJ: Scarecrow Press.

- "Heretical Psychology: On the Scope and Substance of Psychical Research", in A.H. Linda and R.S. Gertrude (eds.) *Proceedings of the Parapsychological Association*, NJ: Scarecrow Press.
- "Psychology, the Psychoid and Parapsychology" (interview with S.A. Martin), *Quadrant*, 24: 11-23.
- "Foreword", in *Sankara: Humanist, Integrator Poet and Philosopher*, by I.V. Chalapati Rao (pp. ix-xvi), Hyderabad: Telugu University.

1991 "Afterword", in H. Motoyama, *The Correlations Between Psi Energy and Ki*", Tokyo: Human Sciences Press.

- "Consciousness Research and Psi", *Journal of Parapsychology*, 55: 1-43.
- "Effect of ESP Feedback on Subject's Responses to a Personality Questionnaire" (with S.R. Krishna), *Journal of Parapsychology*, 55: 147-58.
- "Exploring Normal–paranormal Interaction with in a Memory–ESP Testing Paradigm" (with H. Kanthamani and John Palmer), *Journal of Parapsychology*, 54: 245-59.
- "Healing, Meditation and Anomalous Mental Phenomena", *Journal of Indian Psychology*, 9: 1-13.
- "Introduction", *The Legacy of L.E. Rhine: A Panel Discussion to Commemorate LER'S Birth Centenary*.
- "Skeptics and Selective Reporting", *Contemporary Psychology*, 36 (11): 1013-14.

1992 "Early History of the Paranormal: An Essay Review of Brain Inglis's 'Natural and Supernatural' ", *Journal of Parapsychology*, 56: 147-62.

- "Meditation and Mind/Matter Interface", in B. Rubik (ed.) *The Interrelationship Between Mind and Matter* (pp. 111-41), Philadelphia: Center for Frontier Sciences, Temple University.
- "The Two Sides of Psi Debate", *Contemporary Psychology*, 37: 1106-08.

1993 "Charles Honorton: A Man of Many Talents", *Journal of the American Society for Psychical Research*, 57: 356-58.

- "Charles Honorton: A Savant of His Own Kind", *Journal of Parapsychology*, 57: 1-6.

- "Consciousness, Awareness, and First-person Perspective", *Behavioral and Brain Sciences,* 16: 407-09.
- "Cultivating Consciousness: Some Conceptual and Methodological Issues", in K.R. Rao (ed.) *Cultivating Consciousness,* Westport, CT: Praeger.
- "C.T.K. Chari (1908-93)", *Journal of the Society for Psychical Research,* 59: 237-40.
- "Demonstration Research and Meta-analysis in Parapsychology" (with S. Krippner, W. Braud, I.L. Child, J. Palmer, M. Schlitz, R. White and J. Utts), *Journal of Parapsychology,* 57: 275-86.
- "Exploring Consciousness: Some Conceptual and Methodological Issues", paper presented at the Third International Symposium on Consciousness and Science, 2-6 January 1993, Olympia, Greece.
- "Karma, Reincarnation and Parapsychology", paper presented at the Conference on Karma, Reincarnation and Past Life Therapy, 18-19 September 1993, California Institute for Human Sciences.
- "Parapsychology and Religion", paper presented at the Parliament of World Religions, 2 September 1993, Chicago.

1994 "Consciousness", in R.J. Corsini (ed.) *Encyclopedia of Parapsychology* (2nd edn.), (vol. 1, pp. 302-06), New York: John Wiley.

- "Introduction", in K.R. Rao (ed.), *Charles Honorton and the Impoverished State of Skepticism: Essays on a Parapsychological Pioneer,* pp 1-6, Jafferson, NC: McFarland.
- "Parapsychology", in R.J. Corsini (ed.) *Encyclopedia of Parapsychology* (2nd edn), (vol. 3, pp. 10-15), New York: John Wiley.

1995 *Human Rights and Social Identity: A Gandhian Perspective,* Centre for Studies in Human Rights and Social Developments, Tirupati: S.V. University.

- *Reforming School Education* (with others), Hyderabad: Government of Andhra Pradesh.
- "Some Reflections on Religion and Anomalies of Consciousness", *Journal of Indian Psychology,* 13: 1-15; also published in *Reviews,* 18(1): 11-18.

1996 "Why Am I an Indian? Reflections on Indian Identity and National Integration", in K.S. Murthy and A. Dasgupta (eds.) *The Perennial Tree* (pp. 354-78), New Delhi: New Age International.

1997 "Some Reflections on Religion and Anomalies of Consciousness", in Charles T. Tart (ed.) *Body, Mind, Spirit* (pp. 68-83).

1998 "Two Faces of Consciousness: A Look at Eastern and Western Perspectives", *Journal of Consciousness Studies*, 5(3): 309-27.

1999 "Does ESP Exist?", *CIHS News Letter*, 6: 3-4.

2000 *Higher Education in India: Ground 00 and Vision 2020* (Dr. Sarvepalli Radhakrishnan Memorial Lecture), Visakhapatnam: Andhra University Press.

2001 "Consciousness Studies: A Survey of Perspectives and Research", in J. Pandey (ed.), *Psychology in India Revisited: Developments in the Discipline* (pp. 19-62), New Delhi: Sage Publications.

- Introduction: Reality, Replicability and Lawfulness of Psi, in K.R. Rao (ed.) *Basic Research in Parapsychology* (pp. 3-37), Jefferson, NC: McFarland.
- "Psi and Self", in P. Howell and J. Hall (eds.) *Self Through Art and Science* (pp. 175-89), First Books Library.

2002 "Bridging Eastern and Western Perspectives on Consciousness", *Journal of Consciousness Studies*, 9(11): 63-68.

2004 "Brain, Mind and Consciousness", *The Theosophist*, 125: 291-99.

- "Centrality of Consciousness in Indian Psychology", in Kireet Joshi and Matthijs Cornellissen (eds.) *Consciousness, Indian Psychology and Yoga* (pp. 53-75), New Delhi: PHISPC, Centre for Studies in Civilizations.
- "Classical Indian Psychology: Lessons for Education, Health and Wellness", in D. Prahladchar (chief ed.) and M.L. Narasimha Murty and Rani Sadisiva Murty (eds.) *Work Culture and Efficiency with Special Reference to Indriyas*, Tirupathi: Rashtriya Sanskrit Vidyapeetha.
- "Knowing and Being: Exploring the Cross-cultural Contours of Consciousness Studies", in Sangeetha Menon et al. (eds.) *Science and Beyond: Cosmology, Consciousness and Technology in the Indic Traditions*, Bangalore: National Institute of Advanced Studies.
- "Long Journey and Lone Memories", in George Victor (ed.) *Philosophical Tradition and Unified Curriculum: Profiles, Perspectives and Syllabus*, New Delhi: D.K. Printworld.

2005 "Introduction", in K.R. Rao and S.B. Marwaha (eds.) *Towards a*

Spiritual Psychology (pp. 1-17), New Delhi: Samvad.

- "Perception, Cognition and Consciousness in Classical Hindu Psychology", *Journal of Consciousness Studies,* 12(3): 3-30.
- "Religiosity and Sense of Well-being: Spiritual Dimensions of Health", in A.K. Dalal and S. Ray (eds.) *Social Dimensions of Health,* Jaipur: Rawat Publications.
- "Scope and Substance of Indian Psychology", in K.R. Rao and S.B. Marwaha (eds.) *Towards a Spiritual Psychology* (pp. 18-40), New Delhi: Samvad.

2006 "A Plea for Promoting Indigenous Cognitive Psychology in India", 2nd International Conference on Cognitive Science, Allahabad, 10-12 December 2006.

- "A Study of the Relationship Between Religion, Personality and the Paranormal", National Conference, Training-cum-Workshop, Visakhapatnam, 3-23 January 2006.
- "An Investigation of Cognitive Anomalies Among College Students", National Conference, Training-cum-Workshop, Visakhapatnam, 3-23 January 2006.
- "Bharatiya-Jiva-Sastra-Sutra" (Principles of Indian Psychology), Inaugural Address, National Seminar on Holistic Paradigms in Psychology: Problems and Prospects, New Delhi: Zakir Hussain College.
- "Consciousness and Cognitive Anomalies", in Sangeetha Menon (ed.) *Consciousness, Experience and Ways of Knowing* (pp. 41-101), Bangalore: National Institute of Advanced Studies.
- "The Relevance of Philosophy to Life in the 21st Century" (paper presented at the International Conference on Relevance of Philosophy to Life in the 21st Century, Colombo, 21 November 2006). *Sri Lanka Journal of Social Sciences,* 29/30 (1-2): 13-41.
- "Theories of Self/Person in Classical Indian Thought", Keynote Address, UGC National Seminar on Relevance of Philosophy in 21st Century, Andhra University, 27 January 2006.

2007 "A Brief Introduction to Indian Psychology", UGC National Seminar-cum-Workshop, St. Joseph's College of Education, November 2007, Guntur, AP, India.

- "Identity and Inclusiveness in Gautama Buddha's Social Philosophy", International Conference on Buddhism (3-5 February 2007), Bodhgaya, Bihar.
- "Indian Psychology Panel Discussion", National Seminar on Indian Psychology: Theories and Models, 26-28 December 2007, VYASA University, Bangalore.
- "Is Indian Psychology Positive?", National Conference on Positive Psychology (28-29 February 2007), Punjab University, Chandigarh.
- *Meditating on the Mandala of Indian Identity* (paper presented at the National Workshop on National Integration and Multiple Identities, Indian Institute of Advanced Studies, Shimla, 15 September 2007), *Journal of Indian Council of Philosophical Research,* 24: 33-65.
- "Principles of Yoga Psychology", Conference on Meditation and Spirituality: Scientific, Conceptual, and Applied Perspectives, Center for Study of Health, Religion and Spirituality, Indiana State University, Terre Haute, Indiana.
- "The Intellectual Legacy of Jawaharlal Nehru", Keynote Address, National Seminar on Jawaharlal Nehru's Philosophy, Policies and Performance: Reflections, Retrospect and Prospects, 3-5 April 2007, Acharya Nagarjuna University, Guntur.
- "The Legacy and Relevance of Lord Buddha", National Seminar on Lord Buddha and His Universe, Indian Institute of Advanced Study, Shimla, 29-30 March 2007.
- "Towards an Inclusive Psychology with Indian Identity", Editorial Conclave, Project of History of Indian Science, Philosophy and Culture, New Delhi, 2 April 2007.
- "Yoga-Advaita Psychology: An Inclusive Psychology for the Future", 17th International Congress on Vedanta, Miami University, Oxford, Ohio, 23 September 2007.

2008 "Buddhist Psychology: Phenomenology of Consciousness", Fifth International Buddhist Conference, K.J. Somaiya Centre for Buddhist Studies, Mumbai, 10 January.

- "Introducing Indian Psychology", in K.R. Rao, A.C. Paranjpe and A.K. Dalal (eds.), *Handbook of Indian Psychology* (pp. 1-18), Delhi: Foundation Books (Cambridge University Press).

- "Psychology in the Advaita Vedanta" (with A.C. Paranjpe), in K.R. Rao, A.C. Paranjpe and A.K. Dalal (eds.) *Handbook of Indian Psychology* (pp. 253-85), Delhi: Foundation Books (Cambridge University Press).
- "Taxonomy of Consciousness", in N. Srinivasan, A.K. Gupta and J. Pandey (eds.) *Advances in Cognitive Science* (vol. 1, pp. 383-423), New Delhi: Sage.
- "Yoga Psychology: Theory and Application" (with A.C. Paranjpe), in K.R. Rao, A.C. Paranjpe and A.K. Dalal (eds.) *Handbook of Indian Psychology* (pp. 186-216), Delhi: Foundation Books (Cambridge University Press).

2009 "Centrality of Consciousness: The BMC Model of the Person" (Patanjali Lecture), University of Massachusetts, Dartmouth, MA.

- "Roadmap to Reform Higher Education: From Radhakrishnan Commission Report to Yashpal Committee Recommendations", Indo-French Joint Seminar on Challenges in Public Higher Education, 21 December 2009, Indian Council of Social Sciences Research, New Delhi.
- "Science and Spirituality: In Search of a Common Ground", Presidential Address, Conference on Science and Spirituality, Ramakrishna Mission Institute of Culture, Golpark, Kolkata, 4 April 2009.
- Violence: A Philosophical Rendezvous (Extracts from the Keynote Address given at National Workshop on National Integration and Identity Violence, North Eastern Hill University, Shillong, 20-23 March 2009); *ICPR Newsletter* (October 2008 – March 2009): 1-6.
- "Yoga Psychology: Towards a Psychology of the Future", Lecture at University of Massachusetts, Dartmouth, 30 April 2009.

2010 "Asian Philosophies in Search of Identity", Presidential Address, 1st Asian Philosophy Congress (6-9 March 2010), New Delhi: Jawaharlal Nehru University, 2010; *ICPR Newsletter* (Jan.-March): 3-5.

- "Cognitive Anomalies: Developing Tests for Screening and Selecting Subjects", in K.R. Rao (ed.) *Yoga and Parapsychology* (pp. 393-496), Delhi: Motilal Banarsidass.
- "Current Scenes of Conflict: Relevance of Gandhi", National Seminar on Current Scenes of Conflict: Gandhian Perspectives for

Resolution, 19-21 March 2010, GITAM University.

- "Indian Psychology: Towards a Psychology of the Future", in D.K. Bhattacharjee (ed.) *Psychology and Education: Indian Perspectives* (pp. 5-33), New Delhi: Indian Council of Educational Research and Training.
- "Paranormal Phenomena and Yoga Psychology and Practice", National Seminar on Parapsychology: From Indian Philosophical Perspectives (4-5 January 2010), Visakhapatnam: Department of Psychology and Parapsychology, Andhra University.
- "Parapsychology and Yoga", in K.R. Rao (ed.) *Yoga and Parapsychology* (pp. 1-41), Delhi: Motilal Banarsidass.
- "Spirituality and Science of Consciousness", International Seminar on Spirituality and Science of Consciousness organized by Ramakrishna Mission Institute of Culture, Kolkata, 8 January 2010.
- "The Question of Post-modern Survival: Empirical Evidence and Theoretical Issues", in K.R. Rao (ed.) *Yoga and Parapsychology* (pp. 261-300), Delhi: Motilal Banarsidass.

2011 "Applied Yoga Psychology: Studies of Neurophysiology of Meditation", *Journal of Consciousness Studies*, 18(11-12): 161-98.

- "Hypnosis, Yoga and Psychic Phenomena", in R. Sharma and B.M. Palan (eds.) *Hypnosis: Psycho-Philosophical Prespectives and Therapeutic Relevance*, New Delhi: Concept Publishing Co.
- "The Indian Perspective of Spirituality", *ICPR Newsletter* (April – Sept. 2011): 5-8.
- "Indian Psychology: Implications and Applications", in R.M.M. Cornelissen, Y. Misra and S. Varma (eds.) *Foundations of Indian Psychology: Theories and Concepts* (vol. 1, pp. 7-26), Delhi: Longman Pearson.
- "Keynote Address": in *Sprituality and Science of Consciousness* (pp. 14-63), Kolkata: Ramakrishna Mission Institute of Culture.
- "Trisula: Trident Model of Person in Indian Psychology", in Girishwar Misra (ed.) *Handbook of Psychology in India*, New Delhi: Oxford University Press.
- "Violence and Nonviolence in Gandhi's Philosophy of Life", *ICPR Newsletter* (Oct. – Dec. 2011): pp. 5-7.

2012 "Bapu and Anna" (editorial), *GITAM Journal of Gandhian Studies*, 1(1): 1-3.

- "Complimentarity of Advaita Non-dualism and Yoga Dualism in Indian Psychology", *Journal of Conciousness Studies*, 19(9-10): 121-42.
- "Gandhi's Touch: Spiritualizing Socialism", *ICPR Newsletter* (Jan. – April 2012): 2-7.
- "Indian Psychology Curriculum: Moving Beyond Borrowed Knowledge", in C. Alvares and S.S. Faruqi (eds.) *Decolonizing the University: The Emerging Quest for Non-Eurocentric Paradigms* (pp. 255-66), Pulan Pinang: Penerbit Universiti Sains Malaysia.
- "Indian Psychology and Positive Psychology", Presidential Address at Seminar on Spirituality and Positive Psychology, 29 September 2012, Kolkata: Ramakrishna Mission Institute of Culture.
- "Marx and the Mahatma" (editorial), *GITAM Journal of Gandhian Studies*, 1(2): 265-76.
- "Parapsychology and Yoga: Theory and Practice", in S. Kakar and J.J. Kripal (eds.) *Seriously Strange: Thinking About Psychic Experiences* (pp. 174-208), New Delhi: Penguin/Viking.
- "Psychology in the Indian Tradition", invited address given at XXXth International Congress of Psychology 2012, Cape Town, South Africa; *Psychological Studies*, 15: 323-30 (October 2012).
- "Spiritual Reconstruction in Philosophy: The Vedantic Way" in G.N. Jha, B.R. Singh, R.P. Singh and D. Mishra (eds.) *Modern Perspectives on Vedanta: Proceedings of the 20th International Congress of Vedanta*, pp. 55-83, New Delhi: D.K. Printworld.
- "Violence and Nonviolence in Gandhi's Philosophy", *GITAM Journal of Gandhian Studies*, 1(1): 131-48.

Contributors

Cornellissen, Mathijs, is a member of the editorial team overseeing the publication of *The Complete Works of Sri Aurobindo*. He teaches integral psychology at the Sri Aurobindo International Centre of Education in Pondicherry. As a qualified physician, he came to India in 1976 to study the confluence of *yoga* and psychotherapy. Together with Neeltje Huppes he founded Mirambika, an experimental teacher training college in New Delhi in 1981. More recently he organized together with Neeltje three major conferences on Indian psychology. He founded the Indian Psychology Institute at Pondicherry in February 2006. His publications include several papers on Indian psychology and two edited volumes, *Consciousness and Its Transformation* and *Indian Psychology, Consciousness and Yoga*, the latter together with Kireet Joshi. He is also the co-editor of *Foundations of Indian Psychology*.
e-mail: matthijs@auromail.net

Dalal, Ajit K., is Professor of Psychology at the University of Allahabad. He has obtained his doctoral degree from the Indian Institute of Technology, Kanpur, and has published in the areas of causal attribution, health beliefs and indigenous psychology. He became the Fulbright Senior Fellow and worked at the University of California, Los Angeles, and at the University of Michigan, Ann Arbor. He is also a recipient of the UGC Career Award, Rockefeller Foundation Award and ICSSR Senior Fellowship. Ajit K. Dalal was the visiting faculty at many places, including the Queen's University, Canada; the National Institute of Health and Family Welfare, New Delhi; the Indian Institute of Management, Ahmedabad; and the Calcutta University, Kolkata. He has published many research articles for books and journals, in addition to seven books, including *Attribution Theory and Research*; *New Directions in Indian Psychology* (vol. 1); and *Social Dimensions of Health*. Presently, he is the editor of the journal *Psychology and Developing Societies* published by Sage.
e-mail: ajitkdalal@gmail.com

Devadoss, T.S., is one of the accomplished scholars in Gandhian philosophy. He joined the Department of Philosophy, University of Madras, and under the inspiring guidance of Prof. T.M.P. Mahadevan, he did his research on Gandhian philosophy and obtained Ph.D. in 1969. His doctoral thesis on "Sarvodaya" was

published by the University of Madras in 1974. T.S. Devadoss was a Member of the Governing Council of ICPR. He was awarded ICPR Emeritus Fellowships and a UGC Emeritus Fellowship. He is the author of several scholarly works which include *Sarvodaya*; *Hindu Family and Marriage*; and *Mahatma Gandhi*. He has to his credit about forty-five research papers published in national and international journals. In due recognition of his contribution to philosophical studies, Devadoss was invited as Visiting Professor at the University of Sasketchavan, Canada; Brock University, Canada; and Birmingham University, UK. During the Post-Centenary of Gandhiji, Devadoss was invited to deliver lectures on Gandhian thought in several universities in USA, Canada and UK. His areas of interest are Gandhian philosophy, peace studies and social philosophy.
e-mail: drtlavanya@gmail.com

Jerry, Solfvin, is adjunct Associate Professor, Center for Indic Studies, University of Massachusetts Dartmouth. He was trained in mathematics (Bridgewater State University), psychology (University of North Carolina & NC Central University) and social science (State University of Utrecht, Netherlands). He was research associate at the Psychical Research Foundation at Duke University. Subsequently he was a faculty member at the Parapsychology Laboratory of the State University of Utrecht, and later directed the parapsychology graduate program at John F. Kennedy University in Orinda, CA. He is a full member of the International Parapsychology Association; and a member of the advisory board of the Rhine Institute in Durham, NC; and University of Massachusetts Dartmouth, MA.
e-mail: jsolfvin@umassd.edu

Kakar, Sudhir, is a well-known psychoanalyst and author. He has been Lecturer at Harvard University, research fellow at Harvard Business School, Professor at IIM, Ahmedabad, and head of the Department of Humanities and Social Sciences at IIT, Delhi. He was senior fellow at the Center for Study of World Religions at Harvard and also visiting professor at the universities of Chicago (1989-92), Harvard, McGill, Melbourne, Hawaii and Vienna. Among the many honours received by Dr Kakar include the Kardiner Award of Columbia University, the Boyer Prize of the American Anthropological Association, Germany's Goethe Medal, the Rockfeller Residency, the Distinguished Service Award of the Indo-American Psychiatric Association, Fellowships of the Institutes of Advanced Study (Princeton and Berlin), and the Bhabha, Nehru and ICSSR National Fellowships in India. He is the author of seventeen books of non-fiction and four novels.
e-mail: sudhir_kakar@rediffmail.com

Kanthamani, H., is a psychology graduate from Mysore University, who attended the National Institute for Mental Health and Neurosciences (NIMHANS) in Bangalore, India, to specialize in clinical psychology. In 1963, she was invited to work as a research fellow in the Duke University Parapsychology Lab. Upon return to India, she has assisted Prof. K.R. Rao in founding the parapsychology programme at Andhra University, where she received her doctorate. In 1971, she returned to the United States and began a long career at the Institute for Parapsychology (FRNM).
e-mail: kanthahanu@yahoo.com

Kristeller, Jean, received her master's degree in clinical and human psychophysiology from the University of Wisconsin, Madison in 1978, and her Ph.D. in clinical psychology with an emphasis in clinical health psychology from Yale University in 1983. Prior to coming to Indiana State University, she was a member of the staff and faculty in the behavioural medicine services at Cambridge Hospital (Harvard Medical School, Department of Psychiatry) and the University of Massachusetts Medical Center (Worcester, MA). Dr Kristeller is interested in the effects of psychological variables on physical health and illness, which has informed much of her research. It has included work with compulsive eating and obesity, smoking, the role of the physician in facilitating health behaviour change, anxiety disorders and the use of meditation as a way to promote self-regulatory processes. She teaches courses on health psychology, psychology of meditation, and advanced clinical research methods. Her current work in the meditation area involves finding out ways to integrate meditative techniques into more comprehensive therapy or support programmes in both the cancer area and in Binge Eating Disorder (BED).
e-mail: Jean.Kristeller@indstate.edu

Misra, Girishwar, is Professor of Psychology and Dean, Research (Humanities & Social Sciences) at the University of Delhi where he has been teaching since 1993. He has been Visiting Professor at the Ruhr University, Germany; ESRC Fellow at Sussex University, UK; and Fulbright-Nehru Lecturer at New School of Social Research, New York. His research interests include deprivation and poverty, self and emotions, and Indian psychology. He is recipient of Fellowship of ICSSR, National Academy of Psychology (NAOP), Fulbright Fellowship, and Pandit Jawaharlal Nehru Award. He is the editor of *Psychological Studies* (Springer). He has been the president of NAOP. He is on the board of advisors of the Asian Association of Cultural and Indigenous Psychology. He has edited *Fifth ICSSR Survey of Psychological Research* and editing its 6th Survey. He has authored/edited over two dozen books including *Applied Social Psychology in India* (Sage); *Psychology and Societal Development* (Concept); *Psychology in India: Advances in Research* (4 vols., Pearson); *Handbook of Psychology in India* (Oxford);

and *Foundations of Indian Psychology* (with Corelissen and Varma) (Pearson).
e-mail: misragirishwar@gmail.com

Pandey, Janak, is currently Vice-Chancellor of Central University of Bihar. He served earlier as Professor of Psychology at Allahabad University and Director, Govind Ballabh Pant Social Science Institute, Allahabad. During his rich and distinguished career, he has been President of the International Association for Cross-cultural Psychology; Fulbright Scholar-in-Residence at Wake Forest University; Visiting Commonwealth Fellow at the University of Manitoba; ICSSR National Fellow; and Dean, Faculty of Arts, Allahabad University. He is a recipient of the Professor V.K.R.V. Rao Award. Professor Pandey has written extensively on social influence processes, and contemporary social and environmental issues that are relevant to socio-economic change in developing countries. Besides having contributed extensively to journals and edited collections, he has previously edited *Perspective on Experimental Social Psychology in India;* the three-volume set entitled *Psychology in India Revisited* series, and has co-edited *Asian Contributions to Cross-Cultural Psychology* and *Handbook of Cross-Cultural Psychology* (vol. 1).
e-mail: janakpandey@cbcs.ac.in

Paranjpe, Anand C., has obtained his Ph.D. from Pune University and conducted post-doctoral research at Harvard University under a Fulbright and Smith-Mundt grant. In 1967 he started teaching at Simon Fraser University in Canada, where he is currently Emeritus Professor of Psychology and Humanities. His major publications include *Theoretical Psychology: The Meeting of East and West* and *Self and Identity in Modern Psychology and Indian Thought*. He co-edited with K.R. Rao and Ajit Dalal the *Handbook of Indian Psychology*.
e-mail: paranjpe@sfu.ca

Pradhan, Ramesh Chandra, teaches philosophy at the University of Hyderabad. He specializes in philosophy of language, philosophy of mind and Wittgenstein. He has published a few books in philosophy and contributed many papers to research journals. He had his Ph.D. from Banaras Hindu University and did his post-doctoral studies at the Oxford University. He was the Member-Secretary of the ICPR, New Delhi, during 2000-03.
e-mail: pradhanrameshchandra@yahoo.com

Raman, V.V., is Emeritus Professor of Physics and Humanities at the Rochester Institute of Technology, Rochester, New York. He obtained his Ph.D. from the University of Paris. He was elected Senior Fellow at the Metanexus Institute (Philadelphia, USA), and Fellow of the International Society for Science and Religion (Cambridge, UK). He is a recipient of the Raja Rao Award from the

Jawaharlal Nehru University (New Delhi, India), and of the Outstanding Scholar Award from the Institute on Religion in an Age of Science (IRAS). Currently, he is serving as President of IRAS. Dr Raman has written extensively on Indic culture, and is the author of several books including *Truth and Tension in Science and Religion; Indic Visions in an Age of Science;* as well as *Variety in Religion and Science.*
e-mail: vvrsps@ritvax.isc.rit.edu , vvrsps@ritvax.rit.edu

Rammohan, Gowri V. has Ph.D. in Parapsychology from Andhra University. She served as Professor in the Department of Psychology and Parapsychology, Andhra University, and retired from her services in January 2012. She published several research papers on parapsychology in national and international journals of repute. She published a book *New Frontiers of Human Science: A Festschrift to Dr. K. Ramakrishna Rao* in honour of K.R. Rao, her teacher and mentor, and released the book on the occasion of Dr Rao's 70th Birthday in 2002. She was the founder Head of the Department of Dance. Dr Gowri is also an accomplished musician in classical music vocal.
e-mail: gowrirammohan@gmail.com

Rao, Hanu, is a clinical psychologist, who has been active in the field of mental health in North Carolina for a long time. He has obtained his master's degree from the Department of Psychology and Parapsychology at Andhra University in 1972, prior to which he served in the Indian Army as a Commissioned Officer. He has a Ph.D. in Psychology from North Carolina State University. He worked as a researcher at the Institute for Parapsychology (FRNM), in the early 1970s.
e-mail: kanthahanu@yahoo.com

Sambasiva Prasad, B., is Director, GITAM Institute for Gandhian Studies, GITAM University, Visakhapatnam. Earlier, he was Professor of Philosophy, at Sri Venkateswara University, Tirupati. His current areas of interest include Gandhian philosophy and peace studies. He was the Hon. Executive Secretary for the Centre for Peace and Nonviolence, Sri Venkateswara University. He has published many research papers in anthologies and journals. He is the Executive Editor for *GITAM Journal of Gandhian Studies.* He had co-ordinated in the execution of the ICPR project on "Phenomenology of Violence", and presently handling the project on "Application of Gandhian Ideas in the Areas of Peace, Conflict Resolution, Rural Development and Higher Education".
e-mail: b.sambasivaprasad@gmail.com

Sharad, Shivantika, is Assistant Professor of Psychology at Vivekananda College, University of Delhi, and is currently on deputation at the Cluster Innovation Centre, University of Delhi. Her doctoral work has been on developing the construct of authenticity. Anchored in the Indian psychological thought, her

publications relate to the meaning and experience of authenticity and the positive outcomes of authentic functioning. Her areas of interest include personality, self and identity; philosophy of science and epistemology; social and cultural psychology; positive psychology; and East–West studies, etc.
e-mail: shivantikasharad@gmail.com

Singh, Karan, is the son of the last ruler of the Princely State of Jammu & Kashmir, Maharaja Hari Singh. Karan Singh served successfully as regent, first and last *Sadar-i-Riyasat* after his father stepped down as the ruler. He served as governor of the state of Jammu & Kashmir from 1965 to 1967. In 1967 he became the youngest-ever member of the Union Cabinet holding the portfolios of Tourism and Civil Aviation. In 1961 after his father's death he surrendered his privy purse and placed the entire sum into a charitable trust.

From 1967 to 1980 and in 1990 Karan Singh served as an MP in the Lok Sabha and he became the Minister of Education and Culture in 1979. In 1989-90, he served as Indian Ambassador to the US; the experience became the subject of a book he wrote, *Brief Sojourn*. Since 1996 he has been an MP in the Rajya Sabha. He served as Chancellor of Banaras Hindu University, Jammu & Kashmir University and NIIT University. Singh received the Padma Vibhushan in 2005.

Tandon, Alok, is a free-lancer and has rich background of sociology, economics and philosophy. He was a fellow of ICSSR and ICPR, and was an awardee of National Merit Scholarship. He was the recipient of Sagar Memorial Prize of Akhil Bhartiya Darshan Parishad in 2009. Alok Tandon authored books on *Man and His Destiny with Special Reference to Marx and Sartre* and *Vikalpa aur Vimarsha*. He has published more than fifty research papers in English and Hindi. He has participated in a number of seminars and conferences. His areas of interests include ethics and social philosophy, existentialism, Marxism, philosophy of science, applied philosophy and cultural discourse.
e-mail: dralokboi@yahoo.com

Vedaparayana, G., is Professor Emeritus, Department of Philosophy, Sri Venkateswara University, Tirupati. He had his masters and Ph.D. from the same university. He also served there as the head of the department for one term. Phenomenology, existentialism, moral philosophy and Madhyamika Buddhism are his areas of specialization. He has also worked on the contemporary Indian thinkers like Mahatma Gandhi, Swami Vivekananda and Jiddu Krishnamurti. He has visited Paris under Indo-French Cultural Exchange Programme sponsored by the Indian Philosophical Council.
e-mail: parayanaveda_49@yahoo.com

Velmans, Max, has been involved in consciousness studies for around thirty-five years, is currently Emeritus Professor of Psychology, Goldsmiths, University of London; Visiting Professor in Consciousness Studies, University of Plymouth; and an academician of the social sciences. His main research focus is on integrating work on the philosophy, cognitive psychology and neuropsychology of consciousness. He has published extensively including *Understanding Consciousness* (2000), which was shortlisted for the British Psychological Society Book Award in 2001 and 2002 and *The Blackwell Companion to Consciousness* (2007).
e-mail: m.velmans@gold.ac.uk

Vohra, Ashok, Professor of Philosophy, University of Delhi, has published more than 150 papers and articles in national and international journals and anthologies. He is the author of *Wittgenstein's Philosophy of Mind* (1986) and is the co-author of *Radhakrishnan: His Life and Ideas* (1990). He has co-edited *The Philosophy of K. Satchidananda Murty* (1996) and *Dharma: The Categorial Imperative* (2005). He has delivered lectures in various universities in India and abroad. He is on the editorial board of *Humanitas Asiatica,* Seoul; *Journal of the Indian Council of Philosophical Research (JICPR); Indian Philosophical Quarterly; Suvidya: Journal of Philosophy and Religion*; and *Indian Journal of Analytic Philosophy*. He writes regularly for the *Times of India, Hindustan Times, The Tribune* and *The Pioneer* on philosophical themes with a view to popularize it.
e-mail: profashokvohra@gmail.com

Index